Up Against the Wall

Up Against the Wall

Violence in the
Making and
Unmaking of the
Black Panther Party

BY CURTIS J. AUSTIN

University of Arkansas Press
Fayetteville   2006

10   09   08   07   06   5   4   3   2   1

Designed by Liz Lester

⊝ The paper used in this publication meets the minimum
requirements of the American National Standard for
Permanence of Paper for Printed Library Materials
Z39.48-1984.

LIBRARY OF CONGRESS
CATALOGING-IN-PUBLICATION DATA

Austin, Curtis J., 1969–
    Up against the wall : violence in the making and
unmaking of the Black Panther Party / by Curtis J.
Austin.—1st ed.
        p.   cm.
    Includes bibliographical references and index.
    ISBN-13: 978-1-55728-827-1 (alk. paper)
    ISBN-10: 1-55728-827-5 (alk. paper)
    1. Black Panther Party—History. 2. Black Panther
Party—Biography. 3. Political violence—United
States—History—20th century. 4. Black power—
United States—History—20th century. 5. African
Americans—Politics and government—20th century.
6. United States—Race relations—History—20th
century. I. Title.
    E185.615.A88   2006
    322.4'20973—dc22
                                2006026040

To my sisters and brothers

CONTENTS

FOREWORD

After years of research that included often difficult-to-obtain interviews with former Black Panther Party members, historian Curtis J. Austin presents his extensive work in *Up Against the Wall: Violence in the Making and Unmaking of the Black Panther Party*. In this book, he uncovers historical evidence related to the often misunderstood facts about the Black Panther Party and offers readers an interesting venue with which to familiarize themselves with pertinent material.

Austin describes how, in the late 1960s and early 1970s, individuals from many areas of the black community joined the Black Panther Party and how it became the most potent political force in the Oakland/San Francisco Bay Area as well as a highly recognized force on the national and international scene. Huey Newton and Bobby Seale, along with hundreds of other young members of this movement, demanded that the U.S. and other governments recognize and respect basic human rights.

In *Up Against the Wall,* many of the controversial aspects of the BPP and the atmosphere of the 1960s and 1970s are graphically illustrated. Curtis Austin not only discusses the violence within the Black Panther Party but, by his very title, describes the position of party members in relationship to the violent acts perpetuated by them and against them and other blacks in America. His book lends a much-needed historical and academic perspective that, based on his interviews with former party members and other research, attempts to explain and put into context the often misunderstood details of the history of the Black Panther Party.

Although former party members' opinions and accounts may differ, what is important here is that Austin provides a valuable framework for open discussion, acknowledges the Black Panther Party's accomplishments as a political force, and recognizes the contributions made and inspired mainly because of love for our people.

This was demonstrated in our programs, which served the basic needs of the black and poor communities. We did this by example, no matter what the personal cost.

The author links the founding of the Black Panther Party to the history of the civil rights movement and takes us down into the Mississippi

Delta, where marches and murders took place as black Americans fought for human and civil rights. The only thing more relentless than the heat of the Delta was black people's determination to be free and their purpose and conviction to be treated with dignity and respect.

Austin's book differs from other analyses of the Black Panther Party in that it is not merely a tell-all about irrelevant personal situations within the party. It does not focus on the sensationalism associated with the party. Neither is his book simply based on autobiographical sketches of prominent party members. What he has accomplished is to provide a detailed view with academic analyses of the tactics and strategies used by the party to promote change in America and the world. He has also chronicled the forces put into play by the American government to stop those changes. He reminds us of the price paid by so many of the Black Panther Party members in the struggle to create those changes.

At the very least, this book allows us an opportunity and forum to openly discuss and recognize the historical significance and contributions made by the Black Panther Party members. Even more significantly, we are encouraged to learn from the history of the Black Panther Party, reflect on how much change is still needed, and discuss how this can best be accomplished. In these times, surely that is of the utmost importance to us all.

ELBERT "BIG MAN" HOWARD
Author, Lecturer, and Activist
Sonoma County, California
April, 2006
An original founding member of the Black Panther Party, member from 1966–1974
Former editor, Black Panther Party newspaper

INTRODUCTION

"Who in the hell are these niggers with these guns?"[1] Bobby Seale, Bobby Hutton, Sherman Forte, and two dozen other compatriots, swathed in black leather and sporting berets and shotguns, marched through the state capitol in Sacramento in search of the California General Assembly. These self-appointed leaders of the fledgling Black Panther Party for Self-Defense, founded in Oakland in October 1966, went to the capitol ostensibly to protest the impending passage of the Mulford Act, a bill designed to prevent private citizens from carrying loaded weapons in public. The date was May 2, 1967, and the Panthers hoped to capitalize on their provocative appearance and bold statement. With the primary purpose of generating national news coverage for a fledgling group of less than thirty self-described revolutionaries, this shrewdly planned publicity stunt succeeded in attracting more recruits and led directly to the party's spread from the Oakland/San Francisco Bay Area to other locales in California and subsequently throughout the nation.

Consequently, many black men and women saw this budding organization as the answer to one of their most pressing problems: the lack of defense against police attacks. Seale described "how smart Brother Huey was when he planned Sacramento," with the explanation that Huey Newton knew the papers would call the Panthers "thugs and hoodlums" but "the brothers on the block, who the man has been calling thugs and hoodlums for 100 years, they're gonna say 'Them's some out of sight thugs and hoodlums up there.' Who is these thugs and hoodlums?" Seale added that Newton knew that blacks would say, "well they've been calling us niggers, thugs, and hoodlums for 400 years, that ain't gon' hurt me, I'm going to check out what these brothers is doing!"[2] The incident launched a movement that would eventually galvanize blacks and whites alike to address the debilitating political and economic subjugation that continued to plague blacks after the passage of civil rights legislation in 1960, 1964, and 1965.

Emphatically impressing upon blacks the importance of self-defense, this tactic succeeded as headlines across the nation described armed blacks entering the legislature. The widespread coverage of the small group dwarfed the coverage given to members of California's "gun lobby," who "were also present registering opposition to the new law."[3]

The decision to move on the capitol grew from a verbal struggle with the Contra Costa County Sheriff's Office about its failure to act in the murder of Richmond resident Denzil Dowell, killed April 1, 1967. The sheriff, Walter Younger, refusing to investigate the incident or to suspend the officer who killed Dowell, flippantly suggested the Panthers and the Dowell family take their grievances to Sacramento. Newton capitalized on this opportunity to act on behalf of the community and to get the publicity his group craved. He wrote later that "the Dowell family only wanted some good to come out of all the grief inflicted on them." He said the Panthers "knew the Dowells would get no better consideration in Sacramento than they had received from [Sheriff] Younger." Their plan, however, was to "raise the encounter to a higher level in the hope of warning people about the dangers in the Mulford bill and the ideas behind it. A national outcry would help the Dowell family by showing them that some good had come from their tragedy; also, it might mobilize our community even more." Knowing "dozens of reporters and photographers haunt the capitol waiting for a story," Newton decided the time was right for the fledgling group to make it big.[4]

After making the decision, Newton instructed Seale on how to handle himself at the capitol. Seale's primary mission was to deliver publicly what was grandly called Executive Mandate Number One, a call for action that carefully explained how and why external violence dictated that blacks take the position of armed self-defense. Newton told Seale and the other Panthers and accompanying community members to fire at anyone who fired on them or who looked like they were going to fire on them. He noted "the main thing was to deliver the message . . . inside the legislature" if possible, "but if it was against the rules to enter" or if they were blocked from entering, he told Seale "to read the message from the capitol steps." Newton also advised Seale that he and the others should "take the arrest" if it came to that, "as long as he had delivered the message."[5]

Once everything had been worked out, the time arrived for them to go. Three separate groups had been assembled to make the trip, including several members of the Dowell family, a group of young blacks led by East Oakland resident Mark Comfort, and members of the Black

Panther Party for Self-Defense. Five years later, Newton revealed that only Comfort's group and the Panthers, excluding Eldridge Cleaver, were armed. It is not clear whether Cleaver went as a member of the party or, as he claimed, in his capacity as a reporter for *Ramparts* magazine. Despite his leadership role in the party, Newton decided it best for him not to go because he remained on probation stemming from the 1964 stabbing of a man named Odell Lee. "Second," he added, "if any arrests were made in Sacramento, someone should be available to raise bail money and whatever else was necessary." He noted that the party insisted he be the one to stay behind to take care of this possibility. Seale wrote in *Seize the Time* that "we voted Huey down and wouldn't let him come" because "we did not want to risk [him] getting shot or anything."[6]

Although it had not been a scorcher in the East Bay, May 2, 1967, turned out to be a hot day in California's Central Valley. The cool winds blowing in from the Pacific made the early part of the drive quite pleasant, but the farther inland they traveled, the hotter it became. This heat would later be blamed when things began to go wrong. The caravan of cars made the eighty-mile trip east without incident. Thirty people, including "six sisters" according to Seale, went along for what turned out to be a road trip of momentous proportions.[7]

Upon arrival at the state capitol in Sacramento, the group boldly parked directly in front of the capitol steps. Emerging from their vehicles as if it were a normal thing for large groups of blacks to be carrying such hardware, the Panthers began loading rounds into the chambers of their firearms, which included pistols, shotguns, and semiautomatic weapons. The guns had not previously been loaded because California Fish and Game laws prohibited the carrying of loaded weapons, other than pistols, in automobiles. This overtly menacing group of armed black people unnerved California governor Ronald Reagan so much that he prematurely ended a speech he had been giving to a youth group on the front lawn of the capitol and made a quick exit. The children, who noticed the spectacle occurring before them, approached members of the Panther contingent and began commenting on their weapons. "Nice thirty-ought six, mister," one of them is reported to have said. "They must have thought we were some kind of gun club," remembered Seale. A news team, which had been previously filming Ronald Reagan's presentation, then began concentrating on the Oakland revolutionaries.[8]

With sixteen-year-old Bobby Hutton on his right and Warren Tucker on his left, Seale proceeded to walk up the front steps of the capitol. All three men openly carried weapons. Seale sported a menacing-looking .45-caliber pistol in a holster on his right hip, Tucker had his .357 Magnum in the same place, and Hutton brazenly displayed his 12-gauge shotgun.[9] At the very moment when he wondered whether to proceed, Seale claims to have overheard a security guard telling two members of his entourage: "you aren't violating anything with your gun, so if you want to, you can go inside." He recalled this statement made up his mind for him.[10]

More than a city block in length and several stories high, the building that houses the California state legislature and the governor's office is an imposing one. Its interior walls are adorned with fine paintings alongside portraits of important state lawmakers and former governors. Shiny, perfectly laid tile flooring makes the rotunda seem even larger than it is. After entering this beautifully appointed structure, the Panther contingent got lost almost immediately.

Seale, who had led the brave souls to Sacramento, "wanted to see the area where a citizen has the right to observe the legislature." He assumed that since assemblyman Don Mulford had authored the bill, they should be looking for the assembly floor. Floating alertly through the capitol building's extra-wide halls, the armed Panthers surprised visitors and statesmen alike. Many simply watched, their open mouths displaying shock and disbelief. The Panthers paid their spectators no mind and proceeded to search for the assembly room.[11]

Growing a little impatient, Seale yelled to the quickly growing contingent of cameramen and reporters now photographing and videotaping the group, "where in the hell's the Assembly? Anybody here know where you go in and observe the Assembly making these laws?" Someone, after a brief moment of silence, yelled back that it was "upstairs on the next floor." The group then proceeded up the winding but wide set of stairs that led to the next floor.

More confusion ensued, but the group finally spotted the entrance-way. Approaching the assembly room, the drama seemed to heighten as the cameramen grew busier and more frantic with their picture-taking and the reporters became less patient and more boisterous with their questions. As the group proceeded, a black man guarding the door to the assembly room suddenly opened it. Seale remembers the gentleman saying, "Come right in sir! You have the gun!" As afraid as he was surprised, the doorkeeper had no idea that he was playing a minor but key role in one of the most electric moments in California history.[12]

At this point, pandemonium ensued. Having entered the assembly chamber, the Panthers and the reporters who surrounded them caused a huge stir. Assemblymen yelled, almost in unison, "what the hell is going on! Get those cameras out of here!" Then when they noticed black men and women carrying weapons they yelled for security to remove the entire contingent. Bobby Hutton immediately had his shotgun taken away as a capitol security team began to usher the group out the door. Hutton screamed as loudly as he could, "Am I under arrest? Am I under arrest? What the hell you got my gun for? If I'm not under arrest you give me my gun back!" All this confusion flooded the now-crowded halls of the capitol building. The Panthers knew that it was perfectly legal to carry unconcealed weapons anywhere in public, including the capitol building —which had hosted National Rifle Association meetings on dozens of occasions. Undaunted, Bobby Seale and his cadre maintained their composure and followed the orders of their escorts, who had by now pushed them onto an elevator and taken them to a small room on the first floor. It was there that one astute and persistent cameraman caught Seale on tape as he read Executive Mandate Number One for all the world to see.[13]

The message explained the reason the Panthers had gone to Sacramento. Seale spoke of the impending Mulford Act, which sought to disarm citizens at the same time that "racist police agencies throughout the country [were] intensifying the terror, brutality, murder and repression of black people." The message delineated what the Panthers described as the murderous violence that the American government had perpetrated against nonwhite people like the Japanese, Native Americans, and Vietnamese. He then compared this violence abroad to the violence that whites perpetrated against blacks, regardless of whether they had been participants in the nonviolent quest for equal rights and justice. "As the aggression of the racist American government escalates in Vietnam," he read, "the police agencies in America escalate the repression of black people throughout the ghettoes of America. Vicious police dogs, cattle prods, and increased patrols have become familiar sights in black communities." Noting that local governments had demonstrated no inclination to halt this brutality, Seale concluded his statement by providing the rationale for armed self-defense. Blacks would be destroyed, he said, if whites were allowed to continue terrorizing them with impunity. According to the statement, the pending Mulford Act brought "the hour of doom one step nearer." The Black Panther Party for Self-Defense served as an example of how blacks throughout the nation could coalesce and protect their communities from outside attack.[14]

The mandate having been read and the weapons returned, the Panthers left the building. As they descended the capitol steps, newsmen asked Seale to read the message again. He complied. Knowing full well that coverage of the event would be widespread, Seale delivered the statement with even more vigor and passion than when he had read it the first time. The caravan of cars then left the capitol building to head back to the Bay.[15]

This final scene, with Seale standing on the capitol steps decked out in his black beret, black leather jacket, and black pants, was flashed across California news screens for the rest of the afternoon and throughout the evening. Chilling video of black men and women defiantly roaming the halls of the capitol building was also shown as thousands of Americans were introduced to the small band of Oakland revolutionaries who would soon be catapulted into the leadership of the black struggle for self-determination. These pictures, and the commentary that accompanied them, struck fear in the hearts of many whites while they simultaneously evoked feelings of love and admiration in the minds of many blacks throughout the nation. This black approval of the bold step the Panthers took would soon be translated into the establishment of Black Panther Party chapters and branches across the nation.

The Black Panther Party for Self-Defense, like most of its Black Power counterparts, sought to address the powerlessness that characterized and circumscribed black ghetto residents. Its leaders understood that more than anything else, black Americans needed to define and determine the destinies of their lives. Insisting they take over and maintain the "cultural and political autonomy of black communities," as Clayborne Carson put it, the Black Panther Party, along with other advocates of Black Power, demonstrated to blacks that the first step toward this all-important goal was self-preservation. The idea that blacks needed to be alive, healthy, and unmolested guided the party's philosophy from its earliest days, through its many transitions, and to the end of its life. Self-defense and control of the institutions in black communities not only became Panther hallmarks, they also acted as magnets that drew blacks to the party. Individuals from the streets, war veterans, college and high school students, small businesspeople, writers, artists, poets, and laborers alike became enthralled by the courageous stand the new organization took. Because of its popularity with the many different segments of African America, the party's influence grew rapidly. Eventually it became a potent political force in the Oakland / San Francisco Bay Area and it subsequently parlayed that strength into a phenomenon that made a profound impact on the national and international scene.

Like other people and organizations before it, the party was called into being by historical precedents and contemporary realities. In effect, it followed the trajectory of African resistance that began in the interior and on the shores of Africa when men and women devised strategies to fight against the barbarous slave trade. These strategies always had complete liberty as their goal.

The central theme of African American history is and has been the struggle for freedom. After whites seized Native Americans' land through force of arms and fraud, they used enslaved Africans to work this land and to make themselves rich. Europeans used the slave trade and the subsequent profits from this free African labor to create an empire as large and as strong as any the world has ever known. Violence and the threat of it was central to the maintenance of the system of slavery. From the very beginning, black people fought to free themselves from these circumstances and used both violent and nonviolent means. That struggle did not end in 1865 when the Thirteenth Amendment outlawed slavery. It continued throughout the rest of the nineteenth century and on into the twentieth century. Like Harriet Tubman, David Walker, the Universal Negro Improvement Association, the National Association for the Advancement of Colored People, Robert Williams, and the Deacons for Defense and Justice, the Black Panther Party was a continuation of that struggle.

The Black Panther Party for Self-Defense emerged at a time when the black freedom movement had become much more militant than it had been during the 1950s and 1960s. This does not mean that blacks had not previously decided that self-defense was necessary to successfully reclaim and maintain their humanity; nor does it mean that political autonomy had not been a goal of the movement. The emergence of this new voice simply indicates that after the brutal experience of Freedom Summer in Mississippi in 1964, after President Lyndon Johnson and his fellow Democrats rejected the Mississippi Freedom Democratic Party's request the same year to be recognized as legitimately constituted challenger of the regular Mississippi delegation, after the urban rebellions of that same year and the two years that followed, and after the widely publicized 1966 James Meredith March through Mississippi turned the phrase "Black Power" into a household term, younger movement activists began to articulate these goals in vastly different ways from either their forbears or their older, more moderate contemporaries. Through its Ten Point Platform and Program, a list of demands including housing, clothing, bread, fair trials, and peace, the BPP tried to lead blacks to the next level of the freedom struggle.[16]

The Sacramento incident epitomized the Panther moment. The party received publicity throughout California and the rest of the nation. Hundreds, then thousands clamored to join. By 1970, it had thirty-two chapters and more than one hundred affiliates across the country. Many more blacks who did not join supported the party's emphasis on armed self-defense. Its allies on the radical left, including Students For A Democratic Society, the Socialist Workers' Party, and the media, gave the BPP a public presence far out of proportion to its numbers, which by most estimates never went higher than five thousand.

By the time the party began its rapid decline as an ultraradical organization in 1972, it had won the hearts and minds of thousands of people around the world. It had also become mired in internal squabbling and internecine warfare. The federal and local infiltration and harassment that ensued left the youthful organization devastated and its members demoralized, incarcerated, and sometimes dead. While not all party members fared so badly, enough did to ensure that the group was virtually unknown by 1982, when it shut down its last community survival program. The members' youthful vigor and dedication to freedom and justice carried the party through those sixteen years.

Once the idea of being black and beautiful became popular, and blacks started emphasizing publicly their cultural heritage, they began to drop the strictly nonviolent approach that had characterized the strategy of previous movement leaders. In effect, the youth, people aged sixteen to twenty-nine, began to take over the movement leadership and to present black demands in terms so uncompromising that the white establishment—and some black leaders—began to label them reverse racists, hot heads, militant demagogues, and traitors to their race, among other things. Stokely Carmichael (who later adopted the name Kwame Ture), Kathleen Cleaver, H. Rap Brown (who later adopted the name Jamil Al-Amin), Ralph Featherstone, Gloria Abernathy, and Ruby Doris Smith Robinson are but a few of the young personalities who began to assert themselves as leaders in this new phase of the struggle.

It was this new approach, coupled with public insistence on armed self-defense, that made the establishment so unwilling to negotiate seriously with these new kids on the block. When one considers that for years people within the movement had debated whether to openly use violence, it becomes clear why the establishment might have been wary of entering into dialogue with people who insisted on adhering to the eye-for-an-eye philosophy. After an increasing number of people in the movement began to question seriously the tactic of nonviolence, establishment leaders found it difficult, then impossible, to explain why violence against blacks and extreme poverty remained as much a reality after the passage of the Civil Rights Act of 1964 and Voting Rights Act of 1965 as it had been before these laws came into being. Because the explanation never materialized, younger blacks began to ask themselves who would lead this new, more radical movement for social change.

Martin Luther King Jr., Bayard Rustin, Ralph Abernathy, Roy Wilkins, and James Farmer balked at a change in tactics; traditional protest measures had secured substantial public support and laws that ostensibly brought about a new day in race relations. Since most movement people understood that established leaders would not, indeed could not, change tactics at a time when things seemed to be improving, the younger, less experienced activists had to answer the question of who was going to lead this next phase of the movement. Would it be the older, more middle-class oriented blacks? Would it be the college-educated, the group W. E. B. DuBois had dubbed the "Talented Tenth?" Would it be the mass of workers who made up the bulk of black America? Or would it be the dispossessed, the unemployed and underemployed people who lived by their wits; those who had no stake in the system, the group that Karl Marx and later Huey Newton dubbed the "lumpen proletariat"?

At the heart of this debate among civil rights activists lay the question of authenticity. They asked themselves which group truly represented the hopes, dreams, and interests of African America. In other words, who could prove their idea of which direction the struggle should move coincided most closely with the overall black mood in America? It took years for movement activists to discover the answers to these and other questions that dogged them as freedom fighters.

Before the Black Panther Party officially disbanded in 1982, however, it succeeded in feeding thousands of hungry children across the country. It first publicized then helped to treat sickle cell anemia, a debilitating blood disease primarily afflicting blacks. Panther Free Health Clinics brought decent healthcare to thousands who were mired in poverty and unable to afford medical care. The BPP pioneered the push for Black Studies programs in high schools, colleges, and universities across the nation. Its Liberation Schools, free busing to prison, free pest control programs, and other services endeared the BPP to black, brown, yellow, red, and some white communities in all regions of the nation. Like the War on Poverty programs that preceded the group's founding, the party assisted countless people in discovering their potential and worth. While few aspects of President Johnson's War on Poverty inspired Panther leaders, they were more than happy to build on the good things they discovered while working in one of Oakland's poverty programs. Like its contemporaries and others before it, the BPP sought to take advantage of the conditions that spawned the party.

The Black Panther Party movement, therefore, did not represent some isolated radical phenomenon. It had firm roots in an ongoing struggle for black civil rights in Oakland as well as the larger African American community. At the same time, however, it signaled a new era in the thinking of blacks nationwide. Like Martin Luther King Jr. and Malcolm X, Huey Newton and Bobby Seale were products of the movement, not creators of a new one. They simply responded to the political leanings of the youth, who after 1964 began to dominate the movement. What they ultimately wanted, like their nonviolent counterparts, was respect for human rights; only their methods differed. While

Seale and Newton were certainly talented individuals, they did not articulate any special brand of militancy. They were men who, at a particular place and time, found the courage to verbalize and to act out what many blacks in America historically longed to say and do in addressing their plight.

This book seeks to offer a critique of these actions through the organization's first six years. From the time of its founding in 1966 to 1972, the party exhibited a militant determination to secure black freedom by any means necessary. This militancy, and the aura of violence that surrounded it, carved out a place in the movement that few organizations could rival. For this reason, the focus here is on the role of violence in the making and unmaking of the most widely known of all the Black Power–era organizations.

Primarily a narrative of the party's early years, this study will show that violence, whether internal or external, rhetorical or real, psychological or physical, constituted the central element driving the group's decision-making processes. We will discover from those most closely associated with the BPP, namely its members and the police, that violence and the threat of it simultaneously made the party a media darling and a hated villain. The party's changing ideology will be illuminated to show that its commitment to violent revolution was short-lived. Oral histories taken from party members will help contextualize these changes and serve as the glue that holds this narrative together. The author has subverted, but not eliminated, the more traditional historical evidence in favor of this method because the story of the Black Panther Party—after forty years—still has not been adequately told. The group's mixed and tragic history constitutes one of the most important narratives of the late 1960s and early 1970s, a period in U.S. history that has yet to be understood. It is the author's intent that this glimpse into one aspect of the party serve as a catalyst to launch the inevitable and crucial process of genuine scholarly examination of this influential and heartbreaking group of black revolutionaries.

In essence, this is a story about the role of violence in the creation, sustenance, and destruction of the Black Panther Party, an organization dedicated to defending and serving the needs of the black community. This approach allows for a much broader discussion of what the BPP represented. When using violence as a lens through which to see the flowering and withering of the most popular and most effective of all the myriad Black Power organizations, it becomes clear that it was not Panther violence but the violence of the state that ultimately determined the tactics of the party in particular and of an era of black protest in general. Furthermore, this approach shows that blacks, particularly members of the BPP, immediately incurred the decidedly violent and deadly wrath of all levels of government after they took full responsibility for their own survival and advancement and after they openly challenged the white monopoly on violence in black communities. This book also highlights the party's internal tension between advocates of a more radical position who insisted on military confrontation with the power structure and those who believed community organizing and alliance building were the first priorities. Finally, it will demonstrate how the group's early emphasis on self-defense, something sorely needed in black communities at the time, left it open to mischaracterization, infiltration, and devastation by local, state, and federal police forces.

As BPP members and other blacks began to believe that their fate was tied up with the fate of the struggling peoples of Africa, Asia, and Latin America, they were compelled to stop viewing themselves as a minority and subsequently to believe that triumphing in their struggle was not only possible, but likely. They concluded that since the majority of the world's population was nonwhite, they had a better than fair chance of coalescing with other oppressed people and winning their complete freedom. Though they made a valiant effort and succeeded in some of their attempts to bring about change, they were wrong in their estimation—sometimes dead wrong.

Finally, the BPP had a profound impact on its members. Depending on what chapter one belonged to, the experience varied. Some were killed. Others were imprisoned, often for life. Still others were psychologically damaged after enduring sieges, raids, shootouts, murdered comrades, and the like. On the other hand, some experienced positive change. The BPP taught uncounted numbers of people to read and write. It gave others valuable skills that they continue to use today. It encouraged many to pursue and acquire a college education.

Even though a demoralized and drug-addicted Huey Newton met a senseless death in 1989 when gang member Tyrone Robinson shot him in the head after a drug dispute, others fared a lot better. Emory Douglas continues to use his skills as a graphic artist with the San Francisco *Sun Reporter*. Kathleen Cleaver now teaches law at Emory University in Atlanta. Carol Rucker owns her own business in Sacramento. BJ works as a labor organizer. Yasmeen Sutton is an accountant for a nonprofit organization in Harlem that serves women in need. Afeni Shakur runs a nonprofit for underprivileged youth. The list of former Panthers whose experiences have translated into livelihoods that allow them to continue serving the people is very long. The story that follows, though tragic in one sense, details how members of the Black Panther Party learned hard lessons in their efforts to secure freedom and justice for all.

CHRONOLOGY OF THE BLACK PANTHER PARTY

1961

Huey Newton meets Bobby Seale at Merritt College in Oakland, California. They later join activist/professor Donald Warden's Afro-American Association.

1964

Freedom Summer in Mississippi. Californians Mario Savio and Tom Hayden, among the nearly one thousand volunteers, become radicalized at the refusal of local, state, and federal agencies to rectify egregious racial discrimination, voter disfranchisement, intimidation, and murder that ran rampant through the Magnolia State. On their return, they help to radicalize the Bay Area and solidify alliances with future members of the soon-to-be-formed Black Panther Party.

1965

Malcolm X is assassinated in the Audubon Ballroom in New York City. In August, the Lowndes County Freedom Organization is founded in Alabama by a coalition of local people and Student Nonviolent Coordinating Committee members. It adopts the image of a pouncing black panther as its symbol.

1966

Huey Newton and Bobby Seale form the Black Panther Party for Self-Defense.

1967

Panthers carry out armed police patrols in Bay Area. They escort Betty Shabazz from San Francisco airport to *Ramparts*, where a major confrontation ending in a standoff between armed Panthers and police takes place. Eldridge Cleaver joins the party and becomes minister of information. The COIN-TELPRO against black nationalists begin, with the BPP as primary target.

Panthers enter the state capitol building in Sacramento and gain national notoriety.

Newton is wounded after an altercation with Oakland police that left Officer John Frey dead and Officer Herbert Haines wounded. The California State Legislature passes the Mulford Act, an antigun law prohibiting the carrying of firearms in any public place or street. This law ends Panther police patrols in Oakland.

1968

Five thousand onlookers cheer the speeches of H. Rap Brown, Bobby Seale, Stokely Carmichael, and a host of others at an event where the BPP merger with SNCC is announced.

Eldridge Cleaver and his wife, Kathleen, flee America, visit Cuba and Paris, then settle in Algiers. An FBI memo details the bureau's plans to cause conflict between Los Angeles panthers and the US organization.

J. Edgar Hoover instructs field agents to take action against the BPP on a national level and to consider how factionalism can be created between local and national leaders. He also instructs his men to neutralize BPP organizational efforts.

1969

The first BPP Free Breakfast for Children Program is initiated at St. Augustine's Church in Oakland. Bunchy Carter and John Huggins, leaders of the Southern California BPP, are killed in a shoot-out on the campus of UCLA.

District Attorney F. S. Hogan announces a twelve-count indictment against twenty-one Black Panther Party leaders in New York on charges of plotting to kill policemen and to bomb police stations, botanical gardens, and department stores. Bail is set at one hundred thousand dollars each. The Chicago chapter begins a free breakfast program that grows from eighty-three to more than 1,100 children in just one week.

J. Edgar Hoover declares "the Black Panther Party, without question, represents the greatest threat to internal security of the country." Stokely Carmichael resigns from the BPP. Panthers implement Liberation Schools, based on the Freedom School model of Mississippi activists.

Eight Panthers are arrested in New Haven, Connecticut, and charged with murder of New York City BPP member Alex Rackley.

Newton is convicted of voluntary manslaughter and sentenced to two to fifteen years in prison. BPP opens international section in Algeria under the aegis of Eldridge Cleaver.

Police raiders murder BPP leaders Fred Hampton, 21 (chairman of the Illinois BPP), and Mark Clark, 22 (minister of defense of the Peoria BPP). LAPD/SWAT and members of BPP fight a four-hour gun battle following a predawn police raid on Panther headquarters.

1970

Huey Newton is set free on a fifty thousand dollar bail after the state Supreme Court reverses his manslaughter conviction. The People's Revolutionary Constitutional Convention is held in Philadelphia. A BPP rally in New Haven, Connecticut, draws twelve thousand to fifteen thousand. Speakers include Chicago Seven defendants Jerry Rubin, Abbie Hoffman, David Dellinger, and David Hilliard. Disorder began following a fiery speech by Rubin and a false report of the arrest of three African Americans. Yale students strike in support of Panthers (including Bobby Seale) on trial, causing class attendance to drop 50 percent to 75 percent.

Jonathan Jackson, George Jackson's seventeen-year-old brother, William Christmas, and Judge Harold Mulvey are killed in an escape attempt from Marin County (California) courthouse. Police trace one of the guns used in the action to Angela Davis and she joined the FBI's Ten Most Wanted List.

1971

Newton and Cleaver split openly on an internationally televised phone call, each calling for the other's expulsion and Cleaver vowing to take over the East Coast wing of the party. Cleaver becomes openly aligned with the Black Liberation Army and strongly identified with more radical wing of the BPP. Cleaver supporters take over various offices in New York City and along the East Coast, including the Corona branch, where the BPP paper distribution was housed. *Black Panther* news circulation surges to over two hundred thousand per week.

BPP conducts its first sickle cell anemia testing. President Richard Nixon subsequently mentions sickle cell in his health message to Congress.

Twelve Panthers found not guilty of attempting to murder five police officers in a New Orleans gun battle that took place the previous year in the notorious Desire Project. George Jackson is killed in San Quentin prison.

Field marshal Robert Webb is murdered in Harlem on the corner of 125th and Seventh streets.

Sam Napier is found tortured and murdered in the Corona branch's office in retaliation for death of Robert Webb.

1972

Huey Newton contends the BPP is "putting down the gun" to work within the system to advance the black community.

Algerian police seal off BPP International headquarters and place those inside under house arrest. The headquarters on Peralta Street closes at the end of the year.

1973

Elaine Brown runs for Oakland City Council; Bobby Seale runs for mayor of Oakland and receives 40 percent of the vote. Though unsuccessful, the BPP shows its strength by registering a large block of voters who later help steer the city in a more progressive direction.

1974

Huey Newton goes into exile in Cuba. Bobby Seale leaves party under mysterious circumstances. Elaine Brown succeeds Newton as chairperson of the BPP.

1975

Eldridge and Kathleen Cleaver return from exile via Paris, France.

1983

After twelve years, Panthers close the Inter-communal Youth Institute (Oakland Community School).

1989

After a drug dispute, Tyrone Robinson kills Huey Newton on the streets of Oakland.

1998

Eldridge Cleaver dies at age 62 in Pomona, California. Stokely Carmichael (Kwame Ture) dies in Guinea, West Africa, at age 57.

Information primarily derived from: http://www.lib.berkeley.edu/MRC/pacificapanthers.html; http://www.itsabouttimebpp.com/; and Taylor, Ula and J. Tarika Lewis, and Mario Van Peebles, "Black Panther Party: A Chronology" in *Panther: A Pictorial History of the Black Panthers and the Story Behind the Film. pp: 177-187* (New York: Newmarket Press, 1995).

CHAPTER 1

Civil Wrongs and the Rise of Black Power

BECAUSE THE BLACK PANTHER PARTY FIT into the context of a nationwide black struggle for human and civil rights, this chapter explores the origins and development of Black Power as a guiding philosophy and presents a history of armed self-defense that unfolds alongside the growing frustrations of younger, more radical activists. Given this context, the Panthers' evolution from the earlier movement becomes readily apparent.

At the time of the founding of the Black Panther Party for Self-Defense in 1966, black communities across the United States still did not enjoy the physical protection police and sheriff's departments provided to most white communities as a matter of course. This reality was especially noticeable when it came to blacks who peaceably protested against the blanket denial of their civil and human rights. Not only could blacks not eat at the same lunch counters or drink out of the same water fountains as whites, but they also, for the most part, did not live in decent homes, attend adequately funded schools, or work at jobs that paid a living wage. When they finally amassed the courage to protest these inequities, they were met with violence, sometimes from white individuals and vigilante groups like the Ku Klux Klan, but most often from brutally racist law enforcement officials who had previously sworn to protect their right to peaceably assemble.

As the forties and fifties turned into the sixties and seventies, blacks' pleas for equal access and equitable treatment to the president(s) of the United States and Justice Department, though commonplace, often went unheeded. Wanting simply to reap the fruits of Americanism that they played a central role in planting in the two world wars, in Korea, and in the fields and factories of America, blacks sought to collect on a debt they believed should have been repaid at least a half century before.

Presidents from Harry Truman to Richard Nixon refused to remove the social, economic, and political barriers that prevented blacks from living lives where these abstractions became reality, effectively paying lip service to justice, equality, and liberty for all. Of course, Truman appointed a Commission on Civil Rights, Dwight Eisenhower federalized the National Guard in Arkansas to ensure the desegregation of Central High School in Little Rock, and Lyndon Johnson helped pass the Civil Rights Act of 1964. President Nixon even increased welfare payments. All these leaders, however, applied band-aids where extensive surgery was needed. None of them came close to addressing the economic inequities that insured blacks' low social status, and they did not attempt to avert the widespread police brutality that permeated black communities. Because of the authorities' failure to act and their subsequent refusal to prevent others from acting up, blacks were left with no alternative but to defend themselves. Because of blacks' insistence on self-defense, white violence, already commonplace, began to increase dramatically.

Early efforts for change in the fifties and sixties, though peaceful, were often met with empty political promises or the passage of frequently unenforced laws. This set of circumstances led to a change in tactics by those who had taken it upon themselves to lead the black freedom movement. Rather than retreating, blacks persevered and seemingly overnight gained the respect and admiration of many of their fellow citizens and a considerable number of supporters and sympathizers throughout the world. The idea that they could affect their own freedom and control their own destiny sparked a fire that could not be put out. Before long, a middle-class-led, integrationist-oriented civil rights movement transformed itself into a youth-led, autonomy-minded effort that became known as the Black Power movement. Some scholars insist that the spark that caused the Black Power movement appeared during and immediately after World War II, but in fact, blacks wanted to and attempted to control their own destinies from the time they were brought to the Americas as chattel. From the work of free black and enslaved people who organized churches and self-help organizations, to black abolitionists like David Walker, blacks had always made the effort to maintain a heightened consciousness and a desire to secure and preserve black power. While it is not expedient to chronicle the rich history of blacks' struggle, an understanding of the more modern antecedents to the rise of the Black Power movement is vital.

Beginning in the post–World War I period, particularly in the early twenties, blacks began to show signs that they truly understood their dilemma in American life. Although they continued to believe that violence used in self-defense was necessary, the emphasis remained on non-violence and peaceful change. Remarkably, even that approach provoked a violent response. While W. E. B. DuBois counseled blacks to demand their human rights and to defend themselves against white attack, Jamaican immigrant Marcus Garvey encouraged his very large following to look to itself and to its African roots for salvation. Both these men encouraged independent black enterprise and the celebration of African identity. Indeed, many blacks were far ahead of them on this score as they erected all-black towns from Mississippi to Oklahoma and fought tirelessly against the legal and extralegal lynchings that characterized this period. Despite the fact that most of these towns were destroyed by jealous and vengeful whites and that lynchings continued to occur through the 1960s, blacks came to see that their willingness to risk life and limb for freedom could have some positive effects.

The 1930s saw the dampening of the spirit of all Americans. The Great Depression ushered in widespread poverty and deprivation for the middle class and poor alike. Blacks, however, continued the struggle for equality. Denied the freedom they had been promised in 1865, blacks maintained their efforts toward inclusion in the body politic. There had in fact been nothing that could be accurately described as "separate but equal" in American life, as had been called for by *Plessey vs. Ferguson,* the 1896 Supreme Court decision creating this dichotomy. From the Southern Tenants Farmers' Union to the National Association for the Advancement of Colored People (NAACP), black activists made it known that their purpose in life was not to be the perennial doormat of white Americans. Though they suffered violent reprisals, blacks continued in their efforts to rid themselves of the shackles of debt peonage, discrimination, illiteracy, and unemployment. Only Adolph Hitler's theft of Czechoslovakia in 1938 and his attack on Poland in the fall of 1939 helped to ease some of this misery. These acts forced the British, Russians, and Americans to coalesce and to respond to the Fuhrer's threat, and World War II began.

Dubbing this campaign a war to save the world for democracy and as an attempt to safeguard and preserve freedom and justice the world over, the Allies unintentionally led many colonized and oppressed people to believe the war was meant to save them. They showed the world that violence was a legitimate tool to use in the fight for freedom. That the Allies did not respond to Hitler's threat with calls for nonviolence led many oppressed people to follow the examples set by these defenders of democracy. Latin Americans, Asians, Africans, and black Americans took this opportunity to begin a push for independence from white rule. While it helped Japanese and German colonies that their masters were under serious attack, black Americans—first through Asa Philip Randolph's March on Washington Movement, then through the many struggles of the Congress of Racial Equality and the NAACP—took the opportunity to demand that they too be given the opportunity to enjoy the fruits of freedom. These struggles led to a sustained organized movement that focused attention on the hypocrisy of American democracy. This refocusing of demands included mass movements, an emphasis on black culture, self-sufficiency, and armed self-defense. By the time the war ended, the momentum from these initial stirrings had grown to the point where they could not easily be contained or co-opted. Because the necessities of war had ushered in the migration of millions of blacks from the South to the North and West, there now existed an opportunity to protest against historical inequities more openly as southern mores no longer stood as barriers. Even when blacks remained in the South, their consciousness and outlook on life had been changed so much as a result of World War II and the changes it wrought that the fear that previously prevented large numbers of them from acting began slowly to subside.[1]

One of the more prominent examples of this dramatic upsurge in black activism is Monroe, North Carolina's NAACP. In the immediate aftermath of World War II, Robert Williams assumed leadership of what at the time was a fledgling branch of this otherwise viable organization. Dedicated to changing racist and oppressive laws through litigation, the NAACP disavowed the use of violence in achieving black equality. The group's leaders and sponsors believed the dark night of black oppression would dawn into a new day if the power structure were compelled to pass and enforce just laws. Williams believed the same thing, only he intended to protect himself, his family and his activist friends with arms if threatened with bodily harm. Williams's stance had materialized as a result of a long tradition of what he liked to call "armed self-reliance."

Historian Timothy B. Tyson, in his masterpiece *Radio Free Dixie,* argued Williams's life served as proof that "'the civil rights movement' and 'the Black Power movement' emerged from the same soil, confronted the same predicaments, and reflected the same quest for African American freedom." Williams, like many before him, insisted on the right of self-defense, and as the leader of Monroe's NAACP, often exercised this right. Though the NAACP's national office in New York suspended this courageous leader for advocating the use of violence, Williams continued to stare down and shoot back at racist policemen, Ku Klux Klansmen, and other elements seeking to terrorize blacks in Union County. Through his works, his courage, and his newspaper, the *Crusader,* Williams helped to create "a new black sense of self" and demonstrated to the world that blacks who defended themselves could survive in hostile environments. Though Williams fled the country to Cuba and later to China, his example influenced the next generation of activists. However, unlike many of those who followed Williams's philosophy, this trailblazer died naturally and not as a result of police bullets. Tyson's interpretation of Williams's life requires historians and scholars of the era to rethink traditional views of Black Power so that it emerges as a revival of past notions rather than a break with the past that introduces something new.[2]

According to Tyson, all the ingredients for Black Power were present in Williams's boyhood North Carolina. He claims the following "historical realities" shaped Williams's "and thousands of other black insurgents'" worldview: "African American cultural resilience; white racial violence . . . the persistent national failure, a century after the fall of slavery, to enforce equal protection of the laws; and the physical and psychological necessity for African American self-defense."[3] Although Tyson's study concentrates on a southern state decades before the formation of the BPP, the same situation confronted black America in the mid-1960s. While Tyson has done a great service to the history of this period, one could carry his argument even further back in time. From the days of the slave trade to the 1960s, blacks fought to ensure their dignity and to defend themselves from outside attack. In essence, what one finds is that the so-called nonviolent phase of the civil rights movement was not a retreat from violence per se, but a necessary tactical, strategic, and philosophical move made primarily by movement leaders who wanted to avoid as much as they could the violence that was sure to come once blacks took to the streets. This momentary lapse into nonviolence represented an effort on the part of movement leaders simultaneously to protect protesters and to ensure their activities garnered the widest media coverage possible. These leaders, however, knew from the beginning their constituents could and would, given the right circumstances, erupt into violence.

As Williams prepared to defend himself and others from the police and the Klan in Monroe in 1955, a particularly god-awful and atrocious act of white reprisal in Money, Mississippi, crystallized the realization that nonviolence was not enough. Roy Bryant and J. W. Milam murdered fifteen-year-old Emmett Till, a Chicago native visiting relatives for the summer. The white Mississippians accused the black Chicagoan of whistling at Carolyn Bryant, Roy's wife. The two men and their accomplices brutally tortured the child and left his body in such terrible condition that his mother "could hardly recognize him." Not only did they split the boy's head open with an ax, but they also gouged out one of his eyes, castrated him, cut out his tongue, and shot him several times. Having finished their gruesome deed, the murderers threw the body in the Tallahatchie River, tying the fan of a cotton gin to Till's neck in hopes that his body would stay on the muddy bottom. After a fisherman discovered Till's body floating in the river, local authorities immediately arrested the murderers. Meanwhile, the teenager's mother insisted on having an open casket funeral so the world might see "what they did to my son." Gruesome pictures of the mutilated youth circulated throughout the country and across the globe, outraging millions. Predictably, the subsequent sham trial ended in acquittal for the killers, who later confessed the murder when a magazine reporter offered them money. After this travesty of justice, an entire generation of young black activists began to see the necessity of fighting racial oppression with all means at their disposal.[4]

A heightened black consciousness emerged in the wake of this tragedy. At this time, many blacks felt enough was enough. This rise in black consciousness meant blacks possessed a weapon they could not be divested of, namely a belief in themselves and their ability to change their own circumstances. They began to understand things would never change if they remained passive. Although this sentiment had been present in parts of the black community prior to the 1950s, it had never been as widespread as it became after Till's horrendous murder.

Using the tactic of nonviolent direct action, blacks in Louisiana, Alabama, Mississippi, and other parts of the South began their effort to desegregate buses, lunch counters, and other places of public accommodation. At the same time, blacks in the North and West began to protest against police brutality, housing and employment discrimination, segregation, and economic stagnation. They also took on the double duty of helping their southern brothers and sisters fight against the Jim Crow laws that circumscribed not only their movements, but also denied them the basic decency due all human beings.

By this time, many black Americans saw newly independent African, Asian, Latin American, and Caribbean countries as models to emulate when gaining their own freedom. Almost overnight, their heroes became Cuba's Fidel Castro, Ghana's Kwame Nkrumah, Kenya's Julius Nyerere, and China's Mao Tse-tung. These new models for freedom-fighting and their newly gained consciousness led many blacks to the understanding that if their movement for liberation were to be effective, they first had to defend themselves from outside attack. Though they adored the leaders and the peoples who struggled in all the Third World countries, American blacks paid particular attention to Africa, where beginning in Sudan in 1956 and in 1957, formerly colonized areas began to emerge as independent nations that fought their way to victory.[5]

Already having been prodded about and made aware of the assault against imperial and colonial domination by the well-traveled Muslim leader Malcolm X, blacks came to see a sort of salvation in a connection with their African counterparts. While they realized their situation differed in many ways from their brothers and sisters in Johannesburg, South Africa, Nairobi, Kenya, Algiers, Algeria, and Accra, Ghana, they seemed also to understand that what they had in common with these struggling people was not only their African roots, but their common enemy. U.S. imperialism in Vietnam, Latin America, and other parts of the world came to be seen as the determining factor that ensured the oppression of all these groups. These two elements coalesced into a movement that eventually culminated with people proclaiming loudly that they were black and proud and that black was indeed beautiful. This self-respect brought with it the responsibility to defend oneself and one's family by any means necessary. As a result, nonviolence as a tactic began to lose its allure.

This latter development in the black movement for social and economic justice is one of its most profound. Blacks' willingness to respond to violent attacks with violence of their own ushered in a new stage of the movement. Love for their family and neighbors now determined their response to attacks rather than fear or the desire to remain nonviolent. Only after blacks decided to identify with their African roots did the movement begin to switch into this higher gear. Before his assassination, Malcolm X, who had been heavily influenced by the teachings of Marcus Garvey, insisted this "was the key to the Black Muslim movement: its concentration on things African. . . . African origins, African languages, African ties." He taught blacks that until they could love themselves, they would not be able to get rid of the oppression that daily circumscribed their lives. This love, in his view, could only come via an identification with who they really were. So rather than being ashamed of their African origins and hating their hair, skin, thick lips, and alleged lack of culture, they should be celebrating those things whites had taught them to hate. Instead of feeling inferior or inadequate as a result of their African origin, many blacks gained confidence, seized the moment, and made a true bid for their liberation.[6] Malcolm X's teachings reached audiences from Harlem to Selma, Alabama, Boston to McComb, Mississippi. Blacks began not only to learn their true history and to identify with it, but to use this newly acquired information as ammunition against the cultural murder that had characterized their lives since the days of slavery. This recognition that they could be identified as something other than misfits, thieves, beggars, or second-class citizens led them to see a newfound unity that could serve as an important weapon in their struggle. In other words, despite the centuries of teachings to the contrary, black people, in the decade between 1957 and 1967, found reason to love themselves and they demonstrated this love by their willingness to lay down their lives for those Africans they now saw as family rather than foe. They saw clearly the possibility of becoming self-sufficient and not relying on whites to provide them with life's necessities. In what social critic Harold Cruse called a revolutionary "act of defiance, blacks 'like Malcolm X' . . . dared to look the white community in the face and say: 'We don't think your civilization is worth the effort of any black man to try to integrate into.'"[7]

This newly acquired love, based on their identification as people of African descent, gave blacks the reservoir of spiritual and mental strength they needed to combat the slings and arrows of an embattled but tenacious Jim Crow system that operated in all regions of the country. It instilled in blacks a willingness not only to fight, while in some cases loving their enemy, but also in some cases to enter into alliances with whomever had their best interests in mind. Although some advocates of Black Power denounced any relationship with whites, others, like the Black Panther Party for Self-Defense, possessed a more inclusive vision that dictated they ally with anyone they saw as the enemy of their enemy. Theirs, therefore, could not be a movement based strictly on race—although race figured heavily into the equation—but more accurately on class and caste. Members of the nascent Black Panther Party realized their struggles were linked with the struggles of poor and working class whites as well as those who had been dispossessed by the vicissitudes of colonialism, racism, and a capitalism so avaricious it sometimes devoured human bodies for profit.

This realization that their struggle should be seen as part and parcel of the worldwide movement against white domination and oppression created an upsurge in activity. Individuals not ordinarily inclined to participate in what heretofore had been dubbed a nonviolent exercise in futility now threw themselves headlong into the fray. Because few northern blacks realized any tangible benefits from the integrationist-oriented, southern-based movement, they saw this widening of black protest as an opportunity to make their skills and talents useful to the black freedom struggle. For example, by 1960, only 234,000 of the nearly twenty-five million U.S. blacks attended any college at all. Throughout the sixties there were only half as many semiskilled jobs as there were black high school dropouts. In effect, neither school nor work had panned out for this strata of society.[8] It still had to deal with the joblessness, poverty, and lack of adequate education that pervaded urban existence. Because they did not have to swear allegiance to the philosophy or tactic of nonviolence, many blacks who became a part of this next phase of protest believed their dedication would not be hampered by the dictates of liberal white allies, who for the most part eschewed violence in the pursuit of human rights. Thomas McCreary, one of the thousands of youths in New York City who joined the Black Power movement, commented that "because the southern movement had bypassed northern youth who had always wanted to participate, Black Power was welcomed with open arms."[9]

Having seen the success of Robert Williams's armed group in Monroe, North Carolina, other groups began to emerge that served as protectors of the unarmed civil rights activists. In Mississippi, activists seeking to integrate schools and public places employed armed guards to protect themselves. Griffin McLaurin, an activist in Covington County, explained that "we formed a little group that was patrolling the community and keeping an eye on our community center. . . . they'd [whites] come in late at night and try to get to the center, but we had our guards. We stood our ground, and whenever we heard something that we thought wasn't right, we had our firepower."[10]

One of the most popular of these armed groups was the Deacons for Defense and Justice. Founded in 1964 in Jonesboro, Louisiana, the Deacons provided protection to civil rights activists seeking to change the status quo in the Pelican State. Like the men who worked with Robert Williams, many of them had served in the military, so they were well-equipped mentally and materially to accomplish their task. They eventually served the civil rights movement throughout the South, providing reconnaissance and security while at the same time warding off racist attackers. Their concept of retaliatory violence indeed helped the civil rights movement remain nonviolent. A. Z. Young, one of the group's members, explained that "If blood is going to be shed," it will be "all kinds, black and white. We are not going to send Negro blood down Columbia [Road] all by itself that's for sure."[11] No activist was ever killed and few were harmed when the Deacons handled security.

By the time the Deacons made their presence felt, others throughout the country had also recognized self-defense, not only as a necessity but as a right to be protected by law. Of course, these advocates of self-defense realized that appealing to conscience and constitutional jurisprudence did little to halt the swinging billy clubs, bats, and chains of racist sheriffs, policemen, and Klansmen. Their solution had not been to outgun their enemies, but to outvote them and to bring about what they hoped would be a peaceful revolution. They believed if they removed racist sheriffs and other politicians who did not have their interests in mind, they could create a situation where a peaceful and legal solution made violent revolution unnecessary. Malcolm X once remarked that of all the imperialist nations, the United States was in the advantageous position of being the only one that had the potential to experience a bloodless revolution. He noted that if whites simply obeyed and enforced their own laws, this feat could be accomplished easily. Many blacks believed wholeheartedly in this position and sought to make it a reality.

During the struggle for human rights in Mississippi in the summer of 1964, the murderous and violent opposition to the movement went a long way toward shaking this belief. The murders of three civil rights workers in Philadelphia, Mississippi, shocked the nation as well as the rich white northern students who had gone to the Magnolia State to help blacks register to vote. Seething with racial violence and a plethora of other injustices, Mississippi was viewed by many Americans as the worst of the racist southern states. In terms of violence, discrimination, and racial hatred, it sat at the top of the list of all other states. To change this reality, movement organizers hoped if whites were hurt or killed in pursuit of civil rights, the government would move to solve the age-old problem. In July 1964, Ku Klux Klansmen, including Sheriff Lawrence Rainey of Neshoba County and his deputy Cecil Price, murdered James Chaney, Andrew Goodman, and Michael Schwerner in an attempt to frighten blacks away from their struggle for equality. The three had gone to Philadelphia, a small town near Meridian in the east-central part of the state, to investigate the bombing of a church that had been used for civil rights meetings. The Klansmen who burned the church were attempting to lure "Mickey" Schwerner into a trap to murder him. When the three left the church and headed back to their headquarters in Meridian, the authorities stopped them and delivered them to their Klan brothers, who summarily executed them. Weeks later, the FBI, state highway patrol, and men from the U.S. Navy stationed at a base near Meridian dug up the bodies from an earthen dam.[12]

These murders, and the dozens that came before them, along with the uncounted beatings activists suffered at the hands of racist whites, forced blacks to question whether America ever intended to live up to its creed of liberty and justice for all. For the moment, however, the activists persevered and continued to push for change by using traditional nonviolent means.

At the end of this crucial summer, blacks who had formed the

Mississippi Freedom Democratic Party sought to be recognized by the national Democrats at the convention in Atlantic City, New Jersey. Even though the all-white Mississippi delegation vowed not to support officially nominated Democrats for president and vice president, the national Democratic Party refused to seat the pleading blacks, led by civil rights stalwart and former sharecropper Fannie Lou Hamer, who promised the group's support to the national Democratic Party. The activists rejected the offer of two seats at large with no voting power, claiming they had not "come all this way for no two seats." This kick in the teeth further soured blacks' enthusiasm for peaceful change. The Mississippi Freedom Democratic Party did not, however, give up on the electoral process. Instead, its members returned to Mississippi and continued organizing. This time, in addition to indigenous Mississippians who had protected activists with arms, a small contingent of members of the Revolutionary Action Movement, an armed group that promised to use violence to bring about political change, went to the Magnolia State and other parts of the South to assist Student Nonviolent Coordinating Committee (SNCC) workers.[13]

As black Mississippians and their allies began to reevaluate their position vis-à-vis the power structure, the idea of using open violence became acceptable to more and more people. At the same time, however, their neighbors to the east began to attract headlines. Blacks in the Alabama "black belt," having learned from both Mississippi's and their own experiences, knew by 1966 that to be armed meant, in many cases, to be alive. The most notable example of this move toward political organizing with the gun as a tool for ensuring success can be found in the 1966 attempt of the Lowndes County (Alabama) Freedom Organization to take power via the ballot box, where their overwhelming numerical majority assured them victory. They arrived at this conclusion based on the fact that blacks outnumbered whites eight to one.

This group of politically savvy activists thought it necessary to organize their own political party—and did so in March 1965. Under the leadership of John Hulette, who had previously organized and led the Lowndes County Christian Movement, thousands in this poverty-stricken black belt enclave rallied to the cause of their own liberation. This organization was designed to effect change in the political process and to push for desegregation of public facilities. After enduring violent oppression and discrimination, its members realized neither the Republican nor the Democratic Party had their best interests in mind. Their understanding of the situation was confirmed when a black man attempting to vote in the previous election was shot and killed. They could point out as an example the fact that only one of the county's twelve thousand black residents was registered to vote—that was John Hulette. Urged on by a small group of SNCC stalwarts that included Stokely Carmichael, Bob Mants, Judy Richardson, and Scott Smith, and encouraged by the newly minted Voting Rights Act of 1965, under which the first federal registrar came to Lowndes County, these black Alabamians decided to attempt what had previously been deemed the impossible, or at least what they had considered "white folks' business," according to Carmichael. He added that once the SNCC team showed black residents the "educational background of most of the white local officials, they realized what a hoax that was" to have believed that "white folks who ran things had knowledge, experience and education that their leaders lacked."[14] Through political education workshops that would later be adopted by the Black Panthers of Oakland, these blacks developed a confidence that compelled them to challenge the all-white Democratic Party that had historically run county politics to the detriment and exclusion of blacks.

Calling its organization the Lowndes County Freedom Organization (LCFO) and utilizing a black panther as its symbol, this group, according to Hulette, did not "want to integrate" but to acquire "power, pure unadulterated political power." According to Hulette, they used the panther as a symbol because it was "a vicious animal . . . that never bothers anything, but when you start pushing him, it moves backwards . . . into his corner, and then he comes out to destroy everything that's before him." He said Lowndes County blacks "have been pushed back through the years . . . deprived of our rights to speak, to move, and to do whatever we wanted to do at all times. And now we are going to start moving." This new party's plan was "to take over the courthouse in Hayneville," the county seat. In an insistent tone of voice, he added, "And whatever it takes to do it, we're going to do it." The LCFO sought to achieve its goal of political representation by running its own slate of officers in the upcoming political campaign. After having been denied access by the regular Democratic Party and, according to Hulette, after having come to terms with the fact that there was "no room for Negroes in the same party as [Governor George] Wallace," they believed this move was their only alternative. Excluding whites from leadership positions, but not from the party itself, the LCFO set out to organize the county's blacks.[15]

Knowing they were going to meet determined opposition in their bid for real power, the members of the LCFO hardly had to discuss their unwritten policy of armed self-defense. Having grown up in and around "bloody Lowndes," these individuals knew of the effect on whites and blacks of a well-armed security apparatus. Indeed, Carmichael recounted, "when night riders started driving by firing guns" at a makeshift "Tent City" that housed blacks who had been evicted because of their participation in the LCFO, "the men and boys posted sentries on the road and returned fire." As in Monroe, North Carolina, nearly a decade before, "the night riding stopped" after this show of force.[16] Group leader John Hulette added that LCFO "is not nonviolent" or even "a protest movement."

"We're out to take power legally, but if we're stopped by the government from doing it legally, we're going to take it the way everyone else took it including the way the Americans took it in the American Revolution." Certain the federal government was not going to protect him and his fellow party members, Hulette told a federal registrar, "if one of our candidates gets touched, we're going to take care of the murderers ourselves."[17] On a fundraising tour, he told a Los Angeles audience that blacks "had never had any protection and today we aren't looking for anybody to protect us. We are going to protect ourselves."[18]

These sentiments portended doom for the slowly splintering civil rights movement as activists openly questioned the usefulness of nonviolence as a tactic. Although this debate had simmered below the movement's surface for years, increased brutality, murders, broken promises, and the slow pace of change compelled many to bring it to the forefront of discussion. Having never been a central tenet of black activism, the Martin Luther King Jr. style of nonviolence began to die in Alabama, the state most notably associated with its birth. LCFO members never considered nonviolent protest important enough to resuscitate, as its life had previously led to the violent deaths of many of their loved ones. Hulette told one Justice Department official, in town to observe the election, that the sheriff had previously forbade the new party to assemble on the courthouse lawn, as provided by the laws of the county. "If shooting takes place," he told the man from Washington, "we are going to stay out here and everybody die together."[19]

Despite the many death threats they received from the Klan and local police officials, LCFO members continued to organize. The results, however, were disappointing. In the end, this fledgling political party failed to seat any of its candidates. Carmichael pointed out that they "discovered on election day that the plantation bosses had completely reversed their tactic" of "running" their blacks "off the plantation for registering."

"Now they were running them off if they didn't. On election day they trucked their field hands in to vote against the Panthers," he noted. He recounted that "of the two thousand newly registered blacks, over nine hundred withstood the threats and cast their votes for the Panthers." Half a decade later their continued organizing led to the election of a black sheriff and county commissioner and gave blacks "eight other contested seats." While initially defeated, the inspiration their political innovation gave to blacks all over the country created quite a stir.

Versions of this Black Panther Party formed elsewhere in places like Los Angeles, San Francisco, Detroit, Chicago, St. Louis, and Oakland. After the Lowndes County action, people who had come from outside the state to help began requesting permission to use the group's name for similar organizations they had created or been a part of in their respective hometowns. California resident and Vietnam veteran Mark Comfort happened to be one of these individuals who went down to Louisiana to help SNCC with security and self-defense. He asked Carmichael if he could use the Panther name and idea to "try to spread it." Carmichael told him it belonged to "the people" so he should "feel free" to use it. Comfort did just that and went back to Oakland and started his own Black Panther Party. He later discovered that other groups throughout the Bay Area liked the Black Panther Party name and idea, too.[20]

In 1966, a Black Panther Party emerged in New York City, with headquarters on Seventh Avenue in Harlem. Like its progenitor, its members believed that "wherever blacks comprised a majority of the population (Like Harlem, Watts, Hough, South Side, Lowndes County, etc.) they should control that area." On August 20, 1966, George M. Miller, a member of this freshly transplanted Black Power organization, wrote to his fellow Harlemites that this new party had formed as a direct result of the action taken in Lowndes County. "This is as it should be," he explained.

Writing in the soulful vernacular of that highly charged era, he hoped to "make a long story short" by proclaiming to the people of this cultural mecca that "the Black Panther Party has arrived in Harlem." Having previously "spread to several cities in the North," he wrote that the party did not seek merely to get votes like its Democratic and Republican Party opponents. He wanted to let them know this was "a social MOVEMENT of BLACK people addressing itself *specifically* to the problems faced by black people living in the midst of white America." Armed self-defense was one of its central tenets.

Going on to explain why blacks needed to pool their resources and coordinate efforts to enhance their unity, Miller discussed the impending action the party had agreed upon. The group planned to make uncompromising demands to the Board of Education about the decayed and atrophied schools their children attended. "Our children are the future," Miller wrote, "so we should be careful what they learn and who teaches them." Expressing grave concern over the issue, he added that "they will mature *either* to become instruments of the white power structure used to keep our people politically unaware and vulnerable, *or* to become proud black men and women with love and concern for their own kind." Referring to the political and social "implications of education in Harlem," the letter implored Harlemites to support the Black Panther Party "in executing OPERATION SHUT DOWN on September 12, 1966."

In its quest for "quality education in Harlem," OPERATION SHUT-DOWN planned to "shut down the public schools in Harlem one by one . . . if the Board failed to comply with all the demands." In a bold move of self-reliance, the Black Panther Party unveiled its plans to teach the children in "liberation schools" established in churches throughout the community. It seemed for the time being the black church remained a rock in a weary land. Going on to list their demands, Miller wrote that the first demand was to ensure that "Afrigan [sic] and African-American history and culture [be] taught in all Central Harlem Public Schools." The group also called for black principals in these schools. Demonstrating a clear understanding of the symbolism that pervades every level of education, the group's final demand called for changing "the names of the public schools so that they reflect the history and achievements of *OUR PEOPLE.*" Repeating the invitation to community members to work with them, the letter ended with the date, location, and time of the next meeting. The urgency of the situation could be seen in Miller's reminder to blacks that "TIME IS RUNNING OUT!" In a final demonstration of sincerity, the party functionary signed the letter "Yours for unity, power, and self-determination." This triumvirate of elements eventually led to relative success for this Black Panther Party and the one that followed it two years later.[21]

In 1966, Carmichael made an open proclamation demanding a dedication to what he called Black Power. This call was heard all over the country, and eventually all over the world. The organizing, struggling, and dying that took place prior to this watershed year must be reexamined, however, before a full understanding of what that cry meant to the people who stood to benefit most from it. Many scholars—Tim Tyson, Charles Payne, and Peniel Joseph, to name a few—have begun the necessary work of reexamining the World War II era in an effort to locate the deep roots of Black Power. Unquestionably, the movement began long before the words "black power" were uttered.

Perhaps this refusal to verbalize such a goal merely indicated the pragmatism of pre-1966 movement leaders. It is revealing to note King's private position on the new phrase. He told Carmichael, who became a national leader of the new movement, after the latter complained about being lambasted in the press over the phrase's implications, that the difference in the mainstream treatment of him and the young firebrand was "simple." Referring to the expression black power, King gently explained to Carmichael that, "Maybe I just don't talk about it." One-time King lieutenant Andrew Young explained that the reverend believed that "if you go around claiming power, the whole society turns on you and crushes you." According to Young, King believed that had been the reason why Jews and Catholics, both powerful entities in American society, "denied" they had any real power. Young concluded of King that "it was not black power that he was against, it was the slogan Black Power, because he said, 'If you really have power you don't need a slogan.'"[22] King must have known that the common enemy he shared with Carmichael—those who maintained capitalism and racism —would be greatly offended by the phrase and their defensiveness would certainly make organizing and negotiating for black rights more difficult, if not impossible.

Then too, blacks who participated in the movement prior to the six-ties probably saw little reason to state the obvious. After all, if blacks could vote and work for the same pay as their white counterparts, then power was a foregone conclusion. They could see that historically these advantages provided whites with plenty of power. Surely, all those people who died trying to register themselves and others to vote or try-ing to integrate public facilities saw their actions as a bid to acquire more power for their communities. They did so even if only to acquire the power to decide. The fact that armed self-defense had been employed for years serves as a testament to the idea that one cannot hope to achieve or maintain power without the requisite willingness to fend off outside attackers. For example, in 1959, seven years before Carmichael uttered his earth-shattering phrase in Greenwood, Mississippi, Martin Luther King Jr., the "apostle of nonviolence" as former attorney general Ramsey Clark called him, convincingly argued that "when the Negro uses force in self-defense, he does not forfeit support—he may even win it, by the courage and self-respect it reflects." Like his role model Mohandas Gandhi, King refused to condemn "[t]he principle of self-defense, even involving weapons and bloodshed." He believed violence used in the name of self-defense was not only "legal" but "moral" as well.[23]

With most movement leaders and their followers agreeing that self-preservation had to take first priority in any struggle, blacks in the years and decades prior to 1966 moved with all deliberate speed to ensure they shared the power that had been promised them in the Constitution and other laws of the land. The fact that no one labeled this phase of the move-ment "Black Power" or that the "civil rights" moniker took precedence over other descriptors says more about those with the power to define such phenomena than it does about the participants' goals and tactics. Neither Martin Luther King Jr., Ralph Abernathy, Roy Wilkins, Bayard Rustin, Fred Shuttlesworth, Ella Baker, Fannie Lou Hamer, nor any other well-known movement figure spoke about the necessity of a civil rights appellation per se. They all, however, spent the better part of their adult lives attempting to transform an oppressed, degraded, and brutalized peo-ple into an organized force that could wield sufficient power to determine the destinies of their lives and the lives of their children. This of course is not to say that these movement icons did not see utility in giving direc-tion to a movement the media had labeled "civil rights." They all believed victory in their morally constituted, nonviolent movement would only come once they successfully fused self-defense with black pride and "independent black political action."[24] Nineteen sixty-six then, happened to be the year that blacks began publicly to articulate, without compromise, their goals and the methods they intended to use to achieve them. This was the year the once-popular James Meredith reemerged on the black activist stage to play yet another decisive role. Previously, in the fall of 1962 in Oxford, Mississippi, Meredith's enrollment at the University of Mississippi had precipitated a three-day riot in which 160 people, including U.S. Marshals, suffered injuries, and two people were killed. Five thousand soldiers from a nearby army division had to be called in to put down the disturbance. This time, however, Meredith pledged to walk, or march, over 150 miles from north Mississippi, just across the state line from Memphis, Tennessee, to the capitol at Jackson in the center of the state. He labeled his one-man venture the March Against Fear. Meredith, described by one contemporary as "a strange, almost eccentric brother," apparently attempted the march "to demonstrate to the people that white violence was nothing they had any longer to fear." Though most might have guessed Meredith would definitely be harassed, probably wounded, and perhaps killed, the veteran integrator of Ole Miss, on June 5, 1966, put whatever reservations he had aside and began his march. A couple of hours after commencing, Aubrey James Norville emerged from a thicket of roadside bushes and unloaded his shotgun into the body of the unsuspecting and exceedingly brave Meredith.[25]

This shooting had the opposite effect of what the assailant intended. Rather than stopping the march, Norville succeeded in attracting more people to it. If that were not bad enough, for Mississippi anyway, these new participants included the leaders of all the major civil rights organizations. Even though moderates like Roy Wilkins and Whitney Young ultimately refused to participate because of the suggested use of an armed contingent of the Deacons for Defense and Justice, most others chose to honor Meredith and carry the march to its conclusion. Martin Luther King Jr. of the religious-based Southern Christian Leadership Conference, Floyd McKissick of the Congress of Racial Equality, and Stokely Carmichael of the SNCC joined forces and pledged to make the march even more meaningful by organizing for change and registering people to vote along the way.[26]

After the dust settled a week after Meredith's shooting, the march resumed. The hot Mississippi summer sun beamed downed on the marchers as they faced taunting crowds of rock and bottle-throwing whites and the more than occasional driver who attempted to run over people in the crowd with a car or truck. The Deacons made a show of force and no one was killed, although King and several others suffered injuries after being hit with flying projectiles. After they were treated, the march resumed. Even though there was a heavy police presence, no whites were arrested for harassing or assaulting the marchers. Every night, the group held a rally to mobilize people in the communities where they camped. Every night large crowds came out to greet the marchers, though, according to Carmichael, most of them just wanted to get a glimpse of King.[27]

As they approached Jackson, the marchers slowly meandered through the Mississippi Delta like Israelites trudging through the desert in search of the promised land. They camped out on the private property of black well-wishers, in public parks, or on school grounds. This strategy worked well until, a week or so into the march, they reached Greenwood, a bastion of segregation under white control in the mostly black Delta. Even though school board members had granted the marchers permission to camp out on the grounds of an all-black elementary school, the Greenwood police tried to prevent the group from doing so. The march leaders, particularly Carmichael, who was well known in Greenwood because of previous organizing there, saw this as "an issue of community control, black power if you will." He remembered that "he told the workers to put up the tent unless the local community leaders stopped them." The marchers argued forcefully with the police and tempers flared. During this exchange, Carmichael must have said something at which police took serious issue because at that point he "was dragged off to jail." Still, he said, "the tent went up."[28]

After several hours and several phone calls from people trying to get Carmichael released, there was a breakthrough. The authorities notified march leaders that they were going to release Carmichael later that evening. He came out "just minutes" before the rally began. Right before he began his speech, Carmichael "passed Mukasa [Willie Ricks]" who told him to "Drop it now. The people are ready. Drop it now." Blacks all over north and central Mississippi were already responding positively to the phrase Black Power. Ricks should have known they were ready because he had been frantically crisscrossing the Delta and other parts of northern and central Mississippi to test the new slogan that came to symbolize the movement. Organizing small rallies and punctuating them with the Black Power slogan, Ricks had worked to prime anxious blacks for the moment. Carmichael knew the moment had come, too, so he wasted little time getting to his point.[29]

Not "in a mood to compromise with racist arrogance," Carmichael remembered emerging onto the stage to thundering applause. There were hundreds of people ready to listen to the beloved "Stokely." Blacks had come from all over central Mississippi, as far away as Yazoo City, Benton, Eden, and Midnight. Some had just left the cotton fields and others still wore their work clothes. They knew their time had come to stand up and make a change, or their very survival might be forfeited. Carmichael turned out to be the night's last speaker, so he had to bring it all home. The speakers before him had been "particularly militant," he remembered. The mood at the "huge" rally had been upbeat, carrying along with it "the spirit of self-assertion." The crowd's "defiance was palpable," Carmichael noted. They were ready to begin to exploit the power in their numbers and they were happy that finally the storm of their long night of discontent had begun to show signs of lifting. Having been in this storm so long, black Mississippians were ready to move to make brighter days for themselves. Most in the crowd believed God had given them the right to do so. They knew the Fifteenth Amendment and civil rights laws, which they hardly benefited from, had guaranteed this right. Carmichael remembered he "looked over" the "embattled" crowd and "told them what they knew, that they could depend only on themselves, their own organized collective strength. Register and vote. The only rights they were likely to get were the ones they took for themselves," he roared.[30]

Cleveland Sellers remembered that "Carmichael let it all hang out" because he was in his element. Carmichael's powerful words electrified the receptive crowd. People clapped their hands, stomped their feet and urged the fiery-eyed, finger-pointing activist on to greater heights. The rally had transformed into something akin to a church meeting. The back-and-forth dynamic between speaker and audience resonated with joy and thanksgiving, with some in the crowd saying amen while others waved their hands or swayed to the rhythm of the night. People's hopes were high and "the spirit of the Lord," as some Mississippians like to call it, seemed to pulsate through the general body. Black Mississippians had come full circle. They felt themselves ready to take the power whites had refused to share for so long, and their attendance testified to the fact that they were indeed not afraid. As menacing Mississippi Highway Patrolmen, sheriffs, and their deputies looked on in disgust, the group affirmed its right to stand up and be heard. They now seemed ready to act on their Christian belief that "with God all things are possible."[31]

Sensing the receptiveness of the now jubilant crowd, Carmichael decided to "drop it" as Ricks had urged him to do at the outset, and drop it he did. He told the eager crowd he had gone to jail twenty-seven times since he had become an activist in 1960. It must have been one time too many. "I ain't going to jail no more!" he shouted. Addressing one of the most pressing problems facing blacks in the Delta (and in northern ghettos for that matter), he exclaimed, "The only way we gonna stop them white men from whippin' us is to take over. We been saying freedom for six years and we ain't got nothing. What we gonna start saying now is Black Power." Like any good black congregation, the crowd roared back to him: "Black Power!" Carmichael knew he had been understood when each time he shouted the new phrase, his captivated audience shouted it back. At this point, a wily Willie Ricks mounted the back of the truck from which Carmichael spoke and asked the crowd, "What do you want?"

"Again and again," wrote Carson, "the audience shouted in unison the slogan that had suddenly galvanized their emotions. 'Black Power! Black Power! Black Power!'" While it is now clear this galvanization had not been so sudden, but rather a result of the heavy spade work Ricks and others had done, it is accurate to say that after this momentous night blacks began to see their struggle in a completely different light. Though they had been working for and toward black power at least since the beginning of World War II, an extremely well-known and respected personality had now given voice, tone, and definition to their hard-fought and often embittering struggle. In essence, their hopes and aspirations had been condensed and clearly articulated, not just for Mississippians or Americans, but for much of the world. For those who lived the experience, rainy days were ending and the sun was about to shine.[32]

To many blacks, the new slogan was a manifesto that meant from then on, they, as a unified group, would concentrate on organized self-sufficiency rather than white largesse. Historian William Chafe accurately pointed out that Black Power advocates in North Carolina struck "at the very base of white control—the power to define what is real and unreal, permissible and impermissible." By organizing those people who historically had little political power and no access to it, they were rejecting "the definition of their proper 'place' handed down by white authorities . . . and undercutting the very foundations of white power. If blacks created their own ground rules," Chafe wrote, "they would cease to be vulnerable to white attempts to divide and conquer them through traditional white rules."[33] These sentiments, agreed upon by many if not most of the younger activists of the period, came to make up the Black Power mystique.

This new militancy, the public declaration of the right to self-defense, and an uncompromising stance on full equality, though not a grand diversion, worked like a strong undercurrent to the more traditional civil rights movement unfolding on television. Although participants in earlier phases of the movement believed wholeheartedly in the importance of cultural awareness and pride, and in the right to self-determination and self-defense, what made the later stage *appear* more radical to the press was the public declaration of these rights. King, Wilkins, Rustin, and other more moderate leaders had concentrated on cautious, deliberate negotiation, compromise, and enjoying the benefits of a fully integrated polity. The later, much younger activists held no such hopes and believed blacks should work with others to dismantle the system and create a new, more equitable society where liberty and justice for all was a reality.

In the decades prior to the Black Power movement, black activists in Mississippi, Louisiana, Alabama, and Georgia had demonstrated a readiness and willingness to use force in self-defense, but they hardly discussed such a program with the media. They must have believed in the idea that actions speak louder than words, and rather than shouting it from the rooftops and on the six o'clock news, they simply did whatever was necessary. After 1966, armed self-defense became a part of the public agenda.

No longer willing to have their agenda set, or even influenced, by whites who might be upset at their delivery or approach to black liberation, these new, younger activists, including Stokley Carmichael, H. Rap Brown, Willie Ricks, Victoria Gray, and later Kathleen Cleaver, Huey

Newton, and Bobby Seale, thought they saw an opportunity to unify blacks around common issues, regardless of class, status, or geographic location. They had, in effect, taken the principles of their predecessors and added a public call for armed self-defense in a daring attempt to claim not only their manhood and womanhood but their dignity and self-respect as well. To augment these principles, they demanded the same right to community control that many white males had enjoyed and taken for granted for centuries. Theirs was a movement that changed the way the powerless interacted with the powerful. So, rather than requesting change, they became duty-bound to bring it about. Carmichael wrote blacks would "[n]o longer pretend to accept, with a grin and shuffle whatever grudging crumbs and concessions the white establishment might feel disposed to toss our way." He believed blacks were ready "to *assert* and *demand* everything that is ours by right, nothing less. That was the politics."[34] First, however, he and other members of SNCC had to deal with white reaction to the bombshell he dropped in Mississippi.

Carmichael recalled after these "two ordinary, unthreatening, everyday words . . . [black power]" were "rendered menacing, sinister, and subversive of public order and stability," he had extreme difficulty traveling. "In short order" he wrote, the two words had "me denied entry into France and Britain, declared persona non grata, and banned in thirty territories of the former British Empire, including" Trinidad, "the country of my birth." Noting how the combination of the words "black" and "power" seemed "incomprehensible" and confusing "to otherwise intelligent and sophisticated Americans, " Carmichael sarcastically stated the concept appeared "entirely beyond the cognitive reach of the white national media and public." While claiming he had "failed to define the term clearly," the media, along with the movement's enemies, began to describe the phrase as separatist, antiwhite, hate-filled, containing violent overtones, and having black supremacy as its ultimate goal. None of these characterizations accurately defined the term, and they derailed any serious discussion of economic inequality, widespread discrimination against blacks in housing, education and employment, and the continued refusal of any level of government to halt the brutal treatment police officials and ordinary white citizens meted out to blacks as a matter of course. These same conditions prevailed in Detroit and Cleveland as well as in Jackson and Birmingham. These wrongs comprised the very issues Black Power sought to address. One might say this lack of understanding about the simple phrase went hand-in-hand with the existing power structure's desire to protect its interests, which included maintenance of the status quo.[35] It seems if any person or group understood black power, it would have been those entities responsible for generating and maintaining white power.

During this turbulent period in 1966, Huey Newton and Bobby Seale formed the Black Panther Party for Self-Defense (BPP) in the ghettos of the Oakland/San Francisco Bay Area. While whites debated among themselves what the Black Power slogan meant, and while Carmichael and others spent countless hours trying to explain what it did not mean, the BPP and other groups began the process of creating the new black man and the new black woman. No longer ashamed of their kinky hair, so-called thick lips, ethnic English, and alleged inferiority, they awakened to a newly discovered love of self that transformed the way they viewed their relationship to their communities. As they sought cultural and psychological self-determination, they used Black Power as the tool to free themselves from what Carmichael described as "a heritage of demeaning definitions imposed on us, over centuries of colonial conditioning by a racist culture." It seemed to work like a charm as the Panther leaders began to provide assistance to the downtrodden of Oakland. They began to recruit literally at the street level.[36]

This grassroots organizing, tested and perfected in Klan strongholds in Mississippi, Alabama, and Georgia, was now going to be used in urban enclaves where the racism had been subtler but no less brutal. This time, however, the brutality was confronted not with love and prayers but with armed self-defense and a closing of ranks designed to help blacks face white racism with a united front. The Black Panther Party, in just a few years, came to represent this effort better than any of the Black Power groups that emerged after the summer of 1966. Having dramatically changed the rules of the game, they were now ready to get on with the business of playing for keeps. They knew their opponents had been doing just that since the game started. The leaders' journey to this particular point in their lives had prepared them for the moment when they led the most dynamic of all the Black Power organizations.

———————

Among a tide of southern immigrants, the Newton family arrived in Oakland in 1945. Like many others, the Newtons moved west because of the promise of jobs and a higher standard of living. Huey Percy Newton, the last of seven children, was only three years old when his family moved to Oakland. Born in Monroe, Louisiana, he was named after Huey Pierce Long, the flamboyant legendary Kingfish and former governor of the Pelican State. According to Walter Newton, Huey's father, Huey Long sponsored many beneficial programs that helped Louisiana blacks: free books in the schools, free commodities for the poor, and public road and bridge construction projects that employed many impoverished blacks. Believing that Long had been a great man, Huey's father named a son after him.[37]

Like many other black families in Oakland, the Newtons moved frequently from one substandard house to another. In his autobiography, *Revolutionary Suicide,* Newton recalled how he often had to sleep in the kitchen of their two-bedroom homes. Also like others in the Bay Area, the Newtons lived amid racial discrimination, inferior schools, and crime-ridden neighborhoods. During his adolescent years, young Huey developed an intense dislike for those individuals in the political power structure, whom he claimed condoned the deplorable ghetto surroundings. It appeared the rapidly increasing layoffs in shipbuilding and other war-related industries meant the Newton family had chosen a bad time to relocate to Oakland. Their hopes of a better future in the West seemed to be dashed by many of the same factors that had prevented their economic and social advancement in the Deep South. Extralegal violence, dilapidated neighborhoods, and inadequate educational facilities mirrored the situation from which they fled. Despite the hardship, the Newtons did not accept their lowly position as being permanent.[38] Like others, they continued to struggle for economic and social advancement. Newton's father used his talents as a Baptist preacher to help the family through these hard times.

Newton remembered growing up feeling uncomfortable, ignorant, and ashamed of his color. He told how he often felt inferior to whites. Commenting on his years in the Oakland public school system, Newton complained that he "did not have one teacher who taught [him] anything relevant to [his] own life experience." He added, "not one instructor ever awoke in me a desire to learn more or question or explore the worlds of literature, science, or history. All they did was try to rob me of the sense of my own uniqueness and worth, and in the process they nearly killed my urge to inquire."[39]

Newton's words, if true, represent an indictment of a public system that often did not serve blacks well. Most of America's inner-city schools, as a matter of practice if not primarily of policy, undereducated or miseducated almost all black students.[40] Newton's description of the Oakland public school system clearly condemns the inadequacy of black Californians' education during this period. Newton had not been the only person to criticize Oakland's public schools.

A 1963 Fair Employment Practices Committee report noted that as late as 1962, only five blacks worked as principals and vice principals out of a total of 139 such administrators in the Oakland public schools. The report also indicated there were only 164 black teachers in the Oakland public school system, out of a total of 1,158 teachers. When one considers that blacks represented some thirty percent of Oakland's population, these numbers hardly show they enjoyed any real representation. The report concluded that the absence of black administrators and teachers tended to exacerbate the public education problem.[41]

In 1959, after Newton graduated from high school, he began to question seriously the inequalities of American society. He wondered why the majority of blacks did not succeed, even though they worked hard all their lives. Perhaps naiveté prevented him from understanding America's promise of prosperity to all who worked hard did not apply to everyone, whether black, white, or any other ethnicity. To be sure, class differences worked to keep many of the poor and uneducated of all races from realizing the American promise, but clearly racism in American economic, political, and social policies worked to keep blacks in their place. With these questions occupying his thoughts, in 1959, Newton entered Merritt College, a small school in Oakland that had once been known as Grove Street College, where he met Bobby G. Seale, who became his friend and comrade-in-arms.[42]

Bobby Seale, born October 22, 1936, in Dallas, Texas, grew up poor in the Lone Star State. His carpentry skills, learned from his father, and drafting skills, acquired in school, did not help pull his family out of poverty. In 1943, the Seales moved west in search of greater economic opportunities and better race relations. While better job opportunities existed in California, the racial situation, in many cases, proved to be worse than the one they had left behind. After construction forced their removal from the Codornices Village housing project, the Seales moved from home to home throughout the Bay Area. Meanwhile, because his parents often separated, young Bobby worked small jobs to help out at home. In his autobiography, Seale remembers "hauling groceries and cutting lawns" to help supplement the family income.[43]

Seale's adolescence resembled that of the average black male in America. Early in his teenage years, however, he became disgruntled with American society and its injustices. Unlike Newton, Seale credits his history courses with providing him insight about America. Although he failed to mention what he learned about blacks, he told how these classes taught him the real truth about how and why American Indians occupied such a low position on the social ladder. Opting not to go to college after high school, Seale joined the Air Force in 1954, where his growing resentment of the federal government and its policies toward blacks and other minorities intensified and eventually turned into hatred.[44]

In 1958, toward the end of his military service, Seale got into trouble with his superior officers for something that had no relationship to his military duties. Seale fell behind on the payments for a six hundred dollar set of drums he purchased in Oakland, and the store that sold him the drums sent a collection agent to his base at Ellsworth in Rapid City, South Dakota. Unfortunately, Seale's commanding officer, a Colonel King, happened to be related to the collection agency's owners. For nearly five months after the collection agency sought payment, the colonel, whose activities included encouraging airmen to honor their debts, threatened to put Seale in jail if he did not pay.[45]

Seale claimed one night he cursed a dispatcher and ransacked his room in anger because a sergeant tried to force him to do work not originally assigned to him. Subsequently, his superiors threatened him with dishonorable discharge. Seale later went to jail because of his continued outbursts and refusal to calm down. While there, he decided to quit the Air Force by going AWOL (absent without leave). Before he could carry out his plans, however, Colonel King had a psychiatrist declare Seale "crazy," court-martialed him, and subsequently gave him a bad conduct discharge. In his autobiography, Seale wrote that the colonel told him

he "was not going to be able to get a job when [he] got out of there."
In his mind, Seale believed the United States government had rejected
him. While Seale is responsible for disobeying orders, the unfair treatment from his commanding officer pushed this situation far beyond the
simple question of repaying a debt.[46]

After he left the Air Force, Seale worked as a sheet metal mechanic
in major aircraft plants on the West Coast, including Kaiser Aerospace
Electronics near Oakland. According to Seale, after several months in
each plant, his superiors found out about his dishonorable discharge and
fired him. He said after approximately a year of such constant rejection
he decided to go to school, working as a comedian for a time to help
defray the costs of his education. Two years later, in 1962, Seale met
Huey Newton at Merritt College and immersed himself in the black
freedom struggle. Newton's activities, outspokenness, and visibility on
campus drew Seale's attention.[47]

When he enrolled at Merritt College in 1959, Newton had joined the
Afro-American Association, a group working to develop a sense of pride
among blacks by concentrating on their history and contributions to
American culture and society. Donald Warden, a University of California,
Berkeley lawyer, had founded the group a year earlier. Newton noted that
for the first time he saw all his turmoil "in terms of racism and exploitation." He claimed this realization attracted him to the rhetoric of socialism, which helped him see the link between racism and capitalism.
Newton claims he confirmed these beliefs when he attended an Afro-
American Association conference featuring Malcolm X as the guest
speaker. Malcolm's familiarity with "the brothers off the block" (pimps,
drug dealers, and numbers runners), his tenacity in standing up for his
convictions, and his insistence on armed self-defense appealed to Newton.
Like Seale, Newton had grown increasingly hostile toward the white
establishment, and consequently began to think about solutions to
America's race problems.[48] Students around campus knew Newton as one
who criticized the administration for ignoring various campus problems,
so Seale, like many other students, gravitated toward him. Newton's influence on campus also stemmed from the fact that he was one of the key
people who helped to develop Merritt's first black history course. This
push for black history at Merritt came quite early. On most American college campuses, black and white, these courses did not become popular or

reach fruition until the mid to late 1960s, after the onset of the Black Power movement.[49]

Seale and Newton subsequently had several meetings, consolidating their friendship and discussing racial matters. During this period, Bobby Seale tried to recruit Newton into the Revolutionary Action Movement (RAM), an organization he had joined earlier. Inspired by the example set by Robert Williams, RAM had been formed in 1962 by Donald Freeman, Max Stanford, and other students from Central State College in Wilberforce, Ohio. Socialist in orientation and dedicated to the armed overthrow of the government, RAM was a revolutionary nationalist group that emphasized African culture and moral transformation as it sought to organize black youth into armed self-defense groups. Quickly discovering its desire for open warfare was not shared by the black masses, RAM members, after being targeted by the FBI and CIA and arrested, then attempted to join existing black nationalist organizations in an effort to influence their programmatic goals. Many found a home in the SNCC and, later, the Black Panther Party. Surprisingly and ironically, the leaders of RAM refused to admit Newton into the organization, although they worked with him to get black history included in the college curriculum. They probably refused him entrance because of a college suspension Newton had received as a result of his speeches criticizing the United States' Cuban policies.[50]

Thousands of blacks entering college for the first time found their exposure to higher education and the resources at their disposal provided them with the raw materials to lead the burgeoning nationwide student movement. According to Newton, the courses he took in college further substantiated his belief that white people were criminals. Like many disaffected blacks, Newton wanted to find a way to beat whites at their own game. Consequently, he studied police science to learn more about the thinking of the law enforcement establishment. He also studied law, first at Oakland City College and later at San Francisco Law School. Newton claims to have pursued these disciplines not to become a lawyer or policeman, but to learn to outsmart the police and the justice system. Shortly thereafter, he entered a life of petty crime. In his autobiography, Newton explained he "equated having money with whiteness . . . and to take what whites called theirs" provided him with "a feeling of real freedom." This feeling of freedom, however, did not last long. Newton's life of crime caught up with him in late 1964, when an Oakland jury found him guilty of assault with a deadly weapon. Newton went to prison for six months, spending most of his time in solitary confinement. Instead of suffering in what the guards called the "soul breaker," Newton claimed he spent his time thinking of ways to help blacks eradicate white oppression.[51]

Upon his release from jail, Newton and Seale (who had been in and out of school and working odd jobs during this period) resumed their friendship and began a serious dialogue concerning solutions to some of the black liberation movement's ideological problems. The two also tried to understand why almost all the established black political organizations experienced such limited success. While it is not clear they found the answer, they soon concluded that only the Organization of Afro-American Unity, founded by Malcolm X, because of its stance on self-defense, portended long-term success. Newton and Seale agreed with Malcolm's conclusion that capitalism and racism were linked by the economic necessity of exploiting colonized people. They also believed Malcolm's assertion that the plight of black Americans and the people of Southeast Asia, Africa, and Latin America were intertwined. Malcolm X, through the organization, had hoped "to unite everyone on the continent of Africa" and "in the Western Hemisphere of African descent into one united force."[52] Once united, according to Malcolm, blacks would boldly assert their right to defend "themselves by whatever means necessary . . . in those areas where the government is either unable or unwilling to protect the lives and property" of black people. The soon-to-be leaders agreed with Malcolm's conclusion that black America was an internal colony mirroring the rest of the colonized world. According to them, blacks, like the Vietnamese or Angolans, had to use violence to rid themselves of this oppressive situation.

Newton and Seale were especially impressed when they learned Malcolm X, in addition to supporting armed self-defense, had forged contacts with the Organization of African Unity, a group founded by influential heads of African countries to foster social, economic, and political improvement on the continent. After he made these contacts, Malcolm X sought to bring the United States before the United Nations on charges of human rights violations. Even though Malcolm's murder in 1965 prevented him from implementing his philosophy, Seale and

Newton believed his solutions "by any means necessary" represented the only viable ones. Their organization later attempted to finish the work Malcolm X started.[53] Newton wrote that he found it difficult to convey "the effect that Malcolm has had on the Black Panther Party" but that the group stood as "a living testament to his life work." He was careful "not to claim that the party has done what Malcolm would have done" but "Malcolm's spirit is in us."[54] Following Malcolm's lead, the Panthers' philosophy included organizing the black community so it could counteract the white domination and exploitation that had been common since the Thirteenth Amendment banned slavery in 1865.

Newton and Seale shared their plans to organize and arm the black community with various groups and individuals in the San Francisco, Oakland, Richmond, and Berkeley areas. Receiving little more than lip service from Bay Area residents, the two returned to Merritt College in 1966 and publicized their ideas through the Soul Students Advisory Council (SSAC), a group that addressed some of the campus problems black students faced. Capitalizing on the strong wave of Black Power sentiment sweeping across American college campuses, Newton and Seale attempted to move the SSAC to a new plateau by recommending that it adopt a program of armed self-defense.[55]

They suggested SSAC members strap on guns and parade along the sidewalk, while other Soul Students conducted a campus rally in support of the newly proposed Afro-American History program. They also suggested group members encourage black opposition to increased police brutality, not just in the Oakland area, but throughout the nation. Newton and Seale also discussed following the police through the black community to help curb police violence. They borrowed this idea from their brethren in Southern California, who, after the Watts riots, which ended in the deaths of nearly forty people and millions of dollars in property damage, organized the Community Alert Patrol to minimize police abuse of black citizens. Rather than a neighborhood watch, it served as a community police watch.

The SSAC rejected Newton and Seale's suggestions, accurately claiming blacks could never survive by violently confronting the police. Opponents pointed to police maltreatment of blacks in the Watts rebellion only a year before. When Newton and Seale presented their idea to the Revolutionary Action Movement, they were met with the same level of resistance. RAM members had been jailed early in the movement and later forced underground because of their violent rhetoric and open display of weapons. They knew of the dangers in taking such a position. Having rejected their plan, Newton recalled, RAM members explained to Newton and Seale that such a move would be "suicidal, that we could not survive a single day patrolling the police." Years later, after the murder and/or incarceration of many of his close friends, Newton understood the wisdom of these dissenting students. At that time, however, he and Seale continued to push their ideas, pointing to what they saw as the failure and rejection of the philosophy of nonviolence favored by Martin Luther King Jr. and the determination of police to employ excessive force in suppressing black protest. They wanted to use weapons "as a recruiting device," according to Newton, and after their "program of self-defense . . . was worked out" they could develop a more encompassing strategy. At this point, the two had no desire to create their own group since, according to Newton, "there were too many organizations already. Our job was to make one of them relevant; that would be contribution enough."[56] They believed armed self-defense had to be the centerpiece, not only because of what they saw happen in Watts a year earlier but because state and local police officials had begun "to carry their shotguns in full view as another way of striking fear into the community." Insisting that the collective consciousness of blacks "was almost at the point of explosion," and that Malcolm's philosophy represented their torchlight to freedom, Newton became "convinced that our time had come."[57] He wrote, "[o]ut of this need sprang the Black Panther Party."

"We had no choice," he concluded, "but to form an organization that would involve the lower class brothers." Newton and Seale casually made their plan in "conversations and discussions" that Newton later labeled their first "political education classes." In an effort to educate themselves, they "read Frantz Fanon's *The Wretched of the Earth,* the four volumes of chairman Mao Tse-tung, and Che Guevara's *Guerrilla Warfare.*" Seeing these men as "kinsmen" because "the oppressor who had controlled them was controlling us," they thought it "necessary to know how they gained their freedom in order to go about getting ours." Not desiring "merely to import ideas and strategies," Newton wrote, "we had to transform what we learned into principles and methods acceptable to the brothers on the block." He added that the writings and speeches of Malcolm X as well as Robert Williams's *Negroes With Guns* "had a great influence on the kind of party we developed."[58]

Newton recounted that sometime in early October of 1966 he stumbled upon the name for the organization. One day, he remembered, he had been reading a pamphlet about voter registration in the South, detailing the efforts of the Lowndes County Freedom Organization in Alabama. Newton was struck by the image of a black panther, the symbol this group used to identify itself. Apparently, the pamphlet explained the party's motivation for employing the sleek but powerful animal because Newton used exactly the same words to describe his and Seale's rationale for using it. He explained that "[t]he panther is a fierce animal, but he will not attack until he is backed in to a corner; then he will strike out." At this point, Newton decided to name their "political vehicle" the Black Panther Party. Seale agreed with the moniker "without discussion" and the two began to move forward. Hoping to avoid "the intellectualizing and rhetoric characteristic of other groups," the two decided "it was time to stop talking and begin organizing." Admitting they had to this point been "as inactive as the others," Newton explained they had to engage in action if they wanted to make an impact.[59]

There could be no action, however, without a clear program to guide the organization. Subsequently Newton and Seale, now minister of defense and chairman of the Black Panther Party, respectively, set out to put their mission in writing. After consulting with hundreds of Oakland residents, the Panther leaders in October 1966 drew up a mission statement. They called this document the *Ten Point Program: What We Want, What We Believe.*

Their program demanded the following: the right of black communities to determine their own destinies; full employment; equal economic opportunities; decent housing and education; the exemption of blacks from the military; an end to police brutality and murder of black people; fair trials; the release of all black men from federal, state, and local jails; social justice; land, bread, and peace. The group's leaders explained that their major political objective was to have "a United Nations supervised plebiscite to be held throughout" the African American community "for the purpose of determining the will of black people as to their national destiny."[60] Of course, this objective took Malcolm X's desire to have the U.S. government investigated and charged with human rights violations one step further. These young radicals were attempting to stay true to the multifaceted attack Malcolm had advocated before his assassination.

This program guided the party after 1966. The Panthers' attempts to implement it provoked a level of calculated political violence by police authorities heretofore unseen in the United States. Undaunted, the Panthers nevertheless confronted directly the local, state, and federal authorities whom they believed oppressed black and poor people. As Lawrence Lader pointed out in *Power on the Left,* the Panthers "designated themselves an armed agency to protect the community, to put the police on notice that if a black were mistreated or a home invaded without legal warrant, black protest would be backed up with bullets."[61] In essence, the group set out not to placate whites or even to gain respect in the minds of liberals who often supported black demands for change, but to win black freedom in any way they could. Unlike other protest groups of the period, the Panthers had little tolerance for any position not consistent with the immediate and total liberation of black and other oppressed people. This unwillingness to compromise or equivocate not only gave them a reputation as being "the baddest niggas on the scene," according to one former Panther, but it also attracted recruits.[62]

The first of these recruits was Robert "Li'l Bobby" Hutton. After moving to Oakland from Arkansas at the age of three, Hutton was soon introduced to the mean streets of urban America. The youngest of seven, Hutton, according to Newton, "had endured the same hardships and humiliations to which so many young blacks in poor communities are subjected." A handsome young man with an infectious smile, he struggled academically, so Hutton often broke school rules to keep himself busy. "Like many of the brothers," wrote Newton, "he had been kicked out of school" during the late fifties. In early 1966, he landed a job at a poverty program housed in the North Oakland Service Center. There he met Seale and began to receive tutoring and other guidance from the Air Force veteran. Essentially illiterate, Hutton learned to read from Seale. He quickly became interested in the problems of blacks and subsequently "became enthusiastic" about the party. As a result, Seale talked to Hutton's parents, and at the age of fifteen Hutton became the nascent organization's first recruit. They designated him party treasurer, although, according to Elbert Howard, another original member, "there was not much money to keep track of."[63] Hutton became an example and a motivation for thousands of youths who eventually joined the party. As people joined, the party apparatus slowly came into being.

In terms of organizational structure, the party had an elaborate system of ranks, titles, and specific duties for its leadership and rank-and-file members. The Central Committee governed the party and made all policy decisions. Some of its members included Huey Newton, Bobby and June Seale, Eldridge and Kathleen Cleaver, David Hilliard, Emory Douglas, John and Ericka Huggins, Elaine Brown, Geronimo Pratt, Alprentice "Bunchy" Carter, Masai Hewitt, and Michael Fultz. These individuals, according to former Panther Emory Douglas, coordinated all the party's activities, discussed and worked out problems, and explained the organization's position on various political issues. Douglas added, however, that "Huey and Bobby had the most influence on the Central Committee," and therefore wielded the most power. Former chairwoman Elaine Brown noted that the leaders referred to this arrangement as "democratic centralism, whereby a central body dictated the work of the whole in its interest."[64] To be sure, this power the leaders had was quite limited; not in Oakland of course, but elsewhere.

The fact is, after the BPP's notoriety in late 1967 and early 1968, other chapters sometimes organized without the Central Committee's consent. Although Central sent people to the new locations, these new Panthers often did what they pleased. There were other times when different situations prevailed in different cities, so the directives of the Oakland office could not always be uniformly followed. Malik Rahim of the New Orleans Panthers expounded on this point when he noted, "the situation [was] different in the South as opposed to the northeast or west, so we had to adapt to different situations."[65] So while reports, money, and other information flowed back and forth on a regular basis, directives from headquarters did not always hold sway over local activities.

The Central Committee organized the party's chapters by state, except in California, where it set up northern and Southern California chapters (see figure 1). Brown explained that "within a chapter were branches, organized by city, and within the branches were sections." Panther leadership divided the sections into subsections and subsections into squads, depending on the size and layout of a city. This paramilitary structure ensured individuals in leadership positions held absolute power over members of the rank-and-file.[66] This autocratic structure eventually encouraged much of the internal violence experienced by party members.

From the beginning, Huey Newton, the leading member of the party, served as minister of defense, the most important office. Its status as the top-level position derived largely from Newton's role as founder and dominant personality in the party's early development. His duties were formulating, overseeing, and implementing defensive policies and procedures. Emory Douglas noted this position "dealt with organizing police patrols in the early days" and later with "anything that had to do with confronting the intimidation of police." Since it existed at both the state and local levels, the holder of this position also supervised defensive operations such as protecting the group's offices and directing target practice.[67]

Bobby Seale, as chairman, stood as second-in-command. His numerous duties included not only supervising the party's operations, but also aiding in the formulation and implementation of the group's political philosophy. In this capacity, Seale formulated campaign strategies, instituted various community service programs, conducted voter registration programs, organized petition drives, and acted as the party's chief spokesman. Traveling throughout the United States and abroad, Seale also raised funds and helped to facilitate alliances with groups such as Students for a Democratic Society, the Peace and Freedom Party, the Student Nonviolent Coordinating Committee, and a host of others.

The position of field marshal was closely connected to the chairman. Holders of this regional position had responsibility for organizing individual chapters and screened new recruits in an effort to weed out informants and *agents provocateurs*. In retrospect, it is clear whatever method they used did not work well. Nevertheless, these individuals were indispensable to chapter defense ministers because of their knowledge of security procedures. Supervising the various sections and subsections of the party, these individuals also handed out assignments for community work. Working directly beneath the field marshals were the section leaders, who acted as listening posts and kept the party abreast of local complaints and desires. In charge of an area that covered five or six city blocks, section leaders helped the elderly by running their

Figure One: HIERARCHY OF THE BLACK PANTHER PARTY

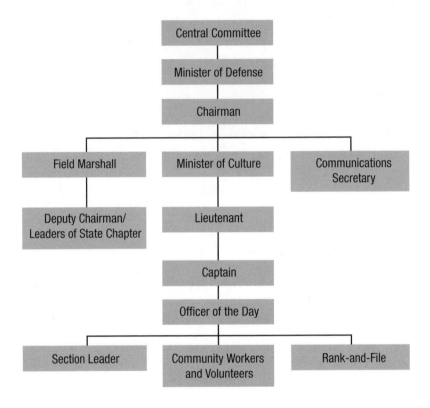

Note: This structure was essentially duplicated at the state level with individuals designated as officer of the day responsible for running local offices.

errands and accompanying them when they cashed their checks (to prevent them from being robbed), organized boycotts and rent strikes, and helped to supervise distribution of the *Black Panther*, the party's official news organ.[68] In this way, the organization successfully built rapport with the communities in which they organized.

Although Tarika Lewis had been the party's first revolutionary artist, it was a man from San Francisco who eventually became most widely known for the images in the Panther paper. Emory Douglas, the party's minister of culture, was primarily responsible for the paper's layout and the very violent depictions found within it. In an interview, Douglas noted that the black ghetto populace "was largely a non-reading group," so his oversized and colorful pictures went a long way in explaining the party's philosophy, goals, and tactics. He added that his work "was a reflection of the art and spirit of the party." What one saw in the paper were various depictions of ghetto life, but with the added dimensions of self-defense and education. The Panthers often drew fire from critics who believed pictures of people killing police and taking their guns would inflame ghetto residents, especially children, into spontaneous violence. While the argument held some truth, these critics failed to offer any solution to the widespread police brutality and murder of blacks in the ghettos who had not been attacking police. While most of Douglas's duties centered on the paper's production, the minister of culture also painted signs, published party literature, and organized the party's entertainment division. Douglas noted that this entertainment consisted mainly of The Lumpen, a singing group organized and produced by the party. Some of its members included Michael Torrence, James Mott, Bill Calhoun, Sandra Reed, and Elaine Brown. Douglas said the famous Motown star Marvin Gaye did the choreography for the group.[69] Indeed, while there were many middle-class blacks who found the party's acceptance of violence deplorable, there were others who actively supported the group by giving their talents, time, and money.

Working closely with the minister of culture and the party's newspaper editor, the minister of information handled the general dissemination of party information. In addition to helping decide the content of news articles, this individual supervised the issuing of party press releases, brochures, and pamphlets. Eldridge Cleaver, author of the popular 1968 book *Soul on Ice*, acted as the party's minister of information from 1966 to 1969. Cleaver was a dynamic and charismatic speaker and often spoke to the press about the daily activities and goals of the party. His many connections with the publishing community also made him useful to the party.[70]

Kathleen Cleaver, former SNCC member and Eldridge's wife, acted as the party's communications secretary, coordinating the group's very complex system of communications. She made sure that all the party's chapters and branches stayed current with the group's official position on federal, state, local, and international issues. She also helped to devise party policy on how information flowed up and down the chain of command.

The BPP's paramilitary structure compelled many Americans to fear and misunderstand the party. The black berets, a popular symbol of revolution during the period, and black leather jackets made the Panthers appear much more menacing than they were in reality. Federal, state, and local government agencies capitalized on these violent undertones and finally forced the party into a battle that proved impossible for it to win.

After discussing a number of pertinent issues with as many ghetto residents as they could, Seale and Newton began trying to convince them to join the budding organization. Attempting to recruit black residents on the basis of a 10–10–10 program, borrowed from SNCC leaders who initially grew close to the new organization, the BPP successfully canvassed entire neighborhoods in many of America's urban ghettoes. Under this arrangement, ten Panthers discussed BPP goals with ten other residents in a ten block radius. These ten did the same and the process continued. One former Panther commented that not only did this program facilitate access to the community, but it also "established places for us to go to which were safe, should the need arise for us to leave one area for security reasons."[71] This need came up as often as the Panthers shot it out with the police. New recruits, therefore, had to learn to be mobile as well as defensive-minded.

———

One of the first people to join the party after Bobby Hutton was Elbert "Big Man" Howard. Like many who later joined, Howard had been born and raised in the South, in his case, Chattanooga, Tennessee. An only child whose father had died before he was two, he joined the Air Force in 1956 to help supplement the meager income his mother derived from "cleaning white folks' houses" and selling bootleg liquor on the weekends. Like all Air Force enlistees, Howard spent his first twelve weeks at Lackland Air Force base in San Antonio, Texas. His test scores to determine what job he worked were high enough for him to choose what he wanted to do in the service. Because he joined the force "to be around airplanes," he opted to become an aircraft mechanic. According to him, his "racist captain talked down to him about what a complicated thing it was" and urged him to try other, less difficult jobs. Thinking "they were going to give me what they want me to have," Howard was not surprised when his job classification did not match his request.[72]

Howard received training as a crash rescue fireman on a base near Burlington, Vermont. After completing this training he left for Europe and spent much of the rest of his time in the Air Force there. He was stationed at Etran Air Force Base in France near Verdun, the site of a famous World War I battle. He recalls frequenting jazz clubs throughout France and Germany and remembers that "many of the European musicians played just like black Americans. Some guy played like Lester Young, some musician played the piano like Earl Garner." It would not have been unusual to hear guys who sounded like "Satchmo and Dizzy Gillespie since they had done these State Department tours during and after the war," he recalled. After a couple of years in France, he had to prepare to leave Europe because "France and the U.S. had a dispute over the weapons storage. France wanted to have some control over some of those weapons and I think the U.S. told them to take a hike." He remembered after this disagreement the French "closed the base down and everybody that had a long time to serve got reassigned to Germany or somewhere." Having already spent four years in the Air Force, his time until discharge was growing short so he took on "a few extra months and got reassigned." Desiring "to check out California," he requested a transfer to Travis Air Force Base, located near Sacramento, not very far from Oakland."[73]

After serving his last eight months in the Bay Area, Howard, who had by then "hooked up with a woman," decided to "hang [there] for a while and see what happens." What happened changed his life and the lives of thousands of other Bay Area blacks. The year was 1960. After securing a job at UARCO Printers, he decided to use his GI Bill benefits to enroll at Merritt College. There he met the future leaders of the Black Panther Party for Self-Defense.

Howard recalled being in the Soul Students Advisory Council with Newton and Seale. Because their interest "went beyond what was being offered in the classroom at the time," Howard explained that he, Newton, and Seale began to have "political education classes after school." They met "at Bobby's mother's house, at Huey's girlfriend's apartment, or at my house in my backyard." As they were "always seeking solutions" to the problems in their community, they "read and discussed the *Red Book,* the writings of DuBois, Fanon, Ho Chi Minh, Che, Castro, and many others." They tried to analyze these writings to see how they applied to their current situation. "In most cases," he recalled, "Huey would lay that shit right out there for you. Make you see it." Because Newton had taken classes in law, he put forth "the idea that we had a legal right to observe the police in our community. And we [had] a right to carry guns." Still not sure of where they were headed, Howard concentrated on his studies, often losing track of Newton and Seale. An altercation with the police made his mind up for him about joining the Panthers.[74]

Believing that life would be fine if he just "kept a job, some money in his pockets, and stayed out of harm's way," Howard proceeded to live the good life. Part of this good life meant spending time with his lady friend and enjoying "the wealth of talented musicians who lived, worked, and played in and around the Bay Area." He remembered that one night after attending a Lou Rawls concert at Don Barksdale's nightclub, he told his date to wait at the door while he retrieved his vehicle. Once he got into his brand new, fire-engine red pickup truck, "with mirrors on both doors," he parked in front of the club to wait for his companion. "There was a white person that I could clearly see parked behind me and white person I could clearly see in front of me," he explained. At this point, he said "Oakland PD pulled up and started writing me a ticket." He emerged from the vehicle and asked the officer: "What's the deal, its white people behind me and some in front of me and you gonna take the middle car and write a ticket and all I'm doing is just waiting to pick up my lady." They exchanged a few words and the officer ordered him "to shut up or some shit" and he responded by saying "fuck you!" At this point, he "jumped in his ride and was about to take off when they sent every police car they had and surrounded me. So they took me and my pickup to jail," he recalled.[75]

Howard's companion contacted Donald Warden, a radio personality and president of Merritt College's Afro-American Association. Warden also had a law degree from the University of California at Berkeley. He made arrangements for Howard's release and eventually they had the issue adjudicated. In the meantime, Howard asked Newton to accompany him to court. Newton agreed, but explained when they got to trial that he would "hang back because Donald Warden doesn't like me and he might get up there and get to acting up or something if he sees me." Howard then went before the judge as Warden presented his case. He recalled that the whole time "the cop was sitting there grinning and carrying on" and the judge said "well, he's probably guilty but I'm gonna dismiss it."

"There is nothing," Howard said, "like the hatred that I felt with them damn cops sitting over there on the side just laughing. Knowing goddamn well I hadn't done anything." On the way back to Newton's girlfriend's apartment after the trial, Howard began asking Newton "about the legality of carrying a weapon and so forth and he ran it down to me." After this altercation, Howard "put a rack in the back of his pickup truck and put his shotgun in there." He remembered thinking that "I'm gonna ride like these fucking rednecks ride and if somebody is out of hand then I don't give a shit, we just gonna get down. I was mad as hell that day," he recalled.

After this, he started working with the Black Panther Party and doing small jobs. In short order, the group opened its office in West Oakland. Howard remembered that "there was hardly anybody in the office in the mornings and it would open when somebody got there." He told Seale to give him a key and he would open up, since his classes were in the afternoon. "I'll hold it down every morning until somebody gets here because people are coming by and they're gonna want to give a donation or talk about how to join up and stuff like that." He remembered that shortly thereafter they "started talking about developing a newspaper" and that he and Bobby Seale were the ones who worked on that. The life of this six-foot-five-inch Air Force veteran changed dramatically after joining this fledgling black nationalist organization.[76]

It had not been police brutality specifically that attracted "Big Man" to the party; it had been his dealings with the police. Even though the judge found him not guilty of any crime, he saw the behavior of the police in court as an affront to his dignity. In addition, he understood like Newton and Seale that blacks in Oakland lived in "deplorable conditions in terms of their treatment by the police." He sincerely believed "the primary job" of the police in Oakland "was to keep black folks down and corralled in the flatlands and out of Claremont or the foothills around Oakland where the well-to-do people lived." Also like the party's founders, he began "to look at those police forces that occupied the flatlands where we lived as occupying forces."[77] Sentiments like these were enough to persuade thousands of blacks to join the organization.

One of these was San Francisco resident Emory Douglas. Douglas was an Arkansas native whose parents moved him from the South to San Francisco. They made the move in an effort to ameliorate his asthma. Douglas, like many of his contemporaries, had been in trouble with the law. In and out of the California Youth Authority juvenile halls and detention centers for petty offenses, he decided to take the advice of one of his probation officers and at the age of seventeen enrolled in college to improve his art skills. Not long after Douglas entered San Francisco City College in 1965, he came into contact with a plethora of black radicals, most of whom were at San Francisco State University, he recalled. Through these individuals he met Newton and Seale. Joining the party in January 1967, he served first as a revolutionary artist, then as minister of culture, a position that allowed him to become a member of the Central Committee, the party's main decision-making body.[78]

"I think Stokely Carmichael's call for Black Power down there in Mississippi was kinda like the spark that lit the prairie fire with the people here in California," Douglas said, "particularly in San Francisco and Oakland. . . . It became like an inspirational kinda thing because of what you'd seen and what you're seeing on TV," remembered the now much more mature revolutionary. He was referring to the "dogs, water hoses, billy clubs, and lynchings." Explaining how many people of his generation had "become frustrated with turning the other cheek," they as young people "wanted to do more." So when the phrase "Black Power" became a part of the national discussion on race and human rights in the United States, "it gave us a sense of pride." As a college student he had already heard Stokely Carmichael, H. Rap Brown, James Forman, "and many other members of SNCC" at San Francisco State and other campuses throughout the Bay Area. Explaining that he had been no stranger to segregation, discrimination, and other hardships associated with growing up poor in the black ghetto, he spoke of how "Black Power was just refreshing because prior to that time we had been referring to ourselves as Negroes. . . . I had even been a member of the Negro Student Association, so when we changed it to the Black Student Association, it gave us a sense of pride." His appetite already whetted for social action, it would not be long before he satisfied this hunger.

Hanging out and working with the likes of Imamu Amiri Baraka, formerly Leroi Jones, the famed revolutionary poet renowned for his work with the Black Arts Repertory Theater, revolutionary poet Marvin X, and other cultural nationalists in San Francisco, Douglas began wearing African garb and learning more about African culture. While these things suited him well, he found himself "hungering for even more."[79] This hunger, however, could not be immediately satisfied as the food he so craved had not yet been prepared. This sustenance turned out to be the Black Panther Party for Self-Defense.

Working in tandem with the Black Panther Party of Northern California, formed by SNCC workers and former members of RAM, Douglas relished the chance to sample that for which he had hungered. This fledgling organization, one of many Black Panther Parties organized after the Lowndes County action, tossed around the idea of bringing Betty Shabazz, Malcolm X's widow, to the Bay Area. Its members asked Douglas to do the artwork for the program if she agreed to come. They were aware that Douglas had done artwork for the Black Student Union at San Francisco State and "had worked with [Amiri] Baraka doing props and that kind of stuff." Capitalizing on his artistic skills, this group employed him and soon thereafter, Douglas met the leaders of the Black Panther Party for Self-Defense.

Before meeting Newton and Seale, he accompanied the northern California group to a session where they tried to persuade Eldridge Cleaver, the BPP's future Minister of Information, to issue the invitation to Malcolm X's widow. The northern California group believed that if Cleaver wrote the letter inviting Betty Shabazz to California, she might say yes. Cleaver, Douglas said, had not only "been a staunch follower of Malcolm in prison" but also had become known for his prolific writing and for publicizing his intention to carry on the work that Malcolm X had started with the Organization of Afro-American Unity. They made contact with the ex-felon turned writer and "he agreed to write the letter," according to Douglas. Sure enough, Shabazz promised to come and the group began to make plans for her visit. At these planning meetings Douglas "heard them talking about brothers coming from Oakland to do security" for Shabazz's visit.

"When the brothers came over to the meeting, who they was talking about doing security, that was Huey and Bobby Seale, and Li'l Bobby [Hutton] . . . Sherman [Forte] and about three or four others. So it was at that particular time, after I heard Bobby and 'nem talk . . . that I knew that's what I wanted to be a part of," reminisced Douglas. Newton and Seale wooed Douglas with their knack for political analysis and their courage and willingness to sacrifice all to gain black liberation. Afterward, Douglas remembered telling Baraka "who was Leroi Jones at that time, that I wanna be part of this and he said OK." Around January 1967, Douglas inquired how he could join the party. They gave him "a little run down" and told him "to come over to Oakland and hang out, ride around and see what's happening." A few days later he caught the bus, went to Newton's house, "woke him up in the morning and started hanging out with them, went on patrol and that's how [he] became involved." Having "found the Panthers' message of aggressive self-reliance and revolutionary action far more persuasive" than the nonviolent movement that he witnessed on television, Douglas cast his lot with an incipient revolutionary organization that soon captured the hearts and minds of black (and some white) youth all over the nation. Placing his decision in the context of the times, he admitted that these nonviolent soldiers had "some helluva courage" to face the "dogs, hoses, and sticks," but at the same time, "we said 'naw, naw that ain't for me.'" He recalls that many of his contemporaries in other parts of the country felt the same way, that "naw, I cain't do that, that ain't my way."[80]

It is interesting to note that all the original members of the party were recent transplants from the South. Their parents accepted the risks and went to California in search of a better life, but found more of the same. The frustration these young men felt was likely different than the despair one might feel having grown up in the same place his parents and grandparents had. Since migration elsewhere was no longer an option, they chose to answer violence with violence. They concluded their forebears had fought the good fight but had used the wrong tools.

Surely the perceived unwavering nonviolence of the civil rights movement left many an urban dweller wondering what they could do to help. For them, the BPP provided that opportunity. What many of these youths had missed was that civil rights workers and their supporters had quietly eked out an existence in the South by defending themselves with arms when the circumstances called for it. They successfully maintained the tradition of defensive violence precisely because it was not a part of their platform. For the first wave of Panthers, retaliatory and defensive violence was a central tenet of the group's art and rhetoric.

What the group and those associated with it miscalculated was the official response their talking up the gun would incur. Though many Panthers knew the authorities would come down as hard as they did, this miscalculation on the part of the leadership had a deleterious effect on the party's growth and development. Once the authorities became convinced of the group's ability to influence others regardless of race or color, they immediately responded with a wrath approaching overkill.

Despite the mistakes they made and the suffering they endured, most surviving Panthers agree with the freedom song that says, "I know the one thing we did right was the day we started to fight." They kept their eyes on the prize and held on to all that was dear to them. All the while, the BPP continued along its collision course with local, state, and federal law enforcement agencies.

CHAPTER 2

The Black Panther Party for Self-Defense

AFTER ABOUT A MONTH OF GOING IN AND out of their office on Fifty-sixth and Grove in Oakland openly displaying their weapons, the moment of truth finally arrived.[1] Bobby Seale wrote that by early 1967 "Huey was on a level where he was ready to organize the black brothers for a righteous revolutionary struggle with guns and force." In addition to its founders, the Black Panther Party's members at this time included Sherman and Reginald Forte, Bobby Hutton, and Elbert Howard. Hoping for the opportunity to demonstrate to the community that their philosophy and tactics helped advance the cause of black liberation, they held political education classes daily in an attempt to bring ideological uniformity to the group. They also had sessions where they learned how to break down, clean, and reassemble weapons, to fire them, and to handle them safely. Newton wrote, "a number of people who [he] knew had just come from Vietnam, and they helped train [the Panthers] in weaponry." Oakland resident John Sloane, who had been in the military, gave the group its first lessons on "field stripping and shooting," according to Seale. (The following chapters further address the Vietnam connection in the following chapters.)

One frigid day in early February 1967, several well-armed Panthers were leaving the office when an Oakland police officer cruised by. The officer continued down the street, radioed to headquarters then quickly made a U-turn and drove back toward the Panthers, who were by then getting into their car to leave. Just as they expected, the police officer pulled behind them. Newton instructed everybody in the car to remain silent because, according to Seale, he said "the minute somebody says something, the man is going to try to arrest you for some jive about interfering with an officer carrying out his duty" or "on a traffic ticket." The people who were "subject to gather around" them would then "think he arrested you because you've got the gun. We want to prove to the people that we've got the right to carry guns and they've got a right to arm themselves and we will exhaust our constitutional right to carry these guns."[2]

Once all the Panthers agreed Newton would do the talking, the scene began to shift. Like a seasoned director, Huey guided the situation through a series of phases that demonstrated his point to the average person. He complied with the officer's request to see his driver's license and verbally confirmed that all the information on it was correct. Not until after the officer asked for Newton's phone number did the situation grow more tense. Huey responded by saying "five," which he said referred to the Fifth Amendment of the Constitution. He told the officer, "I don't have to give you anything but my identification, name and address. So therefore I don't even want to talk to you," and demanded the officer get away from his car and leave him alone. "I don't even want to hear you," he said. Newton proceeded to explicate on the Constitution and a citizen's right "not to testify against himself." Referring to this incident, Seale wrote, "this is where all the shit between the Party and the pigs began."[3]

As the encounter continued to escalate, Newton had his M-1 rifle in full view and Bobby Seale had his 9 mm pistol on the seat beside him. Three other police cars pulled onto the scene. One of the arriving officers inquired about what had been going on and asked if he could take a look at the 9 mm sitting beside Seale. Newton yelled "no" and then told the officer to "Get away from the car. We don't want you around the car and that's all there is to it." With the situation clearly escalating, one of the officers asked Newton, "Who in the hell do you think you are?" to which Newton replied, "who in the hell do you think YOU are? . . . We have a constitutional right to carry the guns anyway, and I don't want to hear it." With his M-1 in tow, Newton proceeded to exit the car. All the policemen immediately retreated a few steps as they watched Newton jack a round into the gun's chamber.

By that point the scene had become electric as dozens of people gathered around, speaking in hushed tones. The police were trying hard to disperse them when Newton told them, "you don't have to move down the street! Don't go anywhere! These pigs can't keep you from observing! You have a right to observe an officer carrying out his duty . . . as long as you stand a reasonable distance away, and you are a reasonable distance."

The police kept trying to move the crowd along, but Newton, thinking quickly, opened the door to the party's office, let them in, and told them to observe as much as they wanted to. They complied as Newton quickly turned to face his adversaries.

Clearly shaken by this ominous display of bravado, the officer in charge asked Newton, "What are you going to do with that gun?" Newton retorted, "What are you going to do with your gun? . . . Because if you try to shoot at me or if you try to take this gun, I'm going to shoot back at you swine." Obviously trying to show the amazed onlookers that the Panthers were fearless, Newton added, "furthermore, you're nothing but a sharecropper anyway. You come from Georgia somewhere, you're downtown making $800.00 a month and you come down here brutalizing and murdering black people in the black communities. They gave you some sergeant stripes and all I say is that you're nothing but a low-life scurvy swine . . . from the racist South somewhere. So if you draw that gun, I'll shoot back at you and blow your brains out." Newton went on for a while "calling the pigs swine, dogs, sharecroppers, bastards, [and] motherfuckers with his M-1 in his hand. And daring them, just daring them. . . . You don't pull your guns on *us*." Witnessing this scene, Seale thought Newton was the "baddest motherfucker in the world."[4]

The confrontation continued as community members watched from the street and the front window of the Panther office. Verbally supporting Newton as if he were a Baptist preacher in a southern church, some of them yelled, "Go head on brother," "Run it down. You know where its at," and "I can dig it." Every time Newton said, "if you shoot at me swine, I'm shooting back," the black spectators in the office responded with, "Tell it, do it, brother." From their reaction, it appeared as if their dream of saying these very words to the police had finally come true. Newton took their supportive response to mean he had been successful in educating people in his community about the necessity of self-defense. Astoundingly, the confrontation ended with the police leaving without making any arrests. Seale later claimed Newton was teaching them to be revolutionaries, letting them know "the gun is where its at and about and in." He went on to explain this was "the very major incident" that got the community to take notice of the new organization of black activists. "After that," he noted, "we really began to patrol pigs then because . . . we got maybe thirteen members in the party that day."[5]

Newton's resoluteness, his knowledge of the law, and the bold manner in which he articulated his position demonstrated to this group of black Oakland onlookers that armed self-defense, at least for the moment, had it merits. The BPP wanted it known that their actions were well within the laws of the city, state, and nation. This insistence on exercising their right to bear arms pitted the members of the Black Panther Party for Self-Defense against the most powerful government on earth. That they could not win in a firefight was beside the point. They simply wanted to demonstrate their desire to enjoy their second amendment rights to bear arms; this was diametrically opposed to a social system that required a degraded, brutalized underclass as a cheap source of labor. In addition, they hoped to infuse a sense of fearlessness into the general black population. They believed if black fear of white authority were overcome, then blacks as a whole could begin to address some of the more pressing issues they faced.

Most of all, however, the upstart organization sought to put police on notice that to continue to brutalize and murder blacks meant they risked bodily harm and possibly even death. Having designated themselves the heirs of Malcolm X, the Panthers insisted brutality should work both ways and that death, if it had to come, should be reciprocal. Bobby Seale, noting the readiness of some blacks to reciprocate, claimed "the ghetto black isn't afraid to stand up to the cops because he already lives with violence. He expects to die any day."[6] While not all ghetto blacks would have agreed with Seale, the urban uprisings that occurred from 1964 to 1966 provided some confirmation that black people, without any formal guidance, would resort to wholesale violence if pushed in that direction. The Panthers sought to capitalize on this readiness to explode. They believed unrestrained rioting and looting should be refocused and redirected into a formal organization and program that would rid the ghetto of white authority, which had of course created the ghetto in the first place. Their desire, in fact, was to channel what they viewed as misguided energy into a potent revolutionary force that protected and served the community.

Arriving at this conclusion meant the Panthers had come one step closer to launching the revolution they hoped would liberate blacks and other oppressed peoples. In October 1966, with their well-thought out Ten Point Platform in hand, they needed to raise money and attract recruits. The BPP platform made this task somewhat easier because they had previously canvassed the community and discovered a majority of the residents wanted things like decent housing, good jobs, adequate education and nourishment, an end to police brutality, the right to control their own communities and ultimately, peace—something neither blacks nor whites had enjoyed much of over the previous three decades. While the BPP also demanded fair trials for blacks, the release of blacks from jails and a United Nations supervised plebiscite so blacks could determine whether they wanted to remain a part of the United States, it had been the former demands they sought to implement immediately.[7] Specifically, they attempted to implement point seven of their program, which demanded an end to police brutality and the murder of blacks.

This decision signaled yet another attempt to attract recruits. Emphasizing that they "obviously [had] to do more than talk to recruit any sizable numbers of street brothers," the Panther leaders boldly moved "to give practical applications of our theory, show them that we were not afraid of weapons and not afraid of death." Hence, they concluded the best way to accomplish their goal was through force of arms. "The way we finally won the brothers over," wrote Newton, "was by patrolling the police with arms." They therefore had to procure the proper "technical equipment," a euphemism party members used when referring to guns.[8]

Using its Ten Point Program and Platform as a guide, the Panthers sought to educate and revolutionize the black community. Because Newton and Seale saw police brutality and murder of blacks as major issues affecting the ghetto, they decided to concentrate first on point seven, which stated:

> We want an immediate end to police brutality and murder of black people. We believe we can end police brutality in our Black community by organizing Black self-defense groups that are dedicated to defending our Black community from racist police oppression and brutality.

Viewing the black community as a series of dispersed colonial outposts on what was otherwise a continent of plenty and the police as an occupying army keeping ghetto subjects pacified, the BPP leaders "recognized that it was ridiculous to report the police to the police." They complained that the relatively few civilian review boards in existence had failed to stop or even slow down police brutality and "the authorities responsible for overseeing the police are police themselves and usually side against the citizens." Newton said that "only by patrolling the police with arms," would blacks "see a change in their behavior."[9] Satisfied that their analysis of the situation had been correct, the group set out to put its theory into practice.

As twenty-odd members of the group carried out their normal daily activities, they implemented their police patrols. Sometimes, according to original member Emory Douglas, their base of operations would be "Bobby or Huey's house or sometimes we would go out from the office when the office was right up the street from Bobby's house." He remembered, "we'd just be hanging out or something, talking, chasing women, talking to people out in the community . . . the whole bit." But then "if we saw something go down, the whole focus would be on that, on what was happening between the brothers and sisters in the community and the police action that was going on." They then went to "stand and observe" and to tell "brothers and sisters that they didn't have to give them anything but their name and address or that they could take the Fifth Amendment." Like good Samaritans, if an individual were arrested, they "would go down and bail them out." Newton recalled because "nobody had ever given them any support or assistance when the police harassed them . . . many citizens came right out of jail and into the party." He claimed, "at first the patrols were a total success."[10]

The police were understandably upset over these Panther patrols. They were being followed by individuals who not only were armed but who were also intent on catching them violating some kind of policy or procedure. Newton claimed the officers were initially "frightened and confused" because "with weapons in our hands, we were no longer their subjects but their equals." Because they stood a safe and legal distance away from an officer and his potential arrestee, there was little police could do to prevent the Panther patrols. Douglas recalled when officers asked "what are you doing with that gun?" Newton articulated "the law to them about the right to bear arms and the whole bit." Douglas recalled, "they knew the law better than the police did." Newton wrote, "I would stand off a little and read the relevant portions of the penal code in a loud voice to all within hearing distance. . . . to educate those who had gathered to observe these incidents."[11] Seale's description of one of these encounters captures the essence of Panther bravado in the early days.

During one of their first patrols in Oakland, Seale remembered he, Newton, and several others had encountered a black man being questioned by the police. When they stopped, Newton stood there with his weapon and told the man that he only had to give his name and address and did not have to answer any questions. Seeing the commotion, a crowd quickly gathered at the scene. When this happened, Newton raised his voice so the onlookers could hear him. He told the man that if he were arrested, the Panthers were going bail him out and that they were there for his protection. The officers told Newton he had no right to be there. Newton responded, according to Seale, by "citing the specifics of the damn law," telling the officer he had a right to observe as the officer carried out his duties. People in the crowd began to murmur and whisper things to each other like "what kind of niggas is these?" and "what they got some sticks or something?" Seale explained that because it had been dark, the people really could not tell whether they had weapons or something else. When the officer ordered the crowd to move, Newton explained they did not have to budge and they had the right to observe the police as long as they stood at least ten feet away. The police officer then carefully lowered the arrested man's head into the car and turned around in disbelief as he saw "a sister there strapped down with a .45 looking like Clint Eastwood or something," remembered Seale. At this point, Newton explained to the crowd that they were the Black Panther Party for Self-Defense and they were there to protect black residents from police brutality. They were also looking to organize blacks so they could begin to enjoy what Seale called "community electoral power." Having witnessed this amazing scene, several people in the crowd followed the Panthers to their office and signed up as members.[12]

Now having to confront a group of well-armed blacks, who by their own admission were bound and determined to rid their neighborhoods of continued brutality, the police responded first with anger and resentment, then with vengeance. They began to arrest Panthers for the slightest offenses. Newton recalled that after being harassed by an officer for about thirty minutes he finally received a ticket for a "faulty license plate" when the officer, not able to find a violation, shook "his rear license plate and a bolt dropped off."[13] By charging others with jaywalking, disturbing the peace, resisting arrest, and a host of similar offenses that are nearly impossible to disprove in a court of law, the police, who were used to wielding complete power in black ghettoes, responded predictably. The confrontations, however, continued to escalate until violence between the police and Panthers inevitably erupted. Newton welcomed such violence, hoping others might join him. If they were going to raise these contradictions, however, the Panthers first had to have weapons.

Acquiring guns turned out to be easy. The familiar story of Newton and Seale buying their first weapon with proceeds from peddling Mao Tse-tung's *The Little Red Book* to University of California Berkeley students, told by Seale in his autobiography and by dozens of other Panthers, is interesting, even colorful, but not necessarily where their *first* guns came from. In fact, Richard Aoki, a Japanese American who identified with the revolutionary fervor of the era, provided Newton and Seale with their first weapons. Seale described Aoki as a "Japanese radical cat" who had ".357 Magnums, 22's, 9mm's, what have you." He later joined the BPP and recruited others into the party. As a member of the Third World Liberation Front, a radical organization seeking change on and off the Berkeley campus, he became instrumental in facilitating coalitions with the BPP and other radical groups. Aoki was a conscientious man who saw the need for revolutionizing those values in American life that Martin Luther King Jr. insisted "needed to be revolutionized." After Seale and Newton reportedly told Aoki that "if he was a real revolutionary" he would let the new revolutionaries have the weapons free of charge, Aoki gave the two "an M-1 and a 9mm." Perhaps this young immigrant resented the fact that his family had been interned as prisoners in concentration camps during World War II. Perhaps he was like millions of others in his generation who saw that American society needed significant change if it were to live up to its ideals of freedom and justice for all. Regardless of his motivation, he played a role in setting in motion a series of events that placed the Bay Area under worldwide scrutiny.[14]

Now that they had guns, the two leaders began securing the necessary recruits. College students themselves, they simply looked around their neighborhoods for what they needed. Because Merritt, or Grove Street College, as it was sometimes called, was situated in the heart of the black community, they easily found people ready and willing to join their new group. After all, they had come on the scene when the black movement was growing more radical by the year. Things had begun to get out of hand. The numerous urban rebellions and the police brutality that spawned them, the poor housing and even poorer education, joblessness, and general lack of respect for black Americans had obviously affected more people than just Newton and Seale. Tarika Lewis, the first woman to join the party in 1967, was a sophomore in high school when the Black Panther Party for Self-Defense formed. She remembers being attracted to the organization because the two leaders were attempting to address issues that affected young and old alike. She stated, "when we saw the Panthers pushing for a Black Studies program at Merritt, we started pushing for one at Tech," the high school she attended in Oakland. She became one of the first Panther artists and took the pseudonym Maatilaba. As Eldridge Cleaver said later, it seemed there would be "a new day in Babylon," a time when people would "move beyond the halting steps" and make the ultimate sacrifice for the cause of black liberation.[15]

Peoples' consciousness of their oppression, and the right to be rid of that oppression, seemed to expand daily. Author William Van Deburg, who analyzed the impact of Black Power on American culture in *New Day in Babylon,* has noted that by this time black pride was in full bloom. This meant blacks had a heightened respect for themselves and their history. In turn, many of them made the decision to stand up and fight, by any means necessary, for their human rights. The Panthers came along and provided what was missing: namely, a tight, sharp, political analysis and a vigorous demonstration of manhood with an emphasis on self-defense. Robert Allen, a writer for the leftist publication the *Guardian,* optimistically concluded that "because of the stress laid on the national question the Panthers are potentially able to mobilize a very wide spectrum of the black population. Because they also understand the nature of class exploitation in U.S. society, the Panthers have been able to work with allies outside the black community and identify enemies within it."[16] The group's most publicized characteristic, however, was an emphasis on the gun as a political tool. Its insistence on defending itself inevitably led to the necessity of picking up the gun.

To understand the growth, development, and demise of the party, one has to understand the magnitude of this final step—this insistence on armed self-defense. Because it led down the path of no return, one can only hope the two leaders thought long and hard about going forward with their public display of weaponry and their scathing verbal attacks on the system, particularly law enforcement personnel, whom they derisively referred to as pigs. The two had to have at least thought about the consequences of their actions. They knew their actions might bring them considerable harm. Seale later pointed out that Newton often admonished him to "remember that we might not ever come back home one day."[17]

What then compelled two obviously talented individuals to take such a drastic step? What made people want to give up life, that most precious of commodities? The answer is simple: a desire to live a life free of violence, whether physical or psychological. The natural human response to violence is a desire to protect one's body. Unlike in the days of slavery, black men and women of the 1960s wanted to make it clear their persons were theirs to control. Like their spiritual mentor Malcolm X, the Panthers advocated freedom from oppression by any means necessary. If they were going to be successful, they had to overcome the violence reserved for them by their enemies in high and low places first.

The Southern Christian Leadership Conference's (SCLC) Bernard Lafayette explained that violence is built into American life because "part of the 'good order of society' is the routine oppression and racism committed against millions of Americans every day." Likewise, in 1969, writer Newton Garver concluded there is "quiet violence in the very operation of the system. . . . A black ghetto in most American cities operates very [much] like any system of slavery. Relatively little overt violence is needed to keep the institutions going, and yet the institution violates the human beings involved because they are systematically denied the options which are open to the vast majority in the society." Systematically depriving people of choices in everyday dealings institutionalizes a kind of violence. "It is as real and as wicked," he wrote, "as the thief with a knife." No one will deny ghetto blacks had been deprived of access to all the things that would have made living there unnecessary. The BPP decided black people's dignity and autonomy had been denied long enough. Its efforts to reverse this trend brought it face-to-face with the American government, which Martin Luther King Jr. described as "the greatest purveyor of violence on the face of the earth."[18]

Like their southern counterparts, Newton and Seale recognized that the freedom America advertised for both domestic and foreign consumption did not exist in their communities. They, along with thousands of others, believed the only way to affirm life was to be willing to give it up for the greater good. While neither Newton nor Seale died as a result of their revolutionary stance (though both came close to death on numerous occasions), they always viewed sudden death as more than a possibility. Herein lies the genius of the Black Panther Party. The group's leaders observed, analyzed, and articulated the extremely trying conditions under which most blacks lived. They then formulated extreme solutions to these problems. These solutions determined the organization's fate. Newton sincerely believed that "[w]hen unified and consistent, theory and action constitute a solid foundation for resolving our problems."[19]

Never in the history of America had blacks moved in such a radical fashion to solve their own problems. While their Ten Point Platform demanded housing, bread, freedom, justice, and peace, Panthers found it neither necessary nor expedient to wait until these things materialized. The Panthers asked for what they wanted then went to work to make those things happen. Perhaps they understood King's position that prayer alone is not a substitute for political participation. King, according to author Lewis Baldwin, realized "prayer must always be combined with hard work, intelligence, and sustained action."[20] This sustained action sounded the fire bell in the night for the authorities. Not only were the Panthers trying to strengthen their own communities by adequately feeding, clothing, and educating them, but they also vowed to defend them. When they succeeded in convincing enough people that their actual survival was at stake, they joined with thousands of other activists throughout the country, and indeed the world, and worked to wrest the power to control their own destinies from the comparatively few rich people who held it at the time. While most observers, then and now, accurately considered their attempt a futile one, the Panthers were confident it was not.

To succeed, the Panthers believed they had to educate their target audience. At first, that audience consisted of black people in the Oakland/San Francisco Bay Area. This task turned out not to be so difficult because police brutality and murder of blacks in the Bay Area had been an issue of concern before the Panthers emerged. In fact, the police had killed at least two Bay Area blacks in the months prior to the founding of the party.

In March 1966, an Oakland police officer shot a black man seven times in the back. The alleged crime: trespassing. The man was left paralyzed for life. The same month, a San Francisco police officer shot and killed sixteen-year-old car theft suspect Matthew Johnson. San Francisco police killed another unarmed teenager and car theft suspect in September 1966. Though none of the victims possessed weapons, coroner's inquests and grand juries declared the killings justifiable homicides. The shootings were necessary, the authorities explained, because they happened in self-defense.[21] Like in other regions of the country, this pattern had been developing for decades prior to the sixties. Viewing their community as a classroom from which to teach, the Panther leaders began using primary documents as teaching tools. From the United States Constitution, the Panthers taught blacks they had the right to bear arms. They then utilized the Declaration of Independence to teach people that part of their civic duty was to alter or abolish any system of government that unduly oppressed them. Not content with using just these two documents, they also consulted the California legal code to prove to the people that state and local law gave every citizen over the age of seventeen the right to bear arms in public.

This activity proved too much for law enforcement officers. Understandably, they became outraged, but at the same time they were at a loss about what to do, since they, too, knew the law. Rather than halt the brutality, harassment, and murder of Bay Area blacks, the police continued these practices. Many black residents in turn recognized the need for the Black Panther Party. This same police activity in other parts of the country had a similar effect on black Americans. Safiya Bhukari, who joined the party when it came to New York City, told an interviewer before she passed, "it wasn't the Black Panther Party that made me join the party, it was the New York City Police Department." Bhukari was a middle-class college student who believed wholeheartedly in the American dream prior to "gaining consciousness" and learning how blacks had been systematically denied their rights. Another New York Panther put it more bluntly when he noted, "the police did more recruiting than we did. If you took one of them butt whippings you was going to join something to get that stuff up off you. . . . Every time the police whipped somebody, that was another recruit for the Black Panther Party."[22] It was this recognition that catapulted the organization from the forefront of black protest in the Bay Area onto the stage of history. Before long, the Panther leaders very deliberately created an environment where people understood there was an organization that addressed the issues with which they were most concerned.

Like the movie actors who dominated popular culture in the southern part of their state, the California Panthers not only played main characters and supporting roles, but also choreographed, produced, and directed many of the acts that made up their drama. There was no better place to watch this drama unfold than on the streets where everyone had a front row seat and all the tickets were free. In their debut as directors, the Panthers chose police patrols for their opening act.

Having set the scene with calls for self-determination in 1966, the Panthers dressed extremely well for their parts. With powder blue shirts mostly hidden by their trademark leather jackets, black pants, and black boots, the Panthers struck an awesome but handsome pose. Their black berets, donned in honor of the much loved Argentine revolutionary Che Guevara, gave them a presence that could not be ignored. Slightly cocked to the side, this headgear gave the young revolutionaries a serious and menacing look. The three-piece suits and bow ties of Elijah Muhammad's Nation of Islam were soon overshadowed by these street revolutionaries, whose leather jackets came to symbolize Black Power and armed self-defense. Elbert Howard, one of the first members of the party, told a group of students the party "chose the black leather jackets because it seemed that everybody had one anyway."[23] This uniform, in addition to playing into the organization's paramilitary scheme, also displayed unity. Having taken care to present themselves well, the new organization started its pilot project by demanding local police cease their wanton brutality. To check compliance with this demand, the Panthers, like their unarmed brothers in Southern California's Community Alert Patrol, decided to follow the police with their cameras, tape recorders, law books, shotguns, and pistols. This initial drama determined whether the show went on.

It is clear some blacks in Oakland supported the party, an organization that vowed to defend them from police brutality. Former Panther Bill Brent commented that "there were people of all races who admired the Panthers because of their image as bad blacks who walked around with guns and wouldn't take no shit off the police, and not because of their rhetoric or political promises."[24] Former executive secretary of the

SNCC James Forman wrote, "[t]he call for resistance issued consistently by the Black Panther Party is a heroic effort" when one considers that "thousands of black men and women have suffered at the hands of the pigs, murdered day after day, night after night, without any organized resistance."[25] Of course the police had to respond to this resistance, an open challenge to their heretofore unquestioned authority.

It would be too much of an understatement to say the police did not like the new organization. More important, however, is the fact that their lives, like the lives of so many blacks, were now directly threatened with armed force. This turn of events understandably made police both uneasy and vengeful. One might have guessed police reaction to armed blacks in the 1960s, or at any other time for that matter, would not be good for party members. Policeman clearly outnumbered members of the BPP and they obviously had more training and experience in the use of firearms. If these two facts were not enough to dissuade the Panthers from continuing along this dangerous course, it should be noted the police had the backing of the state National Guard, the Marines at Camp Pendleton near San Diego, and the United States Army and Navy, with men and materiel stationed at a half dozen or more bases along California's Pacific coast. The yearly summer riots had been proof enough that the soldiers from these military bases would be called into duty if necessary. When they arrived, blacks usually wound up dead.

Understanding this set of circumstances, one wonders why the group's members took such chances with their lives. After all, the well-armed Revolutionary Action Movement (RAM), with Peking-based Robert Williams as its titular head, had been harassed, run underground, and finally removed from public view after they advocated solutions similar to the ones the Panthers offered. RAM called for the overthrow of the government by blacks who would succeed by using the time-honored tactic of guerilla warfare. According to historian Robin Kelley, however, "RAM members never attempted to implement Williams' [guerilla tactics] and they never engaged the police or anyone else in armed confrontation. They only wrote about it." It should be added that they often spoke loudly in public about it as well, claiming "a guerrilla war was not only possible but could be won in ninety days."[26] Even though the Panthers had met and talked with RAM members, they insisted public and armed defiance were essential if blacks were to be free of the fear that kept them from taking their freedom.

Why not forsake the gun as a tool of liberation and just concentrate on voter registration, improving neighborhood schools, and getting better jobs? Unlike Robert Williams, whom many blacks hailed as a hero for setting the example of armed self-reliance, they did not view nonviolent direct action as an alternative tactic. In fact, they eschewed nonviolence, claiming it had not worked to improve the lives of most blacks. Noting they were not looking for a fire fight, the Panthers insisted it was their duty to begin the process of protecting the black community.

One of the most significant actions during these early years concerned the protection of small children. For years, a busy intersection in the neighborhood where the Panthers set up their first office in Oakland was the site of accidents that killed or injured several school-aged children. The problem was the thoroughfare had no light to regulate traffic. As a result, speeding vehicles, primarily driven by whites coming in or on their way out of the community and back to their homes in the suburbs, sometimes ran over children. Seale recalled he and Newton "found out that two kids coming from the Santa Fe school" a block away "had been killed and another injured" on this particular corner. Also, "a girl had been killed there around seven months before" and "a young white girl, riding a motorcycle, got hit there, too." BPP leaders, responding to complaints made to them by area residents, began to view this problem as an unnecessary danger.

In early 1967, Panther members, working through the War on Poverty Center where Seale, Newton, and Hutton were employed, subsequently petitioned the Oakland City Council for a traffic light. After having worked diligently to gather the required signatures, they were rebuffed by the council, whose response had been "they couldn't put a traffic light on that corner until late 1968." This decision, they claimed, had been made after the council consulted with street engineers. The Panthers, according to Tarika Lewis, decided to solve the problem by going down to the intersection "with their guns" to direct traffic. "This is exactly what we did," she remembered. When Oakland policemen drove by the intersection and saw what was happening, they decided to take over from the armed Panthers who had been directing traffic. "By the next week," recalled Lewis, "they were digging holes in the ground" in preparation for the installation of a traffic light.[27]

Later in the party's development, when it shifted its emphasis from guns to serving the people, the experience Seale and Newton gained working in the poverty program was put to good use. They certainly used the canvassing techniques and knowledge of the community they had acquired to help support their Free Breakfast for Children Program. In addition to having provided a network of key people and organizations, their work in the poverty center gave them an idea of what it was like working in and for the community, so they did not go into their activities cold. They were therefore able to avoid many of the pitfalls that might have beset them had they been unversed in the technique of grass-roots organizing. In effect, the shift to community programming was a return to the demanding work the Panthers had left so quickly once the national spotlight turned its attention to them. Not that the group was solely introspective, but the Free Huey movement and ensuing trial ensured that a cult of personality developed in the party. Oblivious to much of the ballyhoo, most party members concerned themselves with serving as full-time revolutionaries defending black people and their communities. Indeed, thousands of people all around the country worked to make democracy a reality for Americans, while the defenders of the status quo simultaneously fought them and the war in Vietnam.

For this reason, the Panthers' willingness to defend the black community should be understood in the context of the quickly spreading Black Power movement. The Panthers, like other advocates of this philosophy, sincerely believed they served blacks' best interests. They saw the historic dependence on whites for protection, jobs, education, and housing had yielded very little in the area of tangible gains. (Black Power advocates, of course, were not including the black middle class in their conclusions.) Having reached this point, they began to demonstrate, first to themselves, and then to others, that immediate action, and nothing else, solved their problems.

Panther minister of information Eldridge Cleaver once wrote that "for too long black people have relied upon the analyses and ideologies of others. No other people in the world are in the same position as we are, and no other people in the world can get us out of it except ourselves. . . . There are those who are all too willing to do our thinking for us, even if it gets us killed. However, they are not willing to follow through and do our dying for us." Reiterating the central importance of self-reliance in any struggle for freedom, he concluded, "if thoughts bring about our deaths, let them at least be our own thoughts, so that we will have broken, once and for all, with the flunkeyism of dying for every cause and every error—except our own."[28] Cleaver later escalated this rhetoric and insisted an armed black revolution, with the support of white radicals, was the answer to the problems blacks faced. He became emboldened in this line of thinking after the following incident compelled him to join the BPP.

The San Francisco-based Black Panther Party of Northern California invited the Oakland Black Panther Party for Self-Defense, because of its recent exploits patrolling the police, to serve as security to Betty Shabazz, Malcolm X's widow. This San Francisco group had formed when SNCC members left the South to organize in other areas of the country. It also included former RAM members, who by this time had learned that the open carrying of weapons was one of the quickest ways to end up in jail. Their experiences in Detroit, New York City, and Philadelphia taught them that working in a more clandestine manner served their purposes better than openly challenging the power structure to a fight they could not win.[29] Either way, the organization sought to honor Malcolm X by sponsoring a yearly festival, and they brought his wife to the West Coast so she could legitimize the event. BPP members agreed to assist when it became clear they could provide a much-needed service to the widow of their hero and because the ensuing publicity might help them in their recruiting efforts.

Because Shabazz's life had been threatened on numerous occasions since her husband's death, she had done no long-distance traveling and had not made any public appearances. The Panther contingent was obviously deeply concerned about her personal safety. According to Eldridge Cleaver, in early 1967, she had decided to make the trip because he and members of other "radical organizations in the Bay Area" had decided to use the anniversary of Malcolm's assassination to launch the San Francisco branch of the Organization of Afro American Unity. Her purpose, recalled Cleaver, had been "to give her blessings to a launching of this branch of the OAAU."[30]

Teaming up with the Black Panther Party of Northern California on February 21, 1967, Newton, Seale, and five or six other Panthers convoyed to the San Francisco International Airport. Because they emerged from their vehicles with weapons, they immediately caught the attention of a member of airport security, who almost instantly called local law enforcement officers for backup. Newton explained their mission to airport security personnel, who insisted they could not enter the facility with the weapons. After telling the guard they "were going in whether he liked it or not," Newton pushed the officer aside and the group of Panthers headed for the waiting area near the tarmac where Betty Shabazz's plane was scheduled to arrive. They marched into the airport in a column of twos and arrived at their destination without incident. There was some contentious back and forth between security and the Panthers, but neither side wanted trouble, so the altercation remained strictly verbal.[31]

Once Betty Shabazz got off the plane, they surrounded her and proceeded to escort her to the vehicle that took her to the *Ramparts* magazine office, where she was scheduled to do an interview with Eldridge Cleaver, the magazine's new senior editor. Shabazz remembered exiting the plane and seeing "all of these police lined on each side of the little area where you walk from the plane to the terminal" and thinking someone famous or important had been on the plane. Noticing the Panthers "standing out there dressed militaristically" while one recited "part of the Constitution about carrying firearms," she thought, "Ok I understand." When she saw how organized and serious her escorts were, "it really did something to" her. She remembered saying to herself, "Oh wow. That's just really fantastic." Despite the tension that had developed between the Panthers and the police before Shabazz arrived, both groups, in a sight never to be seen again, escorted the widow outside. The Panthers formed a tight circle around Shabazz while the police and airport security took positions ahead of and behind the group. No other words were exchanged and the Panthers departed for the *Ramparts* office. After getting into the car and being "swept away," Shabazz noted at that point, "I certainly didn't have any fear."[32] Surely the Panthers' willingness to confront the authorities in the face of overwhelming force reminded Shabazz of her late husband's constant calls for blacks to defend themselves by any means necessary.

Arriving at *Ramparts'* Broadway office, more Panthers met with Shabazz and her contingent of security guards. They then escorted their prized guest inside. Not until after the interview ended did trouble begin to brew. Shabazz, for whatever reason, had informed her bodyguard escorts there were to be no pictures or video taken of her. She noticed several police cars and news reporters hovering outside the office door as she prepared to leave for her hotel. Apparently these policemen had decided to follow the group from the airport, and the newsmen, always alert for the hottest news, must have hurried to the scene after learning of the airport incident. At any rate, the group made a move to leave and the excitement began.

When Newton attempted to enforce Shabazz's request by holding a magazine up to one of the reporter's cameras, the man pushed it away and "down into his stomach," according to Seale, who at the time stood next to the Panther leader. Not phased by all the law enforcement personnel standing around, Newton responded by punching the reporter and demanding the police arrest the reporter for assault. "That man assaulted me," Newton exclaimed. "Now why in the hell don't you arrest him? Arrest that man," Seale remembered him saying.

At that point, several policemen unstrapped their weapons in anticipation of something worse happening. Newton, who noticed some of his fellow Panthers had turned their backs on the action to watch Betty Shabazz as she left, then instructed them all to "turn around!" Emphasizing his order and alluding to the many justifiable homicide verdicts for murdered blacks in the area, Newton yelled, "Don't turn your back on these backshooting motherfuckers!" Ordering his men to spread out so they could be prepared for whatever happened next, Newton simultaneously jacked "a shell off into the chamber of his gun." More policemen arrived, so Seale responded by summoning the rest of the Panthers who had remained in the office. Meanwhile, Warren Hinckle, the *Ramparts* editor, tried to defuse the situation by telling the officers things were under control. He failed.

The already tense situation escalated when, according to Seale, one of the policemen "unhooked the strap off the hammer of his pistol," moved toward Newton, and began shouting "Don't point that gun at me! Stop pointing that gun at me!" Newton asked the policeman matter-of-factly if he really wanted to draw his gun. All the while, several other policemen were pleading with their fellow officer to "cool it," but the staring match continued. Speaking as loudly and as clearly as he could under the circumstances, Newton said "OK, you big fat racist pig, draw your gun! Draw it you cowardly dog! I'm waiting." Although only a few seconds had elapsed after this unveiled threat, to those who witnessed the standoff it seemed like a lifetime. Fortunately, cooler heads prevailed. The now-bewildered officer "let out a great big sigh . . . hung his head," and backed off. Reporters captured the entire scene on camera and the Panthers quickly became known throughout the Bay Area black community as a group of hard-nosed revolutionaries who were intent on ending the police intimidation and brutality that had become a common fixture in their communities. Writer Erika Doss noted the calculating Panthers believed protecting Malcolm X's widow had inherent public relations benefits and as such they were "eager to shape their first testing of the media waters around claims to Shabazz." She concluded that the *San Francisco Chronicle,* the city's largest and most popular daily newspaper, "played into Newton's hands" when its story on the harrowing incident was headlined "A Frightening Army."[33]

Although such a gutsy move and the media circulation of it succeeded in attracting new recruits to the organization, Eldridge Cleaver among them, it created an impasse between the police and Panthers. This impasse became irreconcilable and subsequently created a situation where, early on, each group saw the demise of the other as an ultimate goal. The media, sometimes at the urging of the FBI, quickly realized they could help neutralize the youthful organization by portraying it negatively and dismissing any redeeming qualities about it. Either way, macho tactics and posturing created obstacles for the Panthers they never surmounted. Perhaps if every black man, woman, and child had joined the BPP, the group might have stood a chance. Barring that, and some might argue, even if that had been the case, the Panthers started off fighting a losing battle. While no guns were discharged in this particular situation, it did not take long before bullets flew in both directions.

The BPP, despite its members' commitment, courage, and unyielding tenacity, never could have won a war against the police. Against a dozen or so individual officers maybe, but not against any of the police departments in the large cities where it established chapters. Perhaps William Van Deburg said it best when he noted that "in the long run, the Panthers' utilization of the gun as a recruiting device and 'political tool' worked to their disadvantage, inflaming public opinion, skewing news coverage, and spurring a deadly response" from the police and other representatives of the establishment. The BPP's emphasis on community self-defense coupled with its open support of those who engaged in offensive actions against the police, elicited the type of response for which police, especially in the turbulent sixties and seventies, ordinarily trained. Even more importantly, the Panthers, from the very start, lost an unknown number of potential supporters since most Americans, black and white, viewed the killing of police as a crime, regardless of the reason.[34]

Many Americans, however, did not comprehend how difficult life was for the average ghetto dweller. As a result, they were unable to visualize how anyone could find such extreme action acceptable. The comments of one Watts dweller, made two years after the devastating rebellion of 1965, provide a glimpse into this kind of thinking. Claiming these remarks represented "70 per cent of Watts males," a University of California at Los Angeles (UCLA) study recorded the man as having said that "their despair was not grounded in blind hatred," and that poor blacks "couldn't eat civil rights. . . . I am still hungry and a hungry man is a dangerous man." This UCLA study, conducted by sociologists James Watson, Raymond Murphy, and eight others, concluded that "the problems of urban life for the Negro . . . have grown acute." The result of this worsening situation, they claimed, was that "a significant number of Negroes, successful or unsuccessful, are emotionally prepared for violence as a strategy or solution to end the problems of segregation, exploitation, and subordination."[35] One could argue that because the conditions in Watts had proven to be strikingly similar to conditions in all the other cities where rebellions occurred, the sentiments might also have been similar. Police brutality, lack of opportunity, and the realization that opportunity was not forthcoming in the near future led many blacks to conclude that armed self-defense coupled with self-help was the only way to end the despair.

That the youthful Panthers erred mightily when they challenged the U.S. government to an armed confrontation is obvious. Understandable as their anger and desperation might have been, it is important to analyze and explain the poor choices and unworkable strategies that flowed from this initial stance. It makes sense here to turn to Eldridge Cleaver's assumption of power in the party because the San Francisco standoff led to his decision to join and the party followed his philosophy early on.

Cleaver, born in Wabbeseka near Little Rock, Arkansas, moved west, like many blacks of his generation, as a result of his parents desire to leave the South for a chance at a better life. Mechanization had made obsolete the brute strength and unskilled labor of millions of southern blacks. They went north and west to find work, but to their chagrin good jobs were few. Those lucky enough to land jobs found they had been relegated to the lowest paid and most dangerous positions. Their lack of skills made them useless in a rapidly evolving, technologically advancing economy. Little, if anything, in their educational background prepared them for the demands of such a skill-based economy. While a few trickled up into the lower and middle rungs of the middle class by becoming managers or starting their own businesses, the overwhelming majority of this displaced mass of blacks found they had left the frying pan of the South for the fire of the North and West. In other words, their life chances had, more often than not, decreased rather than increased. Eldridge Cleaver's experience mirrors that of thousands of young black males whose parents possessed an endless reserve of dignity, but very little hope for their children, who often found themselves corrupted by the mean streets of urban America.

Before reaching their final destination of Los Angeles, the Cleavers stopped in Phoenix, Arizona. Eldridge's father had been lucky enough to land a job on the Super Chief train that ran between Los Angeles and Chicago. As Phoenix was a stop along the way, he found it expedient to move his family there to impose some sense of normalcy and togetherness. Because there was still not enough money in the household, young Eldridge started shining shoes to help ease the problem. This job represented the first of many negative encounters he had with law enforcement. He remembered the "cops owned the shoeshine boxes. You had to check them out from the stationhouse and paid in advance for the privilege. If you made your own box, the cops would chase you." He was chased many times. He began to develop a hatred for the police, and he transferred this hatred to whites in general. Having won a sports contest, he received "a piece of watermelon" for a prize. Understanding this to be "a deliberate insult to a black child," he remembered that his "bitterness against whites increased."[36]

He fared no better when his parents left Phoenix for Los Angeles in the early forties. Not long after they arrived, his mother and father separated. Cleaver continued to attend school, where he excelled in sports and began to believe he might even get an athletic scholarship. These plans were derailed when he was arrested for burglary and theft as a juvenile. Sent to the Fred C. Nelle School for Boys at Whittier, California, Cleaver did his time and learned to be more careful as a criminal. Or so he thought. He returned to school, but in June 1954 he was arrested for possession of marijuana. According to one news report, he had been caught "by Los Angeles police in a vacant building with three pounds of marijuana in his possession." This time, because he had reached age eighteen and the authorities no longer considered him a juvenile, he bypassed the California Youth Authority and went to Soledad, a maximum security penitentiary. He earned a high school equivalency certificate while incarcerated. Having served two and a half years, he returned home, thinking he had become a smarter criminal. He turned out to be wrong again, as eleven months later he found himself back in California's correctional system. This time, the authorities arrested and convicted Cleaver of rape, assault with intent to commit murder, and assault with a deadly weapon. In 1959, the court sentenced him to one to fourteen years in San Quentin, although he finished his time in Folsom prison.[37]

Cleaver's response to an interviewer who asked him what happened in that particular incident is interesting. He remembers being caught because he "whipped some people on their heads and shot at them and tried to ravish a woman." The details, as reported in the *Los Angeles Times,* are much more revealing. According to *Los Angeles Times* reporter William Drummond, Cleaver, late at night, approached the window of a parked car where a couple sat talking. "Let me in or I'll break it in!" he demanded. Unfortunately, the couple had left the door unlocked so Cleaver easily forced his way inside. He quickly subdued the male by tying him up with tape and then forced the female onto the back seat. After she refused to take her coat off and began struggling with the would-be robber/rapist, "Cleaver struck her on the head with a gun." By this time, however, the boyfriend had freed himself and he, too, began to struggle with Cleaver. Realizing the peril they were in, the male began blowing the horn and the female screamed for help. Cleaver knew his opportunity had passed so he "got out of the car, turned, and fired the gun at the couple. Neither was hit," reported Drummond. Cleaver then fired at the vehicle of another couple who turned on their headlights after catching sight of the commotion. He missed them, too. He also shot at and missed a man who tried chasing him after the struggle in the car ended. Cleaver, who admitted in an interview that he had been "on dope all week long," then "drove a short distance away and crashed into a parked car." Again, Cleaver fired at a man nearby, and again, he missed. Cleaver's dismal performance in this caper would be duplicated many times as he strove to serve as one of the leaders of a revolutionary vanguard organization. According to him, his attempt to "whip off some p——y" happened during a time when he "was on a one man Mau Mau thing" where he went out on weekends and "beat some Hunkies."[38]

In 1968, Cleaver wrote in the best-selling *Soul on Ice* that he had refined his technique of raping by practicing on "black girls in the ghetto ... where dark and vicious deeds appear not as aberrations or deviations from the norm, but as part of the sufficiency of the Evil of the day." Having perfected his style, he "crossed the tracks and sought out white prey." He wrote that he thought of rape "as an insurrectionary act." Since his victims were white, he saw his acts not only as a way to get revenge, but as a way to defile and trample upon the "white man's law" and his values. He believed he had been justified because of "the historical fact of how the white man has used the black woman." This last stint in prison, however, gave him time to be introspective and to realize that he was "wrong" and he "could not approve the act of rape." He no longer felt justified for his crimes and indeed claims to have lost respect for himself. "My pride as a man dissolved and my whole fragile moral structure seemed to collapse, completely shattered. That is why I started to write. To save myself," he said.[39]

Between 1960 and 1965, Cleaver, like Malcolm X before him, began to transform himself in prison. His affiliation with the Nation of Islam no doubt helped with the discipline he needed to accomplish this goal. He soon became a respected leader in prison, organizing work stoppages, strikes, and a successful protest to get black literature in the prison library. Cleaver, by then a follower more of Malcolm X than the Nation's leader Elijah Muhammad, began teaching a class on African American history. Cleaver's activities were part of a growing prison movement that in just a few years would make headlines all over the world. The cases of prison activist George Jackson, the Soledad Brothers, the San Quentin Six, and the Attica prison uprising in New York all demonstrated to the outside world that prisoners had been affected by the freedom movement that had begun sweeping the globe in the years following World War II. Envisioning himself as part of this movement, Cleaver improved his writing and soon began corresponding with Beverly Axelrod, a white San Francisco divorcee, who also happened to be a lawyer.

While his correspondence with Axelrod slowly developed into an affair, Cleaver became more politicized. In the meantime, assassins gunned down his idol, Malcolm X, in 1965. Knowing he might be released soon, he made a pact with several of his Muslim brothers to carry on Malcolm's legacy by resurrecting his short-lived Organization of Afro-American Unity. One of these close associates was Alprentice "Bunchy" Carter, also from Los Angeles. Carter, a leader of the Slausons, one of Los Angeles's largest and toughest street gangs, also became politicized in prison and later founded the Southern California chapter of the Black Panther Party. In any case, while he waited, Cleaver's cultivation of a relationship with Beverly Axelrod began to produce fruit.[40] The savvy Cleaver began to use her to get himself out of jail.

The two began working on a writ of habeas corpus. Axelrod had also begun funneling some of the letters Cleaver wrote her to the editor at *Ramparts* magazine. The editor loved them and subsequently promised to give Cleaver a job when and if he got out of prison. This turned out to be the break he needed as Axelrod began a flurry of activity to get her black lover released. By December of 1966, barely three months after Newton and Seale founded the BPP, Cleaver was on his way home to his new lover and his new job. Cleaver once all but admitted to an *Evergreen* magazine reporter that he had been "gaming" on Axelrod so she would get him out of prison. Not having made her personal acquaintance, he wrote her letters based on the "concept of where white women were at, and what can move them. I wanted to attract her. I didn't have any money to pay her. I only had words, and I used those words . . . and I got out of the penitentiary." He added, "I think she's very angry with me," but then he explained the matter away by saying, "this was the way I was in prison." This instance was not the last time Cleaver used someone in pursuit of his own agenda. Meanwhile, he transferred his parole from Los Angeles to San Francisco and spent the next seven years rallying the masses to revolution.[41]

Cleaver emerged from prison a virtual celebrity. His association with Axelrod and his work at *Ramparts* made him extremely popular with the white liberals in the Bay Area. He capitalized on this attention and support by establishing the Black House in San Francisco. Located in an imposing Vatican-style structure in San Francisco, the Black House was a cultural mecca for the area. Groups from all over the Bay Area went there to discuss and debate issues of importance to blacks in general and the black struggle in particular. The Black House also served as a clearing house for black artists, poets, dancers, and actors. Amiri Baraka, Marvin X, Sonia Sanchez, and a host of others performed there. Cleaver, having established the Black House to provide "a controlled environment where black images were on display—from Frederick Douglas all the way down to Malcolm X," said it "had a very powerful impact on those who came in, and it was a recruiting device." The goal, he said, was consciously to create "a Malcolm X type personality," something he claimed he and others had successfully done with the black history and culture classes he taught while in prison. Sonia Sanchez saw the Black House as the "western extension" of the New York City-based Black Arts Repertory Theatre. She remembered a "fantastic coming together" of Panthers, cultural nationalists, and students who all cooperated and "supported each other."[42]

Due to his association with such a cultural magnet as the Black House, Cleaver's presence began to dominate the area. Standing over six feet tall, his physical appearance was as imposing as his personality. One journalist, condescendingly labeling Cleaver "the Big Man of black America," noted he "towers over people of average height and enjoys so doing." It would not be long before this titanic figure of the Bay Area grew even larger. Cleaver's penchant for public relations, along with his skill as a writer and connections with well-to-do whites, made a marriage between him and the party seem like the perfect move.[43]

Indeed, the BPP's founders had exactly this alliance in mind when they ventured to the office of a local radio station in Oakland to recruit Cleaver. They heard him speaking about the many riots taking place around the country and liked his approach to the problem. Cleaver remembered delivering a "very radical message" that he had "patterned after Malcolm X." Self-defense, unity, and collective action had been the hallmarks of his speech. Newton had also been impressed with the fact that Cleaver had spent time in prison, which he believed gave Cleaver legitimacy. Newton, who had also spent time in jail, probably viewed

Cleaver in this way because of Malcolm X's impact on black prisoners and the slowly burgeoning prison movement that had been begun to take place around the same time. In an effort to recruit the fiery-tongued soon-to-be sixties icon quickly, Newton and Seale, after the radio show ended, asked Cleaver to join their party, which at that point barely had more than twenty members. Cleaver declined, explaining that he had left prison with the intention of reviving Malcolm X's Organization of Afro-American Unity. He told the two fledgling revolutionaries that he and a number of other recently released prisoners "had taken a kind of blood oath on this." He liked "the armed action and all that" but the name "Black Panther Party for Self-Defense didn't really grab" him. Cleaver wanted immediate action against what he described as his imperialist enemies—not to be confused with his white liberal friends—so the self-defense moniker led him to calculate, inaccurately, that the two nearly unknown Panthers were not serious about revolution. Cleaver, though he had only recently moved to northern California, was already in the center of Bay Area progressive politics. His response clearly indicates that the party had not yet captured the public's full attention. According to Cleaver, because the two were not wearing the uniforms for which they eventually became famous, or infamous, and because he had recently met a lot of people who asked that he join their organizations, he "really didn't understand who they were at the time."[44]

Exercising patience, the two stopped pressuring Cleaver. They did however, continue to visit the Black House. Newton believed Cleaver's literary style and public persona would help the party gain a wider audience. He also believed Cleaver to be as sincere a revolutionary as he understood himself to be. On a number of occasions, the subject was revived but Cleaver, according to Bobby Seale, maintained that he was "still checking around . . . trying to see what's happening." Newton wrote that he "had asked Cleaver to join the party a number of times." Not until after Cleaver began working with the Panthers on the Betty Shabazz visit did he reconsider his decision.[45]

Everything fell into place for Cleaver in February 1967 when he witnessed the Panthers face down the police with guns in front of the *Ramparts* office in San Francisco. Newton recalled he "didn't join until after" this confrontation "where the police were afraid to go for their guns." After several long discussions on his position and title in the party, the three agreed that he would be minister of information. After he joined, he was put in charge of the Panther newspaper.[46]

While recruiting Cleaver to a top position in their organization seemed like the right idea at the time, the two leaders actually knew very little about the ex-con-turned-writer. It was years before they realized what they later termed their "mistake." Cleaver's joining the party when he did should have set off alarm bells for Seale and Newton. That he believed, according to Seale and Newton, that the Panthers had armed confrontation with law enforcement as a goal turned out to be a mistake of the highest order. The two leaders intended to use the gun and the rhetoric that accompanied it as recruiting tools, not as ends in themselves. They knew blacks were already in a state of rebellion, so they wanted to organize that energy into more productive ends. Cleaver, however, wanted a fight, and once Newton and Seale went to jail, he led the party in that direction. Cleaver sometimes filled his public remonstrations with calls for the death of policemen, or "pigs" as he and other Panthers referred to them. The party, believing Cleaver knew exactly what he was doing, accepted this vitriolic public speech. Even when he clearly should have been toning down the rhetoric, party leaders left Cleaver to do as he pleased.

One example of this problem of fundamental misunderstanding arose as Newton's trial on attempted murder charges began April 25, 1967. Though this topic will be taken up in more detail in the next chapter, it should be noted that Newton's October 1967 shootout with two Oakland policeman left the Panther leader with four bullet holes in his abdomen, as well as one officer dead and another seriously wounded. Cleaver, in an effort to rally the people behind Newton, circulated a leaflet throughout the black community. The leaflet charged that the police came into the black community with the express intent of murdering someone, that they had "violated the territorial integrity of the black community," and that Newton "had dealt with their transgression in a necessary way." According to Newton, "[t]he leaflet went on to say that Black people are justified in killing all policemen who do this," inferring that Newton "had killed the police officer" as part of a plan. While Newton's family was upset and complained about the leaflet, Newton supported Cleaver, knowing the leaflet could not be used against him and because he thought issuing the leaflet represented a "political act using the trial to heighten the consciousness of the black community." As far as Newton was concerned, "Eldridge was free to write and mobilize the community by any means necessary."[47]

The position Newton took on this issue was undoubtedly a mistake. Cleaver, wrote historian Robin Kelley, eventually came to represent "a wing of the party more interested in guerilla warfare than in rebuilding society or doing the hard work of grassroots organizing." Of course, political organizing was the primary reason the party emerged. The early emphasis on guns and violent rhetoric, however, made this goal less obvious. Cleaver's rhetoric, along with the rhetoric of other party leaders, became increasingly violent and in turn set an example for others to follow. In the wake of this green light by the leadership, rank-and-file members took the opportunity to use language that was not only good for recruitment but threatening to authorities as well. According to William Van Deburg, this "language of the ghetto" or "political rhetoric," as they termed it, intimidated whites and led to major problems for the party.[48] Before these problems became apparent, however, the group became a media sensation.

A violent murder in the Bay Area helped the Panthers to get the exposure they so badly needed if they were to grow. Mark Comfort, who had been a part of the security detail in Lowndes County Alabama when the SNCC helped to organize the first Black Panther Party in 1965, suggested in the spring of 1967 that the Dowell family contact the Black Panther Party for Self-Defense for assistance. Like other black families in the North Richmond area, the Dowells had recently lost a family member to police murder. Less than six months prior to this murder, policemen had killed two other black men in Richmond. On April 1, 1967, a Contra Costa County sheriff's deputy shot Denzil Dowell several times. According to the police, Dowell had stolen a vehicle and had been attempting to evade arrest when they shot him. After killing the unarmed youth, the police left the scene without calling for an ambulance or even bothering to report the incident. Family members, who thought they heard gunshots earlier, discovered Dowell's body several hours later. A grand jury quickly ruled the killing a "justifiable homicide" even though several important questions remained unanswered. For example, the police claimed to have shot Dowell three times, but a coroner's report noted that "he bled to death after being shot ten times."

The family was neither allowed to see the body nor to take possession of the clothing Dowell wore in order to determine how many times he had been shot. Sheriff Walter Younger also refused a request "that the officer who admitted doing the shooting be removed from duty pending an investigation." Because the Dowell family's efforts to get more answers had been hampered by the police and the grand jury, it looked to the BPP for help. When Comfort contacted Newton and Seale, they did not hesitate to accept the request for assistance.[49]

After having gone to Richmond to conduct their own investigation, the Panthers approached the sheriff with their findings. Despite the new information, Sheriff Younger refused to reopen the case and in an off-handed manner suggested that the Panthers approach the legislators in Sacramento if they had a problem with how the legal system operated. After hearing state assemblyman Don Mulford, who called in to a radio show where the Panthers were guests, announce that he would "get" the Panthers with a bill that outlawed the carrying of weapons in public, the group decided to take the sheriff's advice and go to the state capitol in Sacramento to observe the proceedings and register their protest against it.[50]

This decision, and the flurry of media coverage it generated, catapulted the party into the living rooms of millions of Americans. Some of those Americans, particularly the black ones, were so impressed with what they saw that they began requesting party leaders to help them start their own chapters. Newton wrote that soon after that "we had more members than we could handle." The calls were so frequent, he noted, that "we could hardly keep track of the requests. In a matter of months, we went from a small Bay Area group to a national organization."[51]

Newton and Seale subsequently opened branches in Emeryville, Richmond, San Francisco, Marin City, and Berkeley. Their method was to travel around the Bay Area holding mass rallies, explaining their program and attempting to address problems affecting the particular area. In Richmond, for example, the rallies were centered around the death of Denzil Dowell and the desire of black residents in the area to be incorporated into their own city. Hundreds of people attended these rallies as armed Panthers looked on in silence, their black leather jackets signifying that they were the ones in charge. Some stood on rooftops while others stood in yards and at intersections. All the while, Panther speakers elucidated the problems of the day.

They took the position that manhood was central to achieving black liberation. While women, particularly Denzil's mother, were included in the Dowell protests and women were members of the party, the Panthers thought manhood served as a good word to illustrate their points. The word manhood could be used to define both males and females since it signified the willingness and ability to control one's own destiny. The first issue of their newspaper noted the earliest members of the party were "the cream of black manhood." BPP leaders wanted their audience to know the Panthers were "there for their protection" and that the crowds owed it to themselves "to get behind these brothers and let the world know that black people are not stupid fools who are unable to recognize when someone is acting in the best interest of black people." Emphasizing their point, the paper stated: "BLACK MEN!!! It is your duty to your women and children, to your mothers and sisters, to investigate the program of the PARTY. There is no other way. We have tried everything else." Careful not to exclude women, the paper concluded, "Check it out, Black Brothers and Sisters, This is our Day!!!!!" Thousands of blacks heeded the call.

George Dowell, brother of the slain Denzil Dowell, joined the party and became captain of the Richmond branch. "When I listened to Huey and Bobby talk," he told one reporter, "I could tell they were talking from their hearts. A person can tell when another person is telling the truth and that's what all our people been waiting to hear." Summing up the experience of thousands who eventually joined the organization, Dowell noted, "I feel like a man and now I'm acting like a man. I have always had a feeling of wanting to do something for my people and working with a group that I know is working for the people is a dream fulfilled for me." He went on to say that, hearing the Panther leaders speak, "something lifts inside you and you are proud." To be sure, the BPP did not engineer the moment, but it seized the initiative in response to current events and attempted to demonstrate to blacks that their salvation lay in themselves as opposed to more laws or white largesse. Dowell understood that "black people need protection" and insisted that was the reason the Panthers armed themselves. "We are just tired of living like this. We want freedom now," he stated. Understanding the magnitude of the decision the group had made and accepting the consequences, he told the reporter, "I hope it won't come to bloodshed but if it does and if I die, I'll know I did my part."[52] Panther leaders, via mass rallies, intended to convince thousands more that picking up the gun remained blacks' only hope of surviving in what they termed racist America.

At one such rally in San Francisco, held in June 1967, Newton and Seale addressed the youth in Portero Hill, a small black enclave of decaying World War II barracks that, according to one observer, "should have been torn down years ago." Seale, standing atop a garbage can, began to speak and in the process, explained the history and goals of the Black Panther Party. When he finished, he introduced Newton. Newton provided the crowd with a fifteen-minute history of the black struggle in America and began to make parallels with other revolutions. Because the Vietnam War was raging, he used it as an example for blacks to emulate. Explaining "there were only 30 million" Vietnamese, Newton told the crowd that not only did they oust the Japanese and the French, "but now they are kicking hell out of the Americans and you better believe it brothers." He told them blacks must also arm themselves "for defense against the same racist army. . . . Every time you go execute a white racist gestapo cop, you are defending yourself."[53] Clearly, Newton's rhetoric had been aimed at those whose relationships with the police had left something to be desired. Though Newton constantly stressed obeying the law to Panther recruits, his public statements, designed to attract those recruits in the first place, left no room for negotiation when it came to dealing with police officers. During this period of development, black nationalism became a part of the party's philosophy.

Not content to let Newton have the last word, Seale mounted the garbage can once again and began to explain to the crowd that a change in tactics was in order. He referred to the recent upheaval at Hunter's Point, a black community in San Francisco, where, according to reporter Sol Stern, "disorganized" blacks used "halfhearted attempts to fight back against the cops." Like the rebellions that had devastated Watts, Newark, and Harlem in previous years, this one started after an incident of police brutality. Explaining that chaos and disorganization was a waste, Seale told the audience, "Black people can't just mass on the streets and riot. They'll just shoot us down." He suggested that they form small groups and "take care of business." Stern noted that among other things this business included "executing racist cops." As Seale spoke, the crowd shouted to him "that's right" and "you tell it." The crowd obviously agreed with what the party's chairman had been advocating, as they encouraged him to "come with it." He obliged. In very graphic terms, he described "how a couple of bloods can surprise cops on their coffee breaks." Marching up nonchalantly to the unsuspecting officer, they would then, "with righteous power . . . shoot him down—voom, voom, with a 12-gauge shotgun." In his mind, this was "the only way" blacks "were going to overcome." Using their "potential destructive power," he continued, blacks could ensure their demands were met "by making it impossible for the man's system to function." Referring to several factories in the distance, he added, "all we got to do is drop some [Molotov] cocktails in those oil tanks and then watch everything go." Not long after Seale finished, several people in the crowd took membership applications and offered the local captain their names."[54]

It is important to note here that Seale spoke during a time when some of his suggestions had already been taken into consideration. Not only had blacks organized themselves during the Watts rebellion, but they did the same thing in Newark and Detroit in 1967. Both of these cities, after blacks had minor altercations with police, erupted in rebellion. From July 12–17, 1967, blacks in Newark made an attempt to destroy the symbols of white power in their communities. While the looting, burning, and sniping that followed helped them to vent their anger, some twenty-six people were killed. One week later in Detroit a similar, but more destructive, rebellion occurred when police arrested a group of blacks celebrating the return of a Vietnam veteran at the United Community League for Civic Action, which doubled as an after-hours drinking spot. Racial tension had been running high because a few weeks earlier a group of whites in the Rouge Park community had murdered black Vietnam veteran Danny Thomas. When the crowd, which had been watching as some of its members were arrested and taken away in police cars, began to increase rather than decrease, reinforcements were summoned. When backup arrived, local blacks pelted the police cars with rocks and bottles. The tension simmered until five days later when the Motor City experienced, according to one observer, the worst civil disorder in "twentieth century America in terms of what they cost in lives and destruction."[55]

When it became clear the Detroit Police Department, with the help of officers from neighboring departments, could not quell the disturbance, Gov. George Romney requested federal help. A politically astute President Lyndon Johnson quickly granted the request and subsequently used the riot to discredit Romney, who, according to documentary film-maker Henry Hampton, "had been a contender for the Republican presidential nomination at the time of the riot." Johnson supplemented Detroit's three thousand policemen with five hundred state troopers and two thousand members of the Michigan National Guard along with helicopters, tanks, and other armored vehicles. He also dispatched five thousand paratroopers from the mostly black Eighty-second Airborne, known as one of the toughest outfits in the United States military. The irony was not lost on blacks who fought these troops from street to street and building to building. They realized that blacks in the army were being pitted against blacks in the ghettos. The Panthers later recruited heavily from the armed forces. These well-trained special forces took nearly a week to restore order in the Motor City. With stores and factories afire, chaos reigned. One homeowner in the area remem-bered that "everywhere you turned and looked, you could see nothing but flames." Indeed, the destruction spanned some fourteen square miles, or two hundred square blocks, so it became nearly impossible for authorities to attend to all the fires. For the most part, the fires had to burn themselves out because residents shot at firemen who attempted to quench them. A military-imposed curfew did little to prevent those who were determined from inflicting damage. Guerrilla tactics and snip-ing became the choice methods of resistance for some of the city's resi-dents. Howard Becker, an officer in the National Guard at the time, remembered he and his men "consistently" received "sniper fire from buildings" as well as from the streets. They were able to rein in the snipers only after sending in tanks. Snipers fired on them and then they determined from which direction the shots had come. "Once locating a sniper," he noted "the police and guardsmen would go in" and "hus-tle them out of the buildings."[56]

Ignoring the examples of every revolution that came before the six-ties upheavals, former president Dwight Eisenhower, who had never had the occasion to spend much time around black people, commented that people had to be taught that "personal or social problems cannot be solved by violence and defiance of authority." He said he had "the utmost sympathy for any person who has never had a decent chance in life . . . but the fact that society has treated him badly does not give him a right to smash a store window and take what he wants or to attack our police with animal ferocity." Military and police officials, who used heavy-handed tactics to put down the disturbance, apparently held similar feelings.[57]

Detroit resident and congressional representative John Conyers (D-Michigan) remembered that "what really went on was a police riot." Charging that "federal law enforcement agents" had to "restrain Detroit police," he noted they were "unbelievable in their determination to visit excessive violence upon the population." Thinking that a person on a rooftop "might have a gun and would shoot them, they would shoot at them first" regardless of whether they were armed. He concluded, "they were misusing physical force and lethal force because they were angry and they were also frightened."[58]

After order had been restored and the last of the 4,700 paratroopers left the city, forty-one people had been killed, six hundred injured, and more than four thousand arrested. Of 682 damaged buildings, 412 were total losses. The city suffered property losses of more than $45 million. The primary victims, in terms of deaths, injuries, and arrests, had been blacks. The rebellion did, however, have a positive effect on some blacks.

Detroit resident Ed Vaughn encapsulated the feelings of many when he noted it had not been "Black Power that caused the rebellion, it was the lack of power that caused the rebellions around the country. People did not see any hope for themselves." He continued, "After the rebellion was over, our consciousness had been raised . . . and there was a strong sense of brotherhood and sisterhood. We saw a very strong sense of camaraderie in the community."[59] It had been this consciousness and camaraderie on which the Panthers sought to capitalize. If the riot in Detroit had been the only violent eruption in 1967, the Panthers might not have been able to attract widespread support. In reality, at least a dozen cities experienced violence at approximately the same time as Detroit.

The *Sacramento Bee*, located in the city where the Panthers garnered nationwide publicity, reported that this conglomeration of outbursts represented "the most widespread outbreak of racial strife in the nation's history." It noted that other cities where racial violence erupted included Flint and Grand Rapids, Michigan, Toledo, Ohio, Englewood, New Jersey, Cambridge, Massachusetts, Tucson, Arizona, and Houston, Texas. On July 24, 1967, black snipers in Englewood "pinned down 100 policemen for more than an hour before a downpour of rain cooled off a fourth straight night of racial violence." Panther rhetoric later attracted some people who participated in these actions. In another instance, two blacks were killed in Pontiac, Michigan, one when a state legislator, trying to protect his store from looters, shot and killed an intruder. This set of circumstances also served as the basis of the Panther critique of the marriage of business and government. When the BPP spoke of "demagogic politicians and avaricious businessmen," some blacks were able to identify with its analyses and conclusions. Even if Seale had not urged San Francisco blacks to drop Molotov cocktails in large oil storage containers, the twenty-five blacks in Pontiac arrested a month later "after nearly 40 fires were set" would have still done the deed.[60] This fact is simply an indication that the Panthers gathered ammunition for their fiery speeches from some of the daily occurrences in black communities dispersed throughout the United States.

In other words, the "market" for Panther rhetoric was clearly there. A 1971 report by the House Committee on Internal Security noted the Panthers sought to use the mounting incidence of ghetto riots occurring throughout the country as a source of power to destroy what they considered a hostile American government. The report pointed out that the BPP sought to harness this "black wrath and disaffection" to "blackmail the power structure into meeting [its] demands." Rather than engage in "aimless rioting," the report noted, the BPP hoped such a strategy "would give the nation's black minority a kind of 'military' power to back up its demands."[61] Not all the rioting, however, was aimless. The Detroit riot, for example, lasted as long as it did because of guerilla activity. Using automatic weapons and tracer bullets, and supported by rooftop snipers, blacks succeeded in controlling the Kercheval area for nearly three days. They forced out the police and military, who had to regroup and wait for reinforcements.[62] Wholeheartedly supporting this activity, Huey Newton summed up the BPP's strategy and intentions when he wrote, "the only way he [a black person] can become political is to represent what is commonly called a military power—which the BLACK PANTHER PARTY FOR SELF-DEFENSE calls Self-Defense Power. . . . Black People can develop Self-Defense Power by arming themselves from house to house, block to block, community to community throughout the nation." After this had happened, he believed blacks could then "choose a political representative who [would] state to the power structure the desires of the black masses. If the desires [were] not met, the power structure [would] receive a political consequence. We will make it economically non-profitable for the power structure to go on in its oppressive ways. We will then negotiate as equals. There will be a balance between the people who are economically powerful and the people who are economically destructive."[63]

Advocating the need for change as the only way to gain economic well-being had the potential to appeal to a wide range of people, particularly ghetto blacks. The rhetoric of violence was used as a recruiting tool because of the deep truths it embodied. In other words, the *Black Panther* wanted its readers to know that the time had come to do or die. According to Newton, the Panthers sought to increase the tension between the police and black communities throughout the country, believing they could "take the conflict to so high a level that some change had to come." It is no surprise then that the Panthers met the type of repression reserved for enemies in war. He went on to insist that black people's major problem was the unchecked violence spawned by white supremacy. The Panthers, therefore, organized to check this external violence with defensive violence. Attorney Kimberle Crenshaw, who has written extensively on race and crime, pointed out that in situations like this one, "the state could not assume a position of neutrality regarding black people." She argued that "either the coercive mechanism of the state had to be used to support white supremacy or it had to be used to dismantle it."[64] It was unlikely that the state would destroy itself. This fact left the BPP with a choice.

This lack of protection is the reason why a tired Newton, after attending a rally in Richmond, told a reporter the talk "about killing cops is serious." Asked why "stake everything, including the lives of the Panthers on the killing of a couple of cops," Newton replied it "wouldn't be just a couple of cops." In his serious but characteristically mild tone, he calculated "when the time comes, it will be part of a whole national coordinated effort" that they hoped would "force revolutionary changes in the society." To the question of whether Newton was "willing to kill a cop," he responded "yes," and added that when the time came he was "willing to die."[65] Little did Newton know he would soon find himself in a situation where the opportunities to kill and to die presented themselves simultaneously. This incident set off a firestorm of media coverage and BPP activity, first in the Bay Area and California and then around the globe.

It was October 27, 1967, and, according to fellow Panther Tarika Lewis, Huey Newton busied himself celebrating the last day of his probation, which he incurred several years earlier after being convicted of assaulting a man named Odell Lee at a house party. Lee had attacked Newton with a knife after the Panther leader tried on several occasions to solve the confrontation verbally. During a brawl, Newton subsequently took Lee's knife and stabbed him. His probation was over and he had finally paid his debt to society.[66]

The day started with Newton delivering a Black Student Union–hosted speech at San Francisco State University. Requests to start chapters were still pouring in from the aftermath of the Sacramento incident and, with Seale in jail on weapons charges in Sacramento, Newton and Cleaver had to answer as many of the requests as they could. That evening, Newton went to Bosn's Locker, "the bar where [he] started recruiting." He had just finished "a righteous dinner of mustard greens and corn bread with [his] family." Lewis, who was with Newton that night, remembered Newton was happy because his probation would be over. They attended a few parties to mark the occasion. She remembered leaving the last party that night at about four in the morning when they "dropped him off at his girlfriend's house."[67] At this point, he borrowed his girlfriend's car. Laverne Williams owned a Volkswagen beetle that Newton loved to drive. Newton and his longtime friend Gene McKinney, whom he met and picked up at one of the parties, then drove off into the night, headed to West Oakland's thriving black business district, which housed bars, restaurants, and clubs of every sort. After all the partying, they were hungry again, so they went looking "for righteous soul food," according to Newton.[68]

He never got to taste whatever he hungered for. The Oakland police, who by now had the names, addresses, and photos of Panthers, as well as the license plate numbers of all the cars they drove, ensured that his next meal came from the state. As Newton neared his destination, a police officer flagged him with his red lights. Newton, having been stopped some fifty times at this point, assumed this was business as usual and pulled over. It might very well have been, or it could be that

Newton, who had clearly been drinking earlier, had committed a moving violation. Either way, the stop did not end with pleasantries.[69]

After Newton stopped, Officer John Frey radioed the station that "it's a known Black Panther vehicle . . . you might send a unit by." The dispatcher, Clarence Lord, sent Herbert Heanes on the backup call. Meanwhile, Frey had requested Newton's driver's license, which he produced. Details of what happened after this point are fuzzy and contradictory, depending on who one asks. At the trial, Heanes testified that Newton drew a gun from his shirt, shot once at Frey, then commandeered Frey's sidearm and shot Heanes three times and Frey five more times. According to Newton, Frey began by sarcastically saying, "well, well, what do we have here? The great, *great* Huey P. Newton." He then spoke briefly with Heanes, who at some point took McKinney from the passenger seat to the street side of the car. After this Frey returned, opened Newton's door and ordered him out of the car. He then "aggressively" searched the Panther leader in both a "disgusting and thorough manner." Newton, who had exited the car with his lawbook, asked whether he was under arrest and was told no.[70]

The officer told Newton he wanted to "talk" to him, and told him to go to the back of the car. Newton began finding the relevant passages in his lawbook and told the officer that he had no reason to arrest him. By now, having "reached the back door of the second police car," Frey brought Newton "to an abrupt halt." At this point, Newton claimed Frey told him "you can take that book and shove it up your ass, nigger." Stepping in front of Newton, Frey punched him in the face with his left hand. Newton recalled it "was not a direct blow, but more like a straight arm" that sent him "reeling backwards and down on one knee." His lawbook still in his hand, Newton began to rise. At this point, he "saw the officer draw his service revolver, point it at me, and fire." Although Newton remembered hearing "a rapid volley of shots," he had "no idea where they came from." Meanwhile, he said a sensation like "hot boiling soup spill[ed] over his stomach and he blacked out." Newton survived the shootout with four bullet wounds in his abdomen, while one officer, John Frey, lay dead, and the other, Herbert Heanes, lay wounded.[71]

Newton's passenger, Gene McKinney, flagged down a passing vehicle and ordered the driver to take them to David Hilliard's house, which was nearby. Hilliard, a longtime friend of Newton, eventually became the party's chief of staff. For the time being, however, his concern was with the four bullet holes in Newton's midsection and the blood all over his house. He insisted the unconscious but still breathing Newton be taken to the hospital immediately. They rushed him to Kaiser Hospital a few miles away. After doctors and nurses succeeded in getting Newton onto a gurney and found him a room, the police reportedly entered, grabbed his hands, stretched them over his head and handcuffed them to both sides of the gurney. The police then began to beat on the tightening handcuffs as Newton screamed in pain. The doctor, whom Newton begged to make the police stop, told him to shut up. Meanwhile, the police continued beating Newton about the face and head, saying he had killed one of their fellow officers. Because the police officers were spitting on him, he said he spat blood back at them. The doctor placed a towel over his face to prevent this action and the police continued the beating. Newton wrote, "I was still screaming in pain when I passed out completely."[72]

This incident did more for the Black Panther Party than all its speeches and rallies. Newton immediately became a hero in black communities across the country. The fact that a police officer had been killed elevated his stature in the minds of millions of blacks and other minorities who knew from experience the brutality of policemen. This especially had been the case for those involved in some aspect of the freedom struggle. Newton's incarceration and the time leading up to his trial ushered in the era of the party's most significant growth. The words "Free Huey," due to the savvy machinations of Eldridge Cleaver, galvanized an international movement.

CHAPTER 3

Speaking of Violence

VIOLENT RHETORIC HAD TWO MAJOR effects on the BPP. One influenced its growth and the other helped to bring about its destruction. First, it served as a magnet for disaffected youth in America's ghettos. White radicals and student activists also picked up on this current and followed suit with their own violent rhetoric. Second, and more ominously, Panther rhetoric placed a national spotlight on the organization. This media attention eventually worked to the party's detriment as it increasingly concentrated on an exaggerated paramilitary image that portrayed the group's members as gun-toting thugs out to kill white people. The media subsequently used this skewed image of the party, carefully constructed to strike fear in both the white and black public, to help justify the police repression that Panthers constantly contended with after 1967.

Self-defense sometimes spilled over into what appeared to be unprovoked assaults. The line between violence in self-defense and violence for its own sake was very fine. Panther propaganda helped this along, especially since this was an era of violent nationalists driving out hated colonial forces. The rhetoric of revolution emphasized that the mere presence of police as "colonial armies" in itself constituted an attack on blacks. Perhaps what is really surprising is how little of such violence Panther rhetoric provoked, rather than how much. This contention, however, cannot be understood without the knowledge that the BPP was itself a reaction to unprovoked violence, not just toward its members, but toward blacks in general.[1] The government was violent toward the party, and the party was certainly violent—toward some police and elements within various communities—but was not physically violent at all against the government. In the end, however, the virtually unlimited financial, technological, and human assets of local law enforcement agencies, backed up by federal resources including the armed forces, succeeded in convincing the BPP that the government intended to put the Panthers' armed revolution down at any cost. Convinced that they knew how to make a difference, however, the Panthers continued to insist a violent revolution represented the only salvation for blacks and other oppressed minorities. Taking the lead from their esteemed leader and minister of information Eldridge Cleaver, the group said it was working to drive the occupying police from their neighborhoods.[2]

Algerian author and psychiatrist Frantz Fanon, a popular ideologue for black militants of the post–civil rights era, explained that this readiness to employ violence was liberating for oppressed people. "At the level of individuals," according to Fanon, "violence is a cleansing force. It frees the native from his inferiority complex and from his despair and inaction; it makes him fearless and restores his self-respect." It is not surprising, therefore, that the Panthers looked to Fanon's writings for philosophical guidance.[3] Sometimes they, along with a few other disgruntled radicals, made an attempt to put Fanon's theories into action.

Edward Kiernan, president of the Patrolmen's Benevolent Association of New York City, noted in 1970 that he had no doubt the Panthers were responsible for most of the attacks against police during the period. He added, "in other cases, the crimes may have been committed by unstable individuals who came into possession" of the *Black Panther*. Kiernan explained that the paper's "widespread availability" led the police to conclude "the rhetoric of violence triggers the commission of violent acts."[4] On October 9, 1970, Col. David B. Kelly, superintendent of the New Jersey State Police, told the James O. Eastland–led United States Senate Judiciary Committee that police officers in his state "were the victims of 1,087 cases of assault during 1969, an alarming increase of 41 percent" since 1967. William R. McCoy, detective lieutenant of the Detroit Police Department, told the same committee that from January 1 through August 31, 1970, he counted "475 assaults on police officers in Detroit, a net increase of 68.44 percent during the·same period of 1969." E. M. Davis, chief of the Los Angeles Police Department, remarked that "in the early 60s, there were about 30 assaults with firearms on police officers," with the number jumping to eighty-five in 1965. He added that in 1969 alone, Los Angeles experienced "about 150 assaults" on law enforcement officials. This pattern duplicated itself in virtually all of the urban areas where the BPP existed. Although

Panthers did not take part in all of these incidents, many public officials, including mayors, governors, congressmen, and police chiefs, generally believed they either participated in or inspired these acts of violence. Indeed, there is ample evidence, produced by both the federal government and the BPP, that demonstrates Panther complicity in an alarmingly high number of these incidents. Because virtually every police department that dealt with the Panthers held this suspicion, an uncounted number of BPP newspaper salespeople went to jail on charges ranging from loitering and disturbing the peace to refusing to obey orders of police officers, who, without regard to the first amendment, often told Panthers to stop selling the publication.

Kiernan testified that a "Kill the Pigs" campaign was "constantly pressed in The Black Panther newspaper." He cited as an example the September 7, 1968, issue, which suggested to blacks that "the only culture worth keeping was a revolutionary culture," and that this culture could be realized with the use of "dynamite" and "the gun." Continuing his testimony, Kiernan noted if revolutionaries had any doubts about where to obtain guns, all they had to do was to consult the September 5, 1970, issue of the party paper to find a cartoon captioned "Use what you got to get what you need." The cartoon depicted a black man, armed with an ax and thinking of a pistol, about to assault a caricature of a policeman with a pig's face. This cartoon implied that blacks should assault policemen and take their sidearms. In the same vein, Detective McCoy noted that other BPP organizing manuals informed their readers that "many pig departments are stocking up on them [weapons]" and that they should also "check your National Guard for availability." Panthers Masai Hewitt and Eddie Thibideaux admitted that this method of acquiring arms was quite common for the party.[5] Again, it is difficult to substantiate and corroborate claims like these since the involved parties are either dead or unwilling to talk. Claudia Dahlerus and Christian Davenport have done a good job of documenting the difficulties of doing research on the Panthers.[6]

The February 27, 1971, issue of the Black Panther contained a full page of news items highlighting police killings in the United States. The heading read: "News briefs: Guerrilla Attacks in U.S.A.," and an editorial comment described these deaths as "successful executions of fascist police."[7] BPP leaders worked to assure their supporters and potential supporters that they took seriously their self-assigned task as the people's vanguard army. Chief Davis of the Los Angeles Police Department, perhaps exaggerating the matter, explained the urgency of the situation when he told the Senate committee the national government was being overthrown. Apparently frightened, the police chief noted, "we have revolution on the installment plan. It has been going on for several years. It is going on every-day now."[8]

The BPP, between 1967 and 1971, stood as far left politically as any political organization in the United States. Panthers subsequently confirmed their militant convictions by acquiring thousands of weapons for what they believed and hoped was going to be the war many whites had feared since the earliest days of slavery. Elaine Brown graphically described the extent of the Panthers' deadly arsenal when she noted they had pistols, rifles, automatic machine guns, explosive materials and devices, grenade launchers, and "boxes and boxes of ammunition."[9]

Masai Hewitt, Panther minister of education and the father of party chairwoman Elaine Brown's child, claims the party acquired some of this terrifying arsenal through a "connection" he had at Camp Pendleton Marine Base near San Diego, California. He explained that there were people "down there that don't want nothing but money. . . . If that 101 Highway [a major North-South thoroughfare in California] would have supported [an] M-48 tank we'd have had one of them . . . not because we had some genius but because of the terrible way they [screwed] them Marines down there." He contended, "sooner or later," someone would say "hey man, you want to buy a tank? Pick it up on the corner tomorrow." Another former Panther claimed most of their guns "were raided from gun and pawn shops."[10] These activists displayed their willingness to win by any means necessary by liberating weapons from the oppressor's arsenals. Their going down that particular road, however, meant they had to deal with whatever firepower the enemy they so hated threw at them.

The Panthers seemed to have cultivated violent language to sway audiences. It is not surprising, though, that what excited black audiences resulted in fear and hatred among mainstream whites. Wayne Davis, a special agent at the FBI's Washington, D.C., office, noted the Panther's use of violent language had a negative impact. Because law enforcement saw this rhetoric of violence as "disrespectful," "a breakdown in obedience to the laws," and "perhaps the seeds of anarchy," they had to act. When groups used violent phraseology to describe what would happen to police, he added, "you really can't exclude violent revolutionary means."[11] For this reason, the agency infiltrated and did all it could to render the organization powerless.

The Panther rhetoric of death seemed to demonstrate that not living was better than accepting continued repression. Insisting on their right to self-defense, the Panthers chose to risk death rather than continue to be subjected to hostile police forces. By organizing armed patrols in black communities, they hoped to put an end to police harassment and brutality. Their knowledge of the law, coupled with loaded guns and cameras, sent a message to the police that blacks were no longer going to be passive victims. Harboring no illusions about winning a war with the police, however, Hewitt explained "fighting didn't necessarily entail winning." He insisted the Panthers were "not going to be the only ones bleeding when the smoke clears." Robert Bowen, an ex-naval officer and rank-and-file member of the party, described the situation in more detail when he said, "we thought we was going to fuck up the system so bad til America would never be the same. We were definitely going to be the monkey wrench in the machinery." He went on to say that "a win for them was to destroy the Party," but "a win for our side [was] to make one pig bleed or one pig have a nervous breakdown, or one just gets so paranoid he cannot function. And that happened."[12] In effect, the Panthers sought "to erode the morale of the forces of order, and to induce a general climate of collapse."[13] Despite what he considered their valiant attempt, Newton later concluded "it was very wrong and almost criminal for some people in the Party to make the mistake to think that the Black Panthers could overthrow even the police force."[14] This is an important admission from Newton, though by the time the Panther leader made this comment it was too late for a lot of party members. This error early on made the party an inviting target to its enemies and should have been thought out more clearly. All the Panthers interviewed by the author echoed Newton's views on this issue. It is understandable, however, that inexperienced young people forced to make life-and-death decisions on a daily basis might have made mistakes. That these mistakes cost some people their lives haunts some Panther members and drove others to forsake the party altogether. As Hollis Watkins, veteran of the Mississippi civil rights and Black Power movements explained, "they took that self-defense thing too far."[15] For the Panthers, saying it was almost like doing it, since the police reacted with ferocity either way.

Panther rhetoric almost always came across as violent when it referred to established authority. The phrase "off the pig," which referred to the killing of police officers and others affiliated with what the Panthers called "avaricious" capitalists, became a major component of the Panthers' verbal arsenal. Newton explained that in this way the Panthers got "the people" to dehumanize police and other government officials, making it easier to kill them. New York Panther Michael Tabor urged 1960s radicals to dedicate themselves "to the proposition that the only good pig is a dead pig." Redefining the Panther concept of self-defense as a peremptory attack on policemen, Tabor warned his audience of the danger lurking around the corner and noted that "if you don't get him today, he will get you tomorrow." Another Panther, Belinda, made it clear what the Panthers stood for when she said "we are revolutionaries and we will die to protect the rights of the people. We have children, we are human, and we want the same justice as you do." She added, "this is why we have chosen to pick up the gun, to fight for our freedom and our children's freedom because we see this is the only thing the pigs will understand. The gun is the only thing that will free us—gain us our liberation."[16] When the Panthers spoke like this, people listened, especially the authorities.

As a result of a fiery speech he made during a protest rally at the 1968 Democratic Convention in Chicago, an Illinois court leveled federal conspiracy charges against Panther chairman Bobby Seale. The court accused the Panther founder, along with Tom Hayden, Abbie Hoffman, and a host of ranking white leftists, of violating "laws forbidding interstate travel to foment riots and disorder." Seale and the others were blamed for causing the now infamous "police" riots, in which dozens of activists were beaten and several were killed. The court later severed Seale's case because of murder charges he had pending, so it tried him alone. During the trial, Seale repeatedly labeled the judge and the United States justice system racist. He also refused to accept court-appointed attorneys in place of his own lawyer, Charles Garry, who was recovering from surgery in California. After asking Seale to behave himself numerous times, Judge Julius Hoffman ordered bailiffs to chain the Panther leader to his seat, to gag him, and to shut his mouth with duct tape. The legendary Chicago conspiracy trial ended in October 1970 with a dismissal of the conspiracy charges, but Judge Hoffman charged all the defendants with contempt and Seale had to serve three months in jail.[17]

David Hilliard, formerly chief of staff for BPP National Headquarters, went to jail for threatening to kill President Richard Nixon. "We will kill Richard Nixon," he told a crowd of five thousand in San Francisco. Authorities dropped the charges later because the prosecution did not want to divulge information it had obtained from wiretapping and bugging Panther offices and homes. Eldridge Cleaver said of the White House, "I'll burn the motherfucker down." He also threatened "to beat that punk California Governor Ronald Reagan to death." One anonymous Panther argued that "we need black FBI agents to assassinate J. Edgar Hoover . . . and nigger CIA agents should kidnap the Rockefellers and the Kennedys."[18]

While much of this violent talk proved to be ghetto hyperbole, the FBI and local law enforcement agencies were not trained to deal with such language and quite often took what the Panthers said literally. These officials cannot be blamed for being cautious, since the Panthers had shot a number of policemen in the wake of such rhetoric. David Hilliard helped to crystallize the group's violent thrust when, in late 1969, he said "we advocate the very direct overthrow of the government by way of force and violence, by picking up guns and moving against it because we recognize it as being oppressive and . . . we know that the only solution to it is armed struggle."[19] Although the Panthers insisted their goals were admirable, their methods of achieving them left something to be desired. This rhetoric only served to heighten the tension that already existed and thereby made it more difficult for the Panthers involved in carrying out the "revolution" to stay above ground. Because they were constantly under surveillance, these revolutionaries made it easy for police agencies not only to monitor their words, but the effects of those words as well. In some cases, the Panthers knowingly created these situations in an effort to prove their status as the vanguard Black Power organization. Perhaps the Panther leaders wanted to inspire members of what was really a small movement—in terms of membership—with the sense that they were part of something much bigger and could really make a difference. Many blacks, even today, engage in this kind of banter to minimize the fact that there is really little they can do to change the fact that they, despite time, legislation, and a long history of struggle, remain at the bottom of the American social structure.

One of the party's best propagandists was Chicago-based Fred Hampton. In a April 17, 1969, speech entitled "You Can Murder a Liberator, but You Can't Murder Liberation," Hampton exclaimed, "the Black Panther Party is about complete revolution. We not gonna go out there and half do a thing. And you can let the pigs know it." Noting that he realized that some "pigs" were there in the audience in plainclothes feeling "uncomfortable" and engaging in a lot of "weird action," he told the cheering crowd that "all they got to do is come up to 2350 West Madison any day of the week and anybody up there'll let the mother-fuckers know: Yes, we subversive. Yes, we subversive with the bullshit we are confronted with today. Just as subversive as anybody can be subversive. And we think them motherfuckers is the criminals. They the ones always hiding. We are the ones up front, out in the open." Explaining why they "haven't shot it out with some pigs," he said, "if you kill a few, you get a little satisfaction. But when you kill them ALL you get complete satisfaction." They had not moved in that fashion, he said, because their primary goal had been to "organize" and "educate the people." They first needed "to arm the people" and "teach them about revolutionary political power. . . . And when they understand all that we won't be killing no few and getting no little satisfaction, we'll be killing 'em all and getting complete satisfaction."[20] Based on the roar of the crowd and the rapid growth of his popularity, one might say that Hampton spoke for many of his listeners.

Concluding a memoir of her life in the BPP, former Panther Akua Njeri commented on the violent relationship between the police and the BPP. "People were saying we wanted to do too much too soon, too fast. The BPP was not an aggressive force. We didn't go out and attack the pigs, or this government." She said they believed that if they "were brutalized or attacked," they possessed "the right, the responsibility not to turn the other cheek or bend over and see where they can kick us again, but to fight back." She perceived the party as an organization that "symbolized strong black men and women who said we're not going to take this. . . . They're not going to define in what context I can fight for my freedom," she added, "in what context I survive. . . . We stood up and said we have a right to defend ourselves." Clearly believing they had been "under attack" because of the poverty and degradation blacks experienced, she insisted people "recognize that for what it is."[21] These words epitomized the attitudes of many BPP members, the self-proclaimed heirs of Malcolm X. These sentiments, particularly among certain urban blacks during the mid to late 1960s, worked to propel the BPP and the police into a veritable war that ended in the deaths of dozens of people on both sides.[22]

Since few ghetto residents urged the Panthers to pursue a different course, these sentiments seem to indicate that police abuses in the black community were widespread. Another Panther put this idea in perspective when he said, "every nigga in the black community had either experienced police brutality or was very close to someone who had." Indeed, this sentiment summarized the views of most Panthers during the period from 1968 to 1972.[23] To be sure, these excesses continue to be a problem in the black community today. There is still a long way to go in improving relations between police and people of color, often the victims of brutality, imprisonment, and murder. Ali Bey Hassan, a New York Panther and BLA member, commented "that if anything, [police] got a raise" as a result of beating or killing a black person.[24]

Perhaps one of the most succinct utterances regarding the violence the Panthers found themselves immersed in was not issued by a Panther but by one of the party's most ardent supporters. The now-deceased attorney William Kunstler, delivering a speech at the Panther-sponsored United Front Against Fascism Conference on July 19, 1969, told a cheering crowd that defensive violence was not only good, but necessary and legal. In his speech, Kunstler told the crowd a story about the killing of a black man in New Jersey and the response to it.

He began by explaining that "during the Newark rebellion in Plainfield, New Jersey, some Garand M-1 rifles were found missing from the armory." Attempting to speak above the loud applause, he told the crowd that he was happy to report that during the police search for these weapons, "not a single gun was found." Making his point clear, he explained, "there has not been a white policeman in the central ward of Plainfield since July 1967." He then moved on to explain why the black community had been so adamant about keeping the police out of their communities.[25]

Officer John Gleason had entered the black community on a Saturday afternoon and shot Bobby Lee Williams, a black man, in the abdomen. As Gleason attempted to leave the ghetto, Kunstler said, "he was followed by a crowd of black men and women, and a block and a half past the intersection he was stomped to death." Although this description in itself does not qualify as the searing rhetoric that characterized Panther speakers, Kunstler's response to his own story was telling. He told the crowd, "in my opinion he deserved that death." He came to this conclusion after he observed what happened in black communities throughout the country. "The crowd," he intoned, "justifiably, without the necessity of a trial, and in the most dramatic way possible, stomped him to death." Explaining that because the "white power structures preyed upon ghettos the way vultures preyed on meat," blacks in other communities should follow the example set by Plainfield blacks. He insisted murderous policemen "can only be stopped in one way. . . . If he knows that he might fall like Gleason if he violates the rights of black men, women, and children," a policeman might think twice about doing so.[26]

It is striking how similar the rhetoric was between the BPP in the United States and its sister organization in the Pacific Islands, a region no one can deny suffered from ongoing imperial inhumanities. The BPP counterpart in the Pacific Islands held the same position on self-defense as its American model. In a leaflet introducing its Tenants Aid Brigade, the Polynesian Panther Party explained that it and the black community were "tired of being kicked around, exploited and discriminated against, especially by greedy landlords." Telling of incidents where landlords used "heavies" to throw tenants out of high-rent houses "not fit to live in," it proclaimed that the Tenants Aid Brigade was formed to "protect tenants from the rough treatment they receive." To ensure the rough treatment ended, they vowed to "attack their aggressors." Not willing to be kicked around any longer, they noted "we are now kicking back and our kicks will be heavier and harder because we know we are in the right because we have morality and humanity on our side." Will Ilolahia, contact person for the Auckland area Polynesian Panther Party, concluded the statement by urging people to contact the group's Central Headquarters "if they knew of any cases" of abuse.[27]

Even the BPP's underground wing, sometimes erroneously referred to as the Black Liberation Army (BLA), got into the habit. It often issued public statements that were unequivocal about the violence that might befall those who terrorized or otherwise caused harm to people in the black community. This group employed a broad definition of harm that went well beyond simple attacks with guns. In a leaflet titled "Last Warning," the true BLA headquarters in San Francisco sought the attention of "pimps, ho's [sic], howalkers, trickwalkers, bodyguards, tricks, dope pushers, and owners / operators of trick houses. Anyone found guilty of murdering, stealing, or dehumanizing women would be dealt with," the flyer promised. Other offenses included "bringing undesirable characters into the community," providing bad examples for black youth, "molesting and degrading innocent black women in the community," and being agents of the police. Explaining that the people of San Francisco's nearly all-black Fillmore district had already done a good job "waging a just and courageous fight to clean up their community," the note pointed out that the power structure had retaliated "with threats, brutality, and increased vice in the black community." Like their Polynesian comrades, they developed a method to deal with these problems. BLA leadership created Seek Out And Destroy to rid the black community of these undesirable characters. The group claimed that it developed this branch to "seek out and destroy any and all enemies of the people."[28]

"From this day on," declared the flyer, "any of the people mentioned above who are operating in the black community will be shot." Providing what it believed was the rationale for such drastic action, the communiqué noted "this warning is not to be taken lightly because it involves our peoples' lives and our children's futures." To make sure no one misunderstood, it continued, "failure to heed this warning will bring deadly consequences." Having "turned the problem over" to their "special branch," the note indicated that it was indeed an "official statement from the BLA [Headquarters]." Giving the interlopers one last chance, the note concluded: "If you want to live, leave."[29] The party member this group identified most with, Eldridge Cleaver, though out of the country at the time, busied himself trying to get help for his comrades in their war of liberation. He looked to the far east for support.

In one of his most popular diatribes, first written in letter form then delivered by radio address, Cleaver urged black soldiers in Vietnam to go home and fight for black freedom "against the very same pigs who have you over there doing their dirty work for them. . . . Your people need you and your military skills—to help us take our freedom and stop these racist pigs from committing genocide upon us, as they have been doing for the past 400 years." He then told the black soldiers in Vietnam that "you niggers have your minds all messed up about Black organizations or you wouldn't be the flunkies for the White organization—the U.S.A.—for whom you have picked up the gun." He wondered whether they could "dig niggers, brothers and sisters off the block, who have said later for the pigs and have picked up guns in Babylon" to bring about freedom from "the racist yoke of the white man." Cleaver wanted these soldiers to understand that they were "either part of the solution or part of the problem" and that they were "desperately" needed before it got "too late."[30]

Maintaining this position, he urged blacks soldiers not "to carry out the same dirty work against us, in the name of 'Law and Order' that they carried out against the Vietnamese people." Constantly appealing for their aid, Cleaver counseled his black brethren to "either quit the army now, or start destroying it from the inside. . . . Anything else is a compromise and a form of treason against your own people." Lest his words be misunderstood, he told them to "stop killing the Vietnamese people" and "start killing the racist pigs who are over there with you giving you orders." In case they still did not understand, he advised that they "kill General Abrams and his staff, [and] all his officers. Sabotage supplies and equipment or turn them over to the Vietnamese people." Cleaver believed if these steps were taken, blacks could enjoy "freedom and liberation in our lifetime" and "leave behind us a decent world for our children to live in."[31] Despite this noble goal, neither Cleaver nor the organization fared well in trying to change the status quo through such violent means. In effect, by using statements like this one, Cleaver helped assure an alarmed federal government's use of overwhelming force against the BPP.

Viewing the black struggle in America as an integral part of all the liberation struggles taking place around the globe, Cleaver hoped to impress upon his audience the urgency of the matter. He explained to them, "this is the moment in history that our people have been working, praying, fighting and dying for. Now, while the whole world is rising up with arms against our oppressors, we must make a decisive move for our freedom. . . . If we miss this chance, this golden opportunity, who knows when we will get another chance?"[32] Undoubtedly, Cleaver held fast to the notion that the United States could not successfully fight wars and skirmishes abroad while at the same time dealing with guerilla activity on the home front. The problem with this line of reasoning, however, was that most blacks failed to see the utility in the Panthers' position. The ones who agreed left Vietnam and joined the movement for black liberation, not a few of whom joined the Black Panther Party and used their military skills to help try to secure black liberation.

In an effort to draw attention to their cause, the Panthers made an unsuccessful attempt to disrupt American forces in Vietnam by encouraging insubordination. They claimed that United States aggression in Vietnam was no different than police aggression in the ghettos. Agreeing with the Panthers, many black soldiers, at home and abroad, engaged in political agitation. Dwight Rawls, a former Marine stationed in Germany in 1968, told one journalist, "you'll find a black pride overseas as strong as any place back home." According to former Panthers, a number of black soldiers, even while they served abroad, sought membership in the BPP. Not only did these individuals join overseas support groups for the BPP, but many of them joined the party when they returned from their tours of duty.[33] This trend mirrored the one that emerged after World War II more than two decades earlier. Black men learned in war what the streets and plantations could never teach them: military discipline and marksmanship. The pride instilled in a person once he or she learns the art of personal self-defense cannot be underestimated. The black willingness to put life, family, and possessions on the line after learning that oppression in a foreign land mirrored their own circumstances seemed for some a small price to pay for the freedom that awaited.

The contributions these individuals made to the party are immeasurable. Like other members, they used their skills to serve and protect the black community. Their knowledge of armed self-defense ensured, for the most part, that party members knew how to handle themselves in crisis situations. Their willingness to confront external violence with violence of their own meant the black movement had shifted to a higher stage of development, something that had to occur if the high cost of freedom were to be paid. That this stage had been in the incubation period for decades, with flurries of growth in various cities in the North and South, indicated the strategy of armed self-reliance, as Robert Williams termed it, had won an increased number of supporters. The BPP's open recruitment of men with professional military skills became necessary if the party was going to continue to grow and to champion Malcolm X's philosophy of freedom "by any means necessary." With the war in Vietnam monopolizing people's lives as much as their television screens, and with black unemployment and poverty increasing while whites as a whole experienced economic growth, the Panthers' task of accomplishing such a goal was made much easier.

Men like Thomas Jolly and Thomas McCreary in New York City, Malik Rahim in New Orleans, and Geronimo Pratt in Los Angeles are but a smattering of the people who went from fighting in the jungles of Vietnam to fighting in the alleys, roads, and streets of the United States. Still others like Bobby Seale, Elbert Howard of Oakland, and George Edwards of New Haven, Connecticut, who all did peacetime duty in the Air Force, emerged from the military with the willingness to donate their skills to the black struggle for self-determination. While the number of those with military experience is not ascertainable, it is certain that each chapter had several of these veterans. With thirty-two chapters across the country at its height, the number is at least in the low one hundreds. That there could have been as many as five times that number is borne out by oral histories of Panther members.[34] What is more important than the numbers, however, is the contribution these individuals made to the party.

The activities of the BPP, along with those of other militant, dissident, and mostly white radicals, concerned the United States government enough to prompt open Senate hearings on the question of alleged subversion of the armed forces, especially those stationed in Southeast Asia. Claude Pepper of Florida, the chairman of the Committee on Internal Security, explained that the hearings "were initiated in part due to the plethora of rather sensational press accounts of desertion and disorder within the military." He added that "'fragging' style murders of officers and NCOs, deliberate sabotage of military equipment, and a general picture of mass alienation by American servicemen represented the overall theme" of those press accounts. Such issues as "Vietnam, civil rights, and racial discrimination," continued Pepper, "have been highly exploited" by "various Marxist groups" and "subversive elements" like the BPP.[35]

Leaders of the armed forces, therefore, became increasingly suspicious of the BPP. The United States government demonstrated its concern with the BPP when one of the committee members inquired of a high-ranking army officer whether he felt there had been "any effect upon the soldiers" in "connection with a letter from Eldridge Cleaver urging them to go to Vietnam and kill General Abrams and his staff" and "Black Panther urgings to 'turn your guns' on commanding officers." Although the officer answered that he did not know, the question was well-founded since Dr. Robert Landeen, an army psychiatrist, asserted "black radicals" were one of the groups who "quickly resorted to fragging," a term meaning to "threaten, intimidate or kill the NCO with a fragmentation grenade."[36] One GI stated, "these whites think that every time colored guys get together, well he's Panther."[37] They may have held this misconception because the Panthers, in numerous ways, made it known they were recruiting army personnel.

Cleaver made a two-week visit to North Vietnam, where, in a radio broadcast from Hanoi, he urged "black GI's to desert, commit sabotage, and rip-off the commander of the U.S. forces in South Vietnam." In

Photo of a Vietnam Veteran taken in 1969. *Courtesy of Ilka Hartman.*

addition, Huey Newton, shortly after his August 1970 release from prison, offered the National Liberation Front and the Provisional Revolutionary Government of South Vietnam (Vietcong) "an undetermined number of troops" in their "fight against American imperialism." While the deputy commander of the Vietcong in South Vietnam turned down this "concrete assistance," he advised the BPP that its "persistent and ever-developing struggle is the most active support to our resistance against U.S. aggression."[38] This offer of troops hardly seemed plausible, since by this point the Panthers were experiencing extreme difficulty in keeping people in the party. Nevertheless, the Panthers continued to press for an international attack against racism and oppression.

Cleaver, nicknamed "Papa Rage" for his fiery speeches, concluded blacks could best improve their lot by forging "organizational unity and communication with their brothers and allies around the world, on an international basis." He added, "the only lasting salvation for the black American is to do all he can to see to it that the African, Asian, and Latin American nations are free and independent."[39] As David Walker, Martin Delaney, Martin Luther King Jr., Robert Williams, and Malcolm X before them, the Panthers' internationalization of the struggle secured allies and support but also made the federal government's enforcement apparatus that much more intent on destroying the group.

Viewing themselves as "part of the link in the chain of worldwide revolution," the Panthers gave media outlets more wood for the fire when they sought to ally themselves openly with the United States government's arch enemies. For example, Fidel Castro, in the summer of 1968, entertained Panther minister of education George Murray. Castro subsequently supported the Panthers by providing them asylum once they fled the United States to avoid trials on any number of charges. Publisher and attorney Karen Wald, one of the party's prominent white supporters, noted in a letter to Newton that "revolutionary Cubans, and especially black Cubans, are really interested in the BPP, and it is really important to see that there is a constant flow of information down there." The letter also mentioned that there was a music and news show on Radio de Liberacion in Havana "where several programs have been dedicated to the Black Panther Party."[40]

After the press publicized his presence in Cuba in May, 1969, Panther leader Eldridge Cleaver took up residence in Africa and established the

BPP's international headquarters in Algiers, Algeria. He described the section's main task as publicizing internationally the Panther struggle, making alliances with other movements, receiving assistance from other groups, and presenting proposals to the U.N. concerning blacks' status in the United States. The BPP became one of about a dozen liberation movements the Algerian government supported. That government, only a few years earlier, had waged a successful revolution and ousted French colonizers. It subsequently provided the party's international section with financial assistance, living quarters, transportation, and military training.[41]

In yet another overture to their allies abroad, the Panthers made foreign contacts with the North Koreans and the Chinese. In 1969, Cleaver visited North Korea to address the North Korean Conference of Journalists and to set up ties with the North Korean government. After this visit, both the North Korean and the Chinese governments "joined in public expressions of sympathy for black Americans and the Black Panther Party in particular." A congressional investigation of the group revealed that the governments of North Korea and China "concurred with the Panthers that the United States was the world's public enemy number one as a result of its imperialistic foreign policy and fascist domestic programs." A North Korean radio broadcast declared that the people of North Korea "expressed solidarity with the Panthers and [would] actively support and encourage their struggle." In 1970, North Korean Premier Kim Il Sung sent a telegram to the Panthers expressing his personal wishes "for the Panthers' success in their just struggle to abolish . . . racial discrimination and win liberty and emancipation." A September 23, 1970, Chinese international broadcast deplored the United States government's treatment of the party and expressed its support of the group. According to Senate testimony, while Cleaver visited North Korea, "the regime designated August 18, 1970, as an international day of solidarity with the black people of the United States."[42] These gestures went a long way in encouraging Panther recruitment and heightening the level of revolutionary violence.

In the fall of 1970, the Central Committee of the Partido Revolucionario Dominicano, the decision-making body of a Marxist political group led by Peña Gómez, invited Newton to the Dominican Republic to attend "a special meeting to find out what we want and how, what you want and how, and what we can do to help each other." Gomez, who had replaced the party's exiled leader, Juan Bosch, noted that not only did the Dominican people admire and support the Panthers, but they also respected Newton "more than the puppet president Joaquin Balaguer," who they later replaced with the radical Juan Bosch.[43]

In addition to support from governments abroad, the BPP also became the beneficiary of many citizen support groups overseas. Organizations in Britain, Ireland, Norway, Germany, Switzerland, Sweden, and the Netherlands applauded and publicized Panther activities while at the same time giving them financial assistance. Matsuko Ishida, a member of the Committee to Support the Black Panther Party in Tokyo, Japan, after visiting BPP headquarters in Oakland, wrote that many of the protest groups in Japan "learned from your ideas and concrete wisdom necessary for the [survival] programs, and materialized them in their own programs." Finally, the San Francisco-based International Committee to Release Eldridge Cleaver, in addition to its affiliates in New York, Detroit, and Atlanta, had branches in Paris, Rome, London, and Amsterdam.[44] This activity had become so respected abroad that the BPP "catalyzed indigenous insurgent organizations" in England, Bermuda, Israel, Australia, and India. According to Michael Clemons and Charles Jones, "these global social movements also assumed the BPP's confrontational style and stance on political violence." Despite the Panthers' support at home and abroad, several major obstacles stood in the way of their success.[45]

Aside from the obvious logistical problems of dealing with allies and potential allies abroad, the majority of blacks were simply not willing to confront law enforcement and other government agencies violently. Put simply, most blacks had not made the decision and personal commitment to die for black freedom. Addressing this issue, Emory Douglas, the renowned minister of culture for the BPP, pointed out that while there were "people in the community supporting us and saying right on, it was the Panthers who were getting shot and killed, and therefore, this really didn't encourage the people to pick up arms." The BPP, however, did not necessarily need large numbers of recruits to make its presence known in the communities in which it operated. Douglas pointed out that the group did not seek to make every black, poor, or oppressed person a Panther, but simply to bring attention to their cause.[46]

Some people must have been paying attention, because large numbers of blacks either donated money or gave tacit support to the Panthers. Martin Kenner, former Students for a Democratic Society member, accountant, and director of the defense fund for the BPP, noted that the money came in so fast, they "had to hire people to open the envelopes."[47] This support, however, failed to prevent the problems the party found itself faced with on a daily basis. While it did help to pay for travel, supplies, and enormous amounts of bail, the large sums of money did little in helping the Panthers convince the majority of America's blacks that there was actually a war going on inside the United States.

Despite having access to their own media outlet and commanding a nationwide appeal, the BBP was powerless in its ability to persuade most black men and women to pick up the gun. King's version of black protest, though losing popularity in the late sixties and nearly defunct by the early seventies, had more of an appeal than Panther exhortations to shoot and kill the oppressor. Again, the majority of blacks, in all regions of the country, were Christians and on the most basic level did not want to go to hell for committing such a sinful act as murder. Aside from this practical point, most blacks, regardless of whether they participated in the movement, hoped against hope they could integrate the system. They believed if they could simply show racist whites the error of their ways and if blacks were given the opportunity to demonstrate that they were indeed hard workers, full of thrift and common sense, everything would work out fine. They seemed to underestimate the widespread white backlash sweeping the country in the wake of the mid-sixties upheavals. The Panthers held no such illusions. Instead, they believed that violent revolution was the key to black freedom. Whether on the streets or in prison, they urged people to help the BPP foment a revolution.

In a letter to Huey Newton, George Jackson, the former Panther who successfully organized opposing gangs in California's maximum security prison at San Quentin, wrote that "most of these people [blacks] are suffering under the illusion that the pig is a tough guy. . . . We need education in that area." He explained, "the pig is a murderer when he has the upper hand, he's organized, and enjoys the privilege of being able to kill freely, but that doesn't make [police] much more capable than a wolf pack."[48] Here the rhetoric is used to dehumanize the police, making it "OK" to shoot them.

By the time he wrote the letter, Jackson had been imprisoned for ten years on a charge of petty robbery, for which most Californians served less than a year. He had seen at least fifteen of his comrades "justifiably" killed by prison guards. For nearly eight years he had been a model prisoner, but his revolutionary leaning compelled the all-white parole board to deny his release every time he went before it. His cynicism toward the system should be understood in this light. George Jackson became foremost among those calling for a violent solution to the problem of black subjugation. Newton recruited Jackson, sight unseen, when Newton entered prison in 1968 on a manslaughter charge. He heard about the growing prison movement and the militancy of George Jackson, who had been sentenced to one year to life under California's indeterminate sentencing laws. Radicalized in prison, Jackson spent the rest of his life there, dying in an aborted escape attempt in 1971. Before that fateful day, however, he succeeded in recruiting and influencing thousands of prisoners in California and throughout the United States. His best-selling book *Soledad Brother,* detailing his political growth and development, sold over a hundred thousand copies and continues to sell well. The uprising at Attica Penitentiary in New York, the largest of its kind in American history, which resulted in the deaths of dozens of inmates and hostages (guards), began after prisoners protesting Jackson's murder went on a hunger strike. Jackson's close ties with sixties icon Angela Davis gave him a legitimacy that helped catapult the prison movement to the forefront of many people's consciousnesses during the period. Much more militant and powerful than Malcolm X or Eldridge Cleaver had been as prisoners, Jackson remained in solitary confinement for much of the time he spent incarcerated.[49]

Writing his support committee, he outlined the strategy for black liberation. In a particularly eloquent piece of Panther rhetoric, the Panther's prison field marshal wove together several themes. Jackson began by explaining that in the three years before 1970, blacks had been "doing all the dying," so if they had to continue along this course they would. The goal of blacks, he wrote, was to "destroy the U.S. as a modern nation-state, waste its huge power facilities, destroy its communications and

Bobby Seale, chairman of the Black Panther Party, and Ray "Masai" Hewitt, minister of education, in Europe in 1969. *Photo by Ducho Dennis, courtesy of It's About Time.*

transport facilities, stop all production and distribution, sabotage its sewer system and its harbor facilities and if it comes to it, subject its whole population to poison and germ warfare." That Jackson had no way of personally achieving any of these goals, as he was under constant surveillance by Soledad's prison guards, mattered little. This problem seemed incidental, however, and he insisted "[b]lacks can reduce the U.S. to an entire wasteland and graveyard for 250 million idiots. . . . For 500 years," he prophesied, "the smallest living creature won't be able to find anything to subsist on or live under." Undoubtedly, this rhetoric impressed those Panthers itching to fight "the man." Jackson's grandiose rhetoric came easy because neither he nor the Panthers on the outside could do much else to stop the violence, not always physical, that permeated black life. Such talk must have served as an emotional purgative for those who believed in Jackson.

Claiming that "more of the same is out," and that "the days of half measures and supplications are past," he noted, "we will die at the throat of fascism if that alternative is forced on us."[50] Being "cool, calm, and patient" meant to this hardened inmate "clinical, retaliatory, organized, revolutionary violence!!" And "if you're not ready for that," he asked, "what the hell are you doing around me?" These people, he insisted were "in the wrong camp" if they allowed "a jury summons to frighten" them.

Providing some cue as to what should be the correct response to such a "fascist contra-positive mobilizing tact," he queried "do you have any idea what a Tupamaro's [South American indigenous revolutionaries] response to a court summons would be?" Ensuring his part consisted of more than delegating authority, he explained to his comrades "the legal side of all the killing and attempting to kill our enemies will be financed by me [Jackson] through whatever money comes from sales of my writings, the little dramas and films that are projected for the future, whenever and wherever that stuff is sold England to Afghanistan." Pointing out that Newton gave him a department to run, he tried to anticipate disagreement by adding, "this is the way it must be or the purges begin." He wrote, "I am responsible to no one but the Supreme Commander," one of the monikers Newton took after he emerged from prison in 1970. Noting that this committee work should be run out of a large house in "the Blackest, wildest, poorest section" of town "where people aren't much afraid of pigs," Jackson insisted that his cadre "be merciless with phony people." Here, Jackson clearly wanted his reader to be aware of the similarities between fascism and life for blacks in the United States. These similarities stood out starkly in San Quentin's Adjustment Center, a prison inside a prison, the place where California kept its most dangerous (and politically active) inmates. The rhetoric detailing the nation's fatal destruction was also telling. At the time he wrote the letter, Jackson knew he was not getting out of prison so he needed to be as apocalyptic as possible. As a result, he wanted his supporters, who numbered into the thousands, in and outside the party, to believe they had the capacity to make change. If they could not leave the country, as would have been Jackson's choice, then they should at least try to disrupt its operations. That most blacks were not willing to go nearly as far is not surprising since many of them saw the civil and voting rights legislation as the start of a new era in race relations.

Ending his instructions, the "General," as he was (and still is) often referred to by those who knew him, reminded his charges that their goal was "to create the people's army" and "to mobilize against the men who hate us. . . . Our aim is war on the family plan," he counseled, "a shotgun in every hand, a flame-thrower and M-60 for the cadre." With foresight, he agreed that the "Whites" and "Browns" may not "follow our example," but "the mandate is on us, the floor mat of the world." For this reason, he admonished his troops to "stay alive, practice your quick draw and snap shot" and "always shoot for the left eye." Understanding he and his fellow fighters might die in this undertaking, he noted, "the fact should not be allowed to discourage us" since the revolutionaries knew from the beginning that "fascism allows for no challenges that are truly revolutionary. " Still "faint hearts never win decisive battles," he concluded. Therefore, his troops were to "calculate, wait in ambush, and charge from the rear." As practical as any other military leader, he advised them to all "run if it fails to carry."[51] The choice of command rhetoric here helps to distinguish Jackson from someone crying in the dark. That he had the sanction of one of the most powerful black leaders living (Huey Newton) meant that at least some people listened to his orders. Acquiescing to the influential Panther leader gave Jackson an authority that stretched from prisons in California to those in New York. Many black prisoners at the time wanted to become a part of the growing black movement for social change. Jackson helped fulfill this desire and in the process tried to exhort those on the "outside" to act responsibly by following his orders to start the revolution immediately.

Then again, no one wants to be the door mat of the world. Jackson's attempts to get people to act by appealing to their humanity were perhaps the only thing he could do from a maximum security prison. In addition, the practical military advice must have sounded downright reassuring to those who had been in the military. It was succinct enough to stiffen nervous people who might not have known what they were doing. Jackson must have felt the same way American patriot leaders felt when they instructed their usually green revolutionary forces not to shoot until they saw the whites of their enemy's eyes. Those who seriously believed blacks could win their freedom by engaging in armed struggle must have really revered the jailed revolutionary.

The violent rhetoric used by the Panthers undoubtedly had its benefits as thousands of blacks, particularly in urban areas, viewed their bravado as long overdue. These individuals joined in droves and went in believing that confronting occupying police forces would help solve their problems. The emotional release many blacks experienced when hearing the Panthers verbally confront the enemy went a long way in instilling pride in people who for so long had been given few reasons to be proud. A people that had been oppressed for centuries in a myriad of ways now saw the opportunity to get back at their oppressors, at least through words. Mainstream news media, however, held the opposite view.

Unfortunately for the Panthers, these words sent the wrong signal to the opposition. Because a red flag immediately went up in Washington, D.C., when the Panthers picked up guns, their insistence on using these guns to kill the enemy set in motion a chain of events that left the young party beleaguered and with few supporters before very long. Their miscalculation as to how the majority of blacks perceived their low social status left them in a position where, eventually, only the radicals were willing to support them publicly.

Ultimately, the Panthers' rhetoric of violence did them more harm than good. The media took Panthers at their word—and reporters tended to add their own unflattering interpretations of what Panthers said. While the Panthers made no excuses for their insistence on self-defense, they spent an inordinate amount of time trying to explain away their "violent" media image. At rallies and news conferences, Panther spokespeople continually emphasized that they were "not anti-white, but anti-racist, not concerned with the destruction of white people . . . but with serving, defending and liberating black people."[52] The ineffectiveness of these gestures, however, stood out in newsprint.

In sum, the primary thing to understand about violence in regard to the BPP is that much of it was rhetorical flourish. The reality for the most part was to use violence in self-defense, not revolution. Once the group committed itself to the use of defensive violence, local, state, and federal police agencies sought to destroy it—using the Panthers' violent rhetoric as justification. In the process of doing so, the authorities, with the help of the media and politicians ranging from presidents and senators to mayors and city councilmen, painted the BPP as dangerously criminal and violence-prone, therefore deserving of whatever violence authorities used to suppress it. Indeed, the support of government officials was understandable, given the fact that these individuals were very much a part of the system the BPP targeted in overheated public announcements. The Panthers' rhetoric may very well have led to more recruits, but the ensuing war left the organization with a rag-tag army consisting of very few disciplined soldiers capable of waging war against the most powerful military machine on the planet. Despite the disadvantages, the Panthers persevered in their efforts to set a revolutionary example for an increasingly battle-weary black community.

CHAPTER 4

Publicizing the Party

WHEN THE PANTHERS ORGANIZED AGAINST the violence that pervaded black lives, they inadvertently helped to set off a chain of events that eventually led to their violent repression. In 1968, however, the Panthers could not yet see the trajectory of their organization and were too invested to change tactics. Huey Newton's murder trial dramatically demonstrated this fact.

Alameda County authorities charged Newton with first-degree murder, attempted murder, and kidnapping. Jury selection took two weeks. Nearly two hundred people went through the voir dire process. District Attorney Lowell Jensen succeeded in eliminating all five blacks who were prospective alternates, and Charles Garry, Newton's attorney, was not allowed the customary challenge for any of the eliminations. These five blacks were the only individuals challenged by Jensen during selection of alternate jurors. The final jury, hardly representing Newton's peers, consisted of eleven whites and one black, a Bank of America lending officer. Newton surmised that the district attorney chose this "safe black" to help weaken any eventual appeal.[1]

The trial exposed a mountain of evidence that should have acquitted Newton, but it was ignored. The highly charged political overtones of the case made it difficult for Garry to persuade the judge that this evidence should have been used in the jury's deliberations. During the trial, neither Newton nor Gene McKinney, the passenger in Newton's car, testified that the Panther leader had shot the policemen, or that he possessed a weapon.[2] Although Jensen charged Newton with shooting Heanes and Frey with his own 9 mm P-38 pistol, Officer Heanes testified that he never saw a gun in Newton's hand. Equally important, Frey's gun had gone missing since the night of the shooting and neither he nor Newton received neutron activation tests to determine whether they had fired a weapon. An expert testifying for the state noted that the bullets that wounded Frey and Heanes were lead-jacketed, not copper jacketed like 9 mm bullets, "and much heavier than the 92.3 grain lead-core found in those copper-jacketed bullets." In other words, all the shots came from police guns, and no one ever introduced into evidence a 9 mm P-38 pistol.[3]

Despite the prosecution's determination to paint Newton as a brutal murderer, hellbent on killing white people, Garry succeeded in convincing the jury that Frey's killing had not been intentional. In the process, he highlighted the major discrepancies that should have set Newton free. The state charged Newton with shooting both officers. The jury found him guilty of shooting Frey, but not guilty of shooting Heanes. No one has explained this decision. The trial lasted thirty-four days. After all had been said and done, the jury convicted Newton of manslaughter and gave him a sentence of two to fifteen years in prison; he served only three years.[4] The appeals court, in the 51-page decision overturning the verdict, upheld "the assertion of Charles Garry, [Newton's] defense lawyer, that there was prejudicial error in the trial judge's failure to instruct the jury that unconsciousness could be a complete defense to a charge of criminal homicide."[5]

Despite the fact that Newton had been cut off from the public, or rather because of it, the Panthers built a popular base of support throughout the United States. Newton's trial and the "Free Huey" campaign that ensued before, during, and after it helped to swell the party's ranks. Indeed, his incarceration helped popularize the party in ways his being on the streets probably never would have. Thomas McCreary commented, "there were less than thirty Panthers in the party at the time Newton went to jail, he didn't organize a single chapter, that was Eldridge, Bobby, David and Kathleen that built the party." Half joking and half serious, he remarked, "hell, its kinda good he was locked up, he probably would have sabotaged the whole thing."[6] While Newton had been instrumental in establishing several of the Bay Area branches, the point here is clear. Newton's imprisonment worked to the party's advantage. In this sense then, though Newton had not tried to go to jail intentionally, his incarceration worked the same as it had worked for Martin Luther King Jr. and other nonviolent protesters in the South. The only difference is that Newton had no bail he could refuse. He stayed in jail until his trial began in late summer 1968.

Dissatisfied with the manslaughter conviction, two Oakland policemen, drunk at the time, drove by the Panther office on Grove Street on the night of the verdict and shot it up. They were not satisfied with this volley, so they drove down the street, turned around, returned to the office and shot several more times, shredding posters of Newton and Cleaver that adorned the windows. A nearby resident called the police to notify them of what had transpired and the two policemen were promptly arrested and expelled from the force. Ironically, two days before, Newton had instructed all Panthers to remain off the streets to prevent a bloodbath on the day of the verdict. He noted the police "were looking for an excuse" to do bodily harm to Panthers. The authorities must have sensed trouble, too, since several hundred National Guardsmen and State Police sat on the outskirts of town in the days leading up to the verdict. The only violence came from the aforementioned policemen, and Newton was hustled off to his new home at the State Penitentiary in East San Luis Obispo, several hours south of Oakland.[7]

Newton's decision to order all his troops off the street proved momentous. Panthers all over the country had been saying the authorities needed to "Free Huey or the sky's the limit." Many Panthers hoped for the opportunity to retaliate on the police for jailing their leader. Newton and Seale, of course, only used this threatening rhetoric to attract recruits and to publicize the case. When field marshall Don Cox, who called himself "a respectable nigger by day and a guerrilla by night," learned that Newton and Seale had cancelled the plans they made for him and his men to break Newton out of the Alameda County jail, he was livid. When all actions to attack authorities were called off after Newton's conviction, Cox, in charge of all military operations at the time, thought the Panther leaders had misled both the public and the rank-and-file. This disagreement was left to fester for years.[8] Eventually, inner-party politics became fractious, with one faction wanting to organize and prepare the people for the coming revolution and the other wanting to jump-start the same by engaging in guerrilla warfare all over the country. Neither side won and the party itself was the biggest loser in this dispute over philosophy and tactics. For the time being, however, the rank-and-file trusted the leadership's decisions and worked to make the party a viable alternative to the mainstream politics that had compelled blacks to rebel in the first place.

The nearly ten months between the beginning of Newton's trial and the time of his initial incarceration represented a turning point in the organization's historical development. A number of changes took place that made the party simultaneously stronger and more vulnerable to outside attack. Before the end of 1968, the Black Panther Party for Self-Defense dropped the Self-Defense from its name in an effort to demonstrate its wider political concerns. In less than two years, it evolved from a mostly local, revolutionary nationalist group with a limited following to a revolutionary internationalist organization with members and supporters worldwide. Perhaps most importantly, active leadership was transferred from a prudent Huey Newton, who wanted to remain within the confines of the law, to an unrestrained Eldridge Cleaver, who wanted immediate revolution and cared as little for the law as he did for those who enforced it. Although official control of the party remained in the hands of Chairman Bobby Seale and was later transferred to chief of staff David Hilliard, "Cleaver swiftly emerged as the best recognized voice of the Panther Party," observed writer Michael Newton. "Rightly or wrongly," he continued, "his opinions would become the party's opinions, his sins, the party's sins." It was this change that dictated not only the future direction of the party, but also the way it was received by the powers that be. Michael Newton, no relation to Huey Newton, argued that "in the end," Cleaver's "forceful personality would be the rock on which the movement foundered."[9] Before all this became clear, however, Eldridge Cleaver's orchestration of the "Free Huey" movement resulted in the establishment of chapters across the nation as well as in the group's widespread notoriety in California, particularly in the Bay Area.

Nineteen sixty-eight began in violence and the threat of it for the still-young party. On January 16, 1968, Eldridge and Kathleen Cleaver, then the party's communications secretary, and minister of culture Emory Douglas sat talking in the Cleavers' apartment. They had been making plans for an upcoming rally and discussing Newton's defense. The day before, national captain David Hilliard had been arrested at Oakland Technical High School for passing out leaflets. It now seemed that all the leaders were targeted for neutralization. At about three thirty that morning, as the conversation dragged on, there came a loud knock on the door. Eldridge Cleaver yelled "who is it" and the voice on the other side said "police, open up!" Cleaver then asked the police what they wanted, and they responded they wanted to search the premises for illegal weapons.

At this point, Cleaver, yelling through the door, asked if they had a search warrant, to which the police responded, "we don't need one! So open the door!" According to Douglas, Eldridge then told the officers they "would have to break the motherfucker down then." Seconds later, a half dozen black-clad officers of the San Francisco Tactical Squad came crashing through the door and into the Cleavers' living room. Shocked at what had just happened, the occupants were immediately thrown against the wall, had automatic weapons pointed at them, and were told to "shut the hell up!" At the same time, several officers ransacked the apartment in a frantic search for what they called "contraband" and "after several minutes they left, leaving the apartment in a shambles." Before they left, they confiscated what they thought was an illegal weapon, as Cleaver was an ex-felon and was forbidden by state law to own a gun. The gun turned out to belong to Kathleen Cleaver, who had legally purchased it from a local gun shop.[10]

The Panther leaders were determined that harassment and threats were not going to keep them from their major goal: amassing support to "Free Huey." Their treatment by the police did, however, heighten the tension between the two groups. With the Mulford Act in effect at the end of 1967, Panthers could not legally carry loaded weapons in public, so they were at a major disadvantage if they had to deal with the police outside their homes. To be sure, this act was not much different from the nineteenth century Black Codes passed during Reconstruction that forbade blacks' possession of weapons. Blacks had been disarmed by fearful whites after the Civil War in an effort to maintain a cheap labor force and to ensure that they could not defend themselves against the myriad violent attacks that were sure to come. Newton wrote of this situation in one of his many directives issued from jail. He said, "an unarmed people are subject to slavery at any time." Newton and his fellow Panthers undoubtedly believed the gun served as a great equalizer between themselves and those who policed them. They insisted on their right to self-defense, however, and intended to publicize their position by rallying around their jailed minister of defense.

On February 17, 1968, more than five thousand blacks and other minorities filtered into the Oakland Auditorium. They went to attend a "Free Huey" rally, which happened to fall on Newton's birthday. The Panthers placed a wicker chair in the middle of the stage, in which

Newton had taken a picture holding a spear in one hand and a shotgun in the other, with African shields in the background. Seale explained this chair was "exemplifying the right to self-defense." This image of Newton, who donned the signature Panther beret, had been circulated in the United States and throughout the world, so placing the chair on the stage "made a very big impact," according to Seale. H. Rap Brown, Stokely Carmichael, and James Forman, all leaders in the Student Nonviolent Coordinating Committee (SNCC), attended. Eldridge Cleaver announced a merger of the two organizations while Carmichael, who spoke after Cleaver, described it as a working coalition. This coming together with the SNCC represented an important coalition if they could make it work. The fiery speeches made it sound like they were on to something big. H. Rap Brown, on probation from an East Coast fracas, explained to the crowd "there was no such thing as a second class citizen," because "you are either free or you are a slave." He then reminded blacks what they needed to do to secure freedom. The fact that he had become famous for saying violence was as American as cherry pie was not lost on the cheering crowd. Carmichael spoke highly of the imprisoned Newton while Seale explained to the audience that "it was time that people learn that the Black Panther Party had not been jiving anybody" and that they were serious about making revolution. The authorities needed to free Huey or "the sky's the limit," he said, not once but several times throughout the evening. A resounding success, the rally helped bring in ten thousand dollars for Newton's defense team, led by white lawyer Charles Garry, who had tried some thirty capital cases and won them all.[11]

One week later, on February 25, 1968, at two in the morning, Bobby Seale, like Eldridge Cleaver before him, had an unscheduled meeting with the local authorities. The police arrested Seale and his wife, Artie, at this late hour because, they contended, an anonymous tipster had informed them that he overheard a group of people planning a murder. Officer Edward Coyne "crouched in the darkness outside Seale's window" with his "ear pressed to the glass," according to Michael Newton. He later testified that someone in the apartment said "got to be a killing" and that he heard "the distinctive click of weapons being loaded."[12]

The Seales had just ended a meeting where they discussed with other Panthers plans for Newton's legal defense. These other Panthers, including chief of staff David Hilliard, Arthur Coltrale, and Alprentice "Bunchy" Carter, were arrested when they emerged from the Seales' home and piled into their car. The police surprised and quickly surrounded them. Searching the men, they discovered they were all armed and in violation of the new, Panther-inspired Mulford Act. The police arrested the three and placed them in police cars to await their comrades, whom they captured next. Going back to Seale's house to complete the mission, the police arrived and knocked on the door. Seale asked who it was, the police identified themselves and told him that they wanted to talk to him as they had heard about a disturbance in the area. Seale had heard no disturbance, he told the police. If they wanted to talk with someone about a disturbance, he suggested they speak with the landlord upstairs. As Seale opened the door to point out the landlord's residence, the police came crashing through the door, stuck a shotgun in Seale's midsection and pointed pistols and a rifle at his wife Artie. Seale screamed, "Don't kill my wife, don't kill my wife!" as the rest of the police officers searched the house. A voice from the back very quickly said "got it" and emerged with a sawed-off shotgun. Police subsequently claimed to have found a .45 automatic with the serial numbers shaved off. Seale and his wife were promptly arrested, and along with the other Panthers, taken off to jail.

It took them a year, but all parties were acquitted of conspiracy to murder and weapons possession because of faulty arrests and lack of evidence. Superior court judge Lionel Wilson, according to Michael Newton, ruled the arrests illegal and described "the eavesdropping evidence of Officer Coyne as 'at times inconsistent with other credible evidence, at times evasive.'" The judge "publicly chastised Coyne for displaying 'a convenient memory which was unusually sharp when helpful to his case and not so sharp otherwise.'"[13]

The police, however, did admit in court that they had been eavesdropping on the Panthers. If true, they must have overheard the group discuss the ten thousand dollars that a recent rally had raised for Newton's defense. By the end of the same week, some twenty-four Panthers had been arrested with bail that added up to nearly nine thousand dollars. Seale surmised the police were trying to drain the party of funds while simultaneously taking Panther leadership out of circulation. These tactics foreshadowed police treatment of the Panthers nationwide.[14]

Newton responded to the break-ins with Executive Mandate Number Three. In it he stated that officers of the law, whom he labeled outlaws and gangsters, had illegally entered Seale's and Cleaver's homes. He delineated other "serious threats from certain racist elements of White

Huey P. Newton in East Oakland, August, 1971. *Photo by Ducho Dennis, courtesy of It's About Time.*

America, including the Oakland, Berkeley, and San Francisco Pig Departments." Insisting that party members stay alert at all times, Newton wrote, "we cannot determine when any of these elements or a combination of them may move to implement these threats." He briefly told the story of the mafia-initiated St. Valentine's Day Massacre in the twenties, when gangsters dressed up as policemen and killed rival mafia members after catching them off guard. "We will not fall victim to another St. Valentine's Day Massacre. Therefore those who approach our doors in the manner of outlaws; who seek to enter our homes illegally, unlawfully and in a rowdy fashion; those who kick our doors down with no authority and seek to ransack our homes in violation of our HUMAN RIGHTS will henceforth be treated as outlaws, as gangsters, as evil-doers." He explained that party members had no way to determine that someone in a uniform involved in a forced entry of their homes was in fact a policeman. "He is acting like a lawbreaker," Newton wrote, "and we must make an appropriate response." All members were therefore mandated to "acquire the technical equipment to defend their homes and their dependents. . . . Any member of the party having such technical equipment who fails to defend his threshold shall be expelled from the party for Life."[15]

Emory Douglas emphasized that Newton's intent with this mandate had not been aggressive. He simply "wanted us to draw the line at the threshold of our doors," where it remained legal to possess firearms. That all citizens have the right to self-defense is indisputable. An imprisoned Newton, however, might have inadvertently brought on a lot of death and destruction with this mandate. He certainly could not predict the future, but he had to know that the police, who for the most part despised the Panthers, were not swayed by militant decrees. His order meant that those Panthers who wanted to be in the party at all costs and who shared the same beliefs as Newton sometimes chose to shoot it out with the police rather than accept a legal battle, which, odds were, the Panthers would win. This mandate also encouraged an already offensive-minded Eldridge Cleaver to rally willing troops to a military engagement that could not be won under the circumstances. While some of those willing made themselves known in Oakland, an entire cadre of them were developed and trained in Southern California.

The first chapter outside the Bay Area was in Los Angeles, founded in the last days of 1967. Organized primarily by former gang member Alprentice "Bunchy" Carter, the chapter grew to be one of the largest and strongest. Carter had been in the penitentiary with Eldridge Cleaver. Both men, along with hundreds of others in the prison, followed the teachings of Malcolm X and promised that, upon their release, they would do all they could to carry on the martyr's legacy. They made good on their promises. Cleaver joined Newton and Seale in their call for black control of black communities by any means necessary. Carter had participated in Los Angeles's Community Alert Patrol, a program designed to monitor LAPD traffic stops and to prevent police brutality and murder of citizens. Carter and Cleaver eventually reunited and the two worked together for two years in an effort to build a viable organization to solve the problem of black powerlessness.[16]

Throughout mid-1967, Carter visited the Oakland/San Francisco Bay area to talk with Cleaver about coordinating efforts in the struggle to attain freedom, justice, and equality for blacks. Cleaver, not quite sure he could trust Newton with whatever plans he had, asked Emory Douglas, who knew of the visits, not to tell Newton about them. His reservations were unfounded as Newton, from the very start, had recruited men off the street to engage in clandestine operations, much the like the ones Carter had pulled as an LA gang member. Eventually, however, Cleaver introduced Carter to Newton and presented the Panther leader with his plan to place Carter at the head of what would soon become the Los Angeles–based Southern California chapter of the BPP. After several discussions, Newton agreed that Carter was revolutionary material and authorized the opening of the Los Angeles chapter.

Los Angeles, California, is a different city altogether from Oakland. With its Spanish-planted palm trees, scenic views, and Hollywood lifestyles, its public persona is one of glitz, glamour, and the good life. Those who lived there knew this to be a facade, especially the black population, whose majority had arrived from the South less than three decades before. Two years before, in 1965, the city had been the site of one of the worst race rebellions in United States history. The widespread police violence and other social maladies that caused the Watts riots apparently were enough for thousands of Los Angelinos to "organize and plan once the rebellion got under way," according to the McCone

Report that summed up a government investigation of the upheaval. It seems that men ranging from fourteen years of age to thirty-five distributed "inflammatory handbills" and large quantities of Molotov cocktails. Moving in cars throughout the areas of greatest destruction, the novice rebels wreaked havoc on the city's infrastructure. Thirty-four people were killed, mostly by police attempting to stop looters from fleeing. Ronald Freeman, who later joined the Black Panther Party, took part in the rebellion. He said that "most of the people who were killed were stragglers who had come to the scene too late to capitalize on the snipers that were holding the police off."[17]

After Watts went up flames, a half dozen other outlying areas experienced racial upheaval. San Diego, Pasadena, Pacoima, San Pedro, Wilmington, and Long Beach also exploded. The Southern California region, particularly in south–central Los Angeles, was rife with black, Asian, Hispanic, Chicano, Latino, and some white people who were willing to engage in mass violence. The LAPD had been charged with keeping order in this volatile area. It was a department that prided itself on how well it did its job.

Since the late forties, the LAPD had been, according to writers Norman Klein and Martin Schiesl, "arranged along semi-military lines so as to maintain strict command and control." Marine Corps Gen. William A. Norton was assigned to do this job in 1948 after years of investigations exposed widespread corruption. Nearly twenty years later, Chief Thomas Reddin still "retained the military model" and promised to use "all available methods in dealing with a potential danger." In 1967, after his officers violently clubbed some 1,300 marchers in an anti–Vietnam War rally, Chief Reddin, "responding to charges of police brutality at a press conference, claimed that the march developed into an unlawful assembly and the department's 'beautiful plan' to disperse large crowds had been 'well executed.'" When the Black Panther Party arrived in late 1967, it became immediately clear that the LAPD could not tolerate another paramilitary organization in its midst, especially one that despised police brutality and threatened to defend blacks by returning offense for offense.[18]

When Carter formed the Black Panther Party in Los Angeles, he first joined with SNCC members who had started an organization of the same name. In fact, Stokely Carmichael had been in on the ground floor of this organization, as he had been with the northern California group, trying to make real his wish to see his brand of struggle spread from the South and into the North and West. Once Carter became leader of the LA chapter, he enjoyed plenty of success attracting recruits. Even after the rebellions, according to the McCone Report, blacks in Los Angeles made daily exhortations "to take the most extreme and even illegal remedies to right a wide variety of wrongs, real and supposed." Perhaps they did so because the police chief and his staff "strongly opposed the notion of a review board" and "described the idea as a communist plot" when faced with demands to remedy police brutality and other misconduct." Carter took some of these people, from a population of 650,000, and shaped them into a cadre of well-organized soldiers willing to sacrifice all for the sake of black freedom. From the very beginning, according to reporter/author Martin Schiesl, they "trailed squad cars through the ghetto and threatened citizen's arrest of brutal officers." Having set up its office on Central Avenue, in the heart of the black ghetto, Carter, designated deputy minister of defense of the Southern California chapter, and his crew were ready to prove that they believed in Malcolm X's dictum to obtain black freedom "by any means necessary."[19]

Like Newton and Seale, Carter was a product of urban California's mean streets. Unlike the other two, however, Carter had been the leader of the Renegades, the hardcore contingent of the Slausons, one of the largest of many gangs that proliferated the city. Transforming "loyal members of his street organization, ex-inmates, and other Los Angeles street gangs from the gangster mentality to revolutionary consciousness," wrote scholar Akinyele Umoja, Carter handed the party "an autonomous collective of radicalized street forces" ready to do battle with the LAPD. Almost immediately, added Umoja, Carter "made it his responsibility to organize an underground Panther cadre" that "carried out secret operations to support the work of the BPP in Los Angeles."[20]

Since the activity was secret, it is hard to know exactly what these individuals did. Based on their revolutionary leanings, previous affiliations, and clear disdain for the establishment, it is not too far-fetched to conclude that violence, robbery, and gunplay made up at least a part of this activity. After all, Newton had organized a similar clandestine arm in Oakland and it is not likely that he forbade Carter, much more experienced in this area than he, from doing likewise. Indeed, Carter's "Wolves," the name Panthers assigned his underground members, became quite legendary for their exploits within the party. This element in the party's infrastructure, in conjunction with a heavy-handed police response to the BPP, did not help to staunch the flow of blood that became commonplace between the LAPD and Panther members. It might have even ensured that flow. The killing started in March 1968 when Arthur "Glen" Morris, Carter's brother, was killed by federal agents operating in tandem with the LAPD. At least ten other LA Panthers fell victim to police bullets before the party ended in Southern California.[21]

The Panthers represented but a microcosm of what was happening around them. The anti–Vietnam War protests, which often ended in violence, encouraged them not only because they too stood against the illegal and ill-advised war, but also because it served as proof that at least some of their white counterparts were willing to join them in opposing U.S. domination. They lived in a world where student protests erupted every day. In some instances, these protests turned violent, further encouraging at least some of the group's members.

For example, in 1968, there were eight major bombings or attempted bombings, mostly of Reserve Officer Training Corps facilities or labs where military-related research was being conducted. Berkeley and other law enforcement officials confiscated more than one thousand sticks of dynamite, over two hundred pistols, rifles, shotguns, and other weapons, and dozens of Molotov cocktails. According to one government report, authorities also confiscated materials for making these deadly incendiary devices "including bottles, gasoline, and primer cords, a sort of fuse used to set off high-powered explosives. . . . These explosives and weapons have been found in caches stored in the Berkeley Hills, in apartments, in cars, [and] garages." Dozens of arsons and attempted arsons caused nearly one million dollars in damage in the Berkeley area. In one incident, two California Highway Patrolmen were firebombed, according to the report, "while standing at the intersection of Bancroft and Telegraph during the June 28–July 3 riots of 1968." Both officers were "engulfed in flames and suffered serious burns requiring lengthy hospitalization." In addition to this incident, the report said, "one Berkeley policeman was shot and dozens more were fired at by unknown assailants." When Panther spokesmen talked about "killing pigs," the power structure had real-life examples to which it could refer. For this reason, the radical organization was able to ensure an influx of recruits. It also guaranteed the police repression that authorities insisted was demanded by the circumstances.[22]

With Seale in jail on the charges stemming from his arrest in Sacramento after the Panthers left the capitol, and Newton incarcerated on a manslaughter conviction, Eldridge Cleaver took the reins of the party. He moved quickly. Getting Newton out of jail was top priority. He therefore had to raise money and support. With his close ties to white leftists throughout the Bay Area, he first appealed to members of the Peace and Freedom Party (PFP), who for some time had been having difficulty procuring the required votes to get candidates on the state ballot. White leftists in the Bay Area founded the Peace and Freedom Party in 1968, prior to the national elections. Because it lacked the nearly fifty thousand votes to become eligible for a place on the California ballot, the PFP agreed to a working alliance with the Black Panther Party. All it had to do to get the votes was to agree to back the "Free Huey" campaign. The PFP did so and became a political entity in the Bear Flag Republic and eleven other states, including Connecticut, Massachusetts, New York, Ohio, Pennsylvania, Rhode Island, Texas, and Wisconsin. A PFP pamphlet claimed the group was "permanently independent from the Democrat and Republican parties" and "committed to immediate unconditional withdrawal from Vietnam." A quid pro quo struck between the two organizations signaled the beginning of a public relations stunt so successful that black people as far away as New Zealand joined in the call to "Free Huey" by forming the Black Panther Party of New Zealand. Cleaver and the Panthers badly needed the sound truck owned by the PFP and they were able to get it by quickly registering thousands of black voters and signing them up as members of the PFP.[23]

The Panthers were willing to ally with the PFP because it agreed to make supporting "the Black Liberation Movement in its struggle for equality and self-determination" part of its platform. In a statement outlining its goals, it noted that "racism and colonialism are prime symptoms of the sickness of American society. We unequivocably support the principles of equality and self-determination which are manifested in the Black Power movement in the United States and the revolutions for national liberation throughout the world." The Panthers could not have been more in agreement with their progressive white allies. The PFP also gave its support to poor people, workers, students, "and other groups in their struggle for economic justice and control over those institutions which dominate their lives." It added that the right to unite for mutual protection, to strike and to demonstrate is an inviolable part of that struggle."[24] Satisfied with the direction of this new third party and quite sure that it could remain in control of its own program, the BPP decided to take the plunge into coalition politics.

At the PFP's founding convention, held March 15–17 1968, some one thousand delegates and alternates attended, Bobby Seale and Eldridge Cleaver among them. Cleaver gave the keynote address, claiming the Panthers entered into this "very narrow coalition" to "put the establishment uptight and put black lackeys of the Republican and Democratic parties out of business." Insisting they were going to pull people out of the two major parties, Cleaver intoned that they intended to "send the jackass back to the farm and the elephant back to the zoo." Seale tried to disabuse convention delegates, which included Chicano and labor caucuses, of the notion that the Panthers were racist. "We are not concerned with color," he said. "The Black Panther Party for Self-Defense is not racist—racists come out of your community . . . you must stop it there." Trying to clarify the difference between their goals and the PFP's, he stated "You hate the war in Vietnam. We hate the oppressive conditions we live under. We would prefer non-antagonistic contradictions [but] self-defense is not murder! Huey P. Newton must be freed!"[25]

Not all PFP delegates agreed with BPP insistence on a "by any means necessary" program of action. The initial vote on a resolution reading "Free Huey Newton Now and Free Huey Newton By Any Means Necessary" brought disagreement to the surface between the Panthers and some whites who apparently took the "peace" in the Peace and Freedom Party literally. "By Any Means Necessary" was defeated 227 to 223. Free Speech Movement leader and former Berkeley student Mario Savio represented the majority when he explained, "without discussion of the means . . . the political point is to free him . . . it is not appropriate to write carte blanche." Contra Costa County PFP leader Bob Avakian argued in favor of the "any means" slogan when he said Newton's case represented the struggle of black people to defend themselves and survive, by any means necessary. "If we free Huey," he surmised, "we can free everybody." After the first vote, Seale approached the microphone to remind delegates that he had spoken clearly in support of the slogan.

Addressing the contradiction in the question, he yelled "what's wrong with a gun? What's so damn wrong with a gun?" Michael Gomez, the Chicano Caucus leader from Hayward, hammered out a compromise slogan after threatening to walk out with his Chicano delegation if blacks decided to walk out. Having won by a three-to-one majority, the final slogan read "Free Huey Newton By Any Means Which Will Advance the Black Liberation Movement." According to news reporter Don Newton, "three or four members of [the] Young People for Peace and Freedom [Party] walked out after saying that the vote proved PFP was not really interested in peace."[26]

This debate over the use of violence in word and deed signaled the first of many occasions when BPP members lost public support. Despite the disagreement over terms, the alliance, shaky from the start since both sides entered it with selfish motives, gave the BPP an opportunity to reach potential recruits and supporters in the Bay Area and throughout the country. Its thousands of mostly white supporters and workers, who brought with them typewriters, mimeograph machines, offices, and dollars, along with its ability to advertise and publicize widely, made allying with them worth the PR risk in the mind of some Panther leaders. In the end, Cleaver was put forth as the PFP's candidate for president and Peggy Terry was his vice-presidential running mate. Newton, from jail, ran for Congress in California's seventh Congressional District while Bobby Seale and Kathleen Cleaver ran for assembly seats in Oakland.

From the very beginning, the Panthers alienated potential black supporters because of the party's alliance with white organizations. In an atmosphere where Black Power advocates called for autonomy and an end to white influence and at a time when protest organizations were in the process of ridding themselves of whites, the Panthers' choice of white allies seemed curious. The BPP, however, argued that it was not white people per se who caused the problems they sought to solve. Because the leaders of oppressive institutions happened to be white did not mean all whites participated in or even agreed with the oppression, they argued. Nevertheless, black Americans in the late sixties and early seventies were slow to accept this rationale. When they looked around and saw the problems plaguing their communities, they saw white complicity. Because unresponsive politicians and school board members, brutal police and unfair merchants all had white skin, most blacks readily assumed that whites in general were the problem. The fact that millions of poor whites suffered similar indignities under American capitalism mattered little to ghetto blacks, whose contacts with whites occurred primarily in police stations, court rooms, and exploitative economic situations. Many of these blacks seriously questioned the alliance between Panthers and whites, while others outright rejected it on the grounds that black liberation could not succeed with the enemy in its camp. It was on this issue that the BPP's relationship with SNCC, especially Stokely Carmichael, foundered.

Realizing that it needed all the help it could get, the BPP sought allies in other places. Having taken its name from the SNCC-inspired Lowndes County freedom organization's symbol, Panther leaders naturally reached out to people in SNCC. James Forman, SNCC's chairman at the time, wrote that when the BPP started, SNCC "felt a clear political need for relations with and support for such organizations as the Black Panther Party." Experiencing what he termed "severe repression" at the time, he added, "we doubted how long we could survive; we had to support every emerging Black Power group in the country so that if we did go under, others could carry on the work we had started." It had been in this spirit and under these circumstances, he said, that SNCC members "Stokely Carmichael, George Ware, and H. Rap Brown talked with the group on various occasions in 1966 and early 1967." Forman noted that the SNCC "worked to rally support for the Panthers when they went to the state legislature in Sacramento, guns in hand, to oppose changes in the California gun laws." According to Forman, because the SNCC had been "too trapped" in its "own contradictions to build" such a party themselves, some SNCC leaders looked to it as the next best thing. With funds decreasing by the day as a result of their new radicalism and their blacks-only (in leadership) policy, Forman saw the emergence of the BPP as "the extension of work many of us in SNCC had been doing over the past seven years and a natural outgrowth of the intense struggle that had been waged since 1960." Forman believed the party would grow rapidly because it clearly spoke about the need for armed self-defense and revolution at the same time that black militancy increased. He also thought the "symbolic effect" of Newton's incarceration "for the murder of a policeman was tremendous."[27]

BPP leaders, quite humble in the beginning, reciprocated Forman's admiration. Party members, especially Newton and Seale, thought of the veteran radical organization as a sort of prototype for the structure they had in mind. They hoped to be able to reach and to organize as many people as the SNCC had. Panther leaders saw the bravery of SNCC members as something special. They knew SNCC members had been standing up to racists in Mississippi and Alabama with arms for years. The Panthers hoped the SNCC could bring its administrative and organizing ability to the party and make it a viable national organization. Newton believed that "combining their work in the South and ours in the North would give the forces of Black liberation a powerful striking force." They also wanted "access to their duplicating equipment," wrote Newton.[28]

The BPP hoped to make Stokely Carmichael, quickly growing in popularity at this time, the party's prime minister, thereby giving him and the SNCC control of their organization. Newton wrote that he, Cleaver, and Seale were "in full agreement about . . . whatever places in the administration they had for us." Forman disagreed with the move, explaining that the BPP was not yet a national organization and a title like that would seem presumptuous. He also explained some of the SNCC's internal differences, highlighting the split between Carmichael and H. Rap Brown, SNCC's new chairman, and saying that if anything they should be given equal status, lest the split be exacerbated. To forestall additional problems, Newton decided to name Carmichael the first prime minister of the Afro American nation, then later field marshal. H. Rap Brown became the minister of justice and James Forman would serve as the minister of foreign affairs. Even though Newton made this decision some time in the early summer of 1967, the working alliance did not begin to materialize until February of the following year, when the official announcement came at the birthday rally that raised money for the defense fund of the imprisoned Huey Newton. The relationship was short-lived.[29]

Cleaver drew the responsibility of handling the details of the merger. Already intent on building the organization the way he saw fit, now that Newton was in jail, Cleaver sought to do what he thought was best for the rapidly growing organization. What he thought was best, however, clashed with what his potential ally thought was best. The disagreement was first over descriptors: how would the SNCC-Panther relationship be defined? Would it be a "working alliance," as the SNCC wanted or a "merger," as Cleaver insisted? In a July meeting of the two groups, the question came to a head in a heated discussion. In a room full of revolutionaries, egos were easily bruised. It is not clear what exact words were used that night, but it is clear that the tension rose to a point where violence and the threat of it became a central part of the unfolding scene. Federal authorities noted that members of the Black Panther Party entered Forman's office and an argument ensued. According to a *New York Times* story about the incident, "one of them produced a pistol and put it into Mr. Forman's mouth. He squeezed the trigger three times. The gun went click, click, click. It was unloaded." Forman denied this incident ever took place and said he called Cleaver to alert him of the danger, that the *Times* "article was written to create a fratricidal situation between our two organizations." Cleaver concurred but never spoke to Forman again, even though the two had agreed to issue a joint statement denying "the lie" the *Times* had spread.[30] Most Panthers and those associated with them are understandably silent on this situation.

Some claim that in the incident Forman was just roughed up a little, not threatened with a gun. One New York Panther, who had previously been a member of the SNCC contingent in New York, said, "they just went up there and kicked his butt that's all. He was supposed to set up a meeting with United Nations representatives and he didn't do his job." Forman denied the incident took place the way it was reported in the media, but he did confirm "there had been serious differences between the Panthers and myself, and between the Panthers and SNCC, some nearly involving gun play." Describing one meeting, though it was not clear it was the same July meeting mentioned in the *Times* story, Forman remarked, "it had been a rough meeting." Minister of culture and revolutionary artist Emory Douglas, who attended one of these meetings, remembered "one time Cleaver took some bullets out of his pocket and put them on the table." He then told Forman "they were his, or were for him, or something like that." He insists Cleaver was simply joking with Forman and that "he was always doing stuff like that." He said even though it was a joke, "Forman didn't see it that way." Forman wrote that Cleaver insisted the two groups merge and he did so "in a clearly hostile fashion." This incident created problems that became so serious Forman later resigned, saying, "too much had happened in California and New York for me to trust certain forces in the

Black Panther Party at that time. I had never worked in an organization where I felt my personal security and safety were threatened by internal elements and I did not intend to start doing so then."[31] Clearly, Cleaver's aggressiveness turned Forman off and the threat of violence seemed real enough for him to remove himself from harm's way. A similar situation occurred with Stokely Carmichael.

The differences Panthers had with Carmichael were more ideological in nature. It is important to note that like the Panther alliance with the Peace and Freedom Party, the partnership with the SNCC was based on the fact that "the other group could offer it something it needed," remembered Carmichael. He spoke of it as being "pure self-interest." SNCC members thought the Panthers "could be [the] channel into the Northern urban struggle" where "the action was heating up." In Carmichael's mind, Panther association with the SNCC granted the newer group "a certain legitimacy in struggle" since "they lacked leadership and real political experience." Carmichael added that the Panthers had "no history and no precedent in American politics" and "found themselves in midair, 'learning to fly on the way down.'" When it became clear that everybody's interests were not going to be served, things turned sour. In a huff, Carmichael, like Forman, resigned his position in the BPP, arguing that the party was too hierarchical, too militaristic, and too bold in its open display of guns. The Forman incident angered him and began the unraveling of his relationship with the party. The final straw came when the two sides disagreed over whether the alliance with whites was a good idea. Carmichael's position was that it was not and that blacks should close ranks before deciding whether to take such action.[32]

Cleaver disagreed, claiming that Carmichael possessed an unreasonable fear of being controlled by any white allies because of his experience in the SNCC. It was understandable, Cleaver wrote in an open letter after Carmichael's resignation, "that you [could] have those fears. . . . because most of your years in SNCC were spent under precisely those conditions." Cleaver added that the Panthers were "able to sit down with whites and hammer out solutions to our common problems without trembling in our boots about whether or not we might get taken over in the process." There could be no middle ground. The Federal Bureau of Investigation, which by now had infiltrated *agents provocateurs*, informants, and spies into the BPP, capitalized on this disagreement. Since 1967, it had endeavored to "prevent the rise of a messiah who might unify and electrify the black movement." Claiming that Malcolm X had been a perfect candidate for such a position, the memo authorizing FBI agents to act against black leaders noted that Martin Luther King Jr. and Stokley Carmichael were "aspirants to this role." FBI agents therefore had to carry out J. Edgar Hoover's directive.[33]

To prevent any possibility of smooth sailing between the two groups, the FBI, which under its Counter Intelligence Program (COINTELPRO) had already been trailing and spying on Carmichael and other SNCC leaders for years, decided to direct counterintelligence toward Carmichael. Because FBI agents knew, from phone taps and other hidden listening devices, of the rift between the two groups, they decided to contact Carmichael's mother. The FBI phoned the SNCC leader's mother and informed her that the Black Panther Party had a "hit out" on her son. Understandably fearful of what might happen and not knowing that the anonymous caller posing as a friend was a federal agent, she quickly contacted her son. Frantically passing the message along, she begged him to leave town and to remove himself from this volatile situation. She too had read the *New York Times* story about the Forman incident and, whether it had been true or not, believed the Panthers were capable of doing harm to her child. The fact is, Carmichael believed it, too. He had experience, through other SNCC members, of Panther willingness to brandish and use weapons.

Most notable had been a case that developed in San Francisco between the two Bay Area Panther groups. After the 1967 Betty Shabazz incident in San Francisco where Newton's Panthers had teamed up with the Black Panther Party of northern California to escort Malcolm's widow, the two Panther organizations experienced major differences. The northern California organization had been started by SNCC members, some of whom had left Mississippi for the West Coast. Somehow Newton and Seale found out that the BPP of northern California members had used unloaded weapons while providing security for Shabazz. They thought this failure to have live ammunition in their weapons while confronting policemen constituted a major dereliction of duty and that it could have potentially brought great harm to the entire group. Angered over this discovery, several Panthers, with Newton and Seale in the lead, proceeded from Oakland to San Francisco to confront the unsuspecting young militants, who also had a small contingent of Revolutionary Action Movement (RAM) members in their ranks. On arrival, the Panthers found the San Francisco group having a fish fry to raise funds. There was a party-like atmosphere and it continued that way for a while. At some point, Newton and the others confronted members of the other Black Panther Party.[34]

In a very threatening manner and with their guns openly displayed but not pointed at anybody, Newton told the group that it either had to merge with his organization, disband, or change its name. Either way, he said, there was going to be only one Black Panther Party in the Bay Area. Members of the other group first refused the demand. They argued back and forth for a while, trying to feel each other out, wondering if things would escalate. They did not have to wait for long. Newton's Panthers' penchant for being "bad motherfuckers," although it often got them into trouble with the police and other Black Power organizations, grew out of real situations and early on they worked to prove to all comers that the Panthers were running the show. Only action could demonstrate such resolve. Out of the blue, one of the Panthers shot up at the ceiling and then down into the floor. Immediately, according to Mississippi resident and activist Margaret Block, who was at the fish fry that night, the northern California group "told them crazy motherfuckers that they could have the name if they felt that way about it." Satisfied with the outcome, they left and went back to Oakland, leaving the "Paper Panthers" to simmer over what had just occurred.[35]

Even though members of the BPP had not shot anybody, they had threatened to do so and had already physically attacked James Forman, one of the highest ranking and oldest members of the SNCC. So when Carmichael heard from his mother the vicious rumor about his impending murder, which turned out to be an outright lie, he had reason to believe it might be true and therefore reason to take precaution. The Panthers had admittedly not been Boy Scouts and their military theatrics had real-life equivalents that put everybody who might have the occasion to cross them on guard. Not long after speaking with his mother, Carmichael surreptitiously left the country and wound up in Africa.[36]

His relationship with the SNCC strained, Cleaver had no choice but to work with what he had. He threw caution to the wind and, risking violation of his parole, began a whirlwind tour to free the minister of defense of the Black Panther Party. In the process, he set up a nation-wide network of Panther chapters and inspired a generation of black, white, Hispanic, and Asian student activists. Cleaver's best-selling *Soul on Ice,* a collection of essays written in prison and published early in 1968, opened doors in many places. Detailing his transformation from crook to social critic, this work would be read by activists all over the country. He wrote of the "Supermasculine Menial" black man, Vietnam, nationalism, race pride, the New Left, and prospects for improving the relationships between black men and women. Cleaver's charisma and ability to use words to inspire and compel listeners to think deeply made him a major draw for people and organizations desiring to know more about the black struggle in general and the Black Panthers in particular.

Cleaver's writing and oratory kept the party financially afloat during a time of great stress and it portrayed the jailed Newton as a celebrity, hero, and martyr. His expositions on the current political situation, often tinged with witty remarks, pleased crowds everywhere. For example, he wrote to Stokely Carmichael when he was in Africa that "neither one monkey nor a whole boxcar full is gonna stop this show, because this is the final act" and "when the curtain falls, there will be prizes to hand out and we'll see to it that you get yours. Now lick that up Stokely, with your long international tongue."[37] The fact that he, an ex-felon-turned-writer/revolutionary, could articulate the needs and desires of so many people in such a way that first the state of California, then the federal government, wanted him silenced, made him even more attractive. He could talk a blue streak when it came to black liberation and the methods that ought to be used to achieve that goal.

One speech, "Community Imperialism," delivered to an all-black audience in New Haven, Connecticut, in early 1968, is a particularly good example. Attired in his signature powder blue turtleneck sweater, a leather jacket bedecked with "Free Huey" and other Panther buttons and sporting his Cuban sunglasses, Cleaver could move an audience with ease. His well-kempt goatee made him seem more handsome and more menacing than he actually was. Those in the crowd who had seen Malcolm X in person might have easily mistaken Cleaver for the fallen Muslim's younger but darker brother. Both men's height and ability to speak well allowed them to tower over contemporaries, not only physically but in other ways as well. With a sweaty face and the intensity of Fidel Castro, Cleaver told the wildly cheering crowd that blacks were currently "in the phase of community liberation to free our black people from the imperialistic control exercised over them by the racist exploiting cliques within white communities, to free our people, locked up as they are in urban dungeons, from the imperialism of the white suburbs." As the crowd roared in approval, he added that "our communities are colonized and controlled from outside, and it is this control that has to be smashed, broken, shattered by whatever means."[38] Ghetto residents needed little convincing that the rats, racism, and daily denigration they experienced originated from outside their own communities. Cleaver simply reminded them of things about which they were already painfully aware.

He went on to intimate that the voting process, if carried out fairly, would give blacks, who were "20 million to 30 million strong," at least some representation. As it was, he said, "we are gerrymandered" out of the process so well that "we are political beggars." He claimed that black political power was deliberately diluted through this process and in real terms their large numbers meant nothing politically. Dubbing the few black representatives "who have been selected for us by our enemies . . . uncle toms, traitors, and bootlickers," Cleaver told the responsive crowd that because "we have been organized into this poverty, we must organize ourselves out of it." Since businesses, store owners, and merchants had drained the black communities of funds, "making their neat clean suburban communities into showplaces of prosperity and leaving our communities to deteriorate into desolate, poverty-stricken dirty slums," he told the crowd they "had no choice but to move. . . . The survival of our people depends upon our moving, demands that we move." Momentarily referring to a central theme in black American history, he told his listeners that "by struggling against these conditions we are doing nothing more nor less than continuing the struggle of our ancestors, of the generations of black people who have struggled up from slavery." Black people want, need, and must have, he declared, "the power to determine the destiny of our black communities." Several shouted, "go head and tell it brother" or "right on" as the sweat dripped from Cleaver's now shiny black face. Appearing not to mind the hot sun in which they all baked, Cleaver and his audience agreed that Black Power was the only legitimate recourse to black grievances and the BPP, "organized for this purpose and this purpose alone" was the way to achieve such power. He urged them to join the party, since, as black people, it belonged to them. If they would do this, he guaranteed them they could become "a nation-wide force and in the process of doing that we will have won many victories along the way, we will have become a powerful and uptight people, and as cool as we are, we will be out of sight! And you won't find nobody on the face of the planet earth crazy enough, fool enough, to be messing with us."[39] Not long after he left town, blacks formed a BPP chapter in Bridgeport, Connecticut. They joined the party in other places as well.

Cleaver's inspiring speeches left many crowds mesmerized. In addition, he convinced thousands that their manhood was on the line if they did not act soon. By appealing to basic survival instincts, he easily convinced his listeners of the validity of his position. Cleaver, however, wanted to organize blacks into an army that would be willing to kill and die for freedom. The mood of many blacks during the late sixties and early seventies made the Panther leader's job that much easier. The hundreds of rebellions throughout the country made Cleaver hopeful that he could transform this mass of energy into a well-oiled fighting machine. When people joined the party in every locale where he spoke, he truly believed they agreed completely with his philosophy of "revolution in our time." Though many did agree, most blacks were simply glad there was a group of armed black men and women willing to challenge the brutality of the status quo. Their hopes for peace and security did not lie in killing whites, but in creating communities where they could control their own lives without the external interference that had characterized their and their ancestors' experiences.

Many of these new recruits were women. Black women had long made up more than half the membership of civil rights organizations, so participation in the BPP can only be seen as a continuation of a trend that began in the earliest days of slavery. Panther women, along with the men, eventually formed cohesive organizations that wielded power in black communities throughout the country.

Black women's contributions to the group, however, far outweighed their numbers.[40] Along with their male counterparts, Panther women believed that "political power blasts from barrels of guns" and "the gun and marksmanship decide whether [the black] race survives." One Panther woman noted, "we knew that what we were involved in was no play thing." Under the guise of preserving the lives of black people, as suggested by radical activist Robert Williams, these women joined the men in "moving positively against the racist pigs and their degenerate allies, the running dog toms."[41] Tondalela Woolfolk, a former member of both the Harlem and Chicago BPP chapters, admitted she "kind of romanticized the whole thing, to die in the revolution, to die to make things right . . . if that meant that all kinds of power and repression were going to come down on me, fine. Everybody dies anyway," she said.[42]

These women's seriousness about armed struggle had gone unparalleled since Harriet Tubman rescued her family and other slaves from the South. Gloria Abernethy, a former Panther in the Sacramento and Oakland chapters, echoed these sentiments. She said she believed being a Panther represented "a lifelong commitment" and that she "didn't expect to live long" because of the group's revolutionary posture. She concluded, "it was just going to be war, and whatever came up, that's what I would do." Perhaps Elaine Brown best captured these sentiments when she pointed out that being in the party meant "committing your life" and surrendering "something of our selves . . . because we believed that the struggle we were involved in . . . would take our lives." In many ways, it was this paramilitary aspect of the party that inspired the women. As Brown noted, people in the group saw themselves "as part of a whole, and part of an entire process, and that you were a soldier in the army."[43] Party member Sheba Haven noted that she came into the party because she "wanted the black liberation movement to succeed." The police apparently understood these sentiments since they treated Panther women with the same contempt as they did the men. This gender visibility is another one of the characteristics that separated Panthers from other militant groups of the era. The group, while not destroying racism and sexism, helped to create a forum where these issues could at least be discussed. By doing this, Panther leaders and rank-and-file workers were able to recruit females as well as males.

Many of these women, while they worked to overthrow the system, did not believe that this change would occur without violent struggle. To illustrate this belief, rank-and-file member Akua Njeri pointed out in her memoir that "we couldn't vote our freedom. This was the government that was set up and protected by our enemies." Basing her conclusions on history, this Panther must have assumed whites would continue to find ways to foil the power of the black vote. She seriously questioned whether such a government "was going to let [blacks] vote their freedom" and "take over his system."[44] Seattle Panther Vanetta Molson echoed these sentiments when she noted that the BPP wanted to unite and mobilize "all oppressed peoples around the world" since "you can't vote him out 'cause the only people you get to vote for are pigs." Njeri, Molson, and many of their party sisters thought it imperative that poor and minority people recognize that they were "under attack" and therefore "seriously at war" with the American government.[45]

Convinced that their struggle was "first and foremost" a "struggle for survival," Panther women became indispensable not only to the BPP, but to the larger civil rights movement as well. Having taken their positions as "keepers of the dream" in the most radical of the Black Power era groups, Panther women left no doubt that they were willing to bring about change by any means necessary. Kathleen Cleaver pointed out in a *Black Panther* editorial that the decision to resort to defensive violence in pursuit of this change stemmed directly from the persistence of "white racism" and the power structure's use of "guns and bullets" to keep blacks in their place. The revolutionary-turned-lawyer further explained that she could not "relate to a white man" and that her "hostility towards white men" was "unyielding and profound" because black women had been "raped and brutalized and tortured and used by the white man." She argued that there would be no need for an organization like the BPP if there were only "white racists without political power and without guns."[46] Kathleen Cleaver could speak as well as her husband Eldridge, if not better. Perhaps that is why she became the Party's communications secretary. Together the two were able to persuade thousands of people that the oppression blacks had endured for centuries needed to end. Indeed, her husband's speaking ability made him the most visible person in the party for a while.

That Eldridge Cleaver could speak articulately and persuasively could not be denied. It might have been this gift that led Newton to give him as much leeway as he liked. When this occurred, however, Cleaver often laced his speeches with threats of violence against authorities and obscenities that quite often disappointed and turned off some who might have otherwise joined or supported the party. Even if people agreed in principle with Cleaver when he said "Fuck Ronald Reagan," they thought that different words could have been used. After a Berkeley student asked

Brenda Presley, a national headquarters staff person and typist for the BPP news-paper. *Photo by Ducho Dennis, courtesy of It's About Time.*

Bobby Seale why they insisted on dirty words, he responded, "Because the filthiest word I know is 'kill' and this is what other men have done to the Negro for years."[47] Although Newton later came to despise this way of speaking, the party left Cleaver to organize and speak in any way he saw fit for a while. He worked hard at this job and quite often tapped into the souls of black and white folks who wanted to participate in the move-ment but who failed to see the dignity and usefulness in struggling via nonviolent direct action. The proponents of this other tactic, who insisted love was the answer and not violence or the threat of it, took serious issue with Black Power advocates, particularly those in the BPP.

Still, one has to ask, what is it about armed self-defense that is so central to black liberation? The answer may very well be found in psy-chiatrist Frantz Fanon's writings. In a nutshell, he speaks of the cathar-sis of violence. He wrote, "at the level of individuals, violence is a cleansing force. It frees the native from his inferiority complex and from his despair and inaction; it makes him fearless and restores his self-respect."[48] He wrote of how the violent actions of Algerian rebels to achieve their liberation served as an emotional purgative, only it was not fleeting. Now that they had joined the rest of humanity in collectively seeing self-defense as perfectly justified, many blacks immediately dropped their habit of depending on whites for their survival and advancement. The doubt and fear that had only recently kept them toiling at dead-end jobs was transformed into courage to go out and vote, to serve their communities, and to pick up arms in their own defense.

This catharsis for the Panthers, once some sense of organizational structure emerged, seemed to have spread like wildfire after a thirsty news media absorbed then disseminated the most sensational activities of the period. In effect, striking back gave a heretofore powerless people a sense of power. This new sense of power grew into a movement that only a government as powerful as the United States could co-opt, disrupt, and crush. Before that happened, however, the BPP wrote its experiences in the annals of history and the world has not been the same since.

The example set by the BPP, despite the organization's shortcomings, faults, rivalries, and weaknesses, was essentially a good one. At one point

Voter registration was an important organizing tool for the Panthers. *Photo by Ducho Dennis, courtesy of It's About Time.*

in its abridged lifespan, the BPP successfully married the theory and practice required to bring about the liberation of black people and others who had clearly been victims of systemic oppression. Their ideas concerning coalition-building and alliances, political education, armed self-defense, and a celebration of the culture of all oppressed people helped to create a united front that could have proven formidable to any oppressive system of government.

It accomplished this feat through its very readable and often succinct Ten Point Platform and Program. In this document, Newton and Seale delineated the major problems facing the black community and demanded solutions to those problems. What made the BPP different from most other organizations, however, was that the party never waited around for an answer from the primarily nonresponsive power structure. It took its cause to the streets, and sought to bring about temporary solutions until such time that permanent solutions could be implemented. Not knowing when that appointed time would arrive, party members lived and worked as if every day were their last. Many of them had good reason to believe that some day soon they might meet death, that most catholic of all companions. Yasmeen Sutton, a former Panther from the Corona chapter in New York City, confirmed this widespread feeling of impending doom when she explained that life in the party was so hectic, they could hardly find time to discuss each other's private lives. She remembered, "when you think you're going to die and not live tomorrow, . . . there's no time to get involved in things like personal issues." Important as these issues might have been, according to Bullwhip, another Panther, "our eyes were on the prize and the prize was revolution: Freedom Now!" This feeling of impending death existed for several reasons, including its success in organizing blacks and other oppressed minorities into effective political groups.[49] The most important and most noted of all these reasons, however, was the group's emphasis on armed self-defense.

Just like it set up liberation schools to teach community members math and black history, breakfast programs to feed the children, medical clinics to care for the sick, and voter registration drives to foster civic involvement,[50] the organization picked up the gun in an effort to address its demand in point seven of the Ten Point Plan: "We want an immediate end to police brutality and murder of black people." Picking up the gun was one of the first real distinctions between the Panthers and other Black Power organizations. To offer a viable solution to this problem, the Panthers, like so many respected black leaders before them, thought that blacks should band together and arm themselves.

This particular decision dictated the party's direction from early on. The question becomes then, why, after all this time and at a point when things were seemingly getting better, did some blacks decide that arming themselves against the machinations of whites seemed like a good idea? Of course part of the answer is that for most blacks, things were not getting better. According to one survey, the black median income dropped from 57 percent of what whites made in the mid-1950s to 54 percent in 1964 and black unemployment was still twice that of whites.[51] When one takes into account the dilapidated housing and failing schools that blacks had to endure as a matter of course, it becomes clear why there would be at least some level of dissatisfaction with the system. These factors led blacks in urban centers across the United States to burn or otherwise destroy the symbols of their oppression.

Another reason why the Panther founders reached this conclusion about the use of arms is that by 1966, it had become clear that policemen, most of whom were white, were neither going to benevolently protect nor adequately serve black communities. It must have been equally clear that no government body, whether local, state, or federal, had demonstrated a willingness to compel the police to do such a thing. After years of complaining to the very authorities (police chiefs) that often sanctioned police violence against blacks and other poor people, the Panthers, as part of a new generation of activists, decided to be proactive. Viewing the capitalist system from as wide an angle as possible, the Panthers argued it had been the police and other law enforcement agencies that kept blacks from realizing their freedom. Newton noted that "the reasons that I feel very strongly about dealing with the protectors of the system is simply because without this protection from the army, the police, and the military, the institutions could not go on in their exploitation."[52]

One cannot escape the reality that many black people in ghettos throughout the United States lived in perpetual fear of the police. This fear, of course, had been well-founded, since countless blacks had been brutalized and murdered by policemen acting in their capacity as officers of the law. To be sure, the BPP was very careful not to "claim the right to indiscriminate violence." Its leaders insisted that they were "not out to kill white people" and that it had been "the cops who claim[ed] the right to indiscriminate violence and practice it everyday. It is the cops who have been bathing black people in blood and who seem bent on killing off black people." These conditions existed not only in the ghettos and urban areas of the North and West but in the rural South and Midwest as well. Because the environment in which most blacks lived tended to be the same, blacks not only formed chapters in Chicago and Detroit, but in such out-of-the-way locales as Minneapolis; Omaha, Nebraska; Portland, Oregon; and Cleveland, Mississippi. Sol Stern, assistant managing editor of *Ramparts* magazine, pointed out in 1967 that "the voice of the Panthers . . . is increasingly the voice of young ghetto blacks who in city after city this summer have been confronting cops with bricks, bottles, and bullets."[53] Attempting to speak in one voice for blacks throughout the nation, the Panthers said to the police: "Halt in the name of humanity. You shall make no more war on unarmed people. You will not kill another black person and walk the streets of the black community to gloat about it and sneer at the defenseless relatives of your victims. From now on, when you murder a black person . . . you may as well give it up because we will get your ASS and GOD can't hide you."[54]

It had been these sentiments that brought together the original members of the Black Panther Party. They sincerely believed that arming for self-defense would save black people from total destruction and from being treated as second-class citizens. Their experiences in urban America made them revolutionaries, just as the experiences of the SNCC and the Congress of Racial Equality in rural America made many of their members revolutionaries. It is no accident that once the party began to grow and become known, many of its members came from the SNCC, CORE, RAM, and other previously established organizations that had begun to falter for one reason or another. Huey Newton, in explaining "The Correct Handling of a Revolution," stated that "the vanguard party must provide leadership for the people" by teaching "the correct strategic methods of resistance through literature and activities. Moreover, the party should conduct its activities above ground in order to educate the masses." Newton predicted early on that "the party's activities on the surface will be necessarily shortlived."[55]

This rigid ideological position landed party members in serious trouble with the law in city after city throughout the United States. The Panthers' courageous stance, their willingness to die for the liberation of black people, however, presented the power structure with a problem it had not encountered since the days of Gabriel Prosser, Denmark Vesey, David Walker, and Nat Turner. The Panthers believed that their courage, determination, and faith in the people would bring about the revolution that blacks had been praying and waiting for since the slave ship *Jesus* began dropping their ancestors off on the distant shores of a strange New World some three centuries prior. Why did the they think the time was right?

If history is any indication, revolutionary violence, though dangerous and often deadly, has its merits. One cannot help but notice that the creation of the United States of America was a direct result of revolutionary violence. Suffice it to say that there would be no United States of America without the use of this kind of violence. The French, Russian, and Chinese revolutions are also excellent examples whereby one might find merit in revolutionary violence. For the leaders of the Black Panther Party, these antecedents served as good examples for black Americans to follow. In addition, these leaders looked to their own era for examples that might guide them to the heretofore elusive liberation. That blacks were terribly outnumbered seemed not to have affected their planning.

These young and courageous men and women caught sight of the many African liberation movements that had succeeded in defeating and expelling powerful European colonizers. The changes and upheavals wrought by World War II left many of the world's colonial masters without the military and economic resources to maintain their dominance over Third World peoples. The United States and Russia, having emerged as world powers after World War II, began a heated competition, euphemistically dubbed the Cold War, to convince people struggling for independence that their social system could best meet their needs. Black Americans, cognizant of this struggle, used the leverage afforded them by a United States that sought to highlight its democratic credentials in an effort to entice newly independent, nonaligned nations into its camp. Blacks who understood the many links between foreign and domestic relations used every opportunity to prove to the world that democracy, while being touted abroad as the panacea for all social ills, had failed to bring freedom, justice, and equality to blacks in Oakland, Jackson, New

York City, Memphis, Chicago, Los Angeles, Denver, or any other locale where blacks resided. The rhetoric of equality, made necessary by the exigencies of war, was used by colonized peoples throughout the world to justify their struggles, quite often being waged violently. Suffice it to say that the world's colonial masters had not intended these results. World War II, like any other type of violence, made it difficult, and finally impossible, to brazenly deny freedom-seeking people their independence.

Not only had the grip of despotism been weakened in those colonies formerly controlled by Germany and Japan—the war's losers—but the victors also saw their monopoly of power over foreign lands seriously weakened. That German Southwest Africa and China also rid themselves of the burden of colonialism was not surprising, but when French-controlled Algeria and Vietnam and British mandates throughout the Middle East began to show that they too would rebel violently against European colonization, the entire world was forced to take notice. A new day had begun to dawn on those peoples who had for centuries been hobbled in their advancement by the necessities of European- and, increasingly, American-based corporatism.

The emergence of an independent Kenya in East Africa and an independent Ghana in West Africa in the late 1950s provided shining examples for those trying to determine how to free themselves from what they thought were similar situations. Though Ghana was able to avoid the violence often associated with independence, the Mau Mau rebels in Kenya wreaked havoc on their weakened colonial masters. Even closer to home were the successful revolutions throughout Latin America and the Caribbean. The Panthers soon took note of these developments. While the movement in India led by Mahatma Gandhi achieved independence through nonviolence, the Panthers sought to use these other more radical movements as their standard.

Indeed, for many blacks, including Newton, Cuba stood as the most notable example of how revolutionary violence could be employed to bring about peace and security for people willing to make the sacrifice required for all out war against oppression. That the United States government provided aid essential to the Cuban rebels, including money, intelligence, and military hardware, seemed to have been lost on those who viewed the small island as a model for successful guerilla war. Huey Newton had in fact managed to get suspended from school when he made a pro-Cuba speech on the campus of Merritt College.[56] The revolutionary violence inherent in all these independence movements makes it clear that in at least some cases, arming to fight one's oppressor could yield positive results. Put another way, violence used in defense of one's person, home, family, community, and freedom is acceptable to most human beings.

Reading of, hearing about, and viewing the experiences of others on television, the earliest members of the party and thousands of potential recruits came to believe that they could use similar methods in extricating themselves from the iron grip of American segregation, exploitation, discrimination, and brutalization. They believed that by mimicking the Vietnamese and Algerian guerrillas, by studying Che Guevara's and Malcolm X's theories and practices, they could once and for all bring about their own liberation. One might well say that no ethnic group, race, or nation has achieved and maintained its independence by nonviolent means. That such a thing could even happen in a world where capitalism exists seems quite far-fetched, if not altogether absurd. That such a thing has never happened should be evidence enough to demonstrate that the BPP's theory and practice were neither new nor novel. What has crippled, or at the very least, sidetracked, any in-depth public discussion of the BPP's development and demise is most writers' unwillingness to concede that in real life, human beings are enslaved, brutalized, and lynched in exact proportion to their willingness to allow themselves to be enslaved, brutalized, and lynched. That no blacks died under the vigilant and watchful eye of Monroe, North Carolina's Robert Williams testifies to this fact. Indeed, it was in this same tradition that the Black Panther Party for Self-Defense established itself.

The self-defense stance taken by the party's founders is no doubt significant. The two leaders must have surmised that external violence, primarily emanating from police officials and other whites, presented the clearest threat and most present danger to black survival. Although the group almost immediately delved into teaching black history, the importance of African culture, political awareness, and economic self-sufficiency, it knew none of this knowledge was useful without first securing black bodies. This elementary but necessary component of the black struggle, however, has been placed at odds with a media-fueled overreliance on moderation and tactical nonviolence.

The fact is, not even eighteenth-century Quakers counseled Thomas Paine, Benjamin Franklin, Alexander Hamilton, and George Washington to cease their hostilities against the British. Even advocates of peace and passivism recognize the human right to be free at all costs. Small wonder, then, that the Panthers took to heart Malcolm X's now famous statement that from now on in, black people "declare our rights on this earth. . . . to be a human being, to be given the rights of a human being in this society, on this earth, in this day which we intend to bring into existence BY ANY MEANS NECESSARY." [57]

One can see by the gravity of this philosophy, by the weight of these words, that the Panthers had embarked upon an extremely difficult undertaking. Having internalized this philosophy, they gravitated toward a situation where death and suffering were sure to follow, as those who maintained the status quo had no intention of placing blacks on an equal social, economic, or political footing with whites. Indeed, some have described the Panthers' efforts as not only misguided, but as an utter impossibility. Others have labeled them crazed fanatics. Nevertheless, neither the thought nor fear of failure prohibited these soon-to-be hard-core revolutionaries from shying away from the task they had assigned themselves. In their estimations, they were carrying on the good work started by David Walker, John Brown, Gabriel Prosser, and Denmark Vesey.

The BPP, however, unlike its predecessors, had the might of the most technologically and militarily advanced nation in world history as its chief adversary. To enjoy even minimal success, the BPP had to employ the "by any means necessary" approach. This meant their strategy and tactics would include both offense and defense. For the first time in American history, thousands of black men and women proudly and publicly declared their willingness to use all necessary force to protect and preserve the lives of both present and future generations.

This protection initially manifested itself in self-defense. The party taught blacks who were not aware that they could legally carry weapons to prevent harm to themselves. For many blacks who had grown up mostly ignorant of the law, this revelation came as refreshing news. "BJ," who joined the party in Corona (Queens), New York, admitted he "didn't even know that you could [legally] have a shotgun in your house" before the Panthers came along and began teaching the legality of self-defense.[58]

The party, however, did not stop at this basic explanation. They went even further by pointing out to community members that they were duty-bound by the Constitution of the United States to protect themselves. In the early days, one could hear Panthers in bars and nightclubs, on street corners and college campuses, reciting the final words of their Ten Point Platform and Program: "But, when a long train of abuses and usurpations, pursuing invariably the same object, evinces a design to reduce them under absolute despotism, it is their right, it is their duty to throw off such government and to provide new guards for their future security." The Panthers took seriously the constitutional admonition to "alter or abolish" any government that was repressive or that refused to "effect the safety and happiness" of its citizens.

This understanding of their predicament led the party to consider, and to subsequently implement, offensive political violence to complement its defensive posture. It is here that the philosophical waters surrounding the BPP become very murky. For that reason, it is necessary to distinguish or differentiate between the Panthers' application of defensive and offensive political violence.

The BPP, like any military organization, designed its offensive strategy to complement its defensive strategy. Party members knew full well that they could not rely on foundation grants, government subsidies, or proceeds from welfare checks and low-paying jobs to finance their activities. They needed guns, food, transportation, furniture, housing, and later, for their serve-the-people programs, countless other supplies including medicine, shoes, clothing, and buses. While it is true that many of the things they needed came from donations, it is equally true that the Panthers had alternative methods of procuring what they needed to function. From the earliest days of the party, Huey Newton recruited people he had known when he ran in the streets of Oakland. They had been drafted strictly for military/clandestine purposes.[59]

As a rule, only Huey Newton, and occasionally Eldridge Cleaver or other high-ranking party officials, knew these individuals. To be sure, the party did much more than simply fry bacon and make pancakes for hungry children. Because party leaders organized the group in a paramilitary fashion, it operated on a "need to know" basis. Most members to this day remain oblivious to the involvement of such individuals. Emory Douglas commented, "those were Huey's people and responsible only to

Huey, so who knows what they were doing, you'd have to ask them." Newton provided some indication of what they were doing when he wrote in his autobiography, "I tried to transform many of the so-called criminal activities going on in the street into something political. . . . . Instead of trying to eliminate these activities—numbers, hot goods, drugs—I attempted to channel them into significant community actions." He went on to explain that the rise in consciousness among many blacks of the time made some people "feel guilty about exploiting the Black community" so if these "daily activities for survival could be integrated with actions that undermined the established order, he felt good about it." It was not long before "many of the brothers who were burglarizing and participating in similar pursuits began to contribute weapons and material to community defense." Even though they still had "to sell their hot goods to survive," they simultaneously passed "some of the cash on" to the party. "That way," according to Newton, "ripping off became more than just an individual thing."[60] Undoubtedly the police saw things exactly the opposite of how the Panthers did. The illicit activities of a few would later be superimposed on the legal activities of all Panthers and the negative publicity that came along with this mischaracterization eventually caused the BPP to lose support in both the white and black communities.

To be sure, this kind of strategy had its limits. After all, it was not altogether unlikely that these self-appointed revolutionaries would be caught stealing from the rich and giving to the poor. As a practical matter, the tactic opened the party up to too many liabilities, and it could ill afford to spend time rescuing captured revolutionaries who might make deals with the other side. More importantly, an organization like the BPP had to be as righteous and upstanding as it could if it hoped to have an influx of new recruits. Panther strategy in this instance seemed to lend itself to attracting opportunists, who in later years helped ruin the party from the inside. In the mid-1960s, however, Panther leaders believed the times dictated such a policy.

For them, black oppression had gotten beyond compromising with and displaying niceties toward the oppressor. To party leaders, it mattered little what their enemies thought, as in their minds, the power structure had labeled blacks criminals anyway. Anything they did to achieve their freedom, the Panthers considered legitimate. With this outlook, they organized their party along military lines.

The Black Panther Party had always taken seriously the idea that armed confrontation with the enemy was a necessary ingredient for success. Even after the organization put down the gun, deemphasized revolutionary violence, and emphasized its nonviolent community service programs in the early seventies, its revised Ten Point Program declared that black liberation would only come after violent confrontation with oppressors of blacks. After reiterating what it wanted and what it believed, the statement declared, "deliverance from our ills will only come with a basic transformation, a revolution of the fundamental framework of the governing system of the United States of America. . . . Because there has been no evidence that this oppression will wither away on its own, we propose to participate in programs of action designed to rid . . . the society of all forms of oppression." Assuring that it would "struggle in every way, using any means, to achieve these ends," the statement ended with the Panthers declaring their "firm belief that our liberation from oppression will be ultimately effected through violent confrontation with our oppressors."[61] They intended to "dedicate" their lives "to fostering a program that serves these ends and promotes these ideas." The major difference at this point was the fact that the violent talk and the open display of weapons had ceased. In keeping true to its Black Power roots as well as to its origins in the philosophy of Malcolm X, the archetype of that movement, party members continued to believe that only their conviction and "uncompromising action" would "produce the insurrection" needed to combat and overcome "oppression."[62] This philosophy lent itself to unconventional, brazen, and deadly tactics.

It is important to understand that the BPP considered itself a revolutionary organization. As such, its members understood and always kept in mind that, according to many of them, "revolution is illegal." When it comes to details about certain "actions," whether they be bank robberies or the killing of snitches and informants, only so much can be known. None of the surviving Panthers are willing to discuss openly certain activities, since many of their comrades remain in jail and have open cases. Still others, understandably, do not want to incriminate themselves. These facts must be kept in mind throughout since many of the claims will appear to some as lies, embellishments, or falsifications. The fact that there are no police records or newspaper or magazine articles to corroborate some of these claims should be understood because murder, conspiracy to murder, and attempted murder represent no small problems for former Panthers, who since September 11, 2001, have been rounded up by police officers as they turn up the heat in the war on terrorism. The Panthers themselves certainly did not write down such illegal activities in their weekly reports, and if they kept diaries they are keeping them to themselves in the hope they never become public. Consequently, there will be instances where only so much can be known about certain incidents and we may never be able to get at the entire truth since people, as a rule, do not normally volunteer to go to jail or prison.

When the Panthers started pouncing on and annihilating offending policemen and other law enforcement officials, though the attacks were primarily carried out later in the group's short lifespan and by members of a closely related but clandestine Black Liberation Army, they were never seen by the Panthers as having been unprovoked. Although it is clear in some cases that the Panthers initiated the action, they always insisted the police deserved the same treatment they had been meting out to blacks. In *The Correct Handling of a Revolution,* Newton explained the BPP's role had been to teach by example. "When the masses hear that a gestapo policeman has been executed while sipping coffee at a counter," he wrote, "and the revolutionary executioners fled without being traced, the masses will see the validity of this type of approach to resistance."[63] They hoped these offensive assaults would dissuade policemen from continuing their unprovoked attacks on black citizens.

The civil rights movement had failed miserably in persuading the police that beating blacks was a bad idea. One writer accurately noted the movement had not created jobs for the masses or stopped, or even slowed down "the terrorization of the [black] population by the cops" and white vigilantes.[64] Panther Thomas McCreary recalled it had not been difficult at all for the Panthers to see themselves as justified in their actions. He claimed the primary catalyst had been "the killing of children. Them [policemen] throwing fifteen-year-old kids off buildings and it being ruled justifiable homicide. That's what set this whole thing off, a lot of it." Continuing his recollection, he said they decided, "as long as there was going to be wailing and crying in the black household, there would be no peace in the white household. They would have to experience some of that wailing too."[65]

The multidimensional view of self-defense the Panthers held led them to the conclusion that some initiative had to be taken if protection of the black community was going to be effective. Newton provided the following example to explain why the BPP decided to initiate violence for the sake of self-defense:

> You may go to a party and step on someone's shoes and apologize, and if the person accepts the apology, then nothing happens. If you hear something like "An apology won't shine my shoes" then you know he is really saying "I'm going to fight you." So you defend yourself, and in that case striking first would be a defensive act, not an offensive one. You are trying to get an advantage over an opponent who has already declared war.[66]

The party's leadership, viewing police as armed occupiers of the black community, saw police presence in their neighborhoods as an aggressive move. They concluded that they were fully within their rights to attack people who they believed had demonstrated every intention of attacking them. The decision to open this new front in the war for black liberation first brought notoriety, then recruits. Some of these recruits were to be used to take the war to the enemy. Oakland Panther Bill Jennings explained, "you have to take into consideration that we had people [in the party] who had been to the Vietnam War. When they came back, they were ready to go on the offense. . . . They were talking about what we were going to do to bring down the system. The time for talking was over as far as they were concerned."[67]

In other words, they, along with other like-minded members, were ready and willing to be used as the front-line soldiers of this widened war. One writer has noted, "the Panthers were outstanding in their willingness to face jail and even death for their theory." Thomas McCreary put this notion in perspective when he said that like Che Guevara and his comrades, "we were motivated by love" because "basically, we were trying to take a certain amount of the overt, violent oppression that the police was putting on the black community and bring it to us. We felt that since we were trained in those matters that we could deal with that. We wanted to take the heat off the black community."[68]

Because hot spots in Africa, Latin America, and Southeast Asia continued to flare up, the Panthers became convinced their enemy could not fight a multifront war and win. Fidel Castro, one of their heroes, had come to this conclusion some three months before the Black Panther Party formed. According to the *Washington Post,* he told "a wildly cheering rally in Santiago, Cuba: 'The imperialists are making themselves an international police force against the revolutionary movement in the whole world, and in their own country the exploited ones fight and rebel.'" In this trademark three-hour address, he surmised, as did the Panthers, that the United States "can't put out the flame of revolution in the rest of the world when they have that flame in their own country." The famed leader of the Cuban revolution went on to express "a fervent embrace for exploited Negroes in the United States and for combatants in Venezuela, Bolivia, Guatemala, and Vietnam" where "revolutionary guerrillas were active."[69] The political violence the Panthers symbolized made them extremely popular among those who had experienced—personally or through relatives, friends, and neighbors—police brutality.

For the Panthers, taking up arms and shooting policemen seemed at one point to be the right course of action. They later changed their minds. The task here is to provide a critique of this violence and to determine "how it came to pass that men [and women] would do such things."[70]

It does not take a genius to see that blacks operated at a decided disadvantage when it came to challenging militarily the local, state, and federal police forces. This fact is made even clearer when one sees how the BPP attracted fewer than ten thousand of the nearly thirty million blacks in the country at the time. Nevertheless, as one writer pointed out in 1972, "the Panthers, realizing that the masses could not be organized to aggressively confront the police, developed a conscious policy of substituting their own militants for the organized power of the masses."[71]

This outlook, and the practice that followed, predictably led to failure as these justifiably angry but grossly underequipped and outnumbered youngsters had to battle not only the police, but state troopers, the FBI, the National Guard, and the Army as well. Few people, including the Panthers, held the illusion that this strategy in itself would lead to victory and liberation for black people. One writer pointed out that "adventurous black youth joining the Panthers did not see themselves as building a successful social revolution" but anticipated leaving the party in a pine box "with a dead cop to their credit, having done their share to avenge the centuries-old oppression of their people." While the Panthers certainly did not see themselves in such fatalistic terms, they realized they could not win a military victory.[72] Thomas McCreary noted that tactically Panthers "never expected to win a military war against the United States. We knew that at this point [in] time that wasn't going to happen." Instead, he said, their goal had been to "create a situation where black people would be psychologically" prepared "and willing to do this" if the time ever came. They were trying to get people to understand, he continued, "that if we could implant that [willingness to resist] into the young people growing up and get rid of that type of fear [of whites] then we would be alright." Realistically, he concluded, "many of us" did not "expect to be alive to this day."[73] Clearly, the group sought to lead by example, hence its self-described moniker of vanguard party. Its tactics, however, left a lot to be desired.

In fact, the BPP's optimistic view of how to bring about black liberation had several shortcomings. First of all, the outcome of the rebellions in Newark, Harlem, Watts, Chicago, Washington, D.C., and scores of other cities had demonstrated the willingness of the state to kill any and all blacks who failed to cease their violent outbursts. These uprisings had also demonstrated that when the police could no longer handle the rebels, state and federal reinforcements could be swift and deadly. There were other, more substantive, problems with Panther tactics, however.

One of the group's most egregious mistakes early on was allowing members who worked selling papers and doing other public activities to engage in armed expropriations and other more dangerous, illegal activities. While this practice ended as the organization evolved and grew, it caused considerable difficulty for members who, in any case, were new when it came to starting a revolution. Former Panther Sundiata Acoli explained, "party members who functioned openly in the BPP offices, or organized openly in the community, by day might very well have been the same people who carried out armed operations at night. This provided the police with a convenient excuse to make raids on any and all BPP offices, or members' homes, under the pretext that they were looking for suspects, fugitives, weapons and or explosives." Most of the Panthers interviewed failed to comment on this issue while others, like BJ of the Corona chapter and Malik Rahim, are in agreement with Acoli's statement. Acoli likely reached the conclusion that too many members were part of both the aboveground and underground apparatus after thinking about it for the last thirty years, as he has been imprisoned since the early seventies as a result of a shootout with state police on the New Jersey turnpike. This failure to separate the two muddied the distinction and made it easier for enemies to infiltrate the party and to undermine it. While it is clear that this mistaken policy emerged from the inexperience of party leaders and rank-and-file, there should have existed some mechanism to check and balance the group's more obvious shortcomings.[74]

The Panther's reliance on "the brothers off the block" to stand up to what amounted to an onslaught with all the characteristics of overkill was inadequate. Even when factoring in the leadership and technical skills of veterans of foreign wars (World War II, Korea, and Vietnam) who trained this contingent of anxious revolutionaries, the Panthers remained at a decided disadvantage. Group members simply could not wage a successful war against the armed forces, federal agents, and police who met them with a daily barrage of bullets, harassment arrests, false incarcerations, and media assassinations. Nothing in their experiences or training had prepared them for such a war, while their enemy constantly trained to combat grass-roots resistance movements. Party leaders believed this group, the "lumpen proletariat," had what it took to prosecute a war in America because they simply had nothing to lose and because they lived a violent life to begin with. "People who were the most willing" to lay it all on the line tended to be "the criminal element because they're out there doing it already to a certain extent," recalled McCreary. He noted, "we went deep off into the ghetto" for recruits, looking for people "on the shady side of the street." Just as Newton had pointed out about earlier recruits, McCreary added, "them niggas had been shooting their pistols Friday and Saturday night anyway . . . so we'd get them and politicize them." Black people, he insisted, "ain't got no problem with the gun because we been using it for years on each other, but when you start talking about using it on the enemy" people became "psychologically willing to do that sort of thing."[75]

Writer and cleric Joseph Brandt noted that this internal ghetto violence had served "well the purpose of the controlling group" because it created "little need to fear [this] anger being turned outward." Whites, he noted, often only scoffed at the very common "gang wars, family violence, drunken brawls, and high crime rates as long as it did not cross ghetto borders" and was not "directed against the white man's property that [was] located within the minority ghetto itself."[76] The Panthers sought to build on this pent-up anger and to direct it toward building community institutions and self-defense, which in some cases included offensive maneuvers. Their conclusion was it the lumpen best served this role, based on psychiatrist Frantz Fanon's idea that this group would be used against any grass-roots movement if it were not recruited to the movement for liberation, brought the Panthers a lot of heartache and pain.

According to Acoli, "The lumpen tendencies within some members were what the establishment's media (and some party members) played up the most. Lumpen tendencies are associated with lack of discipline, liberal use of alcohol, marijuana, curse words, loose sexual morals, a criminal mentality, and rash actions." He concluded, "these tendencies in some party members provided the media with better opportunities than they otherwise would have had to play up this aspect, and to slander the party, which diverted much attention from much of the positive work done by the BPP."[77] Some of these individuals had a tendency to revert to their old ways, thereby wreaking havoc on internal party dynamics. Oakland Panther Bill Jennings recounted that "we had no problem with brothers that were hustlers, pimps, etc., because they already knew what police brutality was, they could run it down to you." However, he added, some of these people "were crooks" and "they didn't have no love for the people . . . they were victimizing black people in the community and using the party as a front for criminal activity."[78] He explained this had been one of the reasons for the nationwide purge that commenced in 1969. Still, the problems did not stop there.

Using offices inside the ghetto as bases of operations was also a mistake. As a paramilitary organization, it should not have made defending clearly vulnerable offices a matter of policy. Sundiata Acoli echoed these sentiments when he noted this policy "sucked the BPP into taking the unwinnable position of making stationary defenses of BPP offices. . . . small military forces should never adopt as a general action the position of making stationary defenses of offices, homes, buildings, etc." The frequency and quickness with which they were surrounded and attacked should have led them to develop a policy that would have allowed them to move from one headquarters to another with speed and stealth. Instead, the fledgling group constantly found itself defending sandbagged and otherwise well-fortified offices until their limited supplies of ammunition expired.[79]

These shootouts, which often ended in Panther deaths, arrests, and incarceration, did little to provide the group with a military edge in its ongoing war for black liberation. While the aftermath of these confrontations often inspired others to join the party, they failed to demonstrate to the majority of blacks that the Panthers' military solution to their problems had merit. Though many, if not most, blacks were appalled by the treatment they received at the hands of the police, they found the Panthers' methods risky at best and suicidal at worst. Clearly most blacks were willing to continue suffering "while evils were sufferable," or they chose to work within the system for change. Life and prison-free living seemed to trump the occasional dead policeman coupled with a valiant and dramatic stand flashed for a few minutes on the evening news. Times were apparently not hard enough for them to pick up the gun and begin offing pigs. Jennings accurately noted that going on the offensive had been "an incorrect analysis of. . . . the whole situation." The people who pushed this idea, he recalled, "were putting a personal viewpoint of their ideology above the ideology or the reality of the masses." Though "they were frustrated and some would take up guns," he continued, "by and large the majority of black people wasn't to that stage of taking up the gun." From early on "within the organization you had people pushing for organizational standards and then you had people pushing for an offensive kind of thing."[80] Of course it could very well have been self-doubt and fear of failure that led to most blacks' decisions not to join the fight, but most probably viewed it as a numbers game and saw that being outnumbered and outgunned meant certain death. In addition, the majority of blacks, buttressed by their Christian roots, despite ill treatment from the system, did not view killing as an appropriate response. Despite larger-than-life icons like Bayard Rustin and Martin Luther King Jr., who tried to dissuade the group from taking the road of violence, the BPP persisted. Indeed, it was people like King who, moving beyond the constraints of desegregation and voting rights, helped to create the space that the Panthers came to occupy in the growing movement for liberation.

CHAPTER 5

Growth and Transformation

DESPERATELY TRYING TO GIVE THE NATION, and perhaps himself, a better understanding of the new black militancy that captured the hearts and souls of so many blacks, particularly the young, Martin Luther King Jr. proclaimed, "I should have known that in an atmosphere where false promises are daily realities, where acts of unpunished violence towards Negroes are a way of life, nonviolence would eventually be questioned." Though King's conclusion conveys a sincere element of regret, he too had given more than just tacit approval of an individual's right to self-protection and self-preservation. At about the same time that pacifist/activist Bayard Rustin explained that "King's view of nonviolent tactics was almost non-existent when the [Montgomery bus] boycott began," fellow pacifist and one-time King advisor Glenn Smiley wrote that "King's home is an arsenal." As late as 1967, a year after the founding of the BPP, this movement icon commented that questioning "self-defense" falsifies the issue since common law had always guaranteed "the right to defend one's home and one's person when attacked." King also believed early on that if whites lost blood, change would come a lot faster.[1] Indeed, without the insistence on this right, and guns to back it up, the black population would have been dramatically reduced, particularly as a result of the daily white attacks on them throughout the country during this period and in the hundreds of years prior to the modern civil rights movement. By 1967, King had long been aware that some of his constituents questioned the tactic of nonviolence from the very beginning. Indeed, some had flatly rejected it.

This situation created a serious problem because whites, liberal or not, had proven they were unwilling to finance a movement that possessed the potential to effect significant political change and/or a major redistribution of wealth. Movement leaders, therefore, wanted to keep this seething resentment and more than occasional violence to a minimum and certainly out of the news. Not able to do this, they began to lose credibility with their white benefactors and to inadvertently divert new recruits into the more radical Black Power organizations. Despite this major problem, nonviolence as a tactic remained the preference for most participants in the movement. As a result, King continued to stress the idea's merits, regardless of the visible shift in sentiments among many of those he led and desired to lead.

His attempt to graft nonviolent direct action onto working-class issues demonstrated King's belief that for the black struggle to be successful, leaders had to address economics in addition to human rights. This foray into issues outside of civil rights was his last, however. King's spring 1968 visit to Memphis to support and publicize the plight of striking black sanitation employees attempted to show that the dispossessed had the power to determine their own destinies.

It did not help that he had recently fallen into disfavor with his allies by speaking in opposition to the Vietnam War. Most of his black allies, like those in the NAACP and the Urban League, castigated him for taking what they called an unpopular and ill-advised position. King countered that silence could be too easily taken for cowardice, or worse, complicity in the murder of millions of nonwhite people. Embattled, however, this itinerant preacher/activist began to think his days were numbered as a result of the additional enemies he had created by becoming more vocal and by trying to unite those groups who had, up to that point, been struggling separately for the same things.

His idea of a poor people's march on Washington made him a foe of all those who wished to maintain the status quo, including the president and all his men. His trip to Memphis dictated that changes be made to his plan. King sought to make the black garbage collectors' cause a national issue. That they were doing the same job as their white co-workers and being paid one-third their salary was an issue King wanted to use to dramatize the plight of blacks everywhere. The problem had been the same in the North and West as it had been in the South and East. Blacks had been deliberately prevented from controlling the politics and economy of their communities because they were denied the funds that would have allowed them to take the appropriate actions to fix many of the problems poverty fostered. Having been a democratic socialist for some time, King strategically seized the opportunity to move the issue of economic justice from the back burner to the front and began to speak more often about the connection and inseparability of racism and capitalism. He cared so deeply about this cause and respected his friend Rev. Billy Kiles, a leading cleric in Memphis, so much that he vowed to go to Memphis a second time. An earlier visit had ended in violence when a gang called the Invaders (some members of which later joined the BPP) had infiltrated the march, ostensibly at the behest of the Memphis police and the FBI. Seemingly on cue, some of the Invaders, whom King had actually spoken with earlier, began breaking windows and looting stores. An embarrassed King, insisting that nonviolence would win over all doubters, promised to return and did so a week later in April 1968. Memphis turned out to be the great orator's last road trip.[2]

His second march successful, in the sense that there was no violence, King continued on to the church, where he gave a rousing speech on the importance of carrying on even when the way seemed rough. Eerily, he referred to his desire to live a long life while saying that "longevity" had its place. He, however, was "not concerned about that now," he just wanted "to do God's will." Sweating profusely and in a serious but upbeat mood, King prophesied to the congregation about black peoples' prospects for the future. He compared his role to that of the prophet Moses more than three thousand years before. Like the Hebrew patriarch, he would not make it to Canaan, the promised land. In his mind, he was headed to the land of milk and honey, where lions lay with lambs and where there was no crying or pain. King had served his purpose well, and he knew it. The trepidation in his voice went barely perceived by the attentive crowd. Satisfied that he had done all he could in service to God and the struggle for black freedom, a not-quite resigned King headed toward his conclusion.

He spoke of history, courage, love, and perseverance. Ending his sermon, King told the crowd that blacks had "some difficult days ahead . . . but it really doesn't matter with me now. . . . I've been to the mountain top and I've seen the promised land." He told the cheering congregation, composed of hundreds of Christian Mississippi natives who had moved north in search of greener pastures, "I may not get there with you, but I want you to know tonight that we, as a people, will get to the promised land." With that, he concluded his sermon and took his seat. Exhausted afterward, he decided to retire to his hotel room.[3]

Jessie Jackson, an up-and-coming freedom fighter himself at the time, realized that King and his entourage were staying in a white-owned hotel and impressed upon King the symbolic importance of staying in a black hotel. King agreed and the group moved to the black-owned Lorraine Motel. The day was April 4, and King prepared to attend a dinner at a friend's house. At approximately six that evening, King stepped out onto his balcony to get some fresh air. The moment had arrived and James Earl Ray, from high in a building across the street, set his scope sights on this drum major of justice. With his target locked in, the assassin pulled the trigger. A single shot from the high-powered rifle hit King and ripped the right side of his jaw from his face. The dying minister, profusely bleeding, lay unconscious in the arms of Ralph Abernathy, his best friend, who had rushed out to see what happened. Memphis doctors at St. Joseph's Hospital pronounced the nonviolent prophet dead at 7:05 p.m.[4]

King's death set off a wave of rioting throughout the country that lasted for several days. People, frustrated and angry, discharged their previously pent-up rage in a frenzy of burning and looting. BJ, a Brooklyn-born New Yorker whose family later moved to Queens where he eventually joined the Black Panther Party, reminisced about how the Harlem riots started in the wake of King's murder. BJ, now a labor union organizer for Local 1199 and coordinator for Bread And Roses, its cultural arm, had been a small-time drug dealer who, with his partner, had left Queens that night to go up to Harlem "to cop our drugs." Walking up the main street after getting their drugs "on a side street," they decided to do a little window shopping before they boarded the subway back to Queens. He remembered they had been standing in front of A. J. Lester's. "Everybody had to shop at A. J. Lester's," he recalled. "If you were a black brother, a hustler, at that time, you *had* to have something from A. J. Lester's." As they looked inside the store and simultaneously peddled their drugs, they heard a lady scream. "It was an *eerie* scream, one that sent chills through you," he explained. Slowly walking down the street and not quite sure what was happening, they turned around and saw this "old brother, I can't remember if he was a wino or if he was high, but he was just crying," he said. "And maybe it was just emotion, he was shaking and crying and about this time you could hear footsteps, people coming out of the buildings hollering and screaming, 'they killed him, they killed him!'"[5]

Oblivious to the tragic murder in Memphis, BJ and his partner were "on the street, hustling and wondering what they were talking about." They turned around and "all of a sudden," recalled BJ, "the old man [he had seen earlier] picked up a garbage can and threw it at A. J. Lester's." He remembered that the old man had been stumbling the whole while and that "he didn't have that much strength. So the garbage can hit the glass and bounced off into the street." Curious, the two "ran over to the man and said what's the matter, what happened?"

"They killed King, they killed King," he replied and picked up the garbage can again and threw it. It bounced off the window again. At this point they saw and heard "lots of ladies in the street hollering they killed King." BJ explained that he understood what was going on at this point and said "I'll help you, old man. I picked up the garbage can and threw it through the window. All hell broke loose after that."[6]

In the wake of that initial window smashing, Harlem experienced "a full night of rioting." BJ recalled the memory with a pleasurable fondness for having been the one to set off the explosion expressing the black mecca's anger over King's murder. "It was something," he remembered, "like emotion, you could feel the emotion coming from the streets. Reality had set in." When the commotion first started, BJ remembered a news report in which Malcolm X, who had lived in his Queens community, said to King "they gonna kill us brother, they gonna kill both of us." "And my mind said, oh shit, this shit is real. And we started rioting." When the police came, thousands of people had poured into the streets, so they "kinda let the people do their thing." Two black officers stood guard in front of A. J. Lester's and "if you didn't hit it the first time you weren't going back in." He recalled that "they wouldn't bother you if you hit" the white stores because "it was just too many of us. I think the cops started cracking down on people when they started burning, that's when the shit really got serious." [7]

The same scenario was replayed in more than 120 cities, including Washington, D.C., where, in a crude ironic twist, the nearly all-black elite Eighty-second Airborne was called in to protect the White House. Millions watched on television as smoke billowed over the White House and Army troops waded into Baltimore and Chicago. To contain the violence, President Lyndon B. Johnson, reeling from a credibility gap from which he never recovered because of his lies and distortions about the Vietnam War, sent some twenty thousand regular Army troops and activated another twenty thousand National Guardsmen to put down the disturbances. Before it ended, forty-six people were dead, another three thousand injured, and more than twenty thousand arrested nationwide. Many activists and soon-to-be activists believed that nonviolence had died along with Martin Luther King Jr. Black Power advocates especially held this position.

Bobby Seale noted in an interview that the Panthers "were for nonviolence," but King's death confirmed their contention that the movement needed to be revitalized and restructured. He and other Panthers were fuming because the night before King's assassination, a contingent of heavily armed officers broke into their weekly meeting at St. Augustine's Methodist Church, harassed members, and left without arresting anyone or finding the guns they sought. Shortly after the riots, an Oakland reporter asked Seale whether he agreed with the philosophy of nonviolence. Seale retorted: "nonviolence on the part of whom? on the part of racists who've infested the police department? who continue to brutalize and murder black people in the streets? No, we must defend ourselves, like Malcolm said, by any means necessary." [8]

King's murder, according to Kathleen Cleaver, represented "probably the single most significant event in terms of how the Panthers were perceived by the black community." She succinctly described the atmosphere and significance of this rapidly changing era when she noted that "once King was murdered, in April 1968, that kind of ended any public commitment to nonviolent change. It was like, 'well we tried that, and that's what happened.' So even though there were many people, and many black people, who thought nonviolent change was a good thing and the best thing, nobody came out publicly and supported it." Accurately describing the position of many young activists, she added that "nonviolent change was violently rejected. So it was like the Panthers were all of a sudden thrust into the forefront of being the alternative." [9]

While the group's 1967 appearance on the assembly floor in the Sacramento capitol building did more to shape its image in the public's mind than King's assassination, his murder forced many activists and would-be activists to question seriously the efficacy of nonviolence. BPP leaders insisted that the time for nonviolence had passed and a more useful strategy for black liberation needed to be employed. Few, if any, of the people who joined the party after King's assassination disagreed with this position.

With King dead and nonviolent protest receiving less and less publicity, the BPP emerged as somewhat of a media darling. The party became the benchmark for any and all Black Power organizations. In short, the Panthers represented the other side of the civil rights coin. The threatening rhetoric Malcolm X used to describe the alternative to King seemed to have come true overnight after the martyr's assassination. Even in death, King had the ability to influence the freedom struggle being waged. The rioting and destruction that followed provided an ironic epitaph to the life of this most noted disciple of nonviolence.

The BPP, according to several former Panthers and the National Commission on the Causes and Prevention of Violence, a group established by President Richard Nixon to investigate and offer recommendations about the 1960s riots, helped to keep Oakland "cool after the assassination." The group counseled Bay Area blacks to abstain from rioting because, according to it, the police were looking for a reason to shoot them.[10] Instead, the Panthers urged Oakland blacks to join the party and to work through an organization that channeled its energy in the right direction, and thereby addressed their community's needs.

A few Panthers, led by Eldridge Cleaver, instead of practicing what they preached, proceeded to enter into their first running gun battle with the police. Two days after King's assassination, Eldridge Cleaver, Bobby Hutton, the Panther's treasurer, and a host of other Panthers engaged the police in a forty-five minute shoot-out in Oakland. No scholar has determined exactly how this shootout commenced, but one of the more credible versions claims that before the shootout, an African American police informant had warned Cleaver of an impending police raid on the party's headquarters. Because they did have blacks in the police department who sometimes provided them with information, the Panthers believed this misinformation, loaded their guns into three cars, and set out to move them to different locations throughout the Bay Area. It also happened that the group was preparing for a large rally the next day and they were making preparations for that. In the process of transferring people, food, guns, and other supplies throughout East Oakland, Cleaver said he "had to take a piss real badly." He stopped to urinate in public near an intersection, "right along the driver's side," according to him. When he noticed a vehicle coming his way, he "ran around to the other side of the car" and "just continued." The vehicle turned out to be a police cruiser. According to Cleaver, the driver "threw the spotlight" on him and demanded that he

"Come out from behind there!" Everything after that was confusion, as the police claimed the Panthers fired at them and the Panthers claimed the opposite. Either way, when the shooting started, the Panthers and several non-Panthers Cleaver had recruited for the job fled the scene while returning fire. They certainly did not behave like seasoned revolutionaries, and Cleaver's public urination cannot be considered appropriate behavior as the leader of a group of self-proclaimed revolutionaries. If this had been all there was to the incident, it might be fair to characterize Cleaver's action as something other than misguided and unnecessary. But this was not all there was to it.[11]

Cleaver told one interviewer that "everybody all day was talking about taking some action" after King was killed. They discussed shooting up the town or "shooting up the cops" but these ideas were seen as too irrational so they deliberated for another day. "So we put together a little series of events to take place the next night, where we basically went out to ambush the cops," he continued. "But it was an aborted ambush because the cops showed up too soon." He remembered waiting for the police cars to approach the convoy, then they "got out and started shooting. That's what happened. People scattered and ran every which a-way." Other leading Panthers corroborated this version of events. Emory Douglas says he turned Li'l Bobby Hutton down when he called the evening before to ask if he wanted to go out and "do something" in revenge for King's murder. Panther newspaper editor Elbert "Big Man" Howard remembered giving Hutton the shotgun he used the night of the shootout. Over thirty years later, he wondered aloud to a crowd of students "why [Hutton] needed a shotgun." Hutton told Howard he was "going out on patrol," but of course the Oakland-based Panthers had stopped patrolling the police ever since the Mulford Act outlawed the public display of weapons except by law enforcement officers. The group did crisscross the city in an effort to keep blacks from rioting, but it is highly unlikely that a shotgun was necessary for that type of work. If Cleaver truthfully explained what happened that night, it seems fair to say that this small band of obviously unprepared revolutionaries, with Cleaver at the helm, deserves some responsibility for starting the shootout.[12]

Oakland officer Richard Jensen, on duty that night, was the first policeman on the scene. He remembered pulling up behind the Panther vehicle and reaching for his microphone "to run the plate." As he did this, he recalls, "I got shot in my arm, in my back, all kinds of bullets, just like the Fourth of July firecrackers going off. I must have been shot four or five times, and I slumped to the seat of the car." With bullets and glass flying everywhere, his partner "got out of the other side of the car and returned a few of the shots with his .38." He said, "It was like a war going on." Police later counted 157 holes in their car after discovering some thirteen people had been involved in the exchange.[13]

After the shooting started, Cleaver and Hutton fled in the same direction and found refuge in the basement of a nearby house. Not long thereafter, the police found them and riddled the building with bullets and teargas. The house began to fill with smoke from the gas and a rapidly deteriorating roof. For forty-five minutes, the police perforated the walls of the house with heavy gunfire. Meanwhile, Hutton still had his rifle and apparently plenty of ammunition since he returned police fire for the whole forty-five minutes. Even though the odds were clearly against him, the young revolutionary fought back. Unbeknownst to him, time and circumstances ensured the fight would not last.

At some point during the battle, one of the many teargas canisters police fired into the building hit Cleaver in the chest. Hutton removed Cleaver's shirt to check for holes or blood. Their bad luck getting worse, the house then burst into flames, compelling the two to call out to police that they wanted to surrender. Stunned, the police welcomed the offer and allowed it. Unable to breathe, Hutton and a naked Eldridge Cleaver, who disrobed to ensure authorities knew he was unarmed, emerged from the teargas-filled house.

Oakland police officer Gwen Pearson remembered seeing the two men, one of whom was naked, exit the house with their hands up and "walking about five feet apart." He recalled that several policemen "surrounded the two and began escorting them toward police cars" when he noticed "they were pushing Hutton." His partner Ralph Jennings, who had been observing from the top of a nearby building, saw that "they were shoving and kicking him." As they pushed the seventeen-year-old, he stumbled. When he stumbled, one policeman shot him, there was a pause, then several more shots erupted. Cleaver was hit in the leg and Bobby Hutton, after crawling a few feet, lay dead. The coroner's report showed that "Hutton had been shot at least six times—above the right eye, in the mouth, in the chest, in the back, in the arm, and in the legs—

all from close range." The confrontation also resulted in the wounding of two Oakland police officers. According to Pearson, who had served twenty-two years on the force, Hutton "was not trying to escape when he was shot to death." He explained that Hutton "stumbled and brought his hands down" then "there was a series of six to nine shots and Hutton was killed." Pearson told the grand jury what he witnessed but the stenographer's notes were "never transcribed from the shorthand notes and he was not called to testify." Not long after, the Alameda County grand jury issued the customary justifiable homicide verdict it reserved for blacks killed by policemen. As a result of this shootout, an Oakland judge revoked Cleaver's parole and returned him to jail. Almost immediately, the International Committee to Release Eldridge Cleaver formed to help pay the fifty thousand dollars bail set by the judge.[14] Once Cleaver emerged from jail, he feverishly worked to establish chapters in places as unfamiliar to the original Panthers as Omaha, Nebraska, and Des Moines, Iowa, to those as notable as New York City and Chicago.

The murder of Martin Luther King Jr. helped fuel the party's expansion. More and more blacks came to believe nonviolence died with King and armed self-defense represented the best approach. Indeed, most of the chapters formed in 1968 began after King's tragic death.

Even if the Panthers had been left to organize in peace, they still would have found it difficult to win the black freedom they so often talked about. As it turned out, they were not left to organize in peace. The threatening rhetoric against police officers, along with their penchant for real violence, made them a major concern of the federal government. The larger context of violence in which they operated made them a target for neutralization. James Clarke, an expert on race and crime, wrote that after King's assassination whites had increasingly become targets of a "swelling black rage." He noted that before King's murder, there had been "142 documented instances of group violence between blacks and whites." Between April 1968 and the end of 1969, "that number leaped to 659." The rioting during this period accounted for many of those confrontations, but, according to Clarke, "what is also evident in these numbers is what can be described as an undeclared war that had begun between black militants and the police. For the first time in American history, black militants and paramilitary organizations began a sustained effort to single out police officers and white supremacist organizations for attack." The

Panthers served as the unofficial ringleaders, or the "revolutionary van-guard" of these disparate organizations. Not only had they been the most charismatic, but they also proved to be the most effective at organizing young people of all races, including rich and poor whites. Realizing their potential for success and knowing the BPP could not be bought off, the federal government, via its Counter Intelligence Program (COINTEL-PRO), began slowly to destroy the organization from within. By the time the Chicago chapter was formed, the FBI had been monitoring the Panthers for a year.[15]

Beginning in February 1968, FBI agents in San Francisco, working in eight-hour shifts, began intercepting all telephone calls going into and coming out of Panther headquarters. Set up in San Francisco because it was close to BPP national headquarters, this field office became "the control center for the FBI's secret war against the Panthers." Taking note of Panther recruiting successes on the streets among gang members, drop outs, drug dealers, prostitutes, and high school and college stu-dents, FBI director J. Edgar Hoover told a Senate committee that the BPP represented "the greatest threat to the internal security of the coun-try. Schooled in Marxist-Leninist ideology and the teachings of Chinese Communist Mao Tse-Tung," he told the body of lawmakers, "its mem-bers have perpetrated numerous assaults on police officers and have engaged in violent confrontations with police throughout the country." He noted that BPP leaders had been traveling "extensively all over the United States preaching their gospel of hate and violence not only to ghetto residents but to students in colleges, universities and high schools as well!" He told this not-so-incredulous group of senators that "one out of every four black people, including 43% of those under 21, had a 'great respect' for the BPP."[16]

In turn, a worked-up Hoover directed his field agents to step up their attacks on the Panthers. Hoover's lieutenants created a "Rabble Rouser Index" and a "Black Nationalist Photograph Album" "to help local field offices identify rabble-rousers who visited their area." The bureau also cir-culated a "Racial Calendar" in order to "keep track of black nationalist type conferences and . . . racial events and anniversaries." The federal agency charged with domestic intelligence also constructed several facil-ities to be used as detention camps in case of an actual emergency. Clarke noted that the people who would be taken to these camps "included any person who, although not a member of a suspect organization, had 'revolutionary beliefs,' and might, in time of trouble, attempt to interfere with the operations of the government. He showed that "at one time . . . the FBI Security Index listed 26,174 Americans who might be locked up in time of war or emergency." [17] Clearly, some people in government believed that law and order might break down into chaos. The Panthers, on the other hand, hoped it would.

This phase of Panther growth and development was its most dramatic. The group, like Malcolm X before it, allied itself with whites who wanted to support the freedom struggle; it dropped its wholesale attacks against whites and began to emphasize more of a class analysis of society. Its emphasis on Marxist-Leninist doctrine and its repeated espousal of Maoist statements signaled the group's transition from a revolutionary nationalist to a revolutionary internationalist movement. Every Panther member had to study Mao Tse-tung's *Little Red Book* to advance his or her knowledge of peoples' struggle and the revolutionary process. Having chosen communism over capitalism, the BPP invited scorn upon itself, as the Cold War had polarized Americans into those who believed the exaggerated claims of McCarthy-types and those who insisted that the United States obey its own laws and allow its citizens to protest against a nonresponsive system. Anticommunists far outnumbered their opponents, so the Panthers had a difficult go of it. This fact was among the reasons that so few blacks joined the party. In addition, most blacks, who were overwhelmingly Christian, felt more of a connection with the advocates of nonviolence who, like Jesus, emphasized love for their enemy, and not vengeance. Nevertheless, the Panthers persisted and in the process invited a massive resistance that far surpassed the violence of the one that developed in the wake of the *Brown v. Board of Education* decision. More often than not, this resistance came in the guise of billy clubs, bullets, and other forms of overt violence. Not content simply to give up, the Panthers fought back, and in the process garnered worldwide respect while at the same time suffering hundreds of casualties and dozens of deaths. The "Free Huey" movement, though it failed in keeping Newton out of jail, helped to establish the party in all sections of the country.

The 1960s-era riots, sparked primarily by police brutality, along with continued police confrontations with blacks in the Oakland/San Francisco Bay Area made gaining an audience less daunting than it might have otherwise been. The Kerner Commission, appointed by President Johnson to study the causes of rioting in the sixties, made the following assessment:

> We have cited deep hostility between the police and ghetto com-munities as a primary cause of the disorders. . . . In Newark, in Detroit, in Watts, in Harlem—in practically every city that has experienced racial disruption since the summer of 1964—abrasive relationships between police and Negroes and other minority groups have been a major source of grievance, tension and, ulti-mately, disorder. . . . Police misconduct—whether described as bru-tality, harassment, verbal abuse, or discourtesy–cannot be tolerated even if it is infrequent. It contributes directly to the risk of civil dis-order. It is inconsistent with the basic responsibility of a police force in a democracy.[18]

Most law enforcement agencies throughout the country ignored this report and the police carried on with business as usual. The report did, however, provide some insight into some of the deeper issues that led to blacks' decisions to engage in such widespread destruction and may-hem. These riots, or more accurately, rebellions, often had political implications in that they represented a type of political response to civic leaders who had often ignored black demands for change. Though loot-ing became part and parcel of this phenomenon, it should be noted that most black businesses (and they were few) were either left untouched or, if they were burned or robbed, it was by accident.

Writer Robert Fogelson noted that "there is no doubt that the rioters damaged hundreds of buildings, destroyed millions of dollars of property, and devastated whole sections of ghettos. But neither is there any doubt that they burned stores that charged excessive prices or sold inferior goods . . . yet left homes, schools, and churches unharmed." This violent response to deplorable living conditions emerged after the mostly nonviolent civil rights protest of the early sixties failed to bring about significant change in the daily lives of blacks in the North and West. Both violence and nonviolence were used to force the power structure to pay closer attention to the needs and rights of blacks. In the

Andrew Austin educating National Guard troops about the BPP in Berkeley. The soldiers were called out by then governor Ronald Reagan in 1969. *Photo by Ducho Dennis, courtesy of It's About Time.*

end, the rioters as well as the nonviolent soldiers of the movement sought economic parity with their white counterparts and control over the institutions affecting their lives. Bobby Seale pointed out in *Seize the Time* that "the violence of the many riots that occurred before the Black Panther Party was conceived was a strength in producing an organization like the Black Panther Party and also made other organizations more determined to seek a better, more revolutionary ideology to guide the people." He added that recognized black leaders as well as potential ones "could see that so many people were getting killed just because they were without organization." In addition, Bay Area ghetto residents were publicly discussing at least seven known cases of police brutality in 1966, the year the BPP formed.[19] Seale thought that violence was good, but organized violence was even better.

In his attempt to help organize blacks' readiness to confront their tormentors with violence, Seale, along with the oratorically adept Cleaver, sought to expand Panther influence by setting up chapters in other locales. Attempting to gain support for Huey Newton and to spread the word about Bobby Hutton's death, Seale ventured north to the state of Washington, the site of the party's first chapter outside California. Picturesque Seattle is where it all started. As in all other American cities, blacks in Seattle suffered discrimination, exploitation, and an ever-present police brutality. They sought to counteract this reality and to gain control of the institutions that shaped their lives. It had been in this spirit that members of the Black Student Union (BSU) at the University of Washington invited Bobby Seale to speak at their first conference in the spring of 1968. Aaron Dixon, a member of the BSU, met Seale at this conference and soon became captain of the Seattle chapter of the Black Panther Party for Self-Defense.

Born in 1947 in Chicago to parents who had migrated there from Kentucky and Mississippi, Dixon moved to Seattle in 1957. His father, an out-of-work artist and World War II veteran-turned-communist, decided to move the family out to the far northwest when he found a job as a technical illustrator. There had been another reason for the move. "My father did not want us to grow up in Chicago," he said, "because he had three sons and a daughter and he did not want us to grow up and become involved with the Black Stone Rangers. . . . the largest gang in the country" at that time. Once they moved, he remembered how exciting it was to live around Filipinos, Japanese, Chinese, "and all the other nationalities." In 1963, Dixon "volunteered for the busing program" and became one of the first blacks to integrate a white high school in the area. This experience was the first time he had been "confronted with racism. . . . It was ugly, really ugly." As a result, he "left there and went back to [Garfield High] school in the black community . . . where Jimi Hendrix, Quincy Jones, and Bruce Lee graduated."[20]

He remembered Garfield as "a beautiful experience." It was "well-integrated with a lot of Asians who played on the football team and who played instruments like they were black. The Filipinos acted like they were black, the Japanese acted like they were black and to this very day we're real good friends with them," he reminisced. Thinking out loud, he said, "as a matter of fact, one of them joined the Black Panther Party when it started," apparently referring to Richard Aoki.

When asked what made him join the party, Dixon explained that it had a lot to do with his "parents' history and listening to the stories they had to tell." His paternal grandmother told them stories "about her grandmother in slavery and how she got her foot chopped off" for trying to escape a Mississippi plantation. On his mother's side, he heard another "series of stories of a little black slave woman who ended up having all these kids." It was not clear whether Dixon meant that one of his ancestors had been repeatedly raped by a white man, as was common during the period of slavery in Mississippi, or whether she had been used to produce slave children for the master's profit, equally common at the time. His father told stories of being in the army "with all these other Chicago boys" who had been stationed in Mississippi for boot camp. According to him, "they had a riot and had to ship them out of there." No doubt there were many racial confrontations in Mississippi between blacks and whites during the war. Camp Shelby, south of Hattiesburg, had been one of the main training camps, and when northern blacks encountered southern racism, fights, melees, and often killing resulted. When his father returned to America after the war, "he joined the Communist Party. All of that had a lot to do with us joining," Dixon said.[21]

Another reason why he joined the party, he said, was "the fact that we watched the civil rights movement unfold on TV." He remembered that "all my generation watched the assassination of JFK, who to a lot of black people represented a change and some hope. And Medgar Evers got killed, MLK got killed, Robert Kennedy got killed." Those "four political assassinations in one decade . . . helped to shape all of us," he recalled. After graduating from high school in 1967, he and his brother Elmer Dixon joined a series of organizations. Within a year, they had joined the local Student Nonviolent Coordinating Committee (SNCC) chapter and the Black Student Union at the University of Washington. They did "a lot stuff around SNCC," he remembered.

He noted they "were always looking for something" so they could do their part in the black struggle. "SNCC and the BSU were just vehicles to get us to the next level. We were never satisfied with those organizations," he said. The Black Panther Party "really captured our imagination as a real down-to-earth organization" and "seemed to have all the elements that were important." He talked of King's assassination and the impact it had on him and his close friends. Like other black youth, he began to question the usefulness of nonviolence. "The fact that MLK died," he explained, "made us feel right about wanting to be able to say we'll risk our lives" for black freedom. Emphasizing his point, he said they thought "'yeah!, we'll do it.' It was just time for that."[22]

Dixon's path to the party was strikingly similar to that of thousands of other black youths. Desiring to participate but not convinced that nonviolence would bring them the type of freedom they thought they deserved, this group of enterprising young people sought to end oppression in all its forms. As in other parts of the country, Seattle youth came to know police brutality personally and they agreed with the party's early emphasis on the gun as a tool of liberation. Like their comrades eight hundred miles to the south of Seattle, they turned self-defense and self-determination into an infectious rallying point in the Evergreen State.

Organized in April 1968, the Seattle Black Panther Party quickly came to represent those interests important to the black community. Taking on a number of projects brought in recruits and, in the process, the party established a foothold in Seattle's majority black areas. Dixon recalled that "we had about three hundred members in a month, they just came and signed up." As in other areas, they were required to organize by using the Ten Point Program. Also like other chapters, the Seattle branch chose to focus first on education and self-defense—two things sure to endear the party to an embattled and subjugated black community.

The Seattle chapter worked to create committees composed of black residents who had the power to control the hiring and firing process in the schools their children attended. They also wanted to create an avenue through which they could become involved in curriculum planning. The Panthers complained that the lack of black history classes in school meant black students were not getting an adequate education and were not learning about themselves. In March 1968, Aaron Dixon, as advisor to the Black Student Union at Franklin High school, participated in a sit-in with a group of demonstrating students at Franklin. Dixon and two of the BSU leaders were arrested and taken to jail.

That June, an all-white jury convicted them of unlawful assembly. From jail, Dixon wrote "to the Black Community," that he had not received a fair trial because he had not been tried by a jury of his peers, but rather by an entirely white jury that had "no understanding of the average reasoning man of the Black community." Arguing that he had been a victim of "law and order" and "the racism inherent in the American justice system," the Seattle captain explained "the Black Panther Party is against this blatant outgrowth of racism" and that black people "must unite before we can do more." The Panthers' willingness to work with students and community members made them a group that many blacks relied on to help solve problems.[23]

Dixon remembered one incident where a black mother, who had children in a nearly all-white high school, called on them for help. Her children had first been harassed, then beaten by white toughs at the school. "She called on Monday," he said, and "wanted us to come out to the school because the principal wouldn't do anything." The Panthers first informed the woman that they could not make the trip. After all, they were busy with other community concerns like organizing police patrols "to keep an eye on the cops" and demanding "a civilian police-review board, composed of members chosen by the community, with the power to subpoena, obtain police records, and indict cops for brutality." The Panthers had also held several "Free Huey" rallies. Their smartest step, however, had been to organize a grassroots movement and to present two candidates for the state legislature, E. J. Brisker and Curtis Harris, to run for seats in Washington's Thirty-seventh District. They believed at the time that these activities precluded them from helping the pleading mother.[24]

The woman persisted, however, and according to Dixon, "called Monday, Tuesday, Wednesday, and Thursday. And then she called Friday." He remembered that "on Friday, about four or five mothers called saying their kids were getting beat and would we please do something." The Panthers finally relented and agreed to go to the school. Dixon noted that there were "thirteen Panthers in the office and everybody had rifles and shotguns and got in their cars and drove out there." He remembered that some thirty or so policemen were already at the school when they arrived, possibly tipped off by one of the dozens of informants who had joined the party. A sergeant stopped him and said "hey Dixon, you can't take those loaded weapons in there!" Dixon's reply was that the guns were not loaded, "which meant that there wasn't a bullet in the chamber, but they *were* loaded and we walked right on in." Once they entered the school, the Panthers almost immediately encountered the principal in the hall. According to Dixon, "he started running and the brothers went and got him." The principal did what most people would do after seeing thirteen armed men walking the school halls. They caught the principal, took him into an empty room, "sat him down and told him he'd better start protecting those black kids because we were going to protect them. He said okay and we had no more problems after that."

The armed Panthers, satisfied their mission had been accomplished, walked out of the school, entered their cars, and drove carefully as the police trailed them to the black community.[25] "But they didn't do anything," recalled Dixon.

Although the police failed to do anything that day, they did not choose that option every time they encountered the young revolutionaries. On July 29, some eight squad cars arrived at Panther headquarters armed with a search warrant bearing an incorrect address. They were looking for two stolen typewriters. Entering the Panther office, they immediately noticed the two typewriters sitting on a desk, but they rifled through Panther files before they examined the equipment. Once the officers were satisfied the two typewriters were what they had come for, they handcuffed captain Aaron Dixon and Curtis Harris, his co-captain. The police took both men to jail and held them without charges. "My arrest was a bizarre sight," said Dixon, "as the twenty to thirty local gestapo stormed the Panther office and searched around looking through everything and anything."[26]

Residents of the black community immediately caught word of the arrests and began to gather around Panther headquarters, where BPP leaders held a hastily planned press conference. The press conference was short and outlined the chronology of what had happened earlier in the day. Later that evening, blacks held a large protest rally in the community while whites held an equally large demonstration in front of the Seattle public safety building. This building included the police department and jail where Dixon and Harris were being held. As the demonstration unfolded in front of the jail, according to a committee arranged to defend the Panthers, "a cop squirted mace in the face of Aaron Dixon's brother, Elmer Dixon, as he was about to address the demonstrators." A police officer also "slugged" a "white protestor." Predictably, these incidents led to more trouble later in the evening.

That night, the police and members of the black community scuffled as the police tried to break up another unplanned demonstration. Dixon reminisced that the arrests "opened up a series of attacks on the racist dog police by the Black people of the Black community." During the melee, two black youths and seven policemen suffered injuries. In their efforts to quell the disorder, the police employed teargas. When the demonstrators fled the teargas canisters, they broke a number of windows in the downtown area and smashed the windshields of several police cars. Amazingly, the police arrested no one.[27]

The following morning, authorities released Curtis Harris without charge. Dixon, however, remained in jail on a charge of grand larceny by possession "as the head of an organization in whose office an allegedly stolen typewriter was found." The court set Dixon's bail at three thousand dollars, an amount his attorney, Michael Rosen of the American Civil Liberties Union, could not get the judge to reduce. The presiding judge turned down Rosen's plea because of Dixon's "lack of stability." He allegedly made this claim because of "the fact that Dixon was unemployed and unmarried." Released on bail, Dixon returned to the community and continued to organize around the Ten Point Program.[28]

Because "a lot of people were calling the office for different stuff," Dixon said, the Seattle Panthers often found themselves intervening in a plethora of situations. In addition to dealing with police/community relations, Dixon remembered they were sometimes called for "domestic disputes, landlord disputes, you name it. It kind of got out of hand," he said, "because people were calling for everything." The Seattle captain related a story about helping a tenant who had gotten into a dispute with her landlord. "The landlord had taken the door off the apartment," he recalled, "because they hadn't paid their rent." Because Seattle is often wet and cold, the Panthers saw how the missing door made comfort and safety problematic for the renters. Armed as usual, a group of Panthers "went to the landlord's house and got the door and carried the door down the street and put it back on the apartment." He pointed out that neither they nor the renters had any more problems with that particular landlord.[29]

The Seattle Panthers were not immune from the violence that surrounded their comrades in other cities. In fact, on some occasions, they did not follow party protocol and acted on their own. In 1968, they too had been affected by the death of Martin Luther King Jr. and the many riots that ensued that spring and summer. Dixon remembered there had

Seattle Black Panthers at the state capitol in Olympia, Washington. *Courtesy of the Washington State Archives.*

been riots in Seattle as well and they "led to continuous civil disobedience." Dixon recounted that Panther members, blacks not in the party, Asians, poor whites, and Hispanics participated in the riots that swept Seattle between 1968 and 1970. He remembered that *"Newsweek* used to have a chart of the cities that had the most bombings, fire bombings, and the most sniping. Seattle was number one in firebombing and number two in sniping." When asked what role the party or its members played in these incidents, Dixon responded, "probably 99 percent." He laughed shyly. "It was not necessarily something the party was engaged in, or supposed to be engaged in, but it was an opportunity for us to get back at the racist establishment." In a California state government report entitled *Target for Terrorists—an assortment of bombers zero in on business,* E. Patrick McGuire corroborated Dixon's statement when he noted that Seattle "led the nation in bombings-per-capita" and that it experienced "more than forty-five bombings during the first half of 1970 alone." According to the report, law enforcement officials, pointing out what Dixon and thousands of blacks already knew, believed "a large number" of bombings could be "traced to anger and frustration over social issues (the Vietnam War, racial conflict, etc.)."[30]

That party members in Seattle participated in violent uprisings along with hundreds of others should come as no surprise. Their condition was as bad as that of poor blacks in all parts of the country. They too had been discriminated against and denied educational and employment opportunities based on something as inane and irrelevant as the color of their skin. Inspired by the civil rights movement, they believed that stronger action would speed up the coming of that day when all people were free to grow and develop as much as their talents allowed them. Of course, they were wrong in this estimation—significant social change remained years away. Sensing their miscalculation, some activists began to conclude that greater levels of violence on their part would usher in a time when all oppressed people fought together and won their long-hoped-for freedom. At least Eldridge Cleaver and many of his comrades thought this to be the case.

Despite continued black calls for equality, the 1968 Democratic Convention, convened on August 26 in Chicago, went a long way in helping to elect Richard Nixon president. The problem with thinking that armed action helped solve black problems is that whites, both in government and in the suburbs, had had enough of black demands and the violence that seemed to be associated with them. By 1968, a major backlash against black activism had taken shape. The murder of Martin Luther King Jr. and the government's failure to prosecute the shooter, even though FBI officials knew who did it, was just one example of this backlash. The election of Nixon to the presidency signaled the beginning of the end of the reform era that had begun in the years following World War II.

The Democratic National Convention took place in an environment close to open war. Precipitously, Chicago experienced upheavals even before convention delegates came to town. Massive rioting after the King assassination resulted in the deaths of four blacks and serious injuries for almost a hundred more. Mayor Richard Daley instructed his policemen to "shoot to kill any arsonist" and to "shoot to maim or cripple anyone looting a store in our city." That same month students marching to protest the Vietnam War met billy-club-swinging policemen intent on causing serious harm. Daley's spokesman told a reporter "these people have no right to demonstrate or express their views." Once the most promising

Democratic candidate, Robert Kennedy, brother of the martyred John F. Kennedy, was shot and killed in Los Angeles in early June after defeating Eugene McCarthy in the California primary, Daley became even more determined to keep the peace. As a result, he placed his twelve thousand-man police force on twelve-hour shifts and called up six thousand National Guardsmen and an equal number of regular Army troops, who brought with them flamethrowers, grenade launchers, bayonets, gas dispensers, bazookas, rifles, and .30-caliber machine guns.[31]

The ten thousand activists headed to town seemed not to fear this buildup. Mostly college students, they had either worked to elect the dead Kennedy or had supported Senator Eugene McCarthy, who ran on a platform of continuing to fund social programs and bringing peace to Southeast Asia. Still others supported Vice President Hubert Humphrey. None of them would win. On August 26, the first night of the convention, pandemonium broke out.

Black and white delegates from Georgia engaged in a fist fight that spread through much of the convention hall. Conservatives and liberals shouted at each other and threw paper and ice back and forth. A policeman who had been attempting to quell the ruckus slugged CBS reporter Dan Rather and knocked him to the floor. For this, Walter Cronkite labeled the police thugs. The whole thing was captured on television; it sickened many Americans.

Meanwhile, some of the out-of-town protesters attempted to erect a campsite in Lincoln Park when Mayor Daley's curfew went into effect at eleven at night. Police shot teargas into the park and charged the crowd, again with billy clubs swinging. Bystanders, couples going out to dinner, and nearly thirty reporters and cameramen felt the wrath of the Chicago Police Department. The scene was repeated the following night, when the activists assembled at Grant Park and were again met by the Chicago police and the Illinois National Guard. When a group of young men removed the United States flag from a pole and raised a red shirt in its place, the police charged and people scattered. They reassembled across the street from the Chicago Hilton, the hotel that housed convention delegates. When the group marched down Michigan Avenue and approached the police line, the police launched teargas at them and once again began beating every protester they could lay hands on. Before it all ended, policemen had used so much teargas that the vice president had to leave his suite because the gas had infiltrated the vents and floated throughout the building. While more than ninety million Americans watched on television, news reporters, the elderly, doctors, nurses, and politicians were beaten mercilessly by the police. One journalist wrote that "some tried to surrender by putting their hands on their heads" but "as they were marched to vans to be arrested, they were rapped in the genitals by the cops' swinging billies." One activist accurately concluded that "this convention elected Richard Nixon president of the United States tonight."[32]

The massive resistance had come full circle. King's death led to the resurrection of white supremacy as a platform on which to campaign, which had been popular since the early years following the Civil War. The domestic and international policies of the United States had come into sharp conflict with much of the Third World, all of which is non-white. Vietnam represented this policy abroad, while the open attacks on protesters and protest organizations in the United States signaled the government's willingness to use any means necessary to maintain the status quo and the profits that came along with it. When the Panthers emerged, they were able to join a quickly growing movement that sought to bring about revolutionary change in the United States. Change, however, did not come easily and the Panthers, not quite prepared for the onslaught, reaffirmed this fact through years of struggle. Seale and others had traveled to Chicago to throw their lot in with men and women who wanted withdrawal from Vietnam and freedom for black and other oppressed people. In the process, and in the eyes of the establishment, they became a part of the problem, and Richard Daley was sure he had a solution for it.

Nobody wanted to blame Daley for the upheaval he clearly instigated. After all the mayhem had ended and the delegates returned home, city officials busied themselves trying to determine the culprit. The videotapes showing policemen brutally beating young and old alike did not figure into their deliberations. No one accused Mayor Daley of creating the conditions for the violence. In the end, a group of college students and college dropouts, called Yippies (for Youth International Party), led by the likes of Abbie Hoffman and Jerry Rubin, received the blame. Apparently they had given speeches urging activists to riot. They, however, were not the only ones to be blamed for the unrest.

As a result of a fiery speech he made during a protest rally at the 1968 Democratic convention in Chicago, an Illinois court leveled federal conspiracy charges against BPP Chairman Bobby Seale. The court accused the Panther leader, along with Tom Hayden, Abbie Hoffman, and a host of other ranking white leftists, of violating "laws forbidding interstate travel to foment riots and disorder." Seale and seven others, who became known as the Chicago Eight, were blamed for causing the now infamous "police" riots in which dozens of activists were beaten and several were killed.

After asking Seale to behave himself numerous times, Judge Julius Hoffman ordered bailiffs to chain the Panther leader to his seat, to gag him, and to seal his mouth with duct tape. The legendary Chicago conspiracy trial ended in October 1970 with a dismissal of the conspiracy charges, but Judge Hoffman charged all the defendants with contempt and Seale served three months in jail.[33] Like his comrade-in-arms Newton, he and his case(s) became causes célèbres.

A month after Seale's arrest on charges of inciting riot, the Newton trial ended. The "Free Huey" movement had reached a level where people throughout the world had begun to pay attention to what happened to the BPP. Panthers succeeded in convincing many people at home and abroad that blacks had indeed been treated like colonial subjects. They insisted to all that they had a right to defend themselves. They pointed out that the same day as the shootout that ended in Newton's arrest, the police shot and killed an unarmed seventy-year-old black man in Palo Alto, across the Bay from Oakland. They shot him in the back because they claimed he looked "suspicious." In a move that surprised no one, a coroner's inquest ruled the killing "justifiable homicide." A Panther spokesperson said "it was precisely to put a stop to this kind of terrorism that Huey organized the Panthers—around the issue of self-defense."

"If the Panther party was out to kill cops," one reporter noted, "then they have missed thousands of opportunities." On the contrary, the Panthers sought to educate ghetto residents about the need for protection to keep the police from killing them. They could hardly be blamed for wanting to stay alive.

Taking their protest to the courthouse where Newton's trial unfolded, the Panthers made excellent copy. Bedecked in their black uniforms and sporting stylish afros, they, along with other groups like the

Brown Berets, a Mexican organization with similar goals, stood across from and around the courthouse to show their support for Newton. Marching around the courthouse with their gigantic Panther flags waving in the wind, they chanted their songs. The most notable, and by extension, most ominous, had one line that said: Blacks is Beautiful—Free Huey!—Set our Warrior Free—Free Huey! With hundreds of people chanting the lines at the same time and carrying large placards reading "the Sky's the Limit," they seemed like more than a band of militants. The gospel-like sound of the chant gave their cause a spiritual dimension that left many onlookers awestruck. Their seriousness, however, was not lost on the hundreds of police officers who watched as they guarded the courthouse.[34]

At every entrance there were armed, helmeted deputies with sidearms and batons at the ready. They patrolled the halls of the courthouse in uniform and in plain clothes. Policemen with high-powered rifles stood on all the rooftops surrounding the courthouse. Everybody, every day, who entered the courthouse during the trial endured a thorough search. No violence occurred and no one attempted to "Free Huey" physically. Cleaver told one reporter that the Panthers' actions had been based on the resources they had. "If we could take Huey out of jail forcefully we would," he explained, "but right now this simply is not possible."[35] With no choice, Newton stood trial and was forced to leave the decision about whether he went to the gas chamber in the hands of ten white jurors and a Hispanic, all led by a lone black juror who served as foreman. Newton believed it had been the black man who insisted on a verdict of manslaughter and thereby helped the Panther avoid California's death penalty. The group's luck did not end there.

Eldridge Cleaver left jail in June on a writ of habeas corpus. He had been jailed after the Hutton shootout for violation of parole. Superior Court Judge E. Sherwin noted that "the peril to his parole status stemmed from no failure of personal rehabilitation, but from his undue eloquence in pursuing political goals." In an effort to show how disgusted he was with police misconduct, he released the ex-felon on twenty-five dollars bail. It was Cleaver's only victory for a long time. Upon release, Cleaver's primary goal remained that of freeing Huey Newton. In effect, according to his defense committee, "he declared war" and began speaking "all over the country, demanding that the authorities 'Free Huey or the sky is the limit.'" In a jab at his captors who tried feverishly to get the judge's decision overturned, Cleaver told one crowd that he "didn't leave anything in that penitentiary except half my mind and half my soul and that's dead there. . . . That's my debt to society and I don't owe them a thing! They don't have anything coming! Everything they get from now on, they have to take!"[36]

Cleaver, in an effort to spread the word about Newton, tried to keep every speaking engagement he scheduled. He became such a hot commodity on the lecture circuit that student groups at Berkeley invited him to teach a class in the fall of 1968. He accepted and the drama between him, university regents, and Governor Ronald Reagan began.

Cleaver signed a deal with UC Berkeley to deliver ten lectures in a course titled Social Analysis 139X, for which students received five credits. According to *The New Republic,* "some students drew up a plan to afford them insight into the pressures and problems of the ghetto through close study of one man." Then the problems started. University regents, reacting to the Panther hire, refused to grant credit for the course. Governor Ronald Reagan, elected on a "law and order" platform two years before, wanted Cleaver physically removed from the campus. Reagan had reason not to like anything Cleaver did or said, since the Panther had become famous in the Bay Area for leading large crowds of Berkeley students and other whites in "choruses of four letter obscenities mentioning Ronald Reagan," said one government report. According to Emory Douglas, Cleaver even had "nuns chanting Fuck Ronald Reagan." Meanwhile, some students and faculty joined together to oppose the Regents on this issue. The faculty supported continuance of the class by a vote of 668–114.[37]

Cleaver taught the class, but tensions remained high as students did not receive their five credits. The regents changed the rules in their effort to keep Cleaver out of the classroom. They instituted a policy that restricted all nonfaculty to a single appearance in any class. They then ruled that this policy was retroactive and applied it to Cleaver's situation. Superior Court Judge Gordon Miner later dismissed a suit compelling University of California regents to grant academic credit for the course. Before this activity reached it denouement, however, Cleaver visited campuses throughout the Bay Area, attracting recruits and publicizing the Newton case. One of these campuses was San Francisco State University, not far from Cleaver's own neighborhood.[38]

Before he gave his talk in the first week of October, 1968, San

Francisco State students made Cleaver an honorary member of the Associated Students, its legislative body. Once the formalities ended, Cleaver wasted no time hurling invective and obscenities at the "white power structure." Standing in front of two thousand students assembled on the Commons Lawn at SFSU, he took his time attacking Governor Ronald Reagan, Republican Senate candidate Max Raferty, California Assembly Speaker Jessie Unruh, Mayor Joseph Alioto of San Francisco, Chancellor Glen Dumke "and the rest of the pigs that make up the power structure." Urged on with applause, Cleaver offered the crowd a sprinkling of his four-letter gems. Referring to his jailed minister of defense, Cleaver told the crowd "if Huey isn't freed, we're going to free him and we're going to do it with guns." Noticing that one man in the crowd had not been applauding, he said "you pig, standing there in the business suit and crew cut, why aren't you clapping?" A report to Governor Reagan quoted Cleaver as having said "this is the kind of person that would go against the wall when the shooting starts." Cleaver's violence-laced oratory sometimes became even more explicit.[39]

"In order to transform the American social order," he told one crowd, "we have to destroy the present structure of power in the United States, we have to overthrow the government." He claimed that blacks had for too long "been intimidated into not speaking out clearly what our task is." That task, he said, was "the overthrow of the government, which has to be understood as being nothing but the instrument of the ruling class." He then explained to this group of college students that the Panthers were out to "smash the machinery" the ruling class used to "conduct the life of society" in their interest. "The court, the congress, the legislative and the executive branches of the state and federal government," he said, had to be destroyed "by the only means possible, because the only possible means is the means that's necessary, and the only means possible is the violent overthrow of the machinery of the ruling class." To clarify his point, Cleaver shouted that "that means that we will not allow the ruling class to use brutality and force upon us, without using the same force and brutality upon them."[40]

Remaining consistent, he told a crowd of 7,500 college and high school students at Sacramento State's football stadium that politicians and police officers were "criminals" and that "they have no rights which the people are bound to respect." Commenting on Johnson's announcement that he would not run for reelection, he said, "He's going to run. All the pigs are gong to run for their lives, the way Batista ran out of Cuba." They were going to run because the people were "going to rise up against them," and say, as Seale was often heard to say: "Up against the wall motherfuckers. We come for what's ours!" The Panthers' goal, he said, was "a homegrown Yankee doodle dandy version of socialism that could provide a qualitatively good life for the people." Claiming they could have another Boston Tea Party, he explained to the crowd that if this implied anarchy, then "it's better to have anarchy than a system of oppression."[41] This style and tone of language often landed the Panthers in jail or otherwise brought them trouble with the law.

The macho posturing Cleaver and his fellow comrades became famous for sometimes came back to haunt them. The FBI, having recognized the Panthers' magnetism to ghetto youth, began trailing and infiltrating the group with the help of local police departments. Before long, these agencies took Panthers off the streets, and in some cases, took their lives.[42] They wanted Cleaver to be one of the first to go.

Since Cleaver continued to build the BPP, some police and court officers insisted on returning him to jail. In late 1968, they succeeded in having Judge Sherwin's habeas corpus ruling reversed. The courts then ordered Cleaver back to San Quentin for a hearing to determine whether he had violated his parole in the April 6 shootout with police in Oakland when Bobby Hutton was killed. The prison officials concluded that he had. After the Oakland Superior Court scheduled him to report to San Quentin Prison for a parole revocation hearing, Cleaver insisted that the authorities planned to kill him in jail and chose exile instead.[43] He went first to Cuba, then finally to the newly independent north African nation of Algeria.

In late November 1968, Cleaver was due at San Francisco Police Headquarters for his return back to San Quentin. He did not show. Two thousand supporters held a vigil outside his home that night, singing and carrying signs to demonstrate their support for Cleaver's right to remain free. Many in the crowd secretly hoped Cleaver had hunkered down inside his house with a heavily armed contingent of Panthers ready to resist with force any police attempt to arrest him. According to his defense committee, "Cleaver had rejected the idea of a shootout as suicidal and had fled the country."[44]

Cleaver's contact with white radicals in the Bay Area provided him with an out. He decided to rendezvous with two friends, who "six months earlier had discussed establishing a modern-day 'underground railroad' for political fugitives and Vietnam War deserters." One of these friends had come south from his home in Canada to iron out the details, and when they finished they gave Cleaver the code name "Football." Less than three days later at "touchdown. . . . the Canadian waited at the end of the customs immigration turnstile in the Montreal airport when Football arrived." In an elaborate disguise, Cleaver wore a business suit and carried an attaché case. A brown derby and pencil mustache completed the facade and the soon-to-be-fugitive passed through customs undetected. Once he entered the restroom, his Canadian friend followed and they spoke briefly at the urinal. Exiting the bathroom in unison, the two walked right past "the airport office of the Royal Canadian Mounted Police and drove to a safe house downtown."[45]

Having made sure they had not been followed, the Montreal radicals a few days later, "set up a clandestine meeting with a Cuban emissary at a Montreal café, but the rendezvous flopped when the bewildered [Cuban] emissary indicated he had never heard of Eldridge Cleaver or the Black Panther Party." Not discouraged by this setback and the half dozen or so that followed, Cleaver's helpers succeeded in getting "their message through to the Cuban authorities: Football was on his way to Cuba—and much later, to Algeria."[46]

Cleaver's exit ushered in a new phase of development for the party. Because of its activities, it suffered increased police harassment, incarceration, and death. The party also traded in the nationalist mantra and become internationalist. In the process, it also discarded the leather jackets and berets. Too many people dressed like Panthers got into trouble with the law, thereby giving the party an even worse public image. Newton dictated that the Panther uniform only be worn for funerals, rallies, and other special occasions. The party also made alliances with black, white, Asian, Hispanic, and Native American organizations. Soon it designated itself the vanguard and began its attempt to lead the masses toward revolution. Its members were thrust onto the front lines of a war that left dozens jailed for life, many more permanently exiled, uncounted numbers psychologically damaged, and nearly thirty of their number dead, killed by law enforcement officers or their assigns.

CHAPTER 6

Unjustifiable Homicides

FRED HAMPTON, THE RISING CHICAGO leader of the Panthers, possessed a charisma and effectiveness that won him the uncoveted honor of being placed on the FBI's Rabble Rouser Index, a monitoring program set up in August 1967 to "identify individuals prominent in stirring up civil disorders." Born in Shreveport, Louisiana, in 1948, his only crime had been to organize high school students to protest their grievances. Hampton still struck fear in the hearts of those who did not like the idea of armed black men and women airing their grievances so belligerently. His charisma and oratorical skills did not bode well for local, city, and state officials because of his ability "to persuade people that there was injustice," according to former attorney general Ramsey Clark. As late as 1966, Hampton thought nonviolence could be used to achieve certain goals. In suburban Maywood, on the outskirts of Chicago where he grew up, he helped to stave off a violent riot when he persuaded some five hundred young people to march nonviolently in protest against the community's all-white swimming pool. By the time he joined the Panthers, however, Hampton had come to believe nonviolence hurt rather than helped in the struggle for equality and that all people were free to assert their constitutional and human right of self-defense.[1]

Significantly, Hampton stood next in line for national leadership of the BPP. Huey Newton and Bobby Seale waited in jail, as they both faced murder charges. Seale, after being acquitted in the Chicago conspiracy trial, had been framed by FBI and local police agents in New Haven, Connecticut, in the wake of the *provocateur*-induced murder of New York Panther Alex Rackley. Meanwhile, Eldridge Cleaver lived in self-imposed exile in Algeria, and chief of staff David Hilliard remained under indictment for having threatened to kill Richard Nixon. In Los Angeles, leaders John Huggins and Bunchy Carter had been murdered. The entire leadership cadre of the New York State chapter—twenty-one people—languished in jail on ridiculously high one hundred thousand dollar bonds for conspiring to blow up department stores, police stations, banks, botanical gardens, and other structures in New York City (this subject will be examined in the next chapter). Consequently Hampton, with his impressive speaking ability and dynamic leadership, represented the next best choice for national leadership. According to the *Chicago Tribune*, in late 1969 Hampton "spent almost two weeks on the west coast, conferring with top Panther leaders on ways to revamp the party." Not long after this visit, Chicago police and FBI agents finalized plans for the young leader's execution. His silence was mandatory if the FBI were to achieve its goal of destroying the BPP by eradicating the group's leadership. According to one author, it had been precisely because of "the eloquence of its leaders" that the FBI "placed a high priority on actions to sabotage and to discredit" the group.[2]

Not willing to allow the Chicago BPP to grow to its full potential, the local and federal agents sought to cripple the group, which by 1969 had attained widespread popularity in the black community and among white students. This desire to eliminate the organization and its influence manifested itself in pent-up frustrations and murderous intentions. Local and federal authorities decided to use an illegally obtained search warrant to look for weapons as their pretext to enter Hampton's residence. Utilizing a floor plan provided them by FBI informant William O'Neal and supported by fourteen of Chicago's finest, Sgt. Daniel Groth, commander of the Special Prosecutions Unit created to fight gangs, proceeded to launch a massive assault on Fred Hampton's apartment at 2337 West Monroe Street. The extraordinary violence directed at the individuals in this apartment reminded some Panthers who served in the armed services of their tours in Vietnam.

Court records indicate that on December 4, at about four thirty in the morning, Philip Joseph "Gloves" Davis "kicked open the front door and promptly shot Mark Clark point blank in the chest with a .30 caliber M-1 carbine." Killed instantly, Clark's reflexive response discharged the shotgun he held. According to a later investigation, this shot was "the only round fired by the Panthers during the raid."[3]

Immediately following this action, Davis, a black man, and Groth shot unarmed eighteen-year-old Brenda Harris, who lay asleep in a front room bed. The attacking police then went after their intended target.

According to court transcripts, Gorman and Davis, using automatic sub-machine guns, sprayed forty-two shots in the direction of Hampton's bed. Amazingly, only one of the slugs hit Hampton. The second sub-team crashed through the back door as officer Edward Carmody and another unidentified officer entered Hampton's bedroom. They had the following exchange: "That's Fred Hampton. . . . Is he dead? Bring him out . . . He's barely alive; he'll make it." After this exchange, the raiders and the apartment's occupants heard two shots, "both of which were fired point blank into Hampton's head as he lay prone," according to FBI scholars Ward Churchill and Jim Vander Wall. Carmody then stated "he's good and dead now." According to Kenneth O'Reilly, both "bullets exited below Hampton's left ear and through his left throat, and were never found." By the time the raid ended, the police had shot Doc Satchel, Panther minister of health, five times with a machine gun, leaving him in the hospital for a month; Blair Anderson three times—in both thighs and in the base of his penis; and seventeen-year-old Verlina Brewer twice—once in the left buttock and once in the left knee. The police then proceeded to beat the wounded Panthers. Afterward they "dragged [them] bodily to the street" and arrested them on charges of attempted murder and aggravated assault.[4] According to one American Civil Liberties Union lawyer, the police dropped those charges after they struck a deal in which the grand jury declined to return any indictments against the police in exchange for their dropping the attempted murder charges against the seven Panthers who survived the raid.[5] Notably, the police also never produced the alleged illegal weapons they sought.

The murders of Fred Hampton and Mark Clark clearly demonstrate how local police departments and FBI offices worked in tandem to eliminate the BPP as a viable political alternative to the Republican and Democratic parties. Directed from FBI headquarters and with the full knowledge and support of the executive branch, this onslaught aimed at the Panthers was part of a nationwide effort to destroy the organization. Using tactics from harassment arrests and physical surveillance to long-term imprisonment and outright murder, the FBI, through its Counter Intelligence Program, decimated the BPP, forcing it to take a more reformist direction.

Founded in 1956 to combat the alleged threat of domestic communism, COINTELPRO employed these tactics to subdue radicals and other groups and to convince them not to question the establishment and its policies. The government's implementation of this program disrupted and destroyed both militant and moderate individuals and organizations whether they used violent or nonviolent means to protest. This program almost always spawned violence. Particularly, it targeted revolutionaries like Stokely Carmichael, H. Rap Brown, and Maxwell Stanford. It also infiltrated and disrupted nonviolent groups like the Southern Christian Leadership Conference formed by Martin Luther King Jr., Elijah Muhammad's Nation of Islam, and even Lyndon Johnson's Community Action and Head Start programs.[6] Government efforts to disrupt even nonviolent law-abiding organizations demonstrate that some high-ranking and powerful officials sought to discourage any changes in the status quo. While the BPP clearly supported violence in some cases, a significant amount of that violence resulted from the implementation of official government policies. This fact is perhaps the single most important element in understanding the truncated life span of the BPP.

Undoubtedly, the existence of any organization dedicated to significant social change ran counter to the FBI's goals. Mumia Abu-Jamal, a former Philadelphia Panther currently imprisoned as a result of COINTELPRO, believed that the program "was a codification for white supremacy in America because the function of the FBI was to preserve white political, social, and economic supremacy in America." He added that, "in essence, when one looks at the aims and objectives of the federal government through the FBI by way of the COINTELPRO program, what one really sees is a war against black America."[7] Mumia's conclusion, while disconcerting, received a measure of confirmation in the 1980s and 1990s after scholars and other experts engaged in in-depth investigations of COINTELPRO.[8] Some of these authors include Ward Churchill and Jim Vander Wall as well as Kenneth O'Reilly, Noam Chomsky, and the federal government itself. They discovered that FBI agents, often making racist comments as they went along, infiltrated and disrupted every progressive organization in the country. This government infiltration took place whether the organization was national or local, black, white, red, brown, yellow, or other.

Although the bureau formed COINTELPRO in 1956 to guard against the domestic communist menace of the post-World War II era, the agency expanded the program in 1967 to address the black militant threat to the status quo in the United States and abroad. A July 20, 1997, article in the *New York Times* described COINTELPRO as "a campaign of domestic spying, psychological warfare, and dirty tricks."[9] Its architects, however, said the program's goals were to:

1. Prevent a coalition of militant black nationalist groups . . .

2. Prevent the rise of a messiah who could unify and electrify a militant nationalist movement . . . Martin Luther King, Stokely Carmichael, and Elijah Muhammad all aspire[d] to this position . . .

3. Prevent violence on the part of black nationalist groups . . .

4. Prevent militant black nationalist groups and leaders from gaining respectability by discrediting them . . . [and]

5. Prevent the long-range growth of militant black nationalist organizations, especially among youth.[10]

Clearly, J. Edgar Hoover desired the implementation of a plan that ensured that blacks stayed in their place. Violence-prone or not, FBI agents stopped at nothing to prevent the development of political self-sufficiency on the part of black Americans. The fact that the FBI's director held considerable animosity toward blacks and the struggle for equality figured heavily into the agency's decision to use violence in eliminating any militant threat, particularly from the BPP. This policy of violence turned lethal in Chicago, where blacks who were new to the city and the ones who came before them realized they could run from virulent racism, but they certainly could not hide from it.

Southern blacks, primarily from Mississippi, migrated to the Windy City during and after World War II, pulled by the lure of jobs and a better life and pushed by widespread racial violence, racism, bigotry, extremely low wages, poverty, and segregation. When they moved into cities, whites left for suburban areas, leaving the old city cores to decay and to become mired in vice and violence. The police, however, remained, and they made sure these newcomers and their veteran cousins understood who was in charge. They achieved this goal through violence and intimidation.

For example, in the fall of 1969, the Chicago police arrested a man on domestic battery charges and in the process shoved a billy club into his genitals. In response, the man bit the policeman, as he had already been handcuffed, to make him stop. The arresting officer then took him to the station and told him that "I'll teach you to bite a policeman." He then had two fellow officers "[take] the man into another room where they started beating, kicking, and stomping" their still-handcuffed prisoner. The victim, Arthur Cannon, tried to kick back, at which point about "five more policemen" joined in and started kicking him in the stomach and jumping "up and down on his head." Cannon heard one officer say "I like them to holler" and when Cannon screamed in pain, the same person said "That's more like it." When his wife Annie saw him in court she almost fainted at the sight of his badly disfigured face. This type of brutality and sadism is what inspired the BPP to act. Ridgley Hunt, the *Chicago Tribune* correspondent who wrote the story about this incident, surmised "that is police brutality, a practice as old as the Bow Street Runners, as widespread as sin, as widely misunderstood as human nature." He concluded that "the savagery and barbarism of these assaults is not to be compared with the [1968 Chicago Democratic] convention riots, which at least occurred under the bright lights of the television cameras in full view of the public. These occur in secret, and in secret they remain, infinitely more sinister and horrible."[11]

Another case is worth mentioning. In this one, which happened around the same time, the police arrested Edward Shanks, a fifty-five-year-old security guard, for failure to use his turn signal one night after he left work. The police handcuffed him, threw him in the back of an unmarked car, then kicked him in the face and about the body. Having knocked out his dental bridge, the police then proceeded to try to kick him in the groin, whereupon he kept his legs closed and curled up into the fetal position to avoid this torture. They continued beating him until they reached the station, where they pushed the handcuffed Shanks down a flight of stairs. This Star Detective and Security Agency employee's first arrest kept him out of work for six months, and according to him, he had not regained the use of one arm six months later. The court did, however, impose upon Shanks a twenty-five dollar fine for resisting arrest. Windy City law enforcement officials had developed a habit of brutalizing members of their black constituency.

In January 1969, a black Chicago police officer accosted Mrs. Robert L. Barnett for not having a license plate. She explained to him that it had been stolen and that she had notified the police, who in turn gave her a receipt on which to drive legally until she secured a new one. Despite this official written excuse, the officer "dragged her across the street and shoved her against the car so violently that she hit her head." After her face hit the back door, "her glasses fell to the ground, whereupon the officer kicked them away, slammed the woman against the front of the car, then threw the lady on the ground and put his knee in her stomach." Reporter Ridgley Hunt added that "many policemen and reporters believe that black cops surpass whites in harassing black citizens."[12]

In addition to knocking two women (a mother and her daughter, one of whom was pregnant) unconscious during a domestic quarrel, the Chicago police arrested and beat Mr. and Mrs. Clinton Marshall in a quarrel at a restaurant. They then took Mr. Marshall to the police station and beat him again. Marshall said the policeman told him "if you so much as open your mouth I'll shoot your brains out." The officers then transported him to the hospital, where the doctors used eight stitches to sew up the cut in his lip.[13]

The reporter accurately noted that "when a brutal cop beats up a citizen for little or no reason, he will file charges of disorderly conduct, resisting arrest, and either aggravated assault or aggravated battery." He adds that "disorderly conduct is a nebulous charge, hard to disprove, and a logical choice if you can't think of a better reason for arresting a man. Sometimes it means that the defendant had a beard or a loud mouth or was a black man dating a white girl."[14]

Even black policemen in Chicago weighed in on the racism rampant throughout the city and especially taking hold in the police department. Renault Robinson, president of the Afro-American Patrolmen's League, an organization created to address discrimination in the Chicago Police Department, noted that the police department was "racist" and "the result of racism in the police force [was] selective law enforcement, with blacks treated one way and whites another. Noting that even though there were more white criminals in Chicago, he said "more blacks [were] arrested than whites. . . . More blacks for instance, [were] arrested for vice crimes than whites; however, more whites [were] involved in vice crimes than blacks. Whites even control[ed] the vice in the black community," he said. Continued police brutality was "of value to the power structure" because it maintained "that fear thing in black people and [kept] them in their places, instead of seeking their rights."

Insisting that this brutal treatment cease, Renault said his organization could "stop brutality against black people" because, in addition to knowing what was going on, they carried guns and had "the same police powers as white policemen." Renault concluded that "organized black policemen represent black police power" and this power, "with the black community behind it represents a real threat to the power structure's control over the lives of black people."[15] Their outcry did little to stop police brutality in Chicago. Therefore, the BPP found fertile soil in which to grow and flourish.

The Illinois chapter of the BPP, which became one of the largest, strongest, and best known, originated in the months following King's assassination. According to Chicago resident Bobby Rush, currently a Democratic congressman from Illinois, he traveled to Oakland in October 1968 to meet with minister of information Eldridge Cleaver, chairman Bobby Seale, chief of staff David Hilliard and field marshal Don Cox. Rush, a member of SNCC at the time, asked permission to start a BPP branch but was denied, since the Panther leaders told him that "there was already a chapter existing in Chicago and they didn't need another chapter." Rush thought their position "arrogant" because the Panthers they referred to "weren't really doing anything" and "had no office" and could not be contacted. He lived in Chicago and, as an activist, knew the needs and aspirations of the black community. Nevertheless, he returned to the Windy City and continued to organize without the Panther name since he already had the support of Stokely Carmichael. According to scholar Jon Rice, "Bobby Rush, Bob Brown and a few other SNCC activists began touring local city college campuses, looking for recruits to form a branch of the Black Panther Party in Chicago." They found an office on Madison Avenue. Alderman Sammy Rayner, a Chicago businessman and member of the City Council, signed the lease and had the gas turned on for them. Unlike the other Panthers, according to Rush, they had a working telephone.[16]

When two Panthers, who happened to be members of the Central Committee, flying from New York to Oakland, asked a stewardess "whether or not the distance from New York to Oakland was the same as the distance form New York to Cuba," a serious problem arose. The stewardess, according to Rush, " got hysterical, ran to the captain and the captain called in and they landed that plane here in Chicago." There had recently been a rash of hijackings by militants from the United States to Cuba, so airline personnel were on alert for suspicious activity. Thinking they had planned to highjack the plane, authorities, after discovering the two were members of the BPP, took them to the Cook County jail. Apparently the two jailed Panthers called the Oakland headquarters because, according to Rush, Panthers in Oakland called him and said "look, we got two Panthers there in jail, and you're the only telephone number that we have in the city of Chicago, so would you see what's going on and take care of those guys that's in jail." Rush asserted that this incident was "how we became the official chapter of the Black Panther Party in the state of Illinois."[17] He subsequently became the minister of defense.

The other group of Panthers originated in the East Garfield area of the city by SNCC organizers Bob Brown, Drew Ferguson, and Jewel Cook, who had been "younger members of the Deacons for Defense and Justice, and local young adults, some from the Vice Lord Street gang." According to Rice, after a rally it sponsored in August, this group of Panthers and the one headed by Rush "met that afternoon and decided to merge." By this time in late 1968, Rush had already recruited nineteen-year-old Fred Hampton into the party.[18]

The Chicago chapter was still in its embryonic stage when Hampton joined. Hampton's talents as an effective organizer and "ghetto diplomat" pricked the interest of government agencies charged with preventing Panther growth and / or success. One contemporary observer noted that Hampton had previously organized "a youth chapter of the NAACP at the Proviso East High School," boosting its membership from seventeen to seven hundred. Not long after, the FBI began to monitor his activities and conversations via informants and wiretaps.[19]

Rush was "looking for a dynamic speaker" when he saw Hampton electrify a crowd of several hundred young people at a black leadership conference. "Nonviolence was fine," Hampton thundered, but "the time for self-defense" had come. Hampton had discussed the party with Los Angeles Panther Lennie Eggleston and was interested. Eggleston convinced him "that a movement that transcended race was revolutionary and original." As a result, wrote Rice, Hampton began envisioning "a revolution of the poor, composed of warriors from all 'tribes' uniting to fight the dominant power structure." When Rush, Panther deputy minister of defense, asked Hampton to join his Panther contingent, the "fast-talking, personable . . . and ambitious young man" quickly accepted.[20]

Like its counterparts in other states, the BPP in Illinois contended with the same kind of government pressure to abort its attempt to secure freedom for blacks and other oppressed minorities. In Chicago, as in other cities, the Panthers sought not only the help of radical white students and others on the left, but that of the "lumpen proletariat," that massive layer of humanity that seemed to be on the bottom, at the mercy of those who busied themselves with the exercise of freedom. They quickly found a host of souls willing to join them. The Black Disciples, a South Side gang led by Larry "King" Hoover and David Barksdale, quickly succumbed to Panther overtures. By early 1969, many area residents understood and Fred Hampton concurred that "all Black Disciples are Panthers and all Panthers are Black Disciples."[21] The Disciples had plenty of reason to ally themselves with the Panthers.

They too had been victims of police brutality and their public outcries against police heavy-handedness went unheard by the authorities. Michael Shane, a spokesman for the Disciples, noted that "previous complaints of brutality made by the group either to the Englewood district station or the police internal inspections division had been ignored." In describing the police misconduct, Shane noted that "members of the police canine corps permitted an unprovoked attack by their dogs on Inell Crawford and the following day three Disciples were clubbed with a pistol by an Englewood policeman." There were other "unprovoked beatings," he said. The *Chicago Tribune* noted that "one of the policemen involved already has had 79 brutality complaints lodged against him by the Disciples, none of which had been acted upon."[22] Hampton, then, did not have to do a whole lot of convincing to recruit the members of this street gang. The BPP did not stop there. It had the audacity to look toward this gang's more powerful and much more capable adversary, which occupied adjacent turf.

After he joined the BPP, the FBI figured that Hampton's most serious crime had been the "negotiation" of "a merger between the still-small BPP and a sprawling South Side street gang known as the Blackstone Rangers." Hampton and the Panthers sought to politicize this gang to make their organizing efforts more successful. A successful merger certainly would mean increased revenues for the BPP since the Rangers controlled much of the vice on the South Side. Initially, Panthers believed a coalition was possible because Ranger leader Jeff Fort, born in Aberdeen, Mississippi, in 1947, had for years been attempting to lead his gang toward community building by using the rhetoric of black nationalism and Black Power. His efforts in this regard had been rewarded by the federally funded Office of Economic Opportunity. Program director Sargent Shriver gave the gang $927,000 to help assist the Woodlawn Community in its war on poverty. Shriver had attempted to make good on the dictum of "maximum feasible participation" for the poor in helping to determine the politics of their community. Because this gang already enjoyed a high degree of organization and public respect, albeit forced, Hampton's influence might have been successful in molding it into a formidable political machine.[23]

There is, of course, the possibility that things could have gone awry, even under the best of circumstances. After all, the year before the Panthers emerged in Chicago, Fort had been arrested on murder charges that, while they did not stick, certainly pointed to a potential for serious violence on his part. Eugene Hairston, Fort's second in command, had also been arrested for murder while three Rangers in Shriver's poverty program had been arrested for rape.[24] OEO officials knew of these incidents but for some reason allowed the individuals to remain on the payroll.

In any case, Fort's Rangers were well-armed and predisposed to acts of violence, as are most inner-city street gangs. Senate investigations pointed out that "the Chicago police had linked the Rangers and rival gangs in Chicago to approximately 290 killings from 1965–69." One Chicago police officer told Senate investigators that "the Main 21," the Rangers' governing body, "was responsible for several ritualistic murders of black youths in areas the gang controlled." All this had been made possible by the Rangers' weaponry, which included a deadly array of rifles, shotguns, and revolvers. Just as significant, a Panther absorption of the Rangers would have more than doubled the BPP's national membership.[25] The likelihood that Hampton could have steered the group's criminal proclivities toward purely political ends, in a short period of time, was not very high. As skilled as he was, an open merger with an entity as dangerous and violence-prone as the Rangers would certainly have caused the young revolutionary great grief as gang members are generally not disposed to taking orders from individuals outside their ranks. Despite the odds against them, however, the Panthers continued to make overtures to the gun-toting lumpen elements that made up the Rangers.

By the mid-sixties, gangs like the Disciples and Rangers began shifting their attention away from fighting other gangs and police toward combating poverty, discrimination, and violent disturbances. For example, they accompanied activist Reverend Jesse Jackson and his People United to Save Humanity group when they blocked construction sites on the South Side after companies refused to hire blacks. After the Rangers showed up, blacks received jobs. The same thing occurred during a construction project at the University of Chicago campus. When Jackson tried to back off and avoid confrontation with white workers, Rangers, by then called the Black P Stone Nation, prevented Jackson from leaving and forced him to follow through with the action. Once again, blacks received construction jobs. In 1968, the Rangers had also orchestrated a "no-vote" campaign on the South Side, taking away badly needed votes from a nonresponsive Democratic machine. Because police leaders did not change their image of gangs to suit this changing reality, the mutual hostility that previously existed between the two groups increased.[26]

When the Panthers attempted to develop and maintain close relations with these changing organizations, they began to attract heavy police surveillance, simultaneously becoming subject to frequent arrests. Fred Hampton, however, had more than just the Rangers and the already-committed Disciples in mind. He intimated in a meeting with Jeff Fort that "if the Rangers joined the Panthers, then together they would be able to absorb all the other Chicago gangs." Of course, if this had occurred, Hampton might have set an important precedent, especially if he could have moved the gangs away from vice and violence to productive political organizing and grassroots community building. More important, however, such a merger would have created a more formidable, well-armed opposition to the authorities. The fact that gang members were willing to fight police fire with what they called self-defense fire led the law officers to believe that any merger with the openly "violence-prone" Panthers would result in a challenge to the gangs' already established authority. The FBI and other federal agencies had no intention of dealing with thousands of heavily armed, politically conscious youth being urged on by the revolutionary rhetoric and tactics of the BPP. Understanding this possibility, the authorities took bold and imaginative steps to prevent it.[27]

Shortly after Edward Hanrahan became Illinois state's attorney in January 1969, he set up an elite nine-man unit to deal with Chicago's gangs. It became known as the Special Prosecutions Unit and worked very closely with its city-sponsored counterpart, the Gang Intelligence Unit. Rapidly emerging as a major gang-buster, by the summer of 1969, the Special Prosecutions Unit had issued more than two hundred indictments against gang members through its establishment of a special grand jury. The charges ranged from extortion and robbery to intimidation, assault, and murder. Hanrahan relished the unit's success and continued to tout his ability to maintain law and order. In a series of public speeches and radio broadcasts, he explained to thousands how he felt about this mass of black youth, mostly of southern heritage, that had fallen afoul of the law. In a June 20, 1969, address to several hundred black females enrolled in the Neighborhood Youth Corps, he described gang members as "vicious. . . . animals unfit for society." He told the audience that he was only "trying to take the romance out of gangs and let the brutality show through." His audience booed him. Despite his unpopularity with these youth, Hanrahan earned a lot of political clout in the white community.[28] In some white minds, this enterprising public official, like Mayor Daley and President Nixon, only wanted to maintain law and order. The black population, however, felt differently.

Only fourteen percent of white Chicago residents felt there was discrimination in police treatment of blacks and whites whereas 44 percent of blacks saw that disparity. To boot, only one out of ten whites thought police treated blacks unjustly, whereas almost all (nine out of ten) blacks believed the opposite. After it became clear that most whites thought the police were doing a "very good job," Hanrahan saw no problem in adding another nine members to his special unit. These members, particularly Sgt. Daniel Groth, who commanded the December 4, 1969, raid on Hampton's residence, all had serious brutality and misconduct complaints against them.

Hanrahan's war on gangs had at first been accepted as good, but when charges of unnecessary force and excessive imprisonment mounted over time, the public's interest began to decline. Before Hanrahan knew it, criticism of his policy became commonplace. One Disciple spokesman explained that "there is no war on gangs, as the mayor [Richard Daley] states, but a war on black people." *New York Times* reporter John Kifner wrote that "unquestionably, many of the gang members were delinquents . . . and committed a number of crimes. But there were indications that contrary to official pronouncements, violent gang activity was decreasing and to many the campaign seemed questionable; in fact, one Justice Department official privately called it a 'racist purge.'" This purge resulted in a number of police-directed murders in the same neighborhood where the BPP set up its office. Some eleven blacks fell victim to police bullets prior to the Hampton and Clark killings.[29]

Chicago police killed Charles Cox at the Eleventh District Police Station on April 30, 1969. According to a medical examination, he died of two blows to the head. Eugene Moore, who had been with Cox when the police stopped the two on a sidewalk, said that "two officers jumped out and began slapping Cox in the face with an open hand." Having endured a vicious beating in the police precinct later that evening, Cox succumbed to police murder the following morning, after he had spent the night in the station. Authorities took no action on this murder.

The following month, police killed Charles Green after entering his home with a shotgun. Patrolman John Kemp of the Marquette District apparently responded to a call about street-fighting and, after entering Green's home, thought he saw Green trying to attack his partner, Patrolman W. G. Bixby, with a weapon. After hearing the warning, Bixby whirled around and shot the unarmed Green in the abdomen. The Internal Inspection Division concluded that the incident had been "justifiable homicide."

Seventeen-year-old Pedro Medina was also killed in May when policemen in an unmarked car chased him after they thought they saw a bulge in his pocket. Witnesses reported that Medina tripped and fell and when an officer turned him over, he "put one knee in his chest and deliberately shot him in the stomach." After searching the dead teenager, policemen found twenty cents and a fountain pen. Authorities again failed to prosecute anyone or to take any other action on the murder.

In another homicide, this time termed accidental, police shot John Soto in the back of the head. His crime was to help organize the community in an effort to get the city to put up a traffic light at an intersection near the Henry Horner Projects, where two small children had been killed and several wounded in accidents. John's brother, twenty-year-old Sgt. Michael Soto, home on leave from the Vietnam War after winning numerous combat decorations, including the Bronze Star and the Vietnamese Gallantry Cross with Palm, suffered the same fate. Police shot and killed him after a riot broke out in the wake of his brother's funeral. Though Michael Soto was unarmed and trying to escape, police investigators concluded that his death was justifiable. Police officers also killed seventeen-year-old Wayne Black, nineteen-year-old Linda Anderson, seventeen-year-old James Nance, eighteen-year-old Steve Dixon, and fifteen year-old James Alexander.[30]

In a special investigative report authorized by the federal government, NAACP president Roy Wilkins and former U.S. attorney general Ramsey Clark noted that "the troubling question for Chicago's blacks was whether it was possible that so many killings, in so brief a time period, could have been accidental or justified." Many Windy City residents believed "they clearly could not" have been. Although police refused to investigate these murders in most cases, when they did, the ruling of justifiable or accidental homicide only created more enmity and distrust between them and blacks. It had been in this atmosphere that gangs began to turn political. Fred Hampton and the Panthers emerged at a time when widespread violence against blacks was deadly in addition to being common.

After learning in December 1968 that Jeff Fort had been resisting Panther overtures to integrate the two groups, the bureau's Chicago office sought to exacerbate what at the time seemed like minor friction. This office "proposed sending an anonymous letter to Fort, informing him that two prominent leaders of the Chicago BPP made disparaging remarks about his lack of commitment to black people in general." In a memo to FBI headquarters, the Chicago office explained that Fort was "reportedly aware that such remarks have been circulated" and stated that he might retaliate if he found out who made the statements. The Chicago field office then recommended that an informant tell Fort that "[name deleted] and [name deleted] are responsible for these remarks." Presumably, the deleted names were Fred Hampton and Mark Clark. These agents concluded that if Fort knew the Panthers had bad-mouthed him, he would not only refuse BPP overtures to merge, but he would also have the leaders killed.[31]

This document reveals how badly the FBI wanted to destroy the Panthers. Starting a shooting war between these two groups would certainly have absolved the bureau of any blame in a Panther–Ranger confrontation ending in death on both sides. Despite the FBI's instigation of this clandestine use of violence, the Rangers and Panthers never engaged in a wholesale slaughter of each other. David Hilliard summarized this situation when he wrote that the police and FBI employed "every kind of deviousness to put us at one another's throat, [to] make us appear like gangsters and thugs, niggers killing niggers." In the end, it turned out to be this activity that kept the two organizations wary of each other.[32] Considering the experience and resources of FBI agents in leadership positions, it is easy to understand how these youths were so easily manipulated.

The overwhelming majority of Panthers nationwide were younger than nineteen. Caught up in the excitement of the time, they could hardly have been expected to mount a successful offense against an entity (the United States government) that had helped subdue entire nations. Their desire for change outstripped their ability to match weapons with their avowed enemy, which left some demoralized and others dead. The federal government on the other hand, did feel some political pressure to get rid of the Panthers. In response to domestic protest, it used tactics that it developed in past and contemporary foreign wars on citizens barely old enough to vote.

At any rate, the BPP/Ranger relationship centered around a number of tension-filled meetings where each side insisted on the other's loyalty. At a December 18, 1968, meeting attended by approximately thirty Panthers and one hundred Rangers, Fort, according to an FBI informant, told the Panthers that "the Rangers were behind the Panthers but were not to be considered members." Panther leaders Bobby Rush and Fred Hampton, however, continued to press for the groups' integration. The informant noted that Hampton insisted that Fort "couldn't let the man keep the two groups apart." The source also advised headquarters that although "Fort did not appear over anxious to join forces with the Panthers," he also did not want "to terminate meeting for this purpose."[33]

There is no doubt that a successful union would have precipitated deadly confrontations with the Chicago police and the Cook County Sheriff's Department.

The merger failed to materialize and after a heated meeting at a South Side Chicago bar, both organizations issued ultimatums that they each had until December 28, 1968, to join the other. Neither side stated the consequences, but the two groups' militant stance indicated the likelihood of violent repercussions. The FBI capitalized on these recurrent tensions by sending Jeff Fort another anonymous letter. This time the bureau made the letter look as if it had come from a concerned citizen with official ties to neither group. J. Edgar Hoover approved the following letter on January 30, 1969:

> Brother Jeff:
>
> I've spent some time with some Panther friends on the west side lately and I know what's been going on. The brothers that run the Panthers blame you for blocking their thing and there's supposed to be a hit out for you. I'm not a Panther, or a Ranger, just black. From what I see, these Panthers are out for themselves not black people. I think you ought to know what they're up to. I know what I would do if I was you. You might hear from me again.
>
> (sgd.) a black brother you don't know.

The Chicago office explained that the purpose of the letter was "to intensify the degree of animosity between the two groups" in the hopes that Fort retaliated against BPP leadership. This office ironically explained that it decided against sending "a similar letter to the BPP alleging a Ranger plot against BPP leadership." It reasoned that such a letter was unproductive, "principally because the BPP at present is not believed as violence prone as the Rangers to whom violent type activity—shooting and the like—is second nature."[34] This statement gives credence to the Panther contention that much of the violence surrounding the BPP could be traced back to official sources. The hypocrisy involved in painting the organization in such thugish imagery borders on the criminal. If the bureau had made it known to police departments that it did not see the BPP as being a group of murderous thugs, local police officials might not have found it necessary to jail and incapacitate individual members and chapters.

This office's failure to provoke the Panthers indicates that the BPP had not drunk from the cup of violence from which the media so often accused it of drinking. The bureau clearly realized the group did not represent the natural killers portrayed by it and the media. To be fair, planned, thoughtful violence should be equally unacceptable. Most party members, however, never engaged in violence. Since violence played an integral part in the federal government's war against the group, the government's activities certainly had to be perceived as justified. A gang war fabricated by the FBI and its operatives might have served this purpose well. The general public had not only been led to believe that the Panthers were detrimental to most whites, but to other blacks as well. This gang war, however, to the chagrin of J. Edgar Hoover and other intelligence officials, failed to come to fruition. The Hampton-led Panthers, perhaps realizing that protracted black-on-black warfare ran counter to their goals, eventually worked out a truce with the Rangers. To avoid exacerbating the "enmity and distrust" between the two groups after the truce, the BPP, according to one congressional report, "decided not to conduct activity (like selling papers) or attempt to recruit in Ranger territory."[35] After this truce, Fred Hampton continued his work in other parts of the city organizing ghetto residents for political participation and instituting community welfare, medical, and educational programs.[36]

When the Black Stone Rangers and their traditional enemies, the Black Disciples, joined with the Panthers at a May 1969 news conference to announce a truce, they hit the media and the Chicago Police Department with a bombshell. The three groups issued a public statement declaring that "now, we are all one army."[37] Once these groups sought to coalesce in an effort to combat police violence, state, local, and federal authorities created machinery to thwart and to destroy them individually and organizationally.

Authorities were also greatly concerned about the effectiveness of the party and Hampton in using the media, especially its own newspaper. The police regularly harassed BPP newspaper sellers in Chicago. Authorities also sabotaged a number of Panther speaking engagements, including one instance when police arrested Hampton at a TV station prior to a scheduled appearance.[38] The FBI supplied "cooperative news media" in the area "with a steady stream of discrediting stories." In their crusade against the Panthers, federal agents, claims civil liberties attorney Frank Donner, also planned to use "established and reliable sources in the television and/or radio field to prepare programs discrediting the BPP."[39] As during the earlier civil rights movement, depending on locale, some reporters rallied to the side of government and portrayed the non-violent activists as hotheads and hoodlums being led around by their communist sponsors. Media outlets, often owned by major corporations, almost never delved into in-depth analyses of black poverty and its causes. This lack of credible coverage encouraged many viewers to think of the activists as criminals and therefore deserving of brutal police actions. Because Hampton was such an energetic leader though, the media blitz against him proved ineffectual, as more and more ghetto blacks and white radicals rallied to support the BPP.[40]

After the plan to incite a rift between the Panthers and the Rangers failed to achieve the desired results, the FBI, along with state and local police agencies in the Chicago area, added another dimension to its counterintelligence arsenal. Late in 1968, the FBI had William O'Neal infiltrate the Chicago chapter. The bureau promised to drop charges of interstate car theft and impersonation of an officer against this recent parolee, who feared going back to jail. The FBI also promised O'Neal a monthly stipend, and by the time this counterintelligence program ended, the FBI had paid him over thirty thousand dollars, an amazingly high sum considering the cost of living during that period.[41]

O'Neal explained that John Mitchell, his FBI handler, allowed him to become a Panther before he became an FBI informant. Noting that he "didn't go right in rifling drawers," the informant told an interviewer that agent Mitchell directed him into the group, "backed off," and "let them work on me a while. And slowly, it worked, I became a Black Panther. . . . and lived the life of a Panther." Thinking at first that the group had been just another gang "not unlike the Blackstone Rangers or Cobras," O'Neal quickly discovered that the group was "more sophisticated than a gang" and that "they were into the political scene—the war in Vietnam, Richard Nixon, and specifically, freeing Huey. That was the thing."[42]

After joining the group, O'Neal quickly moved up in the ranks of the BPP and eventually became the Chicago chapter's chief of security and Fred Hampton's personal bodyguard. Unknowingly making him even more of a danger to the group, the party gave O'Neal responsibility for securing arms for the organization. FBI scholars note that "it was his habit to set an example by wearing a .45 automatic in his shoulder holster" and to maintain "a personal inventory of two 12 gauge shotguns and an M-1 carbine 'for security' at BPP headquarters." O'Neal eventually acquired additional weapons, "apparently using falsified documents, and initiated a weapons training program for Party members at a farm in Michigan." The infiltrator also urged Panther members to "always go armed," a move destined to provoke police-Panther confrontations.[43]

O'Neal's activities quite often served as an excuse for police harassment and arrest of party members. These actions included selling drugs, building an electric chair "for ferreting out informants," and urging Panthers to participate in armed robberies and bombings with explosives the FBI had provided. His blatantly violent tendencies eventually became a hallmark of the Chicago chapter. A bureau document indicated that these actions were part of a COINTELPRO assignment that called for "harassing and impelling the criminal activities of the Black Panther Party locally."[43] After it became clear that it needed stronger methods to prevent Hampton from succeeding in Chicago and becoming the primary national spokesperson for the party, the FBI and local police decided to silence the twenty-one-year-old once and for all. In conjunction with the Chicago police, the FBI carefully laid plans to achieve this end, with O'Neal playing the chief role.

In early 1969, O'Neal, one of sixty-seven informants nationwide, gave Special Agent Roy Mitchell a key to Panther headquarters in Chicago. In the months following this action, FBI agents and informers routinely broke in and stole BPP financial records and other materials. They also checked out the Panthers' inventory of guns.

In addition, the FBI ordered O'Neal and other informants to sabotage the organization's widely accepted Free Breakfast for Children Program by destroying food and equipment. Despite their attempts, these tactics failed to achieve the desired goal, and thousands of children throughout the Chicago area continued to attend the Panther-sponsored breakfasts. Oddly, one of the local agents disapproved of these tactics and received this searing rebuke from J. Edgar Hoover:

> You state that the Bureau under the CIP [Counter Intelligence Program] should not attack programs . . . such as the BPP "Breakfast for Children." You state that this is because many prominent "humanitarians," both white and black, are interested in the

program as well as churches which are actively supporting it. You have obviously missed the point. The BPP is not engaged in the "Breakfast for Children" program for humanitarian reasons, including their efforts to create an image of civility, [they want to] assume community control of Negroes, and to fill adolescent children with their insidious poison.[45]

Contrary to popular belief, the Panthers' willingness to use guns to defend themselves and the black community is not what the government feared most. The government knew full well that on any day and at any time it could defeat the Panthers' rag-tag army. It was much more difficult, however, to keep the BPP from organizing blacks to fight against oppression. Federal and local police attacked the breakfast program so vehemently because the Panthers used it to recruit and to indoctrinate community people with its philosophy of self-reliance and armed struggle. To achieve its goal, government agencies had not only to destroy Panther facilities and supplies, but to arrest, beat, imprison, and sometimes kill those responsible for making the Free Breakfast for Children Program work.[46]

Although Hoover's hatred for and fear of the BPP manifests itself in the above memo, he clearly wanted to isolate the group from every possible base of local support. When this tactic failed, the Chicago police attacked the Panther office itself. In early spring 1969, after several policemen claimed they had been shot at from the roof of the Panther's West Madison Street headquarters, dozens of police showed up and began firing on the building. Although only one party member sustained an injury, the Panthers charged that the police—in addition to scattering food, medical supplies, telephones, and filing cabinets over the floor—"took about $1,000 of the party's money" allotted for the free breakfast program and their health care center. When this did not stop Panther organizing, the bureau, going back to its friendly media sources and extralegal activities, attempted to use the press to isolate the Panthers from any potential support they might have received.

Flint Taylor, who as a law student at Northwestern University worked with the Panthers in 1969, noted the violent, racist, gun-toting stereotypes being put out about the Panthers "were a conscious part of COINTEL-PRO." Having dealt with the Panthers on a day-to-day basis, Taylor described them as "real people who had concerns about their lives, about what was happening in their community and also internationally. . . . All were dedicated to the principle of getting oppression off their backs and dealing with police violence and economic justice." Because Panther goals ran contrary to what the bureau stood for, the FBI worked with local law enforcement agencies to eliminate the group. After several police/informant-instigated confrontations with the Panthers in 1969, the FBI drew closer to accomplishing its goal of eradicating the Panthers in Chicago.[47]

O'Neal continued his work of disruption and sabotage, stealing files, starting skirmishes with other groups, and offering Panthers explosives that could be used to blow up armories and "the safe door of a McDonald's he suggested the group rob," according to one reporter writing long after the events.[48] If the FBI's other operations were any indication, these violent tendencies on the part of O'Neal were encouraged by the informant's handlers. The FBI certainly had plenty of time to perfect its tactics. Former SNCC stalwart Stokely Carmichael, who had been an activist since at least 1960, noted that blacks "were a unified force against the local southern sheriffs with their guns and the Ku Klux Klan. But the FBI was able to split us on every conceivable issue with their channels to the press and their informants inside our organization." He soberly concluded that "that's where the real danger was—you were fighting an invisible man."[49] It certainly seemed to be so in the case of the FBI infiltration of the Chicago BPP.

As time elapsed, Hampton became increasingly suspicious of O'Neal's activities, threatening on several occasions to kick him out of the party if he did not cease what Hampton described as counterrevolutionary activities. O'Neal's offenses included suggesting the Panthers use nerve gas and an electric chair to deal with interlopers and informers, an obvious attempt to divert attention away from himself. He also proposed a plan for the BPP to bomb City Hall, using a radio-controlled model airplane he had constructed. This activity went completely beyond the pale of what most Americans considered legitimate political activism, including the Panthers. Hampton, who believed violence should be used only in self-defense, rejected all of these ideas. His conviction that the party should expel O'Neal heightened after these suggestions. Although the group voted to strip O'Neal of his position as chief of security, party members decided not to oust him, a decision that later proved to be a costly mistake.[50] Even if Hampton had acted on his gut feelings, he may very well have been killed anyway. Local and federal authorities hated the BPP and what it stood for. They would have stopped at nothing to discredit and destroy the group. That the Panthers publicly insisted on their right to armed self-defense gave these authorities the much-needed justification to get rid of them by whatever means necessary. When no provocation existed to arrest, imprison, kill, or otherwise harass BPP members, law enforcement officials created one.

In the early morning hours of June 4, 1969, FBI agents and Chicago police officers, led by FBI agent Marlin Johnson, raided the Panther's Chicago headquarters. They claimed they were searching for fugitive George Sams, although they did not possess a search warrant. In New Haven, Connecticut, Sams had directed the torture and ordered the murder of New York City Panther Alex Rackley earlier in the year. FBI agents knew Sams was not there because he walked right past them out of the Panther office, heavily armed, minutes before the raid commenced. Unknown to the Chicago Panthers, Sams was an FBI informer who pretended to be from headquarters in Oakland. Because all Panthers knew the party had been in the middle of a massive purge to rid itself of undesirable elements, Sams told unsuspecting Panthers in several chapters he was there to perform inspections and to straighten people out. When it became clear to all that Sams was not in the office, officers and agents confiscated Panther property and money. They also took a list of Panther contributors, which they later used as leverage for harassing several individuals and groups. At the end of the fake raid, eight Panthers went to jail on charges of harboring a fugitive and possessing illegal weapons. The authorities released all eight individuals on their own recognizance a few days later and dropped all the charges. They had clearly used the raid as a way to harass and intimidate BPP members, perhaps in the hope of provoking a shoot-out.[51]

Police encounters with Panthers also became increasingly violent. On July 16, for example, two Panthers and two policemen engaged in a shootout. Panther Larry Roberson was killed while police arrested Grady Moore and took him to jail. The police charged Moore with attempted murder and interfering with an officer. As with the arrests the previous month, the police soon dropped the charges. The pattern continued nearly three months later when in October the police again raided Panther headquarters. This raid, police contend, came after they responded to "reports of sniper fire." When the police arrived, shooting started. Before long, BPP members, apparently out of ammunition, surrendered. Six Panthers went to jail on charges of attempted murder. Although the police department denied it, Panthers showed pictures of where raiding officers had destroyed their office, setting fire to food meant to be used in the breakfast program as well as medical supplies donated for use in Panther Free Health Clinics. As they had before, the police dropped charges against all these Panthers.[52]

On July 31, 1969, the police engaged in a thirty-minute shootout with the Panthers. After attempting to run a check on guns the Panther security forces carried while patrolling in front of their headquarters, the police fell victim to Panther firepower. Quickly joined by reinforcements, the police entered Panther headquarters and arrested three Panthers. When the episode ended, the Panthers had hit five police officers, one of whom had to be transported to the hospital with a bullet wound in the leg.[53]

Another tragic police-Panther shootout occurred on November 13, 1969. Although the Panthers claimed police attacked them, the police insisted that they "responded to a wife's fear for the safety of her prison-guard husband," after he brawled with Panthers at a bar. The woman told police that she saw the Panthers "lurking in an abandoned building across from the guard's home." The police asserted that when they entered the building, "gunfire fatally wounded one officer and injured another." Before it ended, police reinforcements also suffered casualties. In all, two police officers, Frank Rappaport and John Gilhooly, and one Panther, Spurgeon "Jake" Winters, lay dead, while seven policemen and one Panther suffered minor gunshot wounds. One officer quoted a news release from the local BPP that praised the dead Panther who "defined political power by blowing away racist pig Frank Rappaport and racist pig John Gilhooly and retired eight other reactionary racist pigs before he was shot down." The Panthers in Chicago, a city renowned for its police violence, sought to demonstrate to policemen that violence could work in more ways than one.[54]

Less than a month after the raid of November 13, the FBI and local police used the deaths of Frank Rappaport and John Gilhooly as a pretext for permanently silencing Hampton. Although the bureau identified Hampton as the culprit in these slayings, it knew full well, based on heavy surveillance, that the Panther leader had been out of the city when the killings occurred. Attorney Frank Donner also confirmed the leader was out of town at the time. Despite this fact being common knowledge, the authorities continued to place the blame on Hampton, apparently believing that as leader and spokesman of the organization, he was responsible for the two deaths. O'Neal remembered that "Winters wasn't out there on any official mission for the party," but the BPP "took the heat because Jake Winters was a Black Panther." He knew at this point "that the police would react in some type of way" because his handlers kept asking him for detailed information and as a group, they could "just feel the stepped up surveillance" and "the pressure all the way around." The police, he said, were going to try to avenge the killings because they "wanted to know the locations of weapons caches, . . . if we had explosives, who was staying at what location, who spent the night where."[55]

In an interesting twist, Thomas Lyons, head of Chicago's Gang Intelligence Unit, assigned to "anti-BPP work," canceled a "shooting raid" on the Panther office because he sensed the FBI sought to use him to discredit and destroy the BPP. Lyons apparently fit into that small minority of law enforcement officials who refused to cooperate with the FBI's illegal activities.[56] Indeed, in a follow-up investigation of his own, Lyons discovered that Hampton had nothing to do with the two officers' murders.

Members of the FBI, Gang Intelligence Unit, and the Special Prosecutions Unit worked around Lyons's noncompliance. They eventually decided an arms raid on the Panther office was sufficient reason to enter the apartment unannounced. Edward V. Hanrahan, at the urging of FBI Special Agent Roy Mitchell, secured from Circuit Court Judge Robert Collins, a former employee of Hanrahan, an illegal weapons warrant on December 3, 1969. Had the search warrant been legitimate, United States District Court Judge Joseph Perry might not have later considered the raid illegal. Subsequent court testimony and FBI memos indicate that O'Neal informed his superiors in the bureau that the Panthers "purchased [the guns] on legal Illinois State Gun Registration Cards issued to female BPP members who [had] never been arrested." Despite this information, the bureau, under false pretext, continued to plan for the raid.[57]

In this case, it seems that the government entity set up to safeguard the law was its worst violator. Intent on killing Hampton, FBI agents began studying the floor plan of Hampton's apartment that O'Neal gave them. They also discussed the inventory of Panther armaments. An FBI memo noted that another informant, code named CG T-1, advised them that the Panthers had an array of carbines, shotguns, gas masks, and smoke bombs stored at their West Monroe Street office.[58] This collection of materiel made it clear that the Panthers wanted to be prepared to defend themselves against police or government attack. Gangs, their only other potential enemy, did not usually possess weapons that required gas masks as a defense. It cannot be overstated how the group's readiness for battle kept alive many of its members across the country. At the same time, it obviously increased police fear to the point of hysteria.

In an attempt to ensure the success of their proposed raid, the FBI instructed O'Neal to furnish a list of individuals "most frequently seen at this address." In response, the informant noted that Fred Hampton, Billy "Che" Brooks (deputy minister of information), Ronald "Doc" Satchel (deputy minister of health), Louis Truelock (legal counselor), Alvin Jeffries, Robert Campbell, and numerous female BPP members, including Hampton's pregnant fiancée, Deborah Johnson (now Akua Njeri), occupied the dwelling.[59] The FBI disseminated copies of this memo to the United States Attorney in Chicago, the Chicago branch of the Secret Service, the Office of Special Investigations, and the Region I, 113th Military Intelligence Group headquartered in Evanston, Illinois. In short, the FBI acted just as it might have if it were at war. The bureau anchored the memos with a note stating that "IN VIEW OF THE ABOVE INFORMATION AND PAST ACTIVITIES OF BPP MEMBERS MENTIONED ABOVE ALL SHOULD BE CONSIDERED ARMED AND EXTREMELY DANGEROUS."[60] When this language was coupled with the fact that a Panther was responsible for the deaths of two policemen, it becomes understandable that some officers might have preferred to shoot first and ask questions later. This tack was exactly the course of action they took. In the end, two of the most effective leaders of the Illinois BPP were murdered.

One of these was Mark Clark. Clark came from a large family, the ninth of seventeen children. His upbringing and immediate environment ensured that he liked people and was predisposed to sharing, a useful trait for a member of the BPP. Mark's mother, Fannie Clark, had her hands full when her husband, who pastored Holy Temple Church of

God in Christ, was killed in a Caterpillar Company factory, where he had worked for twenty-eight years. To make ends meet, Mark's mother worked two jobs: one at St. Francis Hospital in Peoria and another as a cleaning woman for well-to-do whites. Only a fair student, but quite talented in art, drama, and speech, Mark failed to finish Manual High School. Like many students, he had disciplinary problems, which, according to one report, included "an alleged assault upon a teacher." Not willing to give up completely on an education, Mark decided to enroll at Illinois Central Junior College in Peoria. Unfortunately, he only completed a few classes before dropping out again.[61]

By his early teens, Clark, along with many of his brothers and sisters, had already become active in Peoria's NAACP, demonstrating against the widespread racial inequality that characterized the small midwestern hamlet. John Gwyn, president of the Illinois NAACP, told one investigator that by the time Clark was thirteen, he was "demonstrating against discrimination in employment, housing and education." Clark, however, was not perfect, and he sometimes found himself in trouble with the law. In 1965, he went to jail for aggravated battery and found himself paying a twenty-five dollar fine for possessing a concealed weapon. Two years later, authorities fined him fifty dollars for violating the city's curfew, set in the aftermath of riots that engulfed the city, just as they had in Detroit and a dozen other cities that year. Donna Cummings, who knew Clark as a result of her work with juveniles, noted that "no one in the world is perfect" and that he joined the party because "in his heart he felt he was doing [it] for his people." Describing the young Panther as one of her children, Cummings noted that "he gave his life for the thing he believed in most."[62]

Sometime in 1968, Clark became the defense captain for the Peoria branch of the BPP. His work, like that of most other party members, consisted of studying two hours a day, attending political education classes, helping to run the group's Free Breakfast for Children Program, and selling the party newspaper. Anthony Harris, another Peoria Panther, accompanied Clark to the Windy City to meet and discuss strategy with other party members. This meeting, held on December 3, 1969, went longer than was planned and as a result Hampton, who chaired the meeting, missed a dinner appointment he and his fiancée, Deborah Johnson, had with Hampton's mother.[63]

With the raid scheduled to take place on December 4, 1969, FBI agents Marlin Johnson and Robert Piper noted in a joint memo to the director that the upcoming raid represented a "positive course of action being effected under the counterintelligence program." Hoover must have been delighted to learn that his subordinates were coming closer to destroying the BPP in Illinois. Since the Blackstone Rangers had failed to take the bait, the FBI had to rely primarily on city and state agencies to do its dirty work. These entities had little compunction about destroying the BPP. State's Attorney Hanrahan, hoping to make political capital on his ability and willingness to maintain law and order in the Windy City, cooperated in every way.[64] He wanted badly to become mayor of Chicago, a prestigious position the entrenched Richard Daley had finally agreed to relinquish. His plans, however, backfired after the Hampton and Clark murders as blacks displayed their disgust with police and government policy. He not only failed in his mayoral bid, he also lost his position as state's attorney. Blacks in Chicago, abandoning the Democratic candidate in a political rebellion, supported liberal Republican Bernard Carey for state's attorney in the 1970 election. According to writer Nicholas Lemann, blacks saw the killings "not as the Sarajevo of the black revolution but as another case of the police killing black people and getting away with it, as they surely wouldn't have if the victims had been white."[65] Hanrahan lost as a result of this change in black voting patterns. Because he directed the raid, the state's attorney paid dearly. Unfortunately, so did Hampton, Clark, and the rest of the Panthers.

In the early morning hours of December 4, 1969, fourteen heavily armed men from the Chicago Police Department's Special Prosecutions Unit (carrying shotguns, submachine guns, carbines, and pistols) left the state's attorney's office in telephone trucks and unmarked cars. They headed toward Fred Hampton's apartment, a block or so from the BPP office. Approaching their destination, Sgt. Daniel Groth, for the first time, alerted "regular" Chicago police officers that a raid on Panther offices was under way and asked them for backup. Earlier, an eight in the evening raid was rejected by FBI agents and Edward Hanrahan. All individuals concerned knew that the apartment was empty at that time and if they had wanted to avoid violence and to confiscate the weapons they claimed to be searching for, they would have conducted the operation in the early evening. Their goal, however, had not been to avoid violence, as indicated by the heavy arsenal they carried. A federal grand jury that investigated the raid later noted "the whole concept of going on a raid in a high crime density area to obtain weapons from known militants—led by a convicted felon believed to be dangerous—with only fourteen men in plainclothes, in the dead of night, with no sound equipment, no lighting equipment, no tear gas, and no plan for dealing with potential resistance, seems ill-conceived." Of course there is much understatement in this conclusion, but the central observation seems accurate. Additionally and unbeknownst to Hampton, William O' Neal drugged the Panther leader with a heavy dose of barbiturates. This measure ensured that the die-hard revolutionary did not retaliate or lead any type of counteroffensive.[66]

Harold Bell, an ex-army officer who dropped out of college and joined the party, was asleep in the living room when he heard two knocks on the door, followed by two gunshots. One of these shots killed twenty-year-old Mark Clark instantly. As Bell immediately rushed to Hampton's side and attempted to wake him, he screamed, "Chairman, Chairman! Wake up! The pigs are vamping! The pigs are vamping!" By this time, Officer Gorman had switched his weapon to full automatic fire and began shooting into a front room closet toward Hampton's bedroom. Following the instructions Groth had issued in the hours before the raid quite well, Officer Gorman told the grand jury he "had faith in the weapon" he wielded and wanted to make sure no Panthers got the opportunity to fire at him or his fellow officers. Hampton's bed vibrated rapidly as automatic fire perforated the mattress. Deborah Johnson, who was eight and a half months pregnant, climbed over Hampton in an attempt to avoid being shot and saw him raise his head. In a daze, he briefly looked around as officers standing in his doorway fired in their direction. Almost as suddenly as he had looked up, he lowered his head back to the mattress, as if fourteen policemen had not been in his living room, kitchen, and doorway firing semiautomatic and automatic weapons. "So, he looked up kind of like this," she gestured to Wilkins and Clark, "and all these pigs were standing at the door just shooting and he laid his head back down like that. I don't know if he was shot then or not. I assumed he was. He didn't move," she concluded.[67]

Bell, pinned down by gunfire, noticed that policemen had entered the back of the house as well. In short order, shotgun blasts and pistol rounds ensured he did not escape. Moving cautiously toward the doorway, a policeman grabbed Bell and pushed him into the kitchen and onto the floor and handcuffed him. At this point, he said, one of the officers put his foot on his neck and "pointed a shotgun in his ear." The whole time he heard officers shooting into Hampton's bedroom. He heard policemen call out "that's Fred Hampton, that's Fred Hampton!"—making it clear this was their intended quarry. At this point, he also heard one of the men say, "we should kill all of the dirty motherfuckers." Dragged bodily from the floor and out the door, Bell claims to have seen Hampton's dead body. "On the way [out] I saw the body," he said, "I saw Fred's body. I saw that he had been shot in the head, and I was told to keep moving, [to] look straight ahead, and taken out and put into a wagon."[68]

Deborah Johnson, directed into the kitchen, found other Panthers there standing around and sitting on the floor. One officer ripped open her nightgown and said: "well what do you know, we have a broad here." Another policeman grabbed her by the hair and shoved her further into the kitchen and out the door in the cold snow-filled Chicago streets.[69] The onslaught ended after the raiders brought out the other Panthers and threw them into police paddy wagons. The Panthers' Chicago leadership had been exterminated for the moment and J. Edgar Hoover could not have been happier. Another group interested in improving the lot of blacks had been severely weakened, and his COINTELPRO seemed to be working like a charm.

Mark Clark died immediately after the invaders shot through the front door and hit him in the heart. The damage to Hampton was much more extensive. He had been shot twice in the head, once in the left shoulder and once in the right forearm. Concluding that Hampton might have been "deliberately selected as the sole target," Wilkins and Clark, in an investigation conducted after the raid, noted that Deborah Johnson and Luis Truelock had been positioned "between Hampton and the line of fire from the north during much of the firing." They concluded that it was highly unlikely "that Hampton could have been hit by fire from that direction while they escaped unscathed."[70]

Among other discoveries made by the commission that investigated the murders was the fact that the police fired nearly one hundred shots that night. "The hour of the raid, the failure to give reasonable warning to the occupants, the over arming of the police, the wildly excessive use of gunfire," the commission said, were "all more suited to a wartime military commando raid than the service of a search warrant." It found no "legal or factual justification" for the overkill and concluded "it is not safe to entrust enforcement of the laws to authorities who permit the use of a machine gun the way the Chicago police did during the episode." Hanrahan, the commission said, was "unworthy of public trust" because he lied when he noted that the raiders "exercised good judgment, considerable restraint, and professional discipline" after being met by the "violent, criminal," and extremely "vicious" BPP members.[71]

Pointing accusing fingers at government investigators after the fact, the commission concluded that the failure of state and local authorities "to employ basic investigative practices such as fingerprinting, preserving evidence, examining all firearms, sealing the premises, and examining and photographing the bodies before removing them, as well as gross errors on the part of these officials in ballistics, autopsy, and other examinations, are professionally inexcusable and can only undermine the confidence and integrity of the police and the legal system." It said the account Hanrahan gave to the *Chicago Tribune* "and the filmed reenactment of the episode by police for CBS-TV, demeaned public office, and violated professional ethics." In a gross understatement, these investigators asserted that local, state, and federal officials "failed to do their duty to protect the lives and rights of citizens. . . . If official violence is to be renounced, the truth must finally overcome our natural reluctance to incriminate government." Commission members hoped their work "would serve that end." Describing this violence emanating from the state as the "most destructive," they noted that the message it sent was "this is our way, we stand for nothing better." The state practiced violence, they surmised, and at the same time taught those seeking change and resisting violence "that there is no alternative." Summing up their conclusions, the commissioners pointed out the common thread "that runs through the violence of B-52 raids in Indochina, police shooting students at Jackson State College in Mississippi, and the slaughter of prisoners and guards at Attica State Penitentiary in New York." They said "we do not value others' lives as we do our own" and "until we understand" that all the aforementioned victims of state-sanctioned violence "are human beings equal in every way to our children and ourselves, we will see no wrong in using violence to control or destroy them."[72]

These findings are interesting because they came as a result of heavy pressure on the government to investigate Hampton's and Clark's murders. Even though a grand jury concluded there were serious discrepancies in the authorities' testimony, it indicted no policemen or FBI agents, who had clearly committed murder. Because of the sham of justice, Panther members refused to testify before the grand jury, claiming the authorities would not believe them and that any future trial might be compromised if they testified. Less than two months after the killings, and after local authorities failed to properly investigate, the Justice Department gave the commission, headed by Wilkins and Clark, authority to look into the tragedy.

Because of the Panthers' radical stance against oppression and police terror, authorities, seeking to maintain black subjugation, used every means to crush them. They accomplished this task with the knowledge that their members would never have to serve time for killing Panthers. One reason, among many others, is that the very body responsible for investigating these incidents was filled with powerful people who vehemently hated the BPP, and who, like the president and the CIA, wanted it eradicated.

Senate hearings concerning this raid noted that the information informant O'Neal supplied "was crucial to the police during their raid." A memo from the Chicago FBI office to headquarters explained that the important logistical and tactical information the FBI obtained prior to the raid "was not available from any other source and subsequently proved to be of tremendous value in that it subsequently saved injury and possible death to police officers participating."[73] The tone and content of the memo indicate that the lives of Hampton and Clark meant little to the authorities.

In the meantime, the FBI paid O'Neal extra for his valuable services. Robert Piper, an agent who helped supervise the operation, requested and received from headquarters a special bonus. In January 1970, "Washington authorized a special payment of $300 as a reward for O'Neal's 'uniquely valuable services.'"[74] O'Neal, after confessing to reporters that he had indeed been an FBI informer, committed suicide in the early 1980s. The FBI's own correspondence and the actions they describe leave no doubt that the leadership elite in the United States stopped at nothing to eliminate meaningful black political organizing.

The fabricated police account of the raid detailed how the Panthers refused them entrance after the announcement of a search warrant, and soon after began firing at them. According to authorities, Fred Hampton fired a .45 pistol the whole time and insisted that the two sides "shoot it out" rather than avoid violent confrontation. The *Chicago Tribune,* which employed individuals "friendly" with the FBI, published this version, complete with pictures of a door panel that purportedly proved that the Panthers repeatedly shot at police. Another group of reporters viewed the apartment and the pictures and proved that the alleged bullet holes were actually nail heads.[75]

Despite this information, on December 8, 1969, State's Attorney Hanrahan conducted a press conference and praised the police for their restraint, bravery, and professional discipline in not killing all the Panthers present. Hanrahan also failed to mention that earlier in the evening O'Neal had drugged Hampton with secobarbital, a chemical used "as a hypnotic and sedative." This fact proved strange since no one had ever known Hampton to use drugs. The evidence emerged after Hampton's autopsy revealed "abnormally high levels of barbiturates" in his blood. O'Neal also testified that he had prepared a late dinner for the group and administered the drug to Hampton through the Kool-Aid he made for them.[76] The authorities apparently hoped to incapacitate the Panther leader to prevent him from retaliating. This one issue however, is far from the only inconsistency in the official report.

"Regardless of what happened," pointed out the *Washington Post,* "there is plenty of other material in this [grand jury] report to convince black militants and many others that the police were less interested in upholding the law and seeing justice done than in getting the Panthers and covering up any illegal tracks they made in getting them." The article also recounted that the 25,000-word grand jury report had noted that the police search of Hampton's apartment had been "unprofessional" and that "the police investigations of the actions of the raiding officers was a whitewash." The grand jury also found the coroner's autopsy "incompetent, that some of the information released by the prosecutor to news media was clearly erroneous, and that the man who made ballistics tests for the police knew they were inadequate (they were also erroneous) but feared for his job if he said so." The leadership of the law enforcement agencies involved in the murders made sure no one tampered with their efforts to rid the Windy City of Fred Hampton and the Panthers. Once again, they did their job well. The success of this raid helped to cripple the BPP in Chicago.[77]

Nevertheless, the surviving Panthers refused to give up without a fight and tried to continue battling within the system. They subsequently took the issue to court. Throughout the 1970s, there were federal grand jury indictments charging conspiracy to obstruct justice against Hanrahan, several police officials, and five policemen, but they all ended in dismissals. The grand jury did, however, contribute useful information about the raid. It estimated that the police fired between eighty-two and one hundred shots—and that only one shot, that of the dying Mark Clark, came from inside the Panther apartment.

After three "official" and highly publicized investigations of the raid and mounting public pressure from citizens and political leaders all over the country, the Chicago grand jury labeled the deaths "justifiable homicides," thereby exonerating the FBI, the Gang Intelligence Unit, and the Special Prosecutions Unit. Afterward, State's Attorney Hanrahan dropped all charges against the Panthers and made a promise to the FBI to remain silent "concerning the facts and nature of FBI involvement in the murders." This turn of events left it up to the victims' families to bring out the truth.[78]

Almost by accident, the families discovered that O'Neal had been an informant. This development gave them the edge they needed. In the summer of 1972, during what newspapers called the "hit squad" trial, O'Neal made his appearance. According to the *Pittsburgh Courier,* "it was principally through this testimony that Stanley Robinson, ex-policeman, was found guilty of murder, and sentenced to three concurrent terms of life imprisonment." During the trial, O'Neal testified "that he was an informant for the FBI and had accompanied Robinson on several of his murderous escapades." The informant told the jury that "he had been in the employ of the FBI since 1969, that he had infiltrated the Black Panther Party, becoming its security chief, reported to FBI agent Roy Mitchell about Panther activities, with the aid of a telephone the FBI conveniently installed in his car." This testimony helped break the case, especially because during the Panther trial, "O'Neal was never called as a witness nor was his name ever mentioned. . . . As far as the government was concerned, he did not even exist," concluded the *Pittsburgh Courier.*[79]

In 1979, after several attempts, attorneys Flint Taylor and Jeff Haas entered a $47.7 million damage suit against Edward V. Hanrahan, et al. The suit alleged "a conspiracy between the FBI and local law enforcement officials and police to illegally deprive the Panthers of their civil rights by destroying their organization, killing and injuring them, then covering up the conspiracy." These lawyers (with the aid of FBI documents supplied them via court order and the Freedom of Information Act) produced enough evidence to prove there had indeed been an FBI conspiracy to murder Hampton and to obstruct justice. A judge subsequently ordered a retrial.[80]

The Justice Department, FBI, Illinois State Attorney's Office, and the Chicago police department all withheld evidence in this new trial. For example, the court discovered several weeks into the trial that of the 1,600 documents in Hampton's file, the FBI and Justice Department "turned over only 57." Judge Joseph Perry scolded the agencies and said "there was no excuse for such flouting of the rules." The defendants appealed to the Supreme Court on the grounds that further probing endangered "the lives of the informants who had participated." The court denied the appeal and again ordered the defendants to produce the documents. The documentary evidence they eventually provided, according to the *Chicago Sun Times,* took up more than thirty feet of file space.[81]

The subsequent trial, without a jury, lasted nearly seven years because of the government's initial refusal to turn over all relevant documents pertaining to the raid. In 1983, Judge John F. Grady ruled that a government conspiracy against the BPP existed and that the plaintiffs' civil rights had been violated. The court awarded the Hampton and Clark families, as well as the other Panthers who were in the apartment, including Hampton's unborn son, a settlement of $1.85 million. Still, not one of the defendants spent a day in jail for these murders and their other crimes. The authorities' eradication of the Chicago BPP demonstrated no compassion for the Panthers' lives and even less respect for the nation's laws against murder and other civil rights violations.[82]

A by-any-means-necessary philosophy undoubtedly guided police authorities in their quest to cripple the popular organization. William C. Sullivan, Hoover's second-in-charge, revealed the FBI's philosophy in a November 1, 1975, deposition to the Senate. He testified that:

During the ten years that I was on the U.S. Intelligence Board, a Board that receives the cream of intelligence for this country from all over the world and inside the United States, never once did I hear anybody, including myself, raise the question: "Is this course of action which we have agreed upon lawful, is it legal, is it ethical or moral?" We never gave any thought to this realm of reasoning, because we were just naturally pragmatists. The one thing we were concerned about was this: will this course of action work, will it get us what we want, will we reach the objective that we desire to reach? [83]

Their pragmatism meant death for those on the other side of the issue. It is clear the FBI and other investigatory agencies charged with suppressing militant activities ignored altogether the rights of some citizens.[84] Even more apparent is the fact that breaking the law to accomplish certain goals had not even been considered, much less deemed, illegal.

Agreeing with an Amnesty International report that described the FBI's tactics as "lawless," *Racial Matters* author Kenneth O'Reilly concluded "political violence was a central part of the FBI response to [the black] struggle" and that it was "something located within the mainstream of government policy towards blacks."[85] It turned out Chicago was not the only city where the government reached into its black bag of deadly tricks. The government's goal of neutralizing and incarcerating effective charismatic Panthers who were able to enlist widespread community support of BPP programs and goals stopped nowhere, including sunny Los Angeles.

Los Angeles, California, was the site of one of the party's strongest chapters. Alprentice "Bunchy" Carter, former gang member and minister of defense of the Southern California chapter, and John Huggins, college student and minister of information, led the chapter. Their charisma and organizing skills placed them high on the bureau's "enemies list." Like others who made the list, these two Panthers ended up dead. Their political organizing on college campuses and elsewhere made them open targets for FBI operatives. Two days before he met fate, Huggins told a crowd at Neyerhoff Park, UCLA's free speech area, that Panthers wanted a Black Studies Program that taught people what they wanted "to know about racist America. When we say Black Studies Program we're dealing with

. . . the survival of a race of people who have been brought to this country, brutalized and mis-educated." He added that the group wanted to coalesce with people and organizations who supported Panther demands and had "solidarity" with their "struggle against capitalism and racism."[86]

On January 17, 1969, 150 members of the University of California, Los Angeles Black Student Union convened on campus to resolve an ongoing dispute over which organization, US or the BPP, decided who became the director of the Black Studies program. Unlike the Panthers, US, a cultural nationalist group organized by Ron Karenga, insisted that a primary emphasis on black pride and black culture were the keys to African American liberation, and thus appealed to the cultural and intellectual elements of the Black Power movement. The US organization generally tried to influence existing black groups rather than to create a national or international movement of its own. The Panthers appealed to a broader, more internationalist-oriented element that sought to take advantage of coalition building and grassroots development.

Karenga explained that "in the beginning, the Panthers and US worked together." He added that the two groups even "used to do community patrol together." Over time, however, the Panthers began to ridicule "Karenga's cultural nationalism, claiming US believed power flowed from the sleeve of a Dashiki and not the barrel of a gun." Huey Newton and the other Panthers agreed that being culturally aware and knowledgeable about one's history was important but they insisted that black freedom would come only through concerted political and armed action. "We have to realize our black heritage in order to give us strength to move on and progress," Newton said, "but as far as returning to the old African culture, it's unnecessary and it's not advantageous in many respects. We believe that culture itself will not liberate us. We're going to need some stronger stuff."[87] By the time of the UCLA tragedy, the two groups had grown to dislike each other and, therefore, vigorously competed for control of the Black Studies program.

The discussion the evening of Carter's death was heated as the two sides disagreed over the Black Studies appointment. While the US organization supported Charles Thomas, a psychologist and director of education at the Watts Health Center, the Panthers supported Harry Edwards, a former San Jose College professor, Ph.D. candidate at the University of Connecticut, who was rumored to be a member of the BPP.

Edwards was popular for helping to organize the protests that made the 1968 Olympics in Mexico so memorable. The winning candidate would assume control of the two hundred thousand dollar yearly budget of the High Potential Program for minorities and the $250,000 annual budget of the Black Studies Program. This position gave its holder considerable sway in the appointment of staff and other important assignments. The successful candidate might also have been the beneficiary of significant consulting fees or honoraria for speaking to others about starting similar programs.

The tension at the meeting was underlined by the presence of five armed Simbas, members of the US elite guard, as well as Carter and Huggins. It was apparent that the students had been swayed by Panther arguments to choose the person the BPP supported for the job. The well-disciplined Simbas sat still and listened intently as Huggins and Carter strongly criticized Karenga.

A few minutes after the meeting ended and most of the people had left the meeting room, all hell broke loose. Carter alerted Huggins to the fact that that one of their "sisters" had been attacked by an US member. The two then went into the lunchroom to confront the US member (Tuwala or Harold Jones), who had accosted the Panther. As the three spoke, Chuchessa (Claude Hubert) emerged from behind the door with his .357 Magnum and shot Huggins in the back, killing him. Carter immediately jumped over a table and chairs and tried to shield himself with Tuwala. His efforts failed as, according to one report, "he was hit by a number of bullets in the chest."[88]

The assailants then made a two-hundred-yard dash across campus to a waiting vehicle that sped them away from the scene. An *Information Digest* report noted that "from its license tags the ownership of the car was subsequently traced to the Black Congress Economic Development Council—a group closely linked with US." Meanwhile, the two Panther leaders lay dying.

In a spring 2002 conversation, Elaine Brown, who was a member of the Los Angeles chapter at the time, Carter's girlfriend, and eventually leader of the entire BPP, informed the author that the shooting started by mistake. She had been standing outside Campbell Hall when an US member asked to speak with her. She refused, insisting that she had to take care of business with the student meeting that had just ended.

A youth gets ready to sell the Panther newspaper. *Photo by Ducho Dennis, courtesy of It's About Time.*

Brown explained that she had recently been in contact with this US member. In fact, he had a crush on her and hoped to take things further. They had spoken on the phone and on campus a few times but that was it. According to Brown, she was flattered by the whole thing, but certainly had no intention of getting involved with the young revolutionary. She had, however, led him on, thinking it harmless.[89]

On the night of the murders, this particular US member became enraged when Brown refused to speak to him and in fact seemed to be giving him the cold shoulder. She told the author the man grabbed her coat, the signature leather jacket worn by Panthers at the time, and snatched her toward him. When he refused to release Brown, she slapped him and jerked away. Before she could leave, however, the US member did her one better and slapped Brown in return. Visibly shaken, and undoubtedly injured by the hard slap, Brown decided she needed help. She told the US member, in no uncertain terms, that he had made a huge mistake, and he had to pay for it.[90]

At this point, Brown marched off into the night, swearing to get someone to take care of the man who had just slapped her. It is not clear whether she vowed to return with Bunchy Carter or not, but everyone present knew that Brown and Carter were in a relationship and that Carter had attended the student meeting. What happened after that point, therefore, is not clear at all. It seems, however, that US members assumed Brown would be returning with Carter, widely known in the Los Angeles area as one of the city's most notorious gang members. As a result, he had cultivated his share of enemies. Many US members, who had been in rival gangs opposing Carter's Slausons, already knew of the Panther leader's penchant for violence. When Brown returned with Carter, US members, fearing that Carter had come to settle the situation violently, launched a preemptive attack and shot Carter and Huggins.[91]

After hours of interrogation, the Los Angeles Police Department finally charged several Los Angeles Panthers, including Geronimo Pratt, Nathaniel Clark, Ericka Huggins (John Huggins's wife), and Elaine Brown, with conspiracy with the intent to commit murder. The police subsequently rounded up and arrested more than seventy-five other area Panthers. They also confiscated an M-1 rifle and two dozen other guns along with several gas masks, a bomb, and a large cache of ammunition. Although all the witnesses that night pointed to the US members as the trigger men, the police refused to arrest any US members. Police claimed to be holding the Panthers to keep them from retaliating against US members.[92]

On January 20, three days after the murders, George Philip Stiner (Ali Sultani) and Larry Joseph Stiner (Sakia) surrendered to the police. Sakia had a bullet in his shoulder when he surrendered at the San Diego airport. At the time they were arrested, the Stiner brothers were on bail for other mischief in Southern California. On February 10, a jury found them guilty of "armed robbery, attempted murder, [and] assault and kidnapping in connection with their involvement in a $4,000.00 bar hold-up in Santa Ana, California [in] March, 1968." A Los Angeles jury found them guilty of the Panther murders in what one commentator described

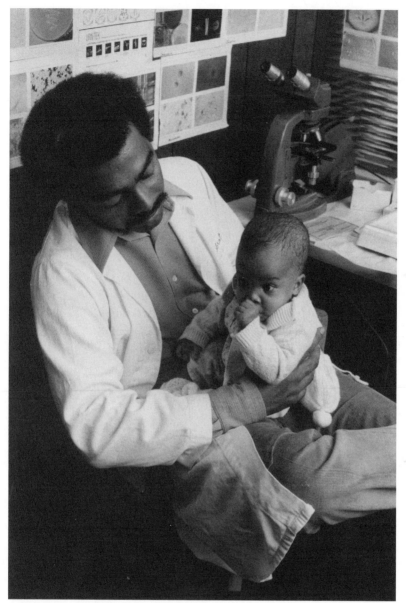

Panther Henry Smith sits with a young child at the George Jackson Clinic. *Photo by Ducho Dennis, courtesy of It's About Time.*

as "a trial that featured the odd sight of Black Panther witnesses [ostensibly at the urging of Elaine Brown] testifying on behalf of the state." The court sentenced them to ten years in the state penitentiary, terms much less lengthy than most murderers received in California during this period. About "four years later the Stiners were transferred to the minimum security section (a very rare action for convicted murderers) at San Quentin, from which they escaped." Claude Hubert, another US member present that night and allegedly involved in the shootings, fled the scene and was never found.[93]

Like FBI operations against the BPP across the country, this one had as its goal the elimination of highly skilled leadership. In this case, it had not been necessary for FBI agents to actually pull the trigger. As long as someone did the job, the results were the same. This intergroup strife did not end at UCLA. These murders sparked a running feud between US and the Panthers that left both groups reeling.

Violent disagreements between US and the Panthers in Southern California ultimately resulted in the killing of a total of four Panthers by US members and a number of "beatings and shootings." A Senate investigation into the local and federal police response to the Panthers several years later revealed "FBI officials were clearly aware of the violent nature of the dispute" and "proudly claimed credit" for it because it provoked "a high degree of unrest" in the ghettos of Southern California. Creating this atmosphere of violence enabled law enforcement officials to use a wide range of tactics in their campaign to destroy the Panther menace.

These extralegal efforts proved to be highly effective. For example, the FBI's Los Angeles field office informed headquarters that US "will be appropriately and discreetly advised of the time and location of BPP activities in order that the two organizations might be brought together and thus grant nature the opportunity to take her course." This sentiment leaves little doubt that the same FBI that flatly refused to protect civil rights workers in Mississippi became duty-bound to destroy radical political organizations and their leadership in other parts of the country. In its conclusions, the Senate investigators chided the chief investigative branch of the federal government for engaging in "lawless tactics" and responding to "deep-seated social problems by fomenting violence and unrest." The report found "equally disturbing . . . the pride" FBI agents "took in claiming credit for the bloodshed that occurred."[94] If one examines this situation closely, the viciousness of the tactics used to destroy the Panthers becomes readily apparent. In short, the violence propagated by official representatives of government agencies had as its goal the maiming and murdering of black activists. Because the Panthers and US were unaware of their manipulation, Hoover and the FBI took this opportunity to inflict even more damage.

One of the FBI's operations consisted of sending fabricated derogatory cartoons to the opposing groups. Examples of these cartoons include one that depicted Ron Karenga studying a checklist of already dead Panthers (John Huggins and Bunchy Carter) and Panthers to be killed (Bobby Seale and David Hilliard). Below the Karenga depiction were chickens, two dead (Huggins and Carter), two alive (Hilliard and Seale), and one in a cage (Newton). Surrounding these chickens hovered a giant cobra-like snake with the initials "US" inscribed on its back. Another caricature "attacked the Los Angeles Panther leader as a bully toward women and children in the Black community," while one "accused the BPP of 'actually instigating' a Los Angeles Police Department raid on US headquarters." One cartoon even "depicted Karenga as an overpowering individual 'who has the BPP completely at his mercy.'" When the FBI began sending negative caricatures of US, supposedly drawn by BPP members, US members retaliated violently. Perhaps overly concerned with the myriad difficulties they encountered daily, neither side understood that

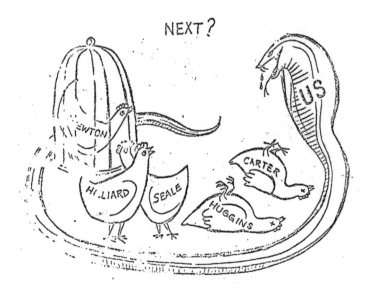

the FBI spent its time exacerbating the problems they had with each other. Undoubtedly the FBI designed these cartoons to cripple both these competing black nationalist organizations.[95]

The same pattern of FBI-fostered violence unfolded between the two groups in San Diego. The most serious of these confrontations occurred August 14–15, 1969, when US members killed Panther Sylvester Bell and critically wounded two others. A few weeks after an US member killed Panther lieutenant John Savage, another Panther, Sylvester Bell, who was selling the Black Panther newspaper in Otto Square in San Diego, was approached by three US members who asked him, "Are you talking about us this week?" Fighting ensued, and when two other Panthers went to Bell's aid, "one of the three members of US drew a gun and fatally shot Bell." After being arrested and tried, "one was convicted of murder, and the two others were convicted as accessories."[96]

An August 20, 1969, memo from the San Diego FBI field office to headquarters observed that "in view of the recent killing of BPP member Sylvester Bell, a new cartoon is being considered in the hopes that it will assist in the continuance of the rift between the BPP and US." FBI agents in San Diego understood how strongly BPP and US members disliked each other at this point and sought to "determine how this situation [could] be capitalized upon for the benefit of the Counterintelligence

PANTHERS ARE BIG AND BRAVE...
SNATCHING DEFENSELESS KIDS

NOW, GERONIMO ... WHO WERE
YOU CALLIN' A PORK CHOP NIGGER?

Program." These groups' opposition to each other provided fertile ground for the FBI to sneak in, cultivate, and harvest seeds of discord in the minds of the radical, and serious, Southern California activists.[97]

Despite FBI efforts to promote violent confrontations between these groups, members from each organization sought to establish a truce. Both groups apparently realized that continued mutual bloodletting ran counter to the goals of the "revolution" they sought to advance. In a March 27, 1969, meeting between the two groups, Walter Wallace, the Panther leader in San Diego, stated that the Panthers "would not hold a grudge against US members for the killing of Huggins and Carter." An April 10, 1969, memo from the San Diego field office to headquarters reported that on April 2, 1969, the two groups had another "friendly" meeting and attempted to work out their differences. Decades later, Panther Emory Douglas explained that both groups worked dili-

HE REALLY WAS A PAPER TIGER

gently to achieve peace and that "it was the power structure that kept them divided."[98] While US and the BPP continued to harbor feelings of distrust for each other, they still believed they fought for the same goals, and therefore hoped to reach some type of common ground. After these groups ceased operating and their members had time to reflect on the turbulent times they lived through, they discovered that external forces kept them from making amends and unifying the struggle.

The FBI proved to be smarter than its enemies in this case and made other plans for the groups. After observing that "tension between the BPP and US appeared to lessen" as a result of these "talks," the San Diego office requested and received "headquarters' approval for three more cartoons

ridiculing the BPP and falsely attributed to US." In the wake of these mailings, the two groups confronted each other in San Diego's Southcrest Park, where "BPP members ran US members off." Bureau agents noted that on the same day (April 4, 1969) "US members broke into a BPP political education meeting and roughed up a female BPP member." The special agent in charge in San Diego "boasted that the cartoons had caused these incidents." Based on information obtained from an FBI informant, the agent told headquarters that the cartoons "are really shaking up the BPP." He added that the cartoons led the Panthers to believe that US was "getting ready to move and this was the cause of the confrontation at Southcrest Park on 4/4/69."[99] Again, the two groups, perhaps blinded by their antagonisms (some of which stemmed from previous gang affiliations), remained unaware of the FBI's manipulation.

THE RIDE OF THE PAPER PANTHER

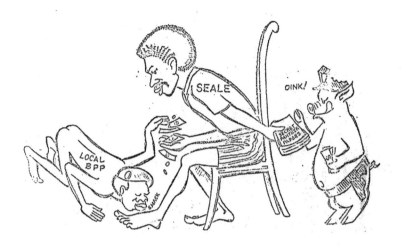

"Do You Want These Cats in Your Community"

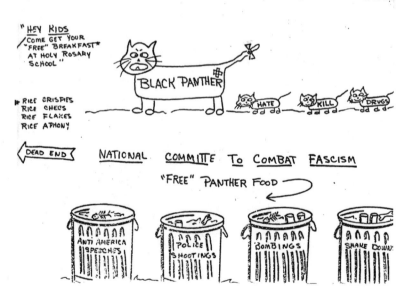

The FBI also sought to discredit both organizations in the eyes of the black community. Pointing out that "the leaders and incidents depicted in the caricatures are known to the general public, particularly among Negroes living in . . . Los Angeles, San Diego, and San Francisco," FBI headquarters informed the San Diego field office that distributing the cartoons was "expected to strengthen" the distrust of both organizations "within the Negro communities." This particular effort, however, failed to achieve its intended goal because Panther and US activities provided beneficial community services and helped to raise the level of pride for the residents they served. Because these urban blacks had often been denied opportunities that boosted their pride and self-esteem, the inner strength and confidence injected into the black community as a result of this radical organizing made people harder to control than the FBI expected.[100] When this tactic failed, FBI agents went back to what worked.

FBI agents in San Diego supplemented their relationship with local law enforcement by conducting "racial briefing sessions" on the Panthers and other militants. These sessions, wherein police departments studied the identities and activities of Panthers and other militants, made officers "more alert," and therefore contributed "to the overall Counter Intelligence program directed against these groups." [101]

In their attempt to destroy the Panthers, police officers in San Diego used traffic warrants as a pretext for a November 20, 1969, raid on BPP headquarters, which, according to the FBI, was being used to hold "sex orgies on almost a nightly basis." In reality, the FBI compelled the police to use these warrants because it feared its informants were in jeopardy. FBI headquarters also informed the San Diego field office that "if there was no legal basis for a raid, it should give this matter further thought and submit other proposals" to bring about success in "the counterintelligence field." The raid by the San Diego police led to the arrest of six people. According to an FBI memo, the police also seized "three shotguns, one of which was stolen, one rifle, four gas masks, and one tear gas canister." The memo stated that informants reported that "[name deleted] has been severely beaten up by other members of the BPP due to the fact that she allowed the officers to enter BPP headquarters the night of the raid." FBI objectives, however, went further than simple arrests and internal confusion. This particular raid succeeded in terminating official BPP activity in San Diego. The San Diego FBI office reported that Panther leaders in Los Angeles dissolved the San Diego branch after this raid. These leaders must have concluded that six individuals could not adequately operate a chapter.[102] The memos clearly indicate the thoroughness of the FBI's coverage of the BPP.

Understanding the bureau's limitations and not wanting to risk discovery, J. Edgar Hoover subsequently instructed agents in Los Angeles to employ counterintelligence measures particularly aimed at crippling the BPP, since it appeared to be the more threatening of the two organizations. In a memo dated November 25, 1968, Hoover intimated that these measures should "fully capitalize upon BPP and US differences as well as to exploit all avenues of creating further dissension within the ranks of the BPP." These other "avenues" included, but were not limited to, the neutralization and incarceration of charismatic Panthers able to enlist widespread community support of BPP programs and goals.[103]

Nowhere was this strategy more evident than in the case of the recently released Geronimo (Ji Jaga) Pratt, commonly referred to by his comrades as "Geronimo" or simply "G." "G" became active in the Los Angeles BPP after he took an early discharge from the army in exchange for two tours of duty in Vietnam, Cambodia, and Laos. He explained that his army service did not result from any feelings of patriotism, but from the mandates of his "elders" who instructed him to join the service to acquire the skills needed to properly conduct the coming war for black liberation. Clearly the ex-officer used his army training in the service of the black struggle. Not long after his release, Pratt, like many veterans, took advantage of his GI Bill benefits. These benefits allowed him to enroll at the University of California at Los Angeles through the High Potential Equal Opportunity Program, originally designed to aid lower-class inner city residents in attending college. This program emerged as a direct result of the 1965 Watts riots. Not long after his entry into the program, Pratt became acquainted with John Huggins and Bunchy Carter, the latter of whom "nurtured a close personal friendship, and recruited [him] into the Party during the fall [of 1968]."[104] Carter, a leader of the Slausons, arguably the most powerful gang in Southern California, had been befriended by Eldridge Cleaver during a stint in jail. Like Malcolm X, Carter used his jail time to refocus his energies and upon his release he stayed true to his vow to transform himself and those around him into politicized guerillas.[105]

In addition to being interested in Pratt because he supported the Black Power movement, the Panthers likely recruited the ex-soldier because of his extensive military training. In addition to being a paratrooper, he was highly trained "in light weapons and irregular warfare." During his tours of duty in Southeast Asia, Pratt "participated in a series of highly classified missions, garnering some eighteen combat decorations—including the Silver Star, Bronze Star (for valor), the Vietnamese Cross of Gallantry and the Purple Heart." These achievements seem more outstanding when one considers that the Louisiana native, who joined the Army in 1965 as a seventeen-year-old, accomplished them before he reached his twenty-first birthday. Pratt's subsequent disenchantment with the war, along with his increasing aversion to the rapidly deteriorating racial crisis in the United States, therefore made him a likely target for Panther recruiters.[106]

After establishing close ties with various members of the national hierarchy as a result of his work on minister of information Eldridge Cleaver's 1968 presidential campaign and on the party's Free Breakfast for Children Program, Pratt gradually began to assert his influence in Southern California. The untimely murder of Bunchy Carter catapulted Pratt into his leadership position in the Los Angeles chapter. Someone "discovered that Carter had left an audio tape (prepared for such an eventuality) designating the ex-GI his successor as head of the LA-BPP." The authors add that "Pratt was also named by Carter to succeed himself and

Huggins as chapter representative on the national Panther Central Committee." Churchill and Vander Wall point out that Pratt's "effective" political work, which included instructing fellow Panthers in the science of office defense and physical training, garnered him the coveted position. After this series of events, the FBI began to target the newly installed Panther leader in many of its COINTELPRO operations.[107]

Designated a Key Black Extremist (KBE) and placed in the FBI's National Security Index, Pratt subsequently became "an individual to be eliminated by local police action." In a memo to G. C. Moore, Charles Brennan, former head of the FBI's Domestic Intelligence Division, explained that the bureau implemented the KBE program to keep track of "key leaders or activists" who insisted on violent revolution in the United States. Subsequently, FBI headquarters disseminated a long list of guidelines and "measures to be taken" against KBEs to "all field offices." Not only were these individuals included in Priority I of the Security Index and placed in the Black Nationalist Photograph Album, but the government also monitored their financial investments, income tax returns, bank accounts, and safe-deposit boxes. FBI headquarters required its field offices to submit reports on all KBEs "every ninety days." It also urged them to employ "initiative and imagination in order that the desired results are achieved." Based on a "total war" philosophy, the FBI's KBE program led the agency to embrace the most extreme measures in neutralizing BPP leaders. One observer noted that "within eight months, three of the top KBE cases were permanently closed." He explained that "Fred Bennet, Black Panther Coordinator of the East Oakland branch office, Samuel Napier, distribution manager for the Black Panther newspaper; and George Jackson, Black Panther Field Marshall and coordinator of the San Quentin branch, had been assassinated."[108] Once again the U.S. government confirmed its faith in the philosophy of kill the head and the body will die. The "inevitable consequence" of Pratt becoming a KBE "was that the new LA-BPP [leader] was placed under intensely close surveillance by the FBI and subjected to a series of unfounded but serious arrests."[109]

Between April and June 1969, the Los Angeles Police Department arrested Pratt at least three times. It is important to note here that the same thing happened to Panther leaders in Chicago, New York, and other cities at the same time. In early April, the authorities charged Pratt with possessing an explosive while driving. The charge brought no conviction because the police failed to produce the alleged evidence of a pipe-bomb and blasting caps. On April 23 LAPD officers arrested Pratt and four other party members, one of whom turned out to be an FBI informant, for the kidnapping of fellow Panther Ollie Taylor. A Los Angeles jury acquitted him of this charge in April 1971. Trial evidence revealed that Taylor had never been kidnapped, although he did endure a vicious pistol whipping by an informant, Julius Butler, on the day of Pratt's arrest. The beating ended only after Pratt intervened. In June, the police arrested Pratt and other party members for the murder of fellow Panther Frank Diggs, whose body had surfaced the previous December in an isolated area south of the Watts community. After this harassment, the police almost immediately dropped the charges.[110] Pratt wrote of this incident that "after the dude who did it turned himself in and the charges were dropped," the police then "rebooked [them] for the possession of explosive devices they had never seen before." In turn, the court set their bail at twenty-five thousand dollars. According to Pratt, the police arrested him primarily to foil a Panther rally and community fundraiser, planned for the following day.[111]

In keeping with its official goal, however, the FBI's desire to eliminate Pratt became even more urgent when the Panther began to play an increasingly active role in the Black Liberation Army (BLA), later named the Afro-American Liberation Army. This organization derived some of its membership from Black Panthers who, for any number of reasons, were driven "underground." For the most part, these members hid out in several cities throughout the country to avoid arrest on real and fabricated criminal charges.[112] After joining this "underground" organization, their primary duty was to engage the police and other government agencies in guerilla war. One BLA member noted that the group wanted to take "the war to the enemy instead of waiting for the enemy to bring the war to us." Another described the group as a decentralized guerrilla army made up of small units "knowledgeable of the particular area in which they operate." He added that one had to be serious about revolution to be admitted. For Pratt, the BLA had a real pan-African connection because "it recognizes our connectedness with Africa, in terms of the history of how Africans were torn away from their homelands and how we, as descendants of those brought to North America as slaves, are

Women of the BPP gather for a political education class in Oakland in 1970. *Photo by Ducho Dennis, courtesy of It's About Time.*

joining, gun in hand, with our comrades, the descendants of those who were left behind to suffer under colonial and neo-colonial domination."[113]

In particular, the FBI, the Department of Defense, and other federal agencies sought to stop Pratt and his comrades before they seriously damaged the American infrastructure, or worse, attracted significant public support for their activities. Pratt's neutralization, therefore, became increasingly important. FBI headquarters then assigned more agents to follow his movements. This assignment took them on a wild and exciting journey.

Pratt described how, in August 1970, the BLA assigned him to organize guerilla units throughout the United States. He added that this program enjoyed success from the start because the young and impoverished blacks he encountered seemed eager to join the Panther's cause. Pratt noted that "these individuals made ideal revolutionaries because their lives on the street had taught them the art of adaptation and survival."[114] The willingness of blacks to join such a radical organization is testament to the extent of deprivation and oppression they experienced on the streets and in the backwoods of America.

Pratt insisted that "one of the main reasons the pigs have been keen on me is that I trained Special Forces at Fort Bragg and endured three wars (four now)." Because of training and experience, Pratt insisted that racist and imperialist actions were easily understood and countered once one understood the general laws of warfare. He went on to write that when the army released him, "guys were being offered high-paying jobs—including myself—by the CIA." Pratt claimed his love for the street life ("pimping and the rest") saved him from both the CIA and an untimely death.[115] His political activities eventually won him a twenty-seven year stay in the California State Prison system.

In 1971, the authorities falsely charged and convicted Pratt of the 1969 robbery and murder of Caroline Olsen, a teacher in Santa Monica, California. Julius Butler, the now infamous *agent provocateur*, provided the crucial evidence that convicted him. Butler claimed that not only had Pratt confessed to him that he murdered the woman, shot her husband, and robbed them of eighteen dollars, but he had also replaced the gun's barrel to avoid detection.[116] Not that Pratt would have divulged this information even to someone he agreed with, but by this point, the Panther leader thoroughly distrusted Butler and is not likely to have provided this information.

The bureau, of course, knew of Pratt's innocence. It had the BPP under heavy surveillance. As a result, FBI agents had recorded the proceedings of a BPP Central Committee meeting in Oakland at the same time that the murder took place. From this surveillance, the FBI knew of Pratt's presence at the meeting, some three hundred miles away from the murder scene. Pratt's team of lawyers, led by Johnnie Cochran, subpoenaed these FBI documents. Pratt's defense team discovered during the trial that the tapes on which these proceedings had been recorded, as well phone taps of calls Pratt made from Oakland to Los Angeles on the day of the murder, were conveniently lost. Thus, Pratt's alibi went unsubstantiated. Months earlier, Pratt and Newton, who had recently been released from prison, had serious personal and ideological disagreements. Newton eventually expelled Pratt because of his bravado and his close associations with Eldridge Cleaver. The FBI knew of this split and capitalized on it by charging Pratt with a two-year-old unsolved murder. With the help of a well-placed informant, the charges stuck.[117] The government's timing proved perfect in this situation. FBI officials knew of the heated disagreements and hatred between the faction of the party that followed Newton and the people who supported Cleaver. The FBI was confident that Newton was not going to allow anyone present at the meeting to testify on Pratt's behalf. As a result, Pratt went to jail for nearly thirty years for a crime the government and the prosecution both knew he did not commit.

In June 1997, however, Everett W. Dickey, a conservative Los Angeles judge appointed by Gov. Ronald Reagan in 1970, reversed the ruling, arguing "the prosecution had suppressed evidence that might have kept him from being convicted." On the witness stand, Butler lied about being an FBI informant, a fact later substantiated by attorney Cochran. FBI records, ironically discovered in the files of the Los Angeles District Attorney prosecuting the case, proved Butler's employment by the bureau from 1969 to 1972. Labeling Butler "a liar and a government informer with a grudge against Pratt," Judge Dickey wrote that "this was not a strong case for the prosecution without the testimony of Butler." One news article noted that "hours after Mr. Pratt was released, Mr. Butler resigned from the board of his church" in Los Angeles and "declined to discuss the case." Nevertheless, Pratt's conviction and sentence achieved the desired effect of furthering the federal government's goal of ruining the BPP's Southern California chapter.[118]

A Senate committee report entitled "The FBI's Covert Action Program to Destroy the Black Panther Party" concluded that "although the claimed purpose of the bureau's COINTELPRO was to prevent violence, some of the FBI's tactics against the BPP were clearly intended to foster violence, and many others could reasonably have been expected to cause violence." This report demonstrated "that the chief investigative branch of the Federal Government, which was charged by law with investigating crimes and preventing criminal conduct, itself engaged in lawless tactics and responded to deep-seated social problems by fomenting violence and unrest." Contemporary observers later came to understand that the federal complicity in much of the violence in which the BPP engaged helped determine the party's demise.[119]

One of the primary goals of the FBI, CIA, and other federal investigative agencies between 1967 and 1972 was to prevent the growth and success of the BPP and other radical political groups. In its efforts to achieve this goal, the federal government (from the executive and judicial branches to the IRS and the army) devised a number of covert operations. These secret activities, exemplified in COINTELPRO, not only involved the use of informants and *agents provocateurs,* but wiretaps and burglaries as well. These endeavors, many of which were clearly questionable ethically and legally, demonstrated the extent of the federal government's commitment to silencing black radical political dissent.[120]

Although other militants qualified as some of the government's targets, by July 1969, it primarily focused on the Panthers. The BPP ultimately became the target of 233 of the total 295 authorized COINTELPRO actions.[121] The bureau must have spent millions on fighting the BPP and its supporters. While it is difficult to pinpoint exactly how much taxpayer money went to these operations, one can assume it took no small amount for the bureau, which admitted in an affidavit to the Church Committee, to collect "between 1,500,000 and 2,000,000 pages of counterintelligence information on the Black Panther Party," of which all but about eighty thousand pages is still classified. This page count did not include files on individual party members, supporters, or contributors to the organization. It is not unreasonable to believe that years of salaries, equipment and other expenditures went into breaking up the BPP. After all, informants and electronic listening devices are expensive.[122] The FBI, nevertheless, needed events to unfold in a certain way to ensure the success of its programs. Despite efforts to cover his tracks, even the esteemed FBI director left some proof of how questionable these activities were.

J. Edgar Hoover, shortly before his death in 1974, expressed the following reservations to his assistant, William Sullivan, concerning his agency's role in domestic surveillance: "For years and years," he wrote, "I have approved opening mail and other similar operations, but no [more]. It is becoming more and more dangerous and we are apt to get caught." Hoover explained he was "not opposed to doing this." Nor was he "opposed to continuing the burglaries and the opening of mail and other similar activities, providing someone higher than myself approves of it." According to the dying director, he no longer wanted "to accept the sole responsibility." He believed "the Attorney General or some high ranking person in the White House" should be responsible. If that happened, he said, "then I will carry out their decision. But I'm not going to accept the responsibility myself anymore, even though I've done it for many years."[123]

This memo demonstrates that Hoover understood the limitations of federal lawlessness and the adverse repercussions that could occur if the facts became public. His admission that burglaries and the like were acceptable also indicates the contempt the number one United States police agency had for the law. In insisting that the blame be placed far away from him, Hoover's note not only shows how cowardly he became over the years, but that other high-ranking officials had knowledge of these clandestine activities, and therefore believed they were essential to maintaining the status quo. The Panthers, like Marcus Garvey, W. E. B. DuBois, Robert Williams, and other black nationalists who came before them, experienced the might of a government determined to maintain its dominance over black life. No matter how hard the Panthers tried, they could not get their operations to run smoothly and without interference from established authority.

CHAPTER 7

Southern Discomfort: Tarheels, Pelicans, Panthers, and Police

PARTLY AS A RESULT OF THE INCREASING pressure to disband, in 1969 the Panthers began using a different organizational tactic. Chief of staff David Hilliard noted that "out of the United Front Against Fascism Conference in July, 1969 came the National Committee to Combat Fascism," which "set up centers of operation in Black and White Communities across the country." These centers were under the control of local residents, and not necessarily the Panthers.[1]

According to the July 25, 1970, issue of *The Black Panther,* these NCCFs acted as "organizing bureaus of the Black Panther Party ONLY." Once an NCCF chapter proved its worthiness via various community initiatives, the national headquarters officially considered it a BPP chapter. For example, in May 1970, the Panther newspaper referred to the Baltimore group as a NCCF. As early as June 1970, the party labeled the same entity a chapter, because, according to one Baltimore Panther, it had proven its worthiness. Interestingly, the BPP allowed whites to become members of these committees, a clear indication that it did not consider all whites to be the enemy. The BPP's class analysis of society, based in the theory of Marxism-Leninism, provided the group bases of support far out of the reach of many of the other Black Power groups of the period (like the Student Nonviolent Coordinating Committee and the Congress of Racial Equality), which insisted that whites be removed from decision-making positions in their organizations.[2] Under this ideology, the BPP saw class as the most important arbiter of conflict and believed that a worldwide revolution of workers was needed to overthrow the capitalists and to institute a dictatorship of the masses.

Despite the group's progressive political views, it continued to have difficulty attracting a large number of blacks. Its alliances with whites turned many of them off. The national white backlash, as indicated by the election of Richard Nixon and the popularity of racist Alabama Gov. George Wallace, who also ran for president in 1968, led an increasing number of blacks to believe whites were indeed their enemies. Attacks on busing, the Civil Rights Act of 1964, and the Voting Rights Act of 1965 convinced many blacks in America that whites had no intention of becoming their friends, particularly not via integration. When the Panthers attempted to look beyond issues of race and began to include whites as a significant part of their base of support, they attempted to fight racism with solidarity while at the same time making up for the lack of black bodies to put on the front lines of their revolutionary advance.

This change in tactics proved especially useful when the party organized in the Deep South. Understanding the historical violence visited upon blacks in the South, one can readily see how the name Black Panther Party might anger keepers of the status quo in places like Memphis, Dallas, Houston, New Orleans, and Greensboro, North Carolina. While the Panthers established NCCFs in all these cities, as well as Cleveland, Mississippi, and Winston-Salem, North Carolina, only the New Orleans and North Carolina branches will be discussed here, because they best illustrate the theme of armed warfare between the police and Panthers.[3]

Panthers created the NCCFs not only to attract more nonblack recruits, but also to address the problem of how rising levels of repression against the party left it with fewer and fewer fighting soldiers. With whites openly working for and with the party, the group expanded into communities it previously had never been able to reach. Their problems, however, increased rather than diminished, causing a downward spiral of violence that eventually destroyed the party. Panthers in Louisiana's bayous, like their comrades in California, found that this reality had no geographic exceptions.

The prevalence of police brutality in New Orleans, along with widespread poverty, unemployment, and rampant discrimination, provided fertile soil for the Panthers. In May 1970, Panther headquarters in Oakland sent Victor Hudson, Harold Holmes, and New Orleans native Stephen Greene to set up a NCCF in New Orleans. As with the establishment of other southern chapters, Geronimo Pratt employed his military skills to help the new organization prepare to go to work. The group opened an office in the black community at 2353 St. Thomas Street. New Orleans's deputy superintendent of police, Louis J. Sirgo, later provided the Senate with a detailed description of how the office operated. There were about "eight persons who [were] the hard core members" and "an office staff of volunteers, including females, consisting of about 40 young people," he recounted. This staff maintained records and files of the organization and typed letters, leaflets and other literature. Noting that the NCCF had "a military type setup," the deputy superintendent pointed out the group designated an armed "officer of the day" to monitor everyone who went in and out of the office. This individual was also responsible for monitoring all police radio calls.[4] Sirgo noted the NCCF quickly made alliances with other leftist groups in the city, namely "the Republic of New Africa, the Progressive Labor Party, and the Tulane Liberation Front, which is a different name for SDS [Students for a Democratic Society] operating at one of our local universities."[5]

Because of the widespread police attacks on Panther offices throughout the country, existing chapters and newly established BPP affiliates (NCCFs) reinforced offices with sandbags, gun portholes, and escape tunnels. Pratt supervised much of this reinforcement throughout the nation. In a February 1998 speech in Jackson, Mississippi, he explained that he and a number of cohorts traveled around the country teaching fellow Panthers these "survival techniques." Panther minister of culture Emory Douglas pointed out that "G was responsible for saving a lot of lives by doing this—that's why they [the police and federal government] wanted him off the streets."[6]

This sandbagging activity on the part of the New Orleans NCCF garnered it an eviction from the 2353 St. Thomas Street headquarters. The party subsequently moved to 3542 Piety Street, near the notorious Desire Project, a federal housing development with some ten thousand residents. Sirgo noted that "this is an impoverished area with [a] high crime rate and boundaries such as a drainage canal and railroad tracks which tend to isolate the area from the rest of the community." Set off like a city within a city, the project's location, according to one newspaper, was in "an area where few buses, and no taxis [went] after dark; of few shops; little police protection and minimal sanitation; of not a single newsstand; of two schools so closely fenced with wire that local children cannot play in the schoolyards after school lets out." This move turned out to be a positive one for the NCCF because, as Sirgo noted, "its membership grew to about 300 persons, mostly young people, many female." He also noted that in addition to fortifying the new head-quarters with sandbags and gun portholes in the front and rear doors, the group also "placed wire over the windows . . . to prevent gas grenades from being thrown in."[7]

After setting up its headquarters, the NCCF followed BPP guidelines and instituted weekly political education classes, set up a breakfast program, sold the party newspaper, put up posters around headquarters and on buildings and telephone poles throughout the area, and engaged in other necessary office work. The Panthers, by providing protection from robbers to the elderly and others and by clearing the community of drug dealers, transformed the Desire Project from one of the most dangerous places in the city to one of the most safe. Malik Rahim, a Vietnam veteran and one of the Panther leaders in New Orleans, recalled that "rapes and break-ins also went down" after the group's arrival.[8] As in other locales, the Panthers believed they had to get violent with those who insisted on bringing violence into the black community. "Once we let them know that that type activity would not be appreciated," Rahim remembered, "they usually got the point and left or did their dirt elsewhere." He added, "there were those who thought they were bad or did not take us seriously so we had to show them." Rahim noted that "showing them" sometimes included a good beating and, in the most extreme cases, some robbers and drug dealers were shot or shot at and then run out of the community.

As this activity continued into 1970, the Panthers simultaneously engaged in the first major incident with the New Orleans Police Department. Officer Raymond Reed, raised in the Desire Project area, arrested two NCCF representatives for placing Panther posters on public property. Sirgo noted that prior to the NCCF organizing in the city, Reed had been "very effective in making arrests of wanted subjects from the area," which likely made him suspect to many residents. NCCF members learned from community residents that Reed customarily harassed the local citizenry. Subsequently, NCCF members painted signs on buildings and distributed leaflets advocating the killing of Officer Reed.[9] One of those leaflets proclaimed that Reed needed to be exposed because he was a "bootlicker, puppet, and nigger pig" who pretended to protect and serve the black community. Claiming that Reed and "White racist components of the N.O. Pig Department are nothing but tools and fools to be used to terrorize the black community and keep Niggers intact," the leaflet informed readers that Reed had "openly showed his hand by unjustly brutalizing brothers on the block and dressing it up by making them look like criminals and he the victim." It further noted that since Reed was a traitor, he deserved "DEATH." The leaflet labeled the black officer a cowardly "Faggot" and said that he was "just like any other Pig and he can bleed." For his crimes against black people, the leaflet said Reed had to be "brought to justice." So that no one was mistaken about the justice he was to receive, it added "he has no choice but to die with the Pigs." Its architect concluded by calling for "All power to the people" and "DEATH TO RAYMOND REED."[10] This brazen declaration of war against one of New Orleans's finest signaled the beginning of a serious confrontation between the Panthers and a police department widely known for its brutality and corruption.

Sirgo told Congress that, at this point, the NOPD "successfully infiltrated two [policemen] into the NCCF organization as community workers." Emory Douglas noted nearly three decades later that this type of infiltration proved simple since the informants who wished to join the party "looked and dressed just like us." He added, "it wasn't like they were strange and funny looking people" and, besides, "if they wanted to come in and sell the paper and do other types of community work, then we didn't care."[11] New Orleans Panther Rahim also noted that they sometimes found informants but chose not to kill or oust them because of their potential value for work and information. He claimed they were used to do grunt work, to retrieve the newspaper from the airport or to run errands for other members of the party.[12] As in many other organizations, however, new recruits had to prove themselves loyal to the party and its goals before the Panther leadership exposed them to sensitive information.

In this case, the Panther leaders suspected the two police agents, Israel Fields and Melvin Howard, who had grown their hair into afros "so that their appearance would be acceptable to the Panthers," according to New Orleans *Times-Picayune* reporter Don Hughes. A member of the community, one of the children, spotted the two going in and out of the local police precinct, and, on several occasions, riding in cars with the police. The child then told the Panthers of this suspicious activity. On September 14, 1970, the Panthers "held a mock trial and determined that the two undercover agents would be killed." What is interesting to note here is that Panther leadership chose not to have the party mete out retribution but turned the two over to the people who lived in the community. Sirgo went on to describe how one of the officers "was severely beaten with a piece of lumber with nails in one end of it." At one point, they "were shoved to the floor and .357 magnums were held to their heads. Then as many as twenty people at a time were allowed to kick and beat the officers, who were forced to wipe up their own blood with their clothing." Afterward, this assembly of more than a hundred people, dubbed "The Peoples' Court," took the agents out of the building to a larger crowd that awaited with "guns, sticks, bottles, pipes, bricks, and chains." Believing they were to be killed soon, the two "jumped from the stairway of the second floor and began their run for life," according to the New Orleans *Times-Picayune.* The awaiting crowd beat them and knocked them to the ground several times before they took off in different directions. They somehow managed to escape. Fields took refuge in a nearby grocery store and Howard, after negotiating a seven-foot fence,[13] "made his way through a drainage canal under houses through backyards until he got to a telephone," said Sirgo. He added that shortly after this incident, "Officer Reed and his partner [Joseph Orticke] were patrolling near the NCCF headquarters when their patrol car came under fire." Shattered glass showered Reed's face and upper body. Despite being wounded, the other officer succeeded in driving the two of them to the hospital. Describing the battle that ensued as "a reign of terror in the Desire area" and explaining that they heard gunfire throughout the night, Sirgo testified "the automobile which the two undercover officers were using was set afire and driven into a canal." He described how "other automobiles were wrecked and burned and used as roadblocks at major intersections leading to the NCCF headquarters." The deputy superintendent noted that the party made its national scope clear when the BPP's "public information officer received a telephone call from UPI" stating that the group's "Oakland chapter issued a release saying that the Black Panther headquarters in New Orleans was under siege by the New Orleans Police Department."[14]

In his Senate testimony a year later, Sirgo explained how in early September 1970, the New Orleans police began to prepare arrest warrants for those responsible for the infiltrators' beatings and search warrants for

NCCF headquarters. He reported that he and his coworkers spent the night's remaining hours preparing a task force because they "were aware of the amount of arms and ammunition located in the headquarters." At the central lockup before the raid, one black policeman told a reporter what they were about to do was "a job" and that "somebody had to do it." A convoy of police buses and cruisers, accompanied by carloads of reporters, then made its way through the downtown rush hour traffic and onto Interstate 10. When the first officers arrived in the Desire area around eight in the morning, heavy gunfire met them before they came within three hundred yards of the building. "My God, it sounds like a war," one policeman exclaimed as "automatic rifle and machine gun fire punctuated the early morning stillness." Along to provide aid and support to the local police were members of the Louisiana State Police and members of the Jefferson Parish Sheriff's Office.[15]

In unequivocal terms, Sirgo exclaimed that "armed combat and open warfare had come to the city of New Orleans." The Panthers used "high powered rifles, automatic weapons, and handguns in their battle against the authorities," noted the *Times-Picayune*. The paper noted that there was a lapse of about four hours "until shooting began again . . . when police attempted to force their way into the two-story building housing the Panthers." According to the police, all they wanted to do was "serve search and arrest warrants on the Panthers,"[16] but the newly purchased armored tank they brought along indicated otherwise. Malik Rahim, who took part in the two-day gun battle, explained that it was a very scary time, but the Panthers had to defend themselves and their offices. He remembered crawling around the headquarters, checking to see if everybody was alright and thinking that "surely a lot of us had been killed because that damned tank out there was rocking those walls." To his surprise, people all over the office who had taken up their prearranged positions yelled out "we all right in here!" in response to his question, "anybody dead in there?" Explaining that the walls in their office had been reinforced with layers and layers of sandbags, he noted that "we surrendered because we had proven our point," which was that blacks could defend themselves, maintain their dignity, and live like real men and women if they only tried. The police, however, thought it was the teargas canisters that forced "the revolutionaries to surrender." Sirgo noted that "small-arms fire continued from other locations in the Desire area," throughout the night.[17]

Panther youth enjoy a meal in 1970 at the Intercommunal Youth Institute. *Photo by Ducho Dennis, courtesy of It's About Time.*

This subsequent shooting could have come from Panthers who had fled to other buildings or from members of the community who supported the BPP. For example, after the Panthers were finally cleared out of the building, "[a] large bottle and rock-throwing crowd gathered and began pushing and shouting" and lifting "clinched fists, a sign indicating support of the Panthers," according to the *Times-Picayune*. The paper added that "the crowd managed to force police officers across a drainage canal bridge on nearby Higgins Blvd. The officers were finally withdrawn at 12:10 p.m."[18] Still others provided medical aid, protection, and shelter for the severely wounded Steve Green, one of the primary people the police sought to arrest. Additional evidence indicating it might have been community residents doing some of the shooting is that many blacks told reporters that they regarded the raid and Panther defense of their office as "the first heroic chapter in the life of the New Orleans chapter." According to the *New York Times*, "others went to the headquarters the following day to get it together for reopening." The paper went on to say that "the nearby community is heavily armed to protect the Panthers."[19]

Amazingly, only one person died in the shootout; he happened to be neither a Panther nor a policeman. The police did, however, arrest more than a dozen people. They booked three women and thirteen men and charged them with attempted murder. All but one of those arrested were between the ages of seventeen and twenty-two. The police also charged a fourteen-year-old boy. According to the *Times-Picayune*, federal agents of the Bureau of Alcohol Tobacco and Firearms division of the Treasury Department "also filed complaints against the 16 for violating the Federal Gun Control Act," as the police had "confiscated 11 shotguns, two revolvers, a M-1 rifle, a training rifle, and a Bowie knife."[20] Had the Panthers and the NCCF not been well-trained to defend themselves against the police and prepared for this eventuality, many lives might have been lost. The Chicago and Los Angeles shootouts clearly demonstrated this fact.

The violence in this episode came about after the police tried to infiltrate an organization that had committed no crime. The Panthers'

Jessica Fountaine, daughter of Gwen Fountaine, Huey Newton's first wife, at the Intercommunal Youth Institute, 1970. *Photo by Ducho Dennis, courtesy of It's About Time.*

response to this violence was to return it in kind. They had no intention of quitting or compromising for the sake of token concessions. Their charge, however, was such that a violent clash with police officials was inevitable.

In November 1970, the police again attempted to evict the Panthers from their Desire headquarters, given to them "by the people," according to NCCF spokesman Harold Holmes. This time, "hundreds of angry Negroes blocked the armored tank, many shouted profanities," noted the *Times Picayune*. After the police, armed with riot guns and wearing bullet-resistant vests, urged the people to move out of the area for their "own safety," the group replied in unison "More power to the people" and began throwing bottles at reporters who watched the fracas from the side of the Community Center.[21] After a five-hour standoff, the police withdrew. Undoubtedly some community members had become fed up with their deplorable living conditions and police maltreatment of New Orleans blacks.

Organizing the community to be politically effective and self-sufficient, this militant group of men and women loudly and publicly spoke out "against the injustice of this society." That they drastically reduced crime in the Desire Project area and made it safe for people to live normal lives again was lost on the authorities. Their violent rhetoric and willingness to die for their convictions presented local law enforcement with a problem they had not had the time or inclination to solve: black people uniting under an agenda not directed or sanctioned by whites. If success came the Panthers' way, the power structure might be drastically and forever changed for the betterment of all the city's residents.

As a result, the New Orleans police chief promised city residents that the police force was not going to allow the NCCF "to get a foothold in the community." An NCCF news release issued after the shootout reported that since the group had arrived in May, the FBI had been warning the mayor and police chief "to cut out the cancer before it spreads." NCCF members explained they "had been evicted from offices twice because of pressure from the city." The note also stated President Richard Nixon used the same words in a letter to university presidents regarding the frequent urban rebellions of the period. Nixon often blamed widespread chaos in the United States on the Panthers, Students for a Democratic Society, and other radical groups. Clearly, established authority viewed the Panthers and others advocating the violent overthrow of the government as arch enemies. As such, these groups had to be dealt with harshly and swiftly.[22]

In its own defense, the NCCF noted that the heavy police response came as a result of their threatening the cops "and the rich who the cops protect." They explained that because they "started a free breakfast for children program, exposed certain cops who terrorized the black community," and "revealed how grocery man Nellie Broussard exploited the community by his high prices . . . the cops here attacked the NCCF chapter." Missing from the Panthers' assessment is that party members, on more than one occasion, threatened to kill policemen who patrolled the black community. The fact that the policemen had been threatening to kill Panthers and other blacks in Desire for a long time mattered little to those who sought to contain the growth of the Panthers and other groups of their ilk.[23] The violence that came in the wake of these threats almost always affected the Panthers negatively.

Calling the police raid on NCCF headquarters a trap designed to provoke the Panthers to commit some lawless act, NCCF spokespersons explained that "no charges were filed" based on the warrants the police eventually obtained and the charges of attempted murder [for firing on police] "were dropped by the city because they knew all along that NCCF members were not guilty." Arguing that what happened in New Orleans was reminiscent of the Los Angeles and Chicago raids, NCCF members complained that "these warrants were only an excuse for the long-planned and eagerly awaited police raid." The group also alleged that the news media had openly become the mouthpiece of the police "in order to spread the lie that the black community is not sympathetic to the NCCF." It is unlikely blacks in the community opposed the NCCF and its goals since most of the community youth participated in the organization's Free Breakfast for Children Program and its Liberation School for the Youth. Attempting to show that the local authorities disapproved of their activities, the NCCF claimed that "some newsmen had the police check their stories before they went to press" while the two entities simultaneously created "a climate of terror where people who were either witnesses to [the shootouts] or who are sympathetic to the NCCF are afraid to speak out."[24]

In the days following the shootout, New Orleans police arrested nearly fifty blacks from the Desire area. An NCCF news release claimed the police were "having a heyday in pinning unsolved crimes on those arrested." The arrestees included Wayne Morris, Larry Patterson, Lionel Ward, and Joseph Batiste, all of whom were college students and members of the NCCF. Others arrested included Charles "Chuckie" Scott, an eighteen-year-old from New York City who had been integral in setting up the New Orleans chapter, Robert Revels and Willie Lee Dawkins of Washington, D.C., George Lloyd of Oakland, and Steve Green, also responsible for helping to organize the chapter. The Panthers who had not been arrested, most of whom were female, opened the office the next day and continued their political organizing.[25] Though the authorities never said it explicitly, they wanted to get rid of the group's many survival programs.

The Free Breakfast for Children Program provided free breakfasts not only to blacks, but also to poor white and Hispanic children. The program provided two basic services in the communities in which it operated: an ongoing supply of food to meet the children's daily needs and periodic mass distributions of food to reach a larger section of the community. During his later years in the party, Eldridge Cleaver greatly diminished the importance of the community service programs, but initially he had explained the need for the programs derived from the basic unmet needs of the people. He said the programs succeeded because "people can readily relate to the need to eat breakfast." Adding that people were "concerned about perpetuating life without food," Cleaver, in agreement with other party members, argued that empty stomachs greatly hindered student production, a phenomenon, they insisted, that led to underachievement in lower-class students. Gauging response to the program in Portland, the Portland *Oregonian* reported that for nearly two years, "the Panthers [had] been winning widespread approval in the . . . community . . . despite financial shortages" and inexperience. Many in the public spoke highly of the programs. Because male and female Panthers were highly visible in the administration of these programs, many of their contemporaries saw them as capable and courageous individuals imbued with the hope and faith necessary to bring about change for themselves and their children.[26]

Claiming the party's "Cardinal Rule" was "have faith in the people

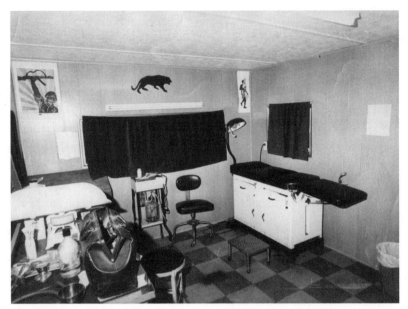

The Black Panther health clinic in Boston, 1971. *Photo by Ducho Dennis, courtesy of It's About Time.*

and faith in the Party," an editorial in the *Black Panther* pointed out the BPP wanted to "overthrow the present imperialistic" system by "providing for the needs of the people." The group's community survival programs represented some of the tools to be used in this struggle. The programs succeeded in attracting support throughout the various communities in which the party operated.[27] Chairman Bobby Seale insisted the party's intended goal was to get the programs started and then "turn them over to the people." Huey Newton pointed out that these survival programs were "only a means of organizing the people in an attempt to lift their consciousness." The programs must have had some positive effect in this respect because there were numerous occasions when police kicked in the doors at the centers where the programs were held. They then destroyed food, files, and equipment, sometimes making it impossible for the programs to continue. In one street battle with Panthers, the Chicago police shot and killed Larry Roberson, the chapter's breakfast coordinator. They hoped his death would diminish the Panthers' effectiveness as community organizers, since the group used the breakfast program to publicize its other goals.[28] Clearly, Roberson's death conformed to the FBI's assumption that to kill the breakfast program would go far toward killing the party.[29]

The degree of success the programs had remains unclear. Seale, Newton, and other Panther leaders claimed to have served more than twenty thousand breakfasts throughout the Bay Area between 1967 and 1972. One Panther noted the party "served about 10,000 breakfasts a day across the country." On the other hand, Newton's successor, Elaine Brown, starkly points out that by 1972, they "found it virtually impossible to feed hungry black people with any regularity because at times we had no access to proper facilities and nearly all the money and energy we . . . mustered were being depleted by our effort to simply keep our people on the street." Residents who lived in the neighborhoods where these programs operated claimed they were well attended.[30]

One of the party's more successful programs was the Oakland Community School, directed by Ericka Huggins, the widow of John Huggins, a Los Angeles Panther leader murdered as a result of the FBI's now infamous Counter Intelligence Program. Located at 6118 East Fourteenth Street, in the heart of East Oakland's black community, the tuition-free school had 120 students in 1975 and continued to operate until 1982. With a curriculum consisting of Spanish, math, reading, writing, and history, the Oakland Community School quickly instilled in the students a strong sense of self-worth and pride. Because the communities adjacent to the school had a sizable Mexican American population, a number of Mexican Americans also attended, as did white and Asian pupils. From the start, the Panthers let the students and their parents know they opposed exploitation from anyone, regardless of color. Ericka Huggins pointed out that "our children don't relate to color, but judge each other as individuals."[31]

The school's twenty-two teachers, ten staff members, and "additional volunteers consisting of welfare mothers, grandmothers," and various other leaders of the black community, eventually became what Huggins described as a model of alternative education. The children's parents actively participated in the school. For example, they provided "aid in the classrooms, offices, cafeteria," and they wrote "proposals to obtain funding," an area in which Panther women played an integral role.[32]

Women played crucial roles in the maintenance of the BPP Free Health Clinics. These medical facilities, which began operating in Oakland in 1969, often started with a single doctor and one nursing student from a nearby university. At first they did little more than refer sick children and elderly people to other doctors for care. As the popularity of these clinics spread and their force of volunteer doctors and nurses increased, the BPP, with whatever resources they had, provided what many observers considered comprehensive health care for their communities.[33]

In their efforts to provide poor communities with health care, Panthers enlisted the help of interns from local medical schools. These individuals, eager to help alleviate some of the suffering in impoverished areas, performed valuable community services free of charge. On occasion, these interns persuaded the doctors they worked under to donate their services to the Panther program. Otherwise, the Panthers simply canvassed the city for people and organizations willing to help. For example, when the Chicago Panthers wanted to establish a Free Health Clinic, Ronald Satchel, a former Vietnam medic who served as the Chicago chapter's minister of health, enlisted the help of "more than 150 nurses, technicians, physicians, and health science students [who had] volunteered to help provide services evenings and all day Sundays."[34]

After the establishment of Free Health Clinics in such cities as Des Moines, Iowa, New York, Detroit, Kansas City, Missouri, Memphis, Chicago, Dallas, Los Angeles, and Oakland, one Panther explained "the Clinics function as model health institutions whose services are geared to meet the needs of Black and other poor people who cannot afford to pay the high fees charged by most doctors in private practices." In his explanation of why the programs were free, Huey Newton remarked he did not feel the Panthers "should get caught up in a lot of embarrassing questions or paperwork which alienate the people." He added that an important goal of the program was "to attempt to get the people to understand the true reasons why they were in need in such an incredibly rich land," an obvious reference to what the BPP considered the "avariciousness" of the American political and economic system.[35]

With multiracial staffs consisting of Asians, blacks, Hispanics, and whites, the clinics not only helped the sick and infirm, but they also demonstrated to many people that the Panthers were not simply out to kill white people, despite the fact that the mainstream media portrayed the group as mad killers. The patrons of these clinics also came from various racial and ethnic backgrounds. Henry Smith, a former coordinator

The Black Panther Party Community Center in West Oakland, 1970. *Photo by Ducho Dennis, courtesy of It's About Time.*

for the People's Free Medical Clinic in Oakland, emphasized this point in an interview when he explained that "we provide medical care equally to all—regardless of their ethnic background or financial status." Dr. Mutulu Shakur, a former member of the New York branch, noted that because health care is essential to human life, he saw no reason why anyone should do without it. Disease and suffering were rampant in ghettos throughout the United States, so the Panthers moved to work out a solution to the problem.[36]

In their efforts to help sustain these clinics, Panthers, many of them trained nurses, not only staffed and solicited support, but also helped to treat their patients with bronchial ailments, high blood pressure, back pain, and the common cold. The better staffed and more sophisticated clinics treated patients with diabetes, tuberculosis, and urinary tract infections. Patients discovered to have heart disease, mental retardation, and other serious conditions were sent to specialists. The clinics' most visible operations, however, were as screening centers for sickle cell anemia. Sickle cell anemia is a disease that overwhelmingly affects black Americans. Their ancestors, from thousands of years of living in Africa, where malaria was common, developed the sickle cell trait to fight this disease—evolving to a point where their blood cells changed shape to prevent malaria from killing them. Instead of being oval like they are in other humans, they turned into an elongated sickle-like shape. The disease had been misdiagnosed in blacks for decades and because of the Panthers, doctors began paying attention to it.

In South Berkeley, Dr. Tolbert Small, a community physician, aided the Panthers in their efforts. David Hilliard pointed out that the party publicized "the problem so successfully that Nixon himself mentioned sickle-cell in his 1968 health message to Congress." He also mentioned the disease in his 1973 Inaugural Address. The BPP eventually set up a Sickle Cell Anemia Research Foundation in an effort to help find a cure for the condition.[37]

Local newspapers and other mainstream publications paid scant or no attention to these Free Health Clinics or any of the other Panther survival programs. It is therefore difficult to prove whether these operations were as successful and effective as the Panthers claimed. Because ghetto residents often had neither access to, nor means to pay for, adequate medical care, these clinics undoubtedly represented some improvements for the neighborhoods in which they served.[38] An article in the New York *Daily World* reported that one Panther Free Health Clinic had "ten doctors, twelve nurses, and two registered technicians." Also staffing the clinic were "a large number of interns who come and help regularly, from medical schools from around the city." Douglas noted that the BPP chapters in Winston-Salem and Memphis provided ambulance services. While a number of the clinics stopped operating by 1972, some clinics continued to function as late as 1976. Still others continue operating today but with non-Panther staff. Regardless of the level of services, the group achieved its goal of showing many poor people that even without adequate resources, they could work together to solve some of their more pressing problems.[39]

Although local, state, and federal officials claimed to have been interested in avoiding violence, they used violence to disrupt and destroy the BPP and its members. The authorities in New Orleans simply outgunned the Panthers and forced them to engage in more peaceful forms of protest or no protest at all. The violence emanating from official sources prompted violence in return. It was this retaliatory violence, however, that gave authorities the justification they needed to rid black communities of the Panther menace. This pattern can be seen in New Orleans and the rest of the Panther chapters established below the Mason-Dixon line, including North Carolina.

The history of Black Panther/NCCF activity in the Tarheel State duplicated what happened in most other states where Panthers became visible. The BPP either started a chapter in a particular locale or authorized a NCCF to help it organize and achieve its goals. In most places, the BPP sought to target the youth of a particular community. In North Carolina, high school and college students represented the bulk of these youngsters. The group's goals remained the same: to set up community service programs in various impoverished areas and to defend black residents from police attacks.

The Greensboro chapter, formed in 1969, was the first chapter in North Carolina. Eric Brown served as captain and Robert Spero as field lieutenant. Harold Avant, one of the field marshals in the Greensboro chapter, told one of his political education classes that as early as January 1969, the group "had a training session on guerrilla tactics on the campus at [historically black North Carolina] A & T University." This campus training session held major implications for the future. Soon after, the Panthers and A&T students found themselves shooting it out with the police and National Guard. This particular conflagration coincided with numerous campus rebellions erupting throughout the United States. As many officials claimed, the BPP played an integral part in fomenting some of these outbreaks.[40]

The FBI knew about the BPP's activities in Greensboro even before the party organized the chapter. A February 17, 1969, memo from FBI director J. Edgar Hoover to the Charlotte division noted that the local office's "investigation of BPP activities in Greensboro shows the value of having informant coverage in a position to report on black extremist activities at their inception." Subsequently, Hoover strongly suggested to his agents that they "should continue this commendable informant development and utilize this instance to illustrate to your Agent personnel the advantages, desirability, and necessity of the development of adequate informant coverage."[41] The saturation with informants of Panther chapters throughout the country significantly contributed to the group's proclivity for violence because these agents had been instructed to encourage Panther violence in whatever way possible. This kind of criminal violence by public officials sworn to uphold the law played a decisive role in crushing the Black Power movement.

Working from one of its bases in Greensboro, the BPP quickly began to spread its image and propaganda throughout the state. Geronimo (Ji Jaga) Pratt, a primary leader of the party's military wing, reminisced during a 1998 speech about going into North Carolina and "teaching the brothers how to properly defend themselves." He stated that some of the men he had trained bought their ammunition from the local sporting goods stores. Often, some of the ammunition was faulty, and when they shot, their guns "would just go pop and not kill anything, so we had to teach them how easy it was to make their own bullets, which were much more effective."[42] Within months, the Panthers caught on like wildfire in the Tarheel State.

A memo from the director's office to Charlotte noted that "a review of BPP activities in the Charlotte division [indicated] that Avant [had] prior connections with the BPP in the New York area." The memo added that Avant went to Greensboro "with Eric Patrick Brown, a student at A&T

State university." Regarding the training session, a February 7, 1969, FBI memo noted that "those in attendance were young, mostly of high school or college age." It claimed Avant told the group "once they attended one meeting of the Black Panther Party, they were brothers and sisters from then on and there was no chance to get out." This statement reflected the truly revolutionary nature of the BPP. Its demand of a lifetime of loyalty, though not enforceable, encouraged potential Panthers to think seriously about the reason they had for wanting to join.[43]

Other BPP chapters in North Carolina experienced similar problems with the police. For example, the Panthers in High Point, much like the Panthers in New Orleans, Omaha, Nebraska, and Greensboro, were grudgingly forced to relocate their headquarters on several occasions. The story is similar to what occurred in most other cities where the group sought to establish itself: the police and FBI encouraged landlords to evict Panthers for any number of infractions, including being members of the BPP. The events in High Point came to a head in the winter of 1971.

FBI agents in Charlotte reported to the Domestic Intelligence Division that sometime around six thirty on a cold February morning the Guilford County Sheriff's Department and High Point police announced to Panthers "over [a] public address system that they were being evicted and gave them ten minutes to get out." A few minutes later, seventeen-year-old Diane Gray Mock came out of the house. Although the Panthers claimed the police started the shooting, the FBI noted that "at about 7:00 a.m. others inside the house started firing and during the shootout, Shaw Cook, a white police officer was critically wounded by a Thirty Thirty caliber bullet." The Panthers also hit two other police officers, although they avoided injury because they wore bulletproof vests. Larry Medley, the only Panther to get hit, went to the hospital with a superficial gunshot wound.[44] This episode was one of the few times when the casualty toll for the police went higher than that of the Panthers.

After this incident, violent confrontations between police and Panthers in High Point declined because the group's leaders were in jail. Randolph Jennings, seventeen, George DeWitt, seventeen, Bradford Lilley, nineteen, and Diane Mock awaited trial on charges of conspiracy to commit the murder of police officers. This moment, according to Pratt and

Emory Douglas, was repeated in other southern states, including Tennessee, Texas, and Georgia. Local, state, and federal agencies, taking advantage of Panther mistakes and youthfulness, succeeded in provoking the Panthers into firefights they had no chance of winning. When the external violence failed, harassment arrests and incarceration followed.[45]

The Panther chapter at Winston-Salem became the strongest chapter in the Tarheel State. Led by area captain Robert Taylor Greer and lieutenant of information Larry Donnell Little, the Winston-Salem Panthers organized in 1969 under the guise of a National Committee to Combat Fascism. Other members included William Rice, lieutenant in charge of BPP newspaper distribution, Nelson Maloy (field lieutenant), Theresa Thomas (finance minister), David Bowman (officer of the day and director of the Children's Liberation School), and Julius Cornell (defense captain, also in charge of Panthers in military training). Establishing its headquarters at 1602 East Fourteenth Street, (after being evicted from two other sites), this NCCF organized a Free Breakfast for Children Program, daily political education classes, a Liberation School (summer camp for kids), and a Free Health Clinic. Local FBI agents noted that the Panthers hoped to use these programs "to win favor and approval of the community at large" and to indoctrinate "the children in Panther psychology and militant activities."[46]

On this point, the FBI came very close to ascribing BPP motives accurately. For those who did not understand the Panthers and their goals, or agree with them, talk of making dramatic changes in the lifestyles of poor people (like securing decent housing and adequate employment) could easily be mistaken for indoctrination. What Panthers really sought, however, was to establish a base of people in black communities across the nation who were willing and able to take control of their own destinies. For example, while giving a talk to one of his political education classes in the summer of 1970, Larry Little stated unequivocally that "there would be a revolution in the near future" and he suggested that his listeners "get a gun, preferably a big gun, such as a .44 magnum" and use it against anyone who harmed them. Little firmly believed life was not worth living without freedom. He explained to one reporter that black people's "desire to live should never supercede our desire to fight for our freedom." The twenty-three year-old former basketball star from Winston-Salem's Reynolds High School also gave an analysis of President

Nixon's policies, ranging from Vietnam to welfare, and made extremely derogatory statements concerning these issues. Pointing out that defense captain Julius Cornell also taught these political education classes, an informant noted that "there are sometimes as high as 30 people in the political education classes with many of these people being from the surrounding communities and not members." An FBI informant noted that in addition to "claiming the Police Department used vicious war type tactics against the Panthers, Little apparently had a strong grudge against Justus Tucker, Winston-Salem's chief of police."[47] The FBI did not mention the source of this grudge.

For several months, NCCF members and police in Winston-Salem avoided violent confrontation. The FBI pointed out that in addition to its community service programs and voter registration drives, the group's "major activities appeared to be their concern [over] various charges against the BPP leadership whose cases have not gone to trial." The bureau indicated that the group in Winston-Salem worked diligently in an effort to raise bond money for the "High Point Four," and to use their forthcoming trial as "a rallying point to gain public support." Other than "agitating at Camp Lejeune, a Marine Corps installation in North Carolina, and [at] Fort Bragg" an army base in Fayetteville, North Carolina, "the BPP members at Winston-Salem continued their work in fixing up their headquarters."[48]

This lull lasted only a short time. Throughout 1970, Panthers, their affiliates, and supporters worked to put together plans to attend plenary sessions of their upcoming Revolutionary People's Constitutional Convention, to be held in Washington, D.C., on November 28, 1970. At this convention, the participants, who included not only Panthers but numerous diverse protest groups like the Students for a Democratic Society, the New University Conference, the Young Socialist Alliance, and several women's groups, hoped to draft a new United States constitution to replace the existing one. The FBI and police in Winston-Salem, however, had other plans for their local NCCF.[49]

Shortly after some sixty NCCF members left Winston-Salem for Washington, D.C., they began to experience mechanical problems with their rented truck. As they pulled off the road at Henderson, North Carolina, the front tire of their truck fell off, and it was not long before the group discovered knife marks in it. In a later investigation, several community residents "confirmed that unknown persons were seen around the truck prior to the commencement of the journey."[50]

When they telephoned Winston-Salem for help, someone told them NCCF headquarters had burned down. An NCCF member stated that undercover police agents firebombed the place. NCCF spokespersons claimed the fire department, instead of trying to extinguish the fire, "completely destroyed the house [and] stole . . . records and some weapons from the office."[51] The authorities undoubtedly intended not only to allow the Panther office to be destroyed, but also to use whatever information it obtained there to force the Panthers out of existence.

NCCF spokespersons also claimed that E. Whitmore, Inc., the towing company that came to their assistance, stated that the truck "could not be repaired and left it on the side of the road." Likewise, the group contacted a mechanic in Greensboro who told them that "the FBI informed [him] not to repair the truck." The FBI, state, and local police, according to the BPP, then "converged on the truck," told the occupants about the destruction of their headquarters, and "proceeded in their usual brutal manner to conduct a search for weapons." Finding no weapons, the authorities left and the NCCF members succeeded in fixing the truck themselves; then they proceeded to Washington and attended the convention. Although no shootout occurred, law enforcement officials clearly sought to sabotage Panther plans and to render their office useless. The BPP in this city, however, decided to continue its community organizing despite the setbacks.[52]

The FBI noted that upon the group's return, the BPP moved its activities to two other locations. In a rather foreboding tone, a memo stated that the group had again "obtained weapons, fortified their headquarters, and sold the Black Panther Party newspaper."[53] In addition to its community activism and antigovernment stance, the group's willingness to act boldly, along with its violent rhetoric, captured law officials' attention. The following excerpt from a Larry Little speech had become par for the course:

> I adhere to violence because my whole life consists of violence in the black community. What happened to the Jews in World War II ain't nothing to what's been happening to black people in the last 400 years in America and in Africa. . . . no honkey can tell me I can't say nothing about violence. And you talk about slavery,

bombings of churches, lynchings, Hiroshima, Nagasaki, Korea, North Vietnam, genocide of American Indians, relocation of the Oriental people in World War II, don't you tell me I can't say nothing about violence."[54]

Clearly, Little sought to link the oppression of others with the oppression blacks experienced at the time. His delivery, however, went a long way not only in scaring whites but in turning many of them against the party. After this occurred, it became easy to jail Panthers on nearly any pretext. Not long after this speech, in early January 1971, three NCCF members (Larry Little, Julius Cornell, and Grady Fuller) landed in jail after the police raided their Twenty-third Street headquarters in an effort to find illegal weapons. Despite this setback, the party in Winston-Salem, which operated an ambulance service, a health clinic, and several other free community programs, continued to operate into the late seventies, when many of its leaders were called out to Oakland to help shore up national headquarters. The violent relationship between Panthers and police also continued well into the mid-1970s until the outnumbered (and outgunned) Panthers were either dead, incarcerated, or too demoralized to fight.[55] Before it disappeared from the headlines, however, the party experienced a phenomenal spurt of progress, which occurred thousands of miles away from Oakland in New York City, one of the most culturally advanced enclaves of blacks in the country.

CHAPTER 8

To the East . . . and Back

BETWEEN 1968 AND 1970, THE BLACK Panther Party spread from northern and Southern California all the way east to New York, Connecticut, Massachusetts, and Maryland. Before reaching the east coast, the party set up chapters and affiliates in places like Denver, Omaha, Nebraska, Kansas City, Missouri, Des Moines, Iowa, Dallas, Detroit, and Toledo and Cleveland, Ohio. In all these locales, the Panthers opposed, both verbally and physically, the police and the forces of business and government that guided and controlled them. This stance almost always ended in violence. Despite the tense situation, the Panthers continued to organize and to coalesce with other groups and individuals that thought the status quo needed to change. The group's widespread activity led to expanded surveillance and counteraction. This response, intimately tied to the prevailing violence between the Panthers and police officials, ensured the Panthers did not reach their goal of complete revolution. The Panthers, however, did not know how things would end by the end of the turbulent sixties. Many still believed that sustained, concerted political action could lead blacks to freedom. The farther east the party spread, the more intense and disciplined Panther action became. The group's culmination in growth, and its establishment in New York, brought with it the development of a cadre of people who believed wholeheartedly in Panther principles and the right of all people to be free.

The New York chapter, formed in mid-1968, was influenced primarily by those closely associated with the Los Angeles chapter. Like other chapters, it emphasized the "Free Huey" movement at first. New York City and its surrounding environs, however, had problems of their own. Eldridge Cleaver, also closely associated with the LA chapter through Bunchy Carter and his close comrade field marshal Don Cox, had an enormous influence on the New York state branch. Cleaver, who spoke in New York at several sites during his presidential bid as a candidate for the Peace and Freedom Party, had the ability to articulate the ills of black society in a way that made people want to take action. Panther Thomas McCreary remembered that when Cleaver was in town people listened because, like Malcolm X, "he was spittin' fire." New York Panther BJ recalled "that was it when he came to P.S. 201 and gave that speech" that electrified the audience and made him think about joining the party. After laying the groundwork, the BPP set up its regional headquarters for the east coast in New York City. Harlem eventually became home to this headquarters. Even though Loudon Ford had been put in charge of the Panther office in Manhattan earlier that summer, a group simultaneously set up in Harlem by Oakland transplant Ron Pennybacker and David Brothers came to dominate the New York scene. Unlike Ford's group, which had been established by SNCC workers during the group's brief dalliance with Stokely Carmichael and James Forman, the Harlem group, according to one author, "attracted a tougher, more militant breed of cat."[1]

Some of these included Afeni Shakur, Lumumba and Zayd Shakur, Dhoruba Bin Wahad (formerly known as Richard Moore), Sundiata Acoli, Chaba Uhn, Michael Cetawayo Tabor, Joan Bird, Cheryl Foster, Safiyah Bhukari, Alex Rackley, and Ali Bey Hassan. Of course, these people represent only a minute sampling of the membership, as the New York chapter eventually grew to more than a thousand members. Stretching from Harlem and the Bronx to Brooklyn, Queens, and Long Island, the BPP found itself immersed in the pressing issues facing blacks in the Big Apple. Cleo Silvers, who joined the party in New York not long after it started, explained that "I was to know every community organization in the Bronx . . . and be involved with those people. I was involved with the community planning board where we would go and make demands in support of the people. That's how deep it was."[2] Silvers's experience in the party is a good example of how the rank-and-file fared in the organization.

The circumstances of her joining are quite interesting. Formerly of Philadelphia, Silvers had been employed as a healthcare worker at Lincoln Hospital in the Bronx. Sometime in 1968, a party member sent her to the Harlem office to join. When she arrived at the headquarters at Seventh Avenue and 125th Street, Panthers Gloria Jean and Afeni Shakur stood on the office steps. Silvers explained to them that she had been sent to join and was immediately told she could not become a Panther because, upon questioning, she did not "know how to wrap a gelee," an African-style head covering popular in the sixties and seventies. Many black women continue to wear them today. Black Harlem's immersion in African culture apparently affected the Panthers as it had affected millions of others. Of course, the two were teasing the potential recruit and having fun doing it. After going inside to retrieve the wrap from the officer of the day, the person in charge of the office on a day-to-day basis, she sat as one of the women wrapped her head. Because they wore the African wraps at the time, they told Silvers, "see, you look like us." Then it was her turn, and according to her, she "wrapped a gelee that day. No mirror no nothing." Proud of her accomplishment, the two informed her that she could become a Panther. After a six-week training period all new recruits had to finish without missing a day, Silvers became a full-fledged member and prepared to go to work.[3]

Silvers "immediately gave up" her job because she could not see how she could do all the party work and maintain it. She noted "you can't sell papers, be up for the breakfast program at 4 a.m., go to the community meetings, work with the children and tutor them after school, go to P.E. classes, cook food, take care of the rest of your colleagues, and have a job. . . . It was just impossible, so I had to quit my job because I wanted to be more involved because of the community aspect of it, the closeness and the unity of the people." Like many Panthers, she lived on the ten cents she got from the sale of each Panther paper she hawked. Though there were many Panthers who maintained their jobs, most quit and became full-time revolutionaries. Their communal living arrangements meant that they shared food and clothes and therefore did not need as much as an individual alone might. With the cost of living being what it was in the sixties and early seventies, it was not difficult to eat adequately and to purchase necessities. As revolutionaries, however, they were all expected to live with less while they became hard-working, politically astute individuals. Silvers noted that political education was central to their development.

She mentioned having to read for two hours every day to be ready for political education class at nine at night. "You had to read your political education material before you get there," she added, "because if Dhoruba asked you a question and you did not know it, you had to do fifty laps around the block." Dhoruba was one of the more outspoken leaders of the party. He was arrested, along with twenty other New York leaders, after being implicated in April 1969 in a police-initiated conspiracy to blow up police stations, botanical gardens, and other public buildings. Apparently, there was no violent discipline in the New York chapter, according to Silvers. She noted that there was too much love for that kind thing to be taking place. "That shit might have happened on the West Coast," she added, "but the brothers taught us love for each other and that you don't harm your comrade." Instead, she explained, the discipline usually included physical exercise. The leadership explained to her that the running was good for her training, especially since she was about to be sent to karate school to learn self-defense.

At this training school, Panther Alex Rackley taught the Harlem Panthers karate and judo. Silvers remembered that when she went to the dojo (karate training school) next door to the office to learn karate, she learned about all kinds of weapons. She noted that "I had stars, I had pins, and I taught the other sisters how to use them. . . . So if a horse run up on you, and you got to get out of the way, you got to get that motherfucker out of your way, guess what, either the police or the horses would fall down. If you put twenty marbles underneath a horses' foot, guess what, the motherfucker is going to break his fucking leg—cause we demonstrating," she laughed.[4] Going to demonstrations and scuffling with the police, however, figured little in the Panthers' daily routine.

In addition to all the activities mentioned above, Silvers also operated as a messenger. She explained that because the police had all the phones tapped "and were listening to everything we said, they [the leaders] had to have secure messages." Bullwhip, another New York Panther, agreed and noted that "they had our phone tapped so much that we stopped paying the bill—and Ma Bell still left them on. . . . As a matter of fact," he added, "way back then, we had three and four way calling and didn't even have to pay because the feds wanted to be sure that they got that information." Indeed, Panther offices all over the country had their phones tapped at one point or another. Transcripts of phone taps fill more than a dozen boxes at the Stanford University archives where Huey Newton's papers are housed. At any rate, after receiving a message, Silvers ran "to the Bronx to another leader's house to take the secure message." She recalled being fast and very good at this job. "They gave me the responsibility to run those messages back and forth," she explained, "because I was quick and I was good and I knew how to state the message" exactly the way it was given. She recalled having to memorize large amounts of information and having to deliver it precisely the way it had been transmitted.[5]

Harlem Panther Cheryl Foster, who served as housing coordinator, kept a diary of her daily activity while in the party. It provides excellent insight into the experience of the average full-time party member in a leadership position. For example, Monday through Friday, she kept the following schedule: Between six and seven in the morning., she exercised, cleaned up, and ate. At seven, she helped at the Free Breakfast Program and by seven thirty, she went to "busy train and bus stops" to sell the Panther paper. At nine, she signed in at the office, received her assignment for the day and by ten she was involved in "section work," which meant anything from helping with police brutality and tenant issues to problems going on in any of a dozen or so local schools. This work was always based on the community's needs. Between noon and one in the afternoon, she engaged in "progressive paper selling." One wonders if she meant aggressive, because of the lunch hour and the many opportunities to sell to workers who ate lunch at this time. From 1:30 to 2:15, she ate lunch and attended a political education class. For the next hour she engaged in more "section work." From 3:45 to 6:30, she sold the paper and at seven she signed in at the office again. Foster and the rest of her comrades then had dinner until eight. From eight thirty to ten thirty, she did "community work, office work," and attended "P.E. class." Though every Panther did not maintain this exact schedule, it is clear rank-and-file party members had their hands full. Indeed, there were many entries in the diary that indicated that the night did not end until two or three in the morning. Paper selling seems to have taken up a lot of time, but the community work also stood out as a priority. There can be no doubt that to be a Panther, one had to be dedicated or get into serious trouble, as the organization had been set up militarily and subordination was not tolerated. After making notations for future "meetings, strategy sessions, and timetables," Foster confirmed this point when she noted at the end of this "list of things to do," that "4 Fuck-ups are to be brought up before staff."[6]

In her position as housing coordinator, Foster kept abreast of the problems tenants in her section encountered with landlords. She sometimes took pictures of dilapidated apartments and demanded that owners maintain housing inhabited by blacks and other people of color in New York City. She spent many hours addressing the Panther demand for housing fit for humans. Along with comrades like Afeni Shakur, who once organized one hundred buildings during a successful rent strike, Foster helped to give hope to thousands of New Yorkers who otherwise had no advocate. Encouraging unity and solidarity, Panthers taught tenants their rights, wrote petitions, organized block meetings, and insisted that health standards be maintained. Because the teaming rats and roaches that occupied the dwellings with the humans sometimes bit children or crawled into people's ears, the Panthers worked long and hard to show blacks that the political system fostered and allowed such misery. When the furnace died in the middle of winter or when there was no hot water for showers, some New York residents began to understand why the Panthers organized. Only by standing up and joining with others to revolutionize certain values in society, the Panthers argued, could poor and oppressed people change their circumstances.[7]

Foster organized rallies, was placed in charge of student organizations throughout the city, worked to free Bobby Seale and New York Panthers arrested for felonies, and fought off the police who tried on several occasions to prevent her from selling the Black Panther Party newspaper. She was one of the many Panthers who tried to bring about justice and equality in the most populous city in the United States.

Her efforts, however, foundered, as internal dissension and external attack ravished the self-appointed vanguard organization. The forces working against the Panthers were almost infinitely stronger than the small group could have imagined. Before long, those forces infiltrated and incapacitated the group of young militants, criminalized the entire organization, and rendered ineffective any violent outbursts on the part of urban guerrillas looking to get even as they attempted to secure black freedom.

In the Big Apple, the infiltration started early on. The New York–based Bureau of Special Services pegged twenty-eight-year old Shaun Dubonnet (born William Fletcher) for an informant early in the party's history. Dubonnet had spent time in fifteen mental institutions and had been diagnosed by psychiatrists as a "chronic paranoid schizophrenic" and a pathological liar before becoming a party member. At the time of his enrollment in the party, the authorities sought him for escaping from a mental institution and Secret Service agents wanted him for threatening the life of the president over the phone. Why and how he became the Panther chief of security in New York City are questions that certainly need to be answered.

This problem, like most others in New York, stemmed from the West Coast, where most of the major decisions originated. The paucity in security checks on party members eventually cost the chapter its life. Many undesirables made their way into the group. While there, they helped rip the party apart by engaging in all manner of illegal and unnecessary activities. Despite the position's sensitivity, West Coast leadership appointed Dubonnet head of security after Cleaver had a problem with the man who previously held the job. They apparently made no attempts to ascertain this person's capability or background.[8] Although Dubonnet's bizarre behavior made Panther leaders wonder if he was a police spy, their attempt to verify their suspicions fell short of success. Panther lieutenant Victor Perez, Dubonnet's immediate superior, planted a false story about killing party opponents in the Ocean Hill–Brownsville dispute over community control of schools, hoping his quarry would expose himself by

Richard Moore, aka Dhoruba Bin Wahad, a member of the New York Black Panther Party and one of the New York Twenty-one. *Photo by Ducho Dennis, courtesy of It's About Time.*

reporting the story to the police. It turns out that the Panthers tried too early, as Dubonnet changed sides only after being arrested for joy riding on New York City streets in a stolen taxi. With the choice of one hundred dollars a week to spy on the Panthers or jail facing him, he instantly agreed to take the money. Before long, FBI informers Roland Hayes, Gene Roberts, and Ralph "Sedan" White found that procuring security positions in the party was an easy thing to do. With former Office of Special Services and former CIA agent Angelo Galante working in tandem with the Bureau of Special Services, it did not take long before the police crashed the party in the Big Apple. Galante had worked for the precursor to the CIA in Italy during World War II, and with the CIA in Korea during the Korean War. At the time he took the job as Panther hunter, he worked on Long Island as an officer in the Army Special Forces. His specialty was "guerilla operations behind enemy lines." With this experience, he helped trap and jail the Panthers in short order and subsequently participated in their premature foundering. As Hayes offered party members crates of dynamite given him by the FBI, Roberts and White worked to trap the New York Panthers in a conspiracy so immense that it took a year-long trial to sort everything out. Before these events took place, however, the New York Panthers made significant headway in the black liberation struggle. They rid many neighborhoods of the heroin menace wreaking havoc on young and old alike. In the process, they created an array of programs that addressed the needs of their constituents: the black communities in New York City and surrounding areas.[9]

Cleo Silvers remembered that the organizing skills of Panther leaders made them targets for those hoping to maintain the status quo. She explained that although they found themselves constantly busy, the leaders "worked harder than we did. They would be up all night planning shit, surveying the conditions of the city," and trying to find solutions to all these problems. For example, she noted that "Dr. Curtis Powell would sit with other doctors and go over all the theories around preventive health care." These were people, she added, who not only talked about sickle cell anemia, but worked to bring about a cure. "There were doctors doing research on this," she said, and they taught Panthers things "and as a result we designed programs that spoke directly to those issues."

Silvers added that Panther leaders retained lawyers like William Kunstler to come to their meetings and to teach them community law

Michael Tabor was a New York Black Panther and part of the New York Twenty-one. *Photo by Ducho Dennis, courtesy of It's About Time.*

so they might deal with some of the issues affecting them. She concluded that "their understanding of how to organize and how to delegate was superb. . . . It was mind boggling for me to see all the shit they was doing."[10]

Thomas McCreary, another New York Panther, who joined after being a member of the SNCC for two years, noted that the party flourished because of the excellent leadership in New York. Like many New York City blacks of his generation, McCreary volunteered for Vietnam in 1965 to avoid being killed in the mean streets of New York, where his family had moved from North Carolina. His nickname, "Blood," came from his escapades as a gang member in the Big Apple. When he went to Vietnam, his unit was dropped off in the Central Highlands near the North Vietnamese border where the Ho Chi Minh Trail began. He saw a lot of action—"they were getting busy up there," he remembered— and went on a lot of search-and-destroy missions. When he entered the party, he noted that the police acted just like he and his fellow soldiers acted when they were in Vietnam. When police raided Panther offices, he noted, "the first thing they would do is destroy all of the food—they were burning cereal up there. . . .They were starting fires, and it reminded me of search and destroy missions in Vietnam. How you going to feed the kids and you ain't go no food?" he asked. "They knew where to hit us," he said. "If you get rid of those programs—'cause those programs get you support from the people"—then it made it easier for the authorities to get rid of them altogether.

"People would come with their children for breakfast and get a meal themselves—we weren't turning anybody down," he noted. "We might talk trash but we weren't turning them down, they were going to get something to eat. . . .We would also clothe the people," he added. They went to all the local cleaners since, according to him, "they got a big sign up there stating 'We are not responsible for your things after thirty days'— then we come down thirty days later and say donate those clothes to us, cause we gonna have a free clothing giveaway—and that afternoon that is what we would do. If a nigga ain't got no winter coat—and it gets cold in New York baby—you gonna be there, and you gonna get a nice coat." People respected them for their charity and willingness to give of them-selves. He added that the leadership and sometimes the rank-and-file went to the churches and asked for the use of their kitchens. "They said yes as long as we agreed to clean up afterwards, most of them anyway. . . . Then you got this nigger on the corner selling this high-priced food, he's gonna give us so much grits for that week. Certain others we gonna go and get so many eggs, and then others some bread" and so on until they had enough food for their Free Breakfast for Children Programs. "Initially," he explained, the relationship between the Panthers and the businesses "was hostile because they did not trust us" and the party's attitude was "we know that you gonna give that merchandise up because you taking the money out of the community at six o'clock when the sun goes down. We know you done made the money and what we asking for ain't much at all. . . . As a matter of fact, we told them they can come down and cook and volunteer themselves if they wanted to see what we were doing with the food. And when they saw that we were sincere, we had them coming to us and offering us help. They would say, 'can you get a truck over there and pick it up?' Be it furniture, clothes, or whatever. We furnished peo-ples apartments, those that needed it, on many occasions."[11]

Silvers noted that people who owned shoe factories "would bring a truckload of shoes, drop it in front of the building and we would size them up and put them outside for the community to come and get them. . . . Bar owners, hustlers, other business people, especially the black businessmen, all contributed, although many of them did not want this known. Our people were so committed that the BPP in Harlem used to take drugs from drug dealers and pour it down the sewer. All the drug dealers were half-scared of the Panthers because we were serious about cleaning up and protecting our communities." As a result, said BJ, a Panther from the Corona (Queens) branch, "they moved the [drug] corner from 125th street all the way down to 116th Street—and yes, [the Panthers] got violent, I think one of them got shot in the leg" for not cooperating. "We had what you would call a safe zone—from 125th to 116th was the safe zone" and anybody who violated it had to deal with the Black Panther Party, "which they did not want to do because we had some serious people out there." Silvers concurred and explained that "even though later on we fell victim to all that stuff—we wasn't having no drugs, we wasn't having violence, we wasn't having no police violence, we was not having no bad education, no rats biting no babies, no bad health care, we wasn't having it up in here, that's why the Harlem community loved us so much." These members said the party leadership let everyone know they were the ones to come to for whatever they needed.[12]

McCreary noted that sometimes the single women in the community came up to the office to ask for help. "And she's got three babies and she got to get downtown to take care of some business. We would say bring them to the office but be back here at five and pick your children up." So when "people had emergencies they would come to us," he said. "The Panther office became the emergency center for damn near everything. It would be a million people in there and everybody wanting some service of some kind." It got to the point, he added, that "the people would get indignant when you told them that you couldn't do something they wanted you to do." When this happened, he recalled, they said, "aw man, I'm going to report you [to the leadership] because you are messing up—you're obviously messing up because you ain't doing your job—stop frontin'! I told you I had this appointment to go to and you telling me you ain't got nobody to keep the kids—well what the hell are you doing? You got all those toys back there in the back, you can go back there every now and then and watch them, you still can work up here in the front." He added that because of the great work the leadership did, "we all became responsible." This effort paid off later when the party needed the community's support. He remembered "whenever the police would raid those offices," community residents "would come into the streets like flies, man. The streets would be full of people—women, children, old people, young people, pimps, hustlers, dope dealers, everybody . . . talking 'bout why y'all messing with them?" Because they gave instead of taking from the people, they always had more support than their membership numbers indicated.[13] For creating such a dynamic organization, the Panther leadership in New York City, and in fact in every other city where the party was established, became targets. The New York Twenty-one, arrested on conspiracy charges because of the city's strategic importance because of the influence they wielded, became a cause célèbre. Rather than scaring people away from the party, the repression increased recruits.

On April 1, 1969, District Attorney Frank Hogan leaked news to the press that his office, along with the New York City Police Department, had uncovered an appalling conspiracy by the Panthers to bomb public buildings and to destroy lives throughout the city of seven million. The following day, New York City police officers charged twenty-one Panthers, all of whom held leadership positions, with a twelve-count indictment for conspiring to murder New York City policemen and to dynamite five midtown department stores, a police precinct, six railroad rights-of-way, and the Bronx Botanical Gardens. The target date of April 6, according to District Attorney Hogan, had been set to coincide with Easter and the anniversary of Bobby Hutton's death in Oakland. Though no actual act was alleged or charged, court authorities set the Panthers' bail at one hundred thousand dollars each.

Authorities kept all the Panthers incarcerated until the trial started a year later. Of these, two were women. Twenty-year-old Joan Bird, who had no previous convictions, had graduated with honors from Cathedral High School, enrolled in Bronx Community College, and started work as a teaching assistant at Public School 175. Twenty-two-year-old Afeni Shakur worked in the Manpower Training Commission, and in addition to the other Panther activities previously mentioned, worked with kindergarten children. Robert Collier had been employed as a staff director at Tompkins Square Community Center, a poverty program, and served as a member of the Lower East Side Planning board. Dr. Curtis Powell worked as a biochemist and was engaged in research at Columbia Presbyterian Medical Center. Thirty-one-year-old Ali Bey Hassan worked with the party as a community educator and organizer. He later emerged as a member of the Black Liberation Army. Lumumba Shakur, twenty-six, worked with the Harlem Community Council. Vietnam veteran Lee Berry, twenty-five, worked as a photographer and actor. However, at the time of his arrest, he was in the hospital suffering from war-induced epilepsy. Poor treatment at the hands of police left him in a coma and unable to stand trial. Twenty-four-year-old Walter Johnson worked in a grocery store and Dhorba Bin Wahad, also twenty-four, worked as a photo letter operator and artist. Twenty-two-year-old Michael "Cetawayo" Tabor worked as an artist for the party. Alan McKiever, nineteen, Eddie Josephs, seventeen, and Lonnie Epps, seventeen, were all high school students.[14] Another minor was on the list, against whom charges were later dropped.

When the police knocked on the door to arrest Nathaniel Burns, he leaped thirty-five feet to the pavement and later wound up in Algeria, site of the party's international headquarters. His codefendants Larry Mack and Thomas Berry, also sought by NYPD, had arrived ahead of him in their attempts to evade arrest. Still other codefendants, Richard Harris and Donald Weems, sat safe in a Newark jail on previous charges of robbery. William King, ex-Marine sergeant and author of *Urban Guerilla Warfare,* and minister of information Zayd Shakur rounded out the list of suspects.

After the arrests, police placed their prisoners in jails throughout the city, confining them in maximum-security facilities. They took this action so the arrested revolutionaries could not collaborate and properly prepare for any eventual trial. It took several days before their lawyers located them all. The extremely high bail the authorities set was unprecedented in New York at the time, especially for people who had not committed any crimes. Writing in the *New York Review* on September 11, 1969, Ronald Steel commented that because the press ensured the Panthers were "generally viewed as an anarchistic band of gun-toting, white-hating thugs," police and federal officials could "abridge their constitutional rights in a way they would not dare use against whites." He concluded that it was "unlikely that members of a white political organization, even the Ku Klux Klan, would be rounded up in the middle of the night, thrown into jails, dispersed around the city, kept under maximum security and even

solitary confinement, detained in prison for months on exorbitant bail
... and charged with plotting irrational actions without the liberal press
voicing its indignation." It happened to the Panthers in New York.
Panthers insist they received such treatment because they had been making progress in building a multiethnic constituency to oppose what they
called a corrupt capitalist system. In addition to their socialist leanings and
their demand for racial justice, the Panthers had significant ties to and
tremendous influence on those Americans who had nothing to lose in
rebelling against their condition. This happened to be especially the case
in New York City, the hub of Panther activity in the east and covering an
area from Providence, Rhode Island, to Winston-Salem, North Carolina.[15]

Indeed, the leadership continued to function while incarcerated.
Through their lawyers, they stayed in constant contact with their people
on the streets. In addition to organizing the inmates who surrounded
them, Silvers noted, "they let us know what was going on. They educated
us while they were in jail—they sent out communiqué number one and
two, telling us what to do, to keep struggling, stay strong, and fight for
us. . . . Sometimes they would get technical and send orders out to you in
the community because one of the persons who was in jail was in charge
of the breakfast program and they would say this breakfast program is
such and such and you had to do this and that. You Brooklyn guys, send
your troops out there to make sure that things were still operating
smoothly." With a twinkle in her eyes and a serious smile, she added,
"they were generals, they were *our* generals. They were like the Central
Committee of New York."[16] The problems they experienced, however,
did not go away just because they were capable people.

Since their arrest in April, a few Panthers had been bailed out in an
effort to rally support for the rest. Dhoruba Bin Wahad, Lumumba
Shakur, Michael "Cetawayo" Tabor, and Afeni Shakur, who was pregnant
with her son Tupac, were among those released. They did an excellent
job helping to organize the defense. This work included staging large rallies where individuals of all political persuasions spoke in support of the
jailed Panthers. Former Students for a Democratic Society member Marty
Kenner became the party's accountant in charge of the defense fund. After
the rest of the twenty-one languished in jail for an entire year, the trial
commenced.

Meanwhile, the "Free Huey" movement had come full circle and accomplished its goal. In August 1970, Huey Newton emerged from prison an icon and a hero. The party he had started four years prior had grown from a Bay Area group vying for attention to an international phenomenon with thousands of members, dozens of chapters, and scores of affiliates, as well as supporters in Europe, Asia, the Middle East, Africa, the Caribbean, and the Pacific Islands. To say the least, he was not prepared for such responsibility and power. He got a taste of what was in store for him when he emerged from the courthouse where he had been kept since leaving prison a few days earlier. A throng of some five thousand awaited him. Black and white, young and old, rich and poor, they all wanted a glimpse of the minister of defense of the Black Panther Party. Upon being released, he and his security team, which included Che Brooks of Chicago, Geronimo Pratt of the Los Angeles chapter, David Hilliard and Bill Jennings of the Oakland chapter, and a half dozen others, had to flee from the crowd. There is a famous picture of Newton standing atop a Volkswagen with his shirt literally being torn away from him. The larger-than-life Panther gleamed in the August sunshine, his muscles, no doubt strengthened while doing push ups in his cell, rippling like Adonis's. A handsome man who looked the part, Newton actually felt overwhelmed and little afraid of the crowd, especially as hundreds of Oakland policemen began approaching. Jennings remembered "it was like we were the Beatles or something and people were chasing us. . . . We got caught and that's how we ended up on top of that car." In fact, Newton had to promise the crowd that he would make a speech at a nearby park to get them to disperse. His admirers took the bait and Newton and his security team fled in the opposite direction.[17]

Newton's respite was short-lived. By 1970, the party had grown tremendously—and too quickly, some would argue. There were any number of internal squabbles threatening to rip it apart at the seams. Sometimes chapters called themselves Panthers but in reality had no relationship with the Oakland headquarters. Troubleshooters crisscrossed the country in an effort to deal with this problem but their efforts were never enough. Even though some members of rogue chapters agreed to go to Oakland and to learn party policy and principles, others refused and continued operating on their own, often getting involved in acts that discredited the BPP. For this reason, in early 1969,

Panther George Edwards in Washington, D.C., in 1970. *Photo by Ducho Dennis, courtesy of It's About Time.*

before the New York Twenty-one arrests and before the Fred Hampton and Mark Clark murders, the party initiated a nationwide purge, dispatching Panther leaders to different parts of the country to whip chapters into shape and to expel undesirable members. This purge worked to their detriment and to the government's advantage.

By the spring of 1970, the FBI learned that Eldridge Cleaver "had accepted as bonafide a fictitious letter stating that BPP leaders in California were seeking to undercut his influence." In April 1970, the FBI sent a letter to Cleaver in Algiers accusing Newton and his followers of plotting against the exiled leader. Each faction (to be discussed later) then ordered the expulsion of the other, resulting in the purging of whole chapters. Indeed, Bobby Seale and the rest of the Panther Central Committee concluded that only through extensive purges could they rid the organization of spies, informants, jackanapes, and *agents provocateurs*.[18]

This purge had a disastrous effect on the party. Not only were some of the best members expelled because of personality clashes, some of the least effective members were left in place because of the unfairness of the purging process. Even worse, the federal government, which had been dogging the Panthers since its early days in an attempt to quash the group, took this opportunity to wreak havoc on the party. Displaying their experience in espionage and counterintelligence, government agents, in chapter after chapter, pretended to be Panthers from headquarters, expelling members and, on a few occasions, disbanding entire chapters. Historian Yohuru Williams wrote that FBI operatives working with local and state authorities attacked BPP chapters "that were new, in bad standing, or feuding with the national headquarters." He added that "a Panther, usually of dubious reputation, would arrive with a message from national headquarters either ordering the target chapter underground or claiming that he had been sent to straighten the chapter out." In addition to creating "an atmosphere of fear and distrust," violent acts against legitimate BPP members were common during these episodes. All this, he wrote, came at a time when "efforts by the national office to bring its chapters under some organizational structure" were at their height.[19] The worst episode in this federal offensive occurred in New Haven, Connecticut.

In the spring of 1969, George Sams, "a clinically diagnosed moron with a reputation for violence," according to Williams, and an escapee from a mental institution in New York, went to Harlem in one of these purging episodes. The New York Twenty-one had recently been arrested and the chapter was in disarray. Sams told unsuspecting New York Panthers, who did not bother to check his credentials with the Oakland headquarters, that he had come to straighten out the chapter and to find out who framed the Panther leaders. While he was there, he beat some members, raped a female Panther, and openly carried a loaded weapon while drinking and smoking heavily. All these activities were against party rules. Had the New York Panthers contacted Oakland, they would have discovered that Sams, introduced to the party by Stokely Carmichael, had been expelled for being the fool he was. Elbert Howard remembered telling David Hilliard that Sams was bad news, as he had "tried to start a fight with a party member" at one of their Bay Area rallies. "No real Panther would be behaving that way," he explained. In fact, Seale had expelled the cantankerous Sams for his improprieties, but he had been reinstated when Carmichael spoke up on his behalf. At any rate, when Sams heard that legitimate Panthers Rory Hithe and Landon Williams were due in New York City for a real inspection, he quickly left. Headed to New Haven, he took unsuspecting twenty-four-year-old Alex Rackley with him.[20]

Elbert "Big Man" Howard, Panther deputy minister of information, and Audrea Jones in Washington, D.C., in 1970. *Photo by Ducho Dennis, courtesy of It's About Time.*

Arriving on May 17, 1969, Sams told New Haven Panthers that he had been sent east from California to inspect and shape up chapters. They too believed him without attempting to verify his credentials with Oakland. Not long after his arrival, Sams resumed his diabolical activities. This time he accused Alex Rackley of having framed the New York Twenty-one. At the time, they were in the home of Warren Kimbro, a leader in the New Haven chapter. Oblivious to what Sams was doing, New Haven Panthers followed in lock step behind Sams's actions. Sams knew that Bobby Seale was due in New Haven to speak at Yale University in a few days. He wanted to create a situation where yet another national Panther leader could be framed for illegal activity unbecoming of a revolutionary. For whatever reason, no one bothered to question his antics. Knowing he had carte blanche, Sams ordered Rackley taken to the basement.[21]

In complete control of the chapter at this point, Sams instructed New Haven Panthers to torture Rackley. Ostensibly he wanted the youth to admit to framing the Panthers. This activity was made all the more plausible because Sams wore a huge .45 pistol and menaced all who threatened his authority. He told Ericka Huggins, who had gone to New Haven to bury her murdered husband John Huggins, to tape record the proceedings so that headquarters would know everybody was following orders. Huggins decided to stay in New Haven after the funeral to help the fledgling chapter, which at the time had barely twenty-five members. She complied with Sams's orders and taped the whole ordeal. Little did they know that the state had asked for the events to be recorded as they wanted to use this recording against the Panthers in a court of law. New Haven Panthers tortured Alex Rackley for days, pistol-whipping him, binding him with coat hangers, and scalding him with boiling water. He refused to admit that he had framed his comrades in New York City. During the entire episode, New Haven police officials and FBI agents listened in, via microphones they had planted in the house, doing nothing to help the hapless youth whom they knew had not been guilty of framing the New York Panthers.[22]

Sams then called New Haven Panther George Edwards, who had joined the party after a stint in the Air Force, to come join the interrogation. Edwards arrived at Kimbro's house not knowing what had transpired. When he entered the basement and saw Rackley's condition, he immediately protested because "the brother had been smacked a few times. So I'm saying what's going on, why am I down here? I'm questioning what's going on with this brother and everybody was standing around all scared because Sams got this gun in his hand." Sams then told Edwards, "look, this is the way it is, this man has violated this, that, and the other." At that point, Edwards began asking more questions and Sams said, "man, why you asking all these questions" and began slapping him in the face saying, "Oh, I heard about you anyway." According to Edwards, Sams then "took that big ass .45 and started waving it in my face, saying get in the corner." Edwards reportedly said to the stunned group of Panthers, "uh oh, y'all know something? Everybody in here is gonna regret this, I see it coming." Sams told Edwards to "shut up," and made him sit in a chair. In the meantime, Edwards remembered, "George Sams told Ericka to ask the questions and she was scared, you can tell. Some of the stuff he [Rackley] was making up and some of it sounded real; he was telling them who they could call, naming high-ranking people in New York, and this, that, and the other" all in an attempt to prove his innocence.[23]

Finally, after Sams could not get Rackley to confess, he told Huggins to "cut off the tape and called for somebody to escort him [Rackley] upstairs and clean him up." He then told everybody that "if anybody asks any questions about if you know what's been done here you say no, of course not." Sams then instructed Panthers Lonnie McLucas and Warren Kimbro to tie up Edwards. They complied "and began saying they were sorry." Edwards told them "you don't have to apologize to me, just make sure you tie me tight. I said, Lonnie, you do what you have to do." At the same time, "Ericka was all messed up behind this thing." He then said, "y'all got me, so what now?" Sams replied, "we gonna find out who you are, nigga, or else."[24]

Then Edwards asked "or else what? You gonna pull the trigger? If so, there's gonna be a price to pay." Again, Sams ordered him to shut up. "If you think there's anything funny about me, pull the trigger," Edwards told Sams. "If I had you like this and I thought you were like this [an informant], I'd do you, I'ma tell you that right now. If I brought you to this level, you wouldn't be here, so do what you got to do, come on with it." At this point, Sams turned the recorder back on and reportedly said, "yeah, so what's your commitment to the struggle, to the Black Panther Party?" When Edwards explained that "on a military level, I'm beyond y'all, I'm trying to knock out communication systems, bank circuits on Wall Street, screw up the stock market, electronic communications, transfer of data, and create economic gridlock in the heart of the beast," they left him alone. Edwards had been an electronics specialist in the Air Force, writing the curriculum for several missile-guidance-systems classes. According to him, he helped to create the first updated and modern guidance systems for nuclear weapons. Other Panthers in the room confirmed that he had such training, and Sams said "well we gonna send this tape to headquarters and see what the verdict is on you." Sams then told Edwards "don't say nothing about this, you are not to ask about him [Rackley], you are to work in the community, every time you leave here we need to know where you are at, when you go home you are to call in, and at the office you are not to go past the first floor and ask no questions about nothing." After he agreed to these terms, they untied Edwards and released him.[25]

The episode, however, did not end there. Sams informed Rackley he had passed all the tests and that he was going to be taken back to New York. Sams, Lonnie McLucas, Warren Kimbro, and Alex Rackley then got into a vehicle, found the interstate, and began driving north out of

New Haven. A relieved Rackley thought he had survived with his life intact until the car stopped near a marsh in Middlefield, Connecticut, some twenty miles north of New Haven. Sams told the tortured Rackley that beyond the bushes, a boat awaited to take him back home. When he began making his way toward the spot Sams pointed to, things turned ugly. According to Williams, "Sams handed Kimbro a .45" and told him to "ice him," referring to Rackley. When Sams insisted that the order had come "from national," Kimbro followed the twenty-four-year-old into the swamp and pumped a bullet into his head. He died immediately. The consummate choreographer, "Sams then gave the gun to Lonnie McLucas and told him to fire a safety shot to make sure Rackley was dead." McLucas then shot the dead Rackley in the chest. When they had finished the deed, the trio abandoned the corpse and took the interstate back to New Haven. After a tip, police found Rackley's body on May 21, 1969, in a deserted wooded area of Middlefield, Connecticut. The tortured cadaver had head and chest wounds and a number of burns. Sams testified that Seale ordered Rackley's death and also named Lonnie McLucas and Warren Kimbro as participants in this action.[26]

Chairman Bobby Seale had given a speech the day before (May 19) in New Haven. The police then arrested Seale, indicted him, and put him on trial with eight other New Haven Panthers, including Ericka Huggins and George Edwards. Because they were bigger targets, Seale and Huggins later had their trials severed from the rest. Sams, after being apprehended in Canada, issued a long statement to the police and "pleaded guilty to second degree murder in the Rackley case," according to a report in the New York Times.[27]

According to the March 14, 1970, issue of the New York Times, a demonstration in support of Seale and Huggins, organized by Yale University students (including Hillary Rodham, future first lady and senator from New York) and local Panthers was attended by some "12,000 to 15,000" people, most of whom were white.[28] Kingman Brewster, Jr., Yale's president at the time, garnered serious criticism from political figures as high up as Vice President Spiro Agnew for noting that he was "skeptical of the ability of black revolutionaries to achieve a fair trial anywhere in the United States."[29] Some three thousand students signed petitions in support of their president for taking such a brave and unusual stand.

Because the judge believed Seale might flee the country as a smattering of other indicted Panthers had, a Connecticut court ordered him held in isolation for eight months while lawyers interviewed 1,550 people in an effort to seat twelve jurors. Before he gave his decision, Judge Harold M. Mulvey stated "it had taken four months" to select a jury. Connecticut State Commissioner of Corrections Ellis C. MacDougall noted that the thirty-three-year-old Seale "would be kept in an individual maximum security cell . . . the strongest facility we have as far as escape opportunities are concerned."[30] They then escorted the chairman to a facility in Montville, Connecticut, home of the state's most secure prison.

The trial began in March 1971, a year after Seale's arrest. After a parade of witnesses from the defense rebutted nearly everything the prosecution advanced, the trial ended with no one really showing who had set this train of events in motion. Sams cracked on the stand and the jury saw him for the fool he was. On May 24, 1971, the jury voted eleven to one for Seale's acquittal. Judge Mulvey explained that the state of Connecticut "had put its best foot forward . . . to prove its cases against these defendants. They have failed to convince a jury of their guilt." He added that "with the massive publicity attendant upon the trial just completed, I find it impossible to believe that an unbiased jury could be selected without superhuman efforts, which this Court, the State, and these defendants should not be called upon either to make or to endure. The motion to dismiss is granted in each case, and the prisoners are discharged forthwith."[31] Though the Panthers won in the courtroom, Sams's actions ostensibly caused the police to raid nearly every chapter in the country in search of fugitives Lonnie McLucas, Warren Kimbro, Rory Hithe, and Sams himself. These raids often led to shootouts and arrests and, in the worst case, to events that led to the murder of Fred Hampton in Chicago. Psycho Sams, as he was known to some Panthers, had done his job well.

In addition to outside interference, another problem that plagued the organization was dissatisfaction with the leadership among the rank-and-file. Today, many former Panthers insist that David Hilliard did an excellent job of presiding over the party while Newton and Seale remained incarcerated. As chief of staff, he oversaw the group's growth in membership and influence and, they believed, did his best to maintain order. His background as a longshoreman, however, had not prepared him to lead an international organization that not only had tremendous influence but was heavily armed. Some accused Hilliard of playing favorites and of providing legal and other kinds of support only to those he liked. Others insisted that he was heavy-handed with the discipline. He had also alienated Eldridge Cleaver, safely ensconced in Algeria. The two rarely agreed on anything, particularly tactics, and before long a rift occurred. To be fair, Hilliard worked diligently with what he had to work with. His mistakes must not be seen solely as a personal failure, but in the larger context of an organization that never quite had the opportunity to grow, reflect, and learn from its mistakes. Panther Thomas McCreary, who had also joined the Black Liberation Army, remembered that at one point things had gotten so bad that, "we didn't even have time to grieve our dead, we were busy stepping over bodies and moving on to the next destination."[32]

Despite the hard times, most party members hoped that all the internal problems would disappear once Newton resumed control. Perhaps the best perspective on this self-inflicted crisis came from Don Cox, field marshal for the entire organization. Cox had helped organize chapters from San Francisco and Los Angeles to Boston and Detroit. He answered only to Newton and Seale, and, once they went to jail, to David Hilliard and his brother June, the assistant chief of staff. One could predict early on that problems might arise because when Cox asked Seale what his duties were, Seale reportedly told him that "whenever you see something that needs done, do it." This kind of leadership was bound to self-destruct in an organization as tension-filled and as heavily armed as the BPP. By 1970, Cox noticed his comrades were operating in fear because "David was then ruling with an iron hand." He wrote that when Panthers attempted to build an escape tunnel under headquarters, "they hit water and had to abandon the project. . . . But they turned that hole that was left into a jail (the People's Jail as it later came to called) where all were put that displeased David." He described June as "the jailer" and said "he carried a blackjack in his pocket and wouldn't hesitate to hit someone in the head with it for the slightest disagreement." This behavior, of course, represented the beginning of the end for the revolutionary organization. Once party members grew afraid to speak and all semblance of democratic centralism disappeared, the leadership became autocratic and self-destructive, leaving plenty of room for the FBI or any other entity to capitalize on such shortcomings.[33]

Hilliard had indeed done as well as he could with what he had to work with. Most Panthers adored and idolized him as "the chief." Those who worked closely with him, however, saw things differently. Hilliard, they said, lived in a better house than other Panthers and wore expensive jewelry and clothes. His detractors argued he only helped those comrades he liked and generally ran the party into the ground with his ineptitude. Most rank-and-file, however, did not even know of the jail and the other problems at headquarters. Additionally, many believed that some of Hilliard's extremism was necessary due to the increasing repression the party came under. Those who saw Hilliard's other side believed he needed to be replaced with someone who had more experience.

By mid-1969, "the only hope" Cox saw for the party "was [Charles] Garry getting Huey out of prison." If the popular lawyer did not prevail, he believed, "there wouldn't be anything left to straighten out." People resigned on a regular basis and the purge had taken its toll, even on those still loyal to the party. "The purge," remembered Bill Jennings, "was very subjective. A person I thought was a good person, some of them [the leaders] might not have thought was a good person, and if they did not like them, they could make trouble for them." Cox concurred with Jennings and asserted that "expulsions were no longer used to clean up the party but were being used to get rid of people David or June didn't like. . . . Then, after they were expelled there would be an article in the Panther paper denouncing them for being an *agent provocateur,* pig, crazy, or something. The Panther paper became a tool of defamation," he concluded. Sometimes, there might be "severe punishment before they were expelled."[34] Clearly, at this point, the party had become cannibalistic and even without government infiltration its leadership did a great job of helping it to self-destruct. Hilliard's authoritarianism and his refusal to take advice from anyone but a select few meant that on Newton's release, the founder had to focus on ironing things out internally rather than concentrating on the advancing of the party's programs.

CHAPTER 9 The Rift

TOWARD THE END OF 1969 AND IN EARLY 1970, a rift began to appear in the BPP. Bobby Seale and Elaine Brown, among others, claimed this rift, primarily between leaders and followers of Huey Newton and Eldridge Cleaver, resulted from ideological differences. Others insist such a division had a natural place in organizations like the BPP and the rift had always existed; only the public did not know it. By 1969, Newton, with many of his closest comrades either dead or in jail, advocated that the Panthers put down their guns and involve themselves in community organizing. They had long since stopped wearing the black leather jackets and berets (except on special occasions) because they thought the uniform made them open targets. Newton and his followers continued to believe violent revolution was inevitable, but they insisted the community had to be organized first. On the other hand, Cleaver, exiled in Algiers, continued to advocate immediate armed rebellion.[1]

The reasons for this rift were many. There had long been a discussion in the party as to who had the right to lead the revolution. Newton and his supporters believed it would be the working class, since it was already well organized, possessed the skills, and had developed the level of consciousness needed to fight such a protracted battle. Cleaver believed it was the "lumpen proletariat" (the unemployed, underemployed, drug dealers, prostitutes, and so on) and that this group should begin immediately in its war with the oppressor. Newton urged caution and patience and insisted the masses needed to be organized before such an undertaking, while Cleaver argued for "revolution in our lifetime." Newton had also been disturbed by Cleaver's impact on party members. David Hilliard noted that Newton complained that "Everybody acts like Eldridge. The profanity. Eldridge's style. Eldridge has taken you guys down this direction. This isn't the way of the party."[2] As for Cleaver, he had little love for Hilliard, so the feeling was probably mutual.

Though he had his own problems and shortcomings, the self-exiled Eldridge Cleaver grew weary of Hilliard's leadership. When a delegation of Panthers went to Algiers in 1970 on its way to tour the Far East and to consolidate the party's international gains, an ugly picture of recrimination, near insanity, and internal destruction began to develop. After touring Korea, Russia, and North Vietnam for two months and meeting the heads of state or other high-ranking officials in those countries, the group settled in back in Algeria. One party member wrote a report of this trip. Its author noted that while in Moscow at a dinner meeting, Cleaver, who had accompanied the group, began a discussion of the left and right wings of the Left Movement and explained "to the entire group how this analysis included the Black Panther Party." In an "outright attack on the Chief of Staff," Cleaver entered into "a long discussion" of what Hilliard had done to the party. He insisted that "certain super-lumpen brothers had been expelled because of David and June Hilliard." Giving a glimpse into Cleaver's state of mind at the time, the report indicated that Cleaver "refused to hear discussion on such foolish acts as the 'great distribution-truck robbery' [of 1968]," excusing "such fool-hardy acts" by saying "at least these brothers were doing something." Obviously Cleaver had reached the point of no return, as there is no possible way to justify robbing a gas station of less than fifty dollars in the middle of the day while driving a delivery truck with the Black Panther Party logo emblazoned on both sides.

Finally, Cleaver told his visiting comrades that "David represented the right wing of the Black Panther Party; that the party was run by Charles Garry; [and] that it was a Breakfast-for-Children Party." At the height of his disgruntlement, he reportedly told the group that to really cleanse and purge the party, someone, he did not say who, "with guts would walk into the National [office] with a gun and demand that David and June Hilliard step down from their position" and "say that you have orders from me. If they refuse to step down, kill them."[3] Though the veracity of this report cannot be verified some thirty-five years later, as Cleaver is dead and the author is unknown, it seems clear that even before Newton's release from prison, the party, while being attacked by the FBI, police, and other outside opponents, was slowly being destroyed from within by those people Newton trusted most.

Another bone of contention had been the widely publicized People's Revolutionary Constitutional Convention, held in late 1970, first in

Philadelphia and again in Washington, D.C. Newton believed these conventions, which required enormous manpower and large amounts of money, were useless since they had no way of implementing any of the ideas delegates proposed. However, because he was fresh out of jail, he went along with Cleaver's plan and eventually gave the opening address, disappointing a crowd of three thousand people who thought he could speak better than he actually did.

Unlike Cleaver, Newton hated to speak in public, partly because he was not very good at it. Because many people had begun to engage in hero worship over the by-now-confused Newton, he felt a need to live up to some of their expectations. Unfortunately, he did not have the proper oratorical skills and most of his public utterances bored his audiences or, at the very least, left them wishing for more. This particular shortcoming could very well have produced jealousy in Newton, especially when it came to Cleaver and other high-ranking party members like Masai Hewitt, who served as minister of education and could speak much better than Newton. Before joining the party, Hewitt had been a member of a number of Marxist groups in Los Angeles. He therefore held a commanding grasp on dialectical materialism and was able to impart this knowledge in a way that even the most unlettered member could understand. Newton, of course, often felt he was being upstaged, and because Hewitt had come out of the Los Angeles chapter, where Cleaver's influence was unquestionable, this made matters worse. Like Cleaver, Hewitt was willing to question some of Newton's policies. Like Hilliard, Newton did not like to be questioned and when Hewitt complained that the Central Committee "had become no more than a rubber stamp" for "Huey's will," Newton demoted Hewitt to a member of the rank-and-file, and, according to Elaine Brown, "assigned Masai to sell Panther newspapers on the street from that point forward."[4] Other Panthers, who will not go on record, say Newton had Hewitt beaten by the Panther goon squad.

The grab for power that characterized the party leadership beginning in 1970 soon ushered in its destruction as a national organization. Newton must have seen some of this coming because he made an attempt to smooth things over with Cleaver. While these events unfolded, disagreements between the New York Panthers and the leaders in Oakland sped the party toward its reckoning with fate.

Since 1969, and perhaps even earlier, tension had been growing between the New York state chapter and headquarters. In the beginning these disagreements were small, even innocuous. For example, Dhoruba had often upset David Hilliard by telephoning the Oakland office collect. Hilliard insisted the practice stop. Dhoruba responded that "we don't have money for a phone," and assured Hilliard the next time he called, it was going to be collect. The issue he called about, however, was more telling. Dhoruba asked Hilliard why articles from New York were not appearing in the newspaper. He mentioned that New York Panthers had submitted several and had not yet seen them in print. Hilliard responded that "a lot of people submit articles so it takes time to get them in." When it became clear that this answer did not satisfy Dhoruba, Hilliard explained that it was not his department and said he needed to check with the people in San Francisco who were in charge of putting the paper out. These differences, however, escalated when some New York members began to implore Newton to allow them a position on the Central Committee. Newton responded that "he would take it into consideration."[5] Of course, Newton considered the idea long enough to know that he was not about to allow such a thing to happen. The unlimited power he held after his release from prison was addictive and he saw no reason to share it with other more capable comrades. New York members resented being ignored, and the seeds of dissension were fertilized.

More problems emerged in New York City between the state chapter and headquarters after the incarceration of the New York Twenty-one. As soon as the leaders went to jail, a host of Panthers from Oakland flooded New York City to help keep the chapter afloat. New York was an important beachhead in the movement since not only did millions of black people reside in the city, but it was also the gateway to the international arena. Party leaders feared that if the New York chapter faltered it meant trouble for the entire east coast. The problem was that when the members from headquarters arrived, they brought their problems with them. New York Panther BJ insisted "the dog had fleas on it when it got here!" Taking the reins of power in the Big Apple, people like Landon Williams, Rory Hithe, and Thomas Jolly demonstrated they had not internalized party principles. According to several New York Panthers, these individuals often displayed chauvinistic attitudes toward Panther women. On several occasions, they attempted to take liberties with some of them. When it became clear that New York Panthers did not tolerate such behavior, tensions rose to a boiling point. One Panther sister had to pull a gun on Landon Williams, who clearly could not take no for an answer after requesting sex. There were other episodes where Panther males had to confront these Oakland Panthers with weapons to get them to stop their advances. This activity certainly did not endear New York Panthers to their leaders from headquarters.[6]

In addition to this problem, Oakland Panthers insisted that those Panthers who wore African headdresses remove them, as that was a manifestation of cultural nationalism, according to the leaders. "Someone from the west coast," explained BJ, "told them to take that shit off." Of course, blacks in Harlem had long been inculcated with African culture, at least since the days of Marcus Garvey and his Universal Negro Improvement Association. This group attempted to impress on blacks the importance of African origins, culture, and religion. With more than twenty million members and New York City as its base, the UNIA represented the largest black mass movement in American history. Though New York Panthers agreed to remove their gelees and other African garb, they resented the order and wondered aloud what kind of leaders they served. BJ remembered that one of the contradictions between the East and West Coast Panthers came once "they made our sisters take off them gelees. We were not cultural nationalists, but we took them off based on principles; but there were hard feelings about doing that. Because in Harlem and New York that was a very cultural thing to do."[7] Though California Panthers like Robert Webb, Elbert "Big Man" Howard, Bobby Seale, and Don Cox were and are held in high esteem by New York Panthers, a majority of those interviewed hold the opinion that most of the leadership from the West Coast did not know how to lead or how to build an organization like the BPP. The fact that many New York Panthers were ideologically closer to Cleaver than to Newton meant that these problems increased the tension that was slowly choking the life out of the party.

The last straw came early in 1971 when Newton expelled members of the New York Twenty-one while they were still in jail. For months, the jailed New York Panthers had disagreed with some of Newton's policies and had written letters to explain their position. They submitted these letters to *The Black Panther* newspaper staff but were rebuffed every time. They never received a reason for why their letters and articles failed to make the paper. Finally, they decided that they had to be heard and sent a letter to the Weather Underground, an offshoot of militant whites who broke from SDS and started a campaign of bombings. Their radical leanings impressed the Panthers and the two groups soon shared money, food, housing, and transportation while they lived underground. The letter from the New York Twenty-one identified the Weather Underground as the vanguard of the revolution since Newton and his supporters had turned reformist. It also castigated Newton for other improprieties.[8] When the Weather Underground published this open letter, Newton immediately expelled its authors for subordination and claimed that they had been counterrevolutionary, a label many sixties radicals used to denote someone they did not like or someone who did something they did not like. More often than not, the slur had nothing to do with politics. Of course, the Panther leadership in New York had done nothing to hinder black progress. Newton's reaction was based on his inability to control and influence the actions of everyone in the party. Though he needed the New York chapter as much as he needed oxygen, Newton's ego did not allow him to accept criticism of any kind. Even if it had, the New York leaders had rejected his leadership, so there was little he could have done aside from being reasonable. By this time, however, Newton was becoming less reasonable by the day.

In the meantime, the year-long trial the New York Panthers endured ended in victory for the Panthers, as they were acquitted of all 121 charges against them. Because they remained in prison for the duration of the trial, they had to be innovative in their defense tactics. They were also helped by government bungling. Trial testimony indicated that several of the Panther leaders had been police agents. Via these conduits, the Bureau of Special Services and the FBI worked to frame leading members of the party by coming up with wild schemes to destroy public property and by offering legitimate Panthers dynamite. Though the presiding judge's home was bombed by members of the Weather Underground as the trial came to a close, the judge seemed not to have tampered with the legal process. The evidence presented by District Attorney Hogan appeared to the jury as if it had been manufactured rather than discovered. Afeni Shakur worked as her own lawyer and astounded the jury with her extensive knowledge of the law and her biting questions during cross-examinations. By the time the Panthers were released, however, the New York state chapter had begun to founder and increasing numbers of its members began to drop out of sight, with many going underground to fight alongside the Black Liberation Army.

Despite the setbacks, Newton tried to hold things together. He wanted to show the public that the party was still strong and that people were not defecting to the more radical wing lead by Cleaver. To prove his point, he decided to speak with Cleaver in a televised international phone hookup on the *Jim Dunbar Show*, a morning program that covered current events in San Francisco. In February 1971, on the night before the call was to take place, Newton phoned Cleaver to make sure he still wanted to participate in the televised call. Newton assured Cleaver that he only wanted to show the world that there had not been a split in the BPP and that no personal material would be discussed. Reluctantly, Cleaver agreed. He did not, however, want to take any chances. He and Newton had been arguing about policy and tactics for some time. These arguments had been taxing on them both. Newton had also begun hearing from other party members that Cleaver killed some Panthers who crossed him in Algiers. This happened at least twice, according to one witness, but maybe even more often. One of the victims had allegedly made advances on Eldridge's wife, Kathleen. Cleaver naturally wondered if Newton might bring some of this dirt out or make up some of his own on live television. Add this possibility to the fact that Cleaver and the others in Algiers no longer trusted Hilliard or Newton—whom they assumed was Hilliard's puppet— and one can see why a live telephone call was a bad idea. Despite the signs that things would deteriorate rapidly, Newton went ahead with the call.[9]

Cleaver opened the conversation by insisting Newton reinstate the ousted Panthers from New York and their supporters on the West Coast, saying their expulsion was "regrettable" and "should not have taken place." Newton denied the request, claiming the eastern Panthers had forgotten the party's original principles and had veered "off into counterproductive avenues of violence and adventurism." Moving beyond this issue, Cleaver criticized the party's "inept" Central Committee and demanded chief of staff David Hilliard be removed from his post. The exiled leader placed sole responsibility on the chief of staff for tearing the party apart "at the seams." Again, Newton refused to entertain Cleaver's suggestion. Cleaver then broke openly with Newton, attacked the community service programs as reformist, and in Newton's view, "frantically tried to coalesce his own followers with transatlantic exhortations for immediate guerrilla warfare." Thereafter, Cleaver announced, he directed the "real" BPP from Algiers.[10]

At that point, the televised part of the long-distance meeting ended. Off the air, Newton accused Cleaver of beating his wife, killing fellow Panthers at the international headquarters in Algiers, and dealing in arms and drugs. In response, Cleaver "expelled" Newton and Hilliard. A few days later his New York followers publicized plans "for an alternate national headquarters in Manhattan." Newton, in turn, expelled Cleaver. The conversation terminated as it had begun, with the two leaders separated by a personal rivalry stemming from the struggle to control the party. An impassable ideological gap had contributed to the leaders' breaking of all ties with each other.[11]

While steady eastward movement had been good for growth, party leaders found it difficult, then finally impossible, to maintain control of thirty-two chapters across the country. With bases in Connecticut, New York, Pennsylvania, Maryland, and a half dozen other eastern seaboard locales, the party had solidified its leadership of the rapidly growing Black Power movement. Its expansion did not come without troubles, however. Before it could make good on its promise to bring liberation to the black masses, the federal government succeeded in weakening it with its counterintelligence tactics. This federal assault, coupled with the group's ability to endanger itself, took its toll on the hopeful revolutionaries. As a result, they, along with their fearless leader, decided to revise their strategy.

This strategy deemphasized the gun and made the growth of black political strength its goal. While that process took effect, the Panthers sought to help blacks maintain themselves with their community survival programs. As with all progress, the BPP turnabout did not come without growing pains.

Some thirty-five years later, it remains difficult and nearly impossible to get Panthers to talk about the controversial aspects of party history. There are some, however, who see the usefulness of telling the story even when it is not necessarily a "good" one. This following series of incidents in the life of a New York Panther certainly shows the party in a light not often seen by outsiders.

BJ, a Corona-based New York Panther who worked with newspaper distribution, postulated that the final breakdown started in earnest when Harlem Panther Zayd Shakur traveled to the West Coast to attempt to make peace between the feuding factions.[12] When he arrived, however, he apparently offended one or several people in leadership because they immediately placed him in the People's Jail located under the headquarters office. One version of what happened, related by Thomas McCreary, says that "they kicked his butt and then put him in jail." Either way, he was immobilized, ensuring that the problem remained unsolved. Apparently, Geronimo Pratt heard about the situation and decided to intervene. According to BJ, Pratt arrived at the People's Jail "and told the brothers guarding Zayd that, 'look I gotta take him to see Huey at Central and they want him there right now.'" They believed him and let him go. McCreary noted that by this time field marshal Robert Webb, who previously lived in California, found out about Shakur's incarceration and went there to straighten things out. When he arrived, he enlisted the help of a few of his friends from Hunters Point in San Francisco and, with Pratt's help, "kicked the guards' butts and broke Zayd out of jail. They really messed them up." Zayd boarded the red-eye flight back to New York City. Upon his arrival in New York, he called a news conference and explained what had happened to him. With the television cameras rolling, he explained Newton's and his cohorts' involvement in drugs, women, and vice in Oakland. This act, of course, ensured Newton's retaliatory response.[13]

Once Cleaver and Newton parted ways in early 1971, the party began to implode. With Cleaver aligned with the Black Liberation Army and having taken complete control of "the Harlem, Brooklyn, and Bronx branches" and a smattering of outposts on the East Coast, things were bound to get worse before they got better—and get worse they did. Several leaders from eastern chapters and branches, soon after Cleaver's defection, held a meeting at the Harlem office. Those present included Paul Coates of the Baltimore chapter, Samuel Napier from across the bridge in Corona, the home base for newspaper distribution, Bashir Hamid of the New Jersey branch, and a dozen or so others. No one but those who attended knows exactly what transpired, but according to BJ, who worked security for the meeting as he waited on his branch partner Samuel Napier, the group made some momentous decisions.

At this meeting, delegates apparently agreed to carve up the East

Robert Webb, Black Panther member and officer of the day in the San Francisco office, 1971. *Photo by Ducho Dennis, courtesy of It's About Time.*

Coast into Newton and Cleaver areas of control. Most party members, however, when confronted with the either-or ultimatum either stayed with Newton or quit the organization. In effect, the party stayed intact with the exception of a few branches and a small number of people from individual chapters. For that reason, it is inaccurate to describe what happened as an East/West split since almost all the East Coast chapters from Rhode Island to North Carolina remained in the Newton camp. Still, the main decision made at the meeting concerned turf. All the delegates agreed that the *Black Panther* newspaper would not be sold in Harlem, Brooklyn, or the Bronx. BJ remembered Napier emerging from the meeting that night enraged, saying "these niggers are crazy, this is the Black Panther Party, they can't do that!" Another Panther was trying to calm him down and get him out of the area because, according to BJ, Paul Coates told Sam "they were getting ready to shoot you." Napier insisted that they would have done no such thing. BJ, born and raised in Brooklyn, knew that the threat had not only been real, but highly likely. Once they drove away, Napier proclaimed "it was a sad day for the Black Panther Party. I hate to lose all these chapters but that's what's happening." BJ concluded, "that's the beginning" of the group's splintering.[14]

BJ remembered that soon after the Harlem meeting, Napier went to Oakland on routine business and attempted to work the situation out while he was there. In the meantime, members of the Harlem branch, under orders from Eldridge Cleaver and Don Cox in Algiers, began to seize branches in New York City. BJ recalled the night it happened at his branch in Corona, the suburb in Queens where Malcolm X and jazz pioneer Louis Armstrong once made their homes.

He and his comrades had been selling papers in the Port Authority until about eleven or so that night. The Port Authority was a central transportation hub where people went to take buses, trains, and cabs to their next destination. Another group of New York Panthers came through headed for New Jersey. BJ thought this was strange because of the late hour and the fact that they were mostly women and children. They yelled "All power to the people" and kept going. Nothing happened at this point but it all made sense to him once the group arrived back at their Northern Boulevard office. "We get back to the office and there were some Panthers there who were not from Corona," he remembered. "In fact it was Twyman Myers, Freddie Hilton, a brother named Hassan, and somebody else I can't remember." He remembered his close comrade Omar Babour just stood there incredulously and explained that "they have taken over." When asked what he meant by that, Babour told BJ to ask Myers, who retorted, "this office is the property of the Black Panther Party International Section and Eldridge Cleaver is the leader." They were then told that they had a choice of going along with Cleaver's program or not. "You are either with us or you are against us," BJ remembered him saying. For the moment, the choice was easy as the people in charge held automatic weapons that everybody knew were loaded. Because the hour was late, most of the Corona Panthers in the office chose to ride out this bizarre storm. There was, however, one exception. A much older brother, also named Omar, decided not to go along with the gun-wielding revolutionaries. A veteran and former World War II paratrooper, this Omar had worked alongside Malcolm X, was from the neighborhood, and handled security for the Corona office. He looked at the men holding the guns and said, "I know you brothers and you know me and this shit is falling apart. This is the same thing that happened to Malcolm and the Muslims and I will not be a part of it, I'm leaving. If you don't want me to leave, shoot me because I'm gone, I quit." After that, BJ said, "he stormed out the door."

The rest of the crew decided to wait until morning to make a decision. According to BJ, when morning arrived, the gunmen made a phone call, "took our guns and split. They just left us there," he said. It is important to note that by this time, the BLA had swung into action. It engaged in bank robberies and other clandestine activity. It also took responsibility for the shooting of several New York City policemen. Twyman Myers and Freddie Hilton were members of this organization, so they could very well have been called off to more pressing business. At any rate, when Napier returned from California, BJ remembered, things "got back in motion, we started selling papers and building a security team to watch us [the Corona Panthers who distributed the *Black Panther*] when we sold papers." They believed they needed the security because of an earlier television newscast in which Zayd Shakur insisted that "seventy-five robots were coming from Oakland to kill" New York Panthers. BJ noted that when the Corona Panthers saw this news clip, "we looked at each other and said damn, there are only two people in here from Oakland and that's Sam and Andrew [Austin]. . . . Seventy-five? I think it was about twelve of us, some came out of Boston, others from D.C., and Philly. They came up for security because there were a lot of threats made at that meeting" in Harlem. They did not "come to do no killing," he said, "they came to protect the paper." As he explained it, they had someone stationed on the next corner keeping an eye on the person who sold the paper. "You had what we called a shadow, or like Geronimo [Pratt] said, a wolf, and this person would watch you all day long and you were supposed to act like you didn't even know 'em." He claimed it worked so well that "at lunch time we would go four blocks away and have lunch together."[15]

After this had gone on for a while, BJ noted that the Harlem Panthers-turned-BLA members were making the news quite often. Sometimes they robbed banks or other establishments and other times they executed police officers. BLA members usually issued communiqués taking credit for and explaining their actions through newspaper outlets or radio stations.

For example, after the New York Twenty-one trial ended, BLA members ran a red light on Riverside Drive near the home of District Attorney Hogan to draw policemen guarding the house into an ambush. The police fell for it and chased the car for several blocks. Once they caught up with the vehicle, they pulled alongside and the driver ducked down in his seat as the passenger opened fire with a .45 caliber submachine gun. The police car crashed into a pole and both officers suffered serious injuries. The following day, local radio stations broadcast a message from the BLA explaining why the incident occurred. To prove the message's authenticity, the culprits sent along the license plate of the getaway car, which police had been searching for since the shooting. When New York City police officers Rocco Laurie, Gregory Foster, Waverly Jones, and Joseph Piagentini were killed near housing projects (not all at the same time), a similar message went out explaining that the suffering and murders of black people had to be avenged. One of the notes read: "This is from the George Jackson Squad of the Black Liberation Army about the pigs wiped out in Lower Manhattan last night. No longer will black people tolerate Attica [the site, in 1971, of the bloodiest prison riot in American history, where unarmed inmates were ambushed from helicopter gun ships after holding hostages in a protest for improvement in prison facilities] and oppression and exploitation and rape of our black community. This is the start of our Spring Offensive. There is more to come. We also dealt with the pigs in Brooklyn. We Remember Attica." They signed the brief note, distributed by United Press International news service, "The George Jackson Squad of the BLA."[16] Not long after this incident, however, BJ and his comrades in Corona heard a news report detailing how the police had "busted a lot of people in the Brooklyn Branch, shot up a few of them and killed one of them." It had been a failed robbery and those not jailed escaped. BJ figured that "the ones that escaped got to be underground, so we decided, OK, we can go to Brooklyn now. So we went to Brooklyn and started selling newspapers."[17]

Soon after this development, BJ, who worked in distribution with Sam Napier, "overheard Sam and Huey talking on the phone one night." When Napier told Newton about the new developments with the Brooklyn turf "and about the arrangements at the meeting," Newton exploded in anger "and started screaming or something because Sam took the phone away from his ear." Later, when Napier related the gist of his conversation with Newton to BJ, he told him "Huey wanted to know why we ain't in

A copy of the Black Panther Party newspaper from 1971. *Courtesy of Bill Jennings/It's About Time.*

Harlem. Harlem is the base of black people in New York and the *Black Panther* needs a presence up in Harlem." BJ noted, "Well that's another fallacy because the base of black people in New York was all over, Queens, Brooklyn, everywhere, we were doing alright, shit we were making our quota." Despite Napier's arguments, Newton demanded the distribution team get papers to Harlem. The party being a paramilitary organization, and "Sam being a stickler for structure and following the rules," it was impossible to ignore Newton's order. In the end, BJ explained, "I was picked to go up there with my wolf. I didn't agree with it at all. I argued against it. We don't need Harlem, let them have Harlem. See I know how New Yorkers are, they are very territorial because we all grew up in gangs and each gang had their own block or own project and if you went into somebody else's neighborhood and don't know nobody they whip your ass, so you know, I didn't want to go to Harlem." According to BJ, "them motherfuckers in California didn't understand that." Newton's insistence on this dangerous and unnecessary move did not bode well for the party. The recently freed power-hungry leader miscalculated the seriousness of his comrades and helped to incapacitate the party.

BJ obeyed the order and made the trip to Harlem. From ten in the morning to five in the evening, he sold the Panther paper, his wolf watching him every minute. At one point, he eyed his wolf and walked over to him to see whether he was ready to go home. His wolf responded, "whatever you wanna do man." BJ told him to go back and take his position and he was "going to sell this one more paper" before leaving. "At that time," he remembered, "here come the Harlem Panthers. One of the Panthers I trained too." His name was Anthony White, "they called him Kimu, and he was killed as a member of the BLA while sitting in a bar in Brooklyn." White walked up to BJ and said in disbelief, "'aw BJ, not you man! What the hell you doing out here, you know better!' I said 'yeah man but I got. . .'" BJ's shadow, or wolf, watched as the entire exchange unfolded, with White in the intersection approaching the sidewalk from where BJ sold his papers. When BJ noticed he had help, he made a little more conversation with White, but "my wolf had the drop on him" by then, he remembered. At this point, BJ said "go for it, get him." White and the wolf were both standing there ready to shoot each other as BJ continued imploring his wolf to "shoot him, I ain't got no gun, shoot him." His wolf, however, apparently did not deem such a drastic measure necessary and made an attempt to defuse the situation. The wolf said, "hold up man, we been out here all day, we getting ready to leave here anyway, right BJ?" BJ answered "yeah, shoot him!" The wolf kept asking BJ, "weren't we leaving?" and finally BJ got the point and agreed. BJ later explained that his wolf and the Harlem Panther "didn't know each other from Adam—this guy was from another state and we brought security in from another state so they wouldn't be recognized. They're standing there in the middle of the street at a standoff, both of them holding their waist belts like it was the OK Corral." Then White said, "OK, that's alright." The wolf then suggested they leave as White barked to them, "don't come back again!"[18] These Panthers narrowly averted a shootout or something worse, simply because Newton wanted the paper to be sold in his sworn enemy's territory. People in Harlem could have easily gotten the papers in other places or through the mail. Stores often volunteered to stock it because it was so popular. For these reasons, Newton's point about having the paper salesmen there physically seems invalid.

When BJ returned to Queens and explained to Napier what happened, he was chastised. "Them same niggers from California," he said, "that don't understand New York, they went off. They thought I was crazy." He explained that he had the paper money and had made his quota, but Napier complained that he "still had ten papers left." When BJ tried to rationalize the situation by reminding Sam that "other motherfuckers walk in here and you give them a hundred [papers] and they come back with thirty-five, you don't say nothing to them!" Ending the argument, Napier told BJ "you ain't shit" and summarily banished him to Greenwich Village to sell papers. "Cool," Sam reportedly said, "I'll get someone else to go up there." That ended it and Napier began the process of finding another team to carry out Newton's nonsensical order.

Because of the heightened security since the rift between Newton and Cleaver, the tension grew and all Panthers "were on a need-to-know" basis when it came to assignments. "We didn't know who went to what corner or where anybody was selling the paper on any given day," explained BJ. The security system became "very sophisticated with vans for the rank-and-file and cars trailing them to watch what happened. A lot of times you would see the car driving around and checking you out, then leave and come back again so they wouldn't be conspicuous. So that's how it went down." The next day, "the very next day, they went out and here come field marshal Robert Webb," he explained. "I guess Kimu told them, yeah get them Panthers out of here, I saw one the other day."

Because BJ had to work in Greenwich Village, where students, hippies, artists, writers, and the well-to-do made their homes, his knowledge of what happened next is second-hand. This fact, of course, makes it less reliable than if he had witnessed the incident. Just like his counterpart the day before, field marshal Robert Webb, sent from San Francisco the previous spring to help shore up the New York chapter while the Twenty-one stood trial, approached the Panthers who were selling papers. This violation of the "rules," especially since two Panthers had been let off the hook the day before, apparently could not go unpunished. There are no newspaper or police reports with an accurate description of the incident and no one who witnessed it came forth. It seems clear, however, that Webb, armed with a fully loaded .357 Magnum, approached the paper salesman; whether he pulled his sidearm and threatened the salesman or not remains unknown. What is known is somebody reacted faster than Webb. In the blink of an eye, twenty-two-year-old Robert Webb lay on a New York City sidewalk at the corner of 125th and Seventh Street, dead of a gunshot wound to the back of his head. It may have been the newspaper salesman's shadow or wolf. Another theory is that a government agent took advantage of the tension to bring the two factions to open warfare. A police source quoted in the *New York Times* said that "a number of local Black Panthers, loyal to the West Coast leadership killed him." Deputy minister of information Zayd Shakur told reporters at a news conference that "Mr. Webb had been shot while attempting to confiscate the reactionary rag sheet from two fools [who] are aligned with the Newton faction." Shakur claimed that Webb had been killed because "he had joined in the local chapter's demand for the resignation or dismissal of Mr. Hilliard," the party's chief of staff.[19]

BJ remembered that when he called the office to check in, he was told that all Panthers had "to get off the street" and that there "had been an incident. I don't quite remember how he said it, but the way he said it, you knew somebody was shot, but you knew it wasn't your people. Everybody that sold papers was supposed to have a safe house in case anything went down. My safe house was my mother's house in Brooklyn."

After he took a train home, he "caught the news that reported a Panther killed. The reason why they said Black Panther was because there had been *Black Panther* newspapers scattered on the ground with blood all over them," he explained. For the next two days, nobody did anything, he remembered. "We took most of the firepower out of the offices and put it in different safe houses in the community because we were looking for a bust. Nothing happened. We said to ourselves, they think we did it, so we know there is going to be some kind of retaliation."

During the following several days consternation abounded, but neither the police nor rival Panthers came looking for those responsible for distribution of the *Black Panther* in New York City. BJ remembered:

> That's the funny part about it. That's the only thing we were worried about because we knew they would have had to come question us because there were stacks of *Black Panther* newspapers there. . . . the police didn't care for the Panthers in Harlem, and if a Harlem Panther got killed it was cool for them. Or the person that shot Robert Webb was an agent and got away with it. If you take that theory, then that means that the FBI perpetuated this violent split with that one action because after that all across the country Panthers were being shot down. I'll be damned if that shit didn't happen until after the murder of Robert Webb. I tend to believe that last theory because they didn't investigate, they didn't do nothing, no questions, no nothing.

The police, according to this Panther, did not ask the party members in charge of distributing the *Black Panther* any questions, including, "where these papers come from?, they yours?"[20] While both of BJ's theories are plausible, it is unlikely that we will ever know the truth about this cold-blooded murder. Police in New York City displayed little inclination to find Webb's killer. After all, BLA members had been killing police for months and Webb had close ties to the BLA. To the police, the BLA and Panthers were one and the same. Then again, Webb could have been murdered by someone trying to protect a comrade. Regardless of who did the killing, this particular murder flung the party into a period of tremendous change and uncertainty.

Preparing themselves for an eventual retaliation, the Corona Panthers increased their security network. Armed security men were placed in the Panther distribution office, one upstairs in the shower and one downstairs in the basement. Another armed man positioned himself in a building across the street and watched the office. These men were never seen by anyone but the officer of the day or other security personnel.

A few days after the Harlem shooting, Napier insisted that newspaper distribution continue. "Circulate to educate," remembered BJ, "was his favorite phrase." The group did not, however, venture to sell the paper in Harlem at this point. They continued to distribute the paper throughout the east coast, from Boston and New Haven, Connecticut, down to Washington, D.C., and Winston-Salem, North Carolina. People from these cities went to Queens once a week to get the papers. "Once a week we were in touch with these brothers and that's how I know how many people defected from the chapters and branches," BJ said. "Because they would say so-and-so had just walked away and said Huey ain't shit you know." Though most accounts of the party describe what happened as a split, BJ explained that there had not been a split, but a defection of a few people. The party continued to grow by starting chapters and adding recruits. "For the amount of people that left that couldn't make it a split," he said.[21]

Once the paper was back up and running, other developments encouraged the Corona Panthers to go back to Harlem. Many in the Harlem chapter had sided with Cleaver, so they supported the BLA. In the process, they also started their own newspaper, calling it *Right On*. BJ recalled that "the Panthers always fantasized about offing the pig," referring to police killings. After one of these murderous escapades, the police captured one of the BLA members and the rest of the Harlem chapter seemed to disappear. Not long after Webb's murder and the increasing number of arrests in the Harlem chapter, BJ remembered Napier saying, "they [the Harlem Panthers turned BLA members] ain't worried about us, they out there carrying the revolution to the white man, they fighting the system, they underground." BJ remembered that because the Panthers and the BLA members were still comrades, every so often they would "get word about who was going underground." The *Right On* newspaper, published under the leadership of Eldridge Cleaver, also gave certain clues about who was doing what, both above and below ground.[22]

It was at this point that Napier asked BJ, "when's the last time you been out there [to Harlem]?" He responded, "Sam, wait, don't go too fast." The native New Yorker in BJ told him that the coast was not yet clear and even though more than a month had passed and Cleaver's supporters in Harlem seemed to have their hands full with evading police all over the country, the time had not yet come for them to try to sell the paper in Harlem. Napier insisted things were safe. Surely the news reports about the BLA shooting it out with the police and robbing bank after bank meant that their minds were on revolution and not retaliation for Webb's murder. Although BJ tried to explain to him how he successfully sold the paper around Queens, Jamaica, Manhattan, and other area locations, Napier would not listen. "You ain't been to mid-town!" he told BJ. At this point, he handed him a bundle of papers and told him to "take these and get out of here!"

BJ did not want to go because he was doing security for the office that day, April 19, 1971. As he left against his will, he watched as Napier put "papers in Omar's hand. Omar had been chief of security and I was his assistant," he added. Prior to this moment, he did all he could to persuade Omar to stay with Napier. Napier, however, reportedly said, "fuck it, ain't nobody gonna fuck with us." BJ remembered that after a while, "if you listen to Sam browbeat your ass, it was hard to take. He told Omar that any person in here for security can be selling papers, I got it, I can handle it. I'm secure," remembered BJ. The loyal Panther guessed that "Omar must have gotten tired of struggling with him and he left." In a moment of sadness, he recalled that "that was it."[23]

It was a bright and sunny spring day. Johnson jumped in the van and went on a route that he had not taken in weeks because of the trouble with the Harlem Panthers. "I got this store in Queens on the way to Harlem" he remembered, "that's right before you get to the Tri-Borough Bridge." He told his driver to wait until they returned to go to that particular store since it was easier to stop there from the other side of the street. When they finally arrived in Harlem, they decided to drive by the Panther office before selling any papers. "Nobody was in there," he said, "it was just deserted. So we got out, running and stumbling with the papers and hurried up and got back in there" for fear they might be noticed by Harlem Panthers. Because the rules dictated that they call in every two hours and let the office know of their location and of any important events, BJ stopped at a pay phone to make the call. "It seems to me like Sam was saying come back to the office," he remembered, "come back to the office right now, and people were telling him to get some more Panthers in here." Then Napier asked him if he remembered to get the store near the Tri-Borough Bridge. What BJ did not know is that several Harlem Panthers and BLA members had been watching the Corona office for over a month, waiting for a chance to get their prey. When everyone, including the security guards, left the office to sell papers, these individuals, including Dhoruba Bin Wahad, Mark Holder, Jamal Josephs, Andrew Jackson, and several others, entered the office with weapons. Initially, they taped the mouths of the children who had been visiting the office and made them lie on the floor. Then they tied up and gagged a female left behind to care for a year-old baby that belonged to Lola, a party member on the run from her parents in Denver. At some point, the assailants tossed the infant out the back door of the office.[24]

As BJ spoke with Napier, who by then was enduring the torture his unexpected visitors meted out, Sam asked if he had stopped "at his favorite store, the one in Queens, the one that sells a hundred papers, did you get that one? When I told him no, you told me to get it on the way back," Napier retorted, "aw you crazy motherfucker forget that shit, come right now!" He and his partner began driving back to Queens and quite quickly reached the Tri-Borough Bridge. They went about two blocks after they crossed the bridge and Johnson began to think, "hold up, Sam is gonna get us in the office and start talking crazy because we didn't get the store, so I said let's get the store." They turned around, went to the store to pick up money and drop off more papers, then headed back to the office. About a block from the office, they heard firetruck sirens behind them. They pulled to the side of the road and let the firetruck pass. As they approached the office, they saw fire coming from what they thought was the storefront next to the office. On getting closer, however, they saw that it was not. "Oh shit, it's the office!" BJ exclaimed, "we've been hit." They immediately pulled over and jumped out of the van. By this time, plumes of fire and thick black smoke billowed out the front window, "like shit you see on TV," BJ remembered.

BJ then went through an apartment building adjacent to the Northern Boulevard office, only blocks from where Malcolm X used to stay, and entered the office through the basement in the rear. He immediately came upon the "sister and she was laying there tied up with tape on her mouth. 'Get the baby, get the baby!' she screamed, 'There's a baby in the backyard.' So I run back and sure enough in the backyard with flames now coming out of the back of the building, there's a baby there." Apparently Lola, the baby's mother, grew weary of sitting in the office and left to sell papers. Because there was another female there who could take care of the child, her leaving did not present a problem. "That's another reason why Sam had to have a woman in there," remembered BJ, "because we had that one baby in there." After BJ retrieved the baby, he untied the woman he had found and sent her and the baby across the street to the van. Before she left, he inquired as to Napier's whereabouts. She said she did not know as she had been tied up and blindfolded the whole time. She explained that they took him to the basement and after BJ asked if he was dead, she told him that she had heard several shots.

At that point, BJ decided that time was running out and that they both needed to leave. They arrived at the van and he told his partner that he thought "they got Sam." As they were pulling off, BJ decided that he needed to call central headquarters in Oakland and let them know what happened. "Biggest mistake of my life," he noted. He telephoned the office and told them what happened, "exactly what she told me and I told them I got the sister and I got the baby out. I said the place is on fire, it's burning up, if he's in there he's a goner and we are getting ready to get out of here." At this point, "some fucking idiot tells me wait a minute brother, go tell the firemen to go down in the basement, he might be stuck down there, he might be trapped." Again, BJ was obliged to follow orders because of the nature of the organization. When he initially called, he asked the person who answered for someone in charge. When the person who responded that he was the officer of the day, BJ said, "I need somebody higher than you, the shit done hit the fan out here, East Coast Distribution is on fire, I need to talk to somebody else!" The response was, "Hold on brother," and almost immediately someone else came to the phone. BJ told people later that he thought it was Don Cox, but then others explained to him that "DC was underground by then and it couldn't have been him." He now assumes that it was David Hilliard. "Then I got that guy," he remembered, "that brother that told me that bullshit and I would have been in a safe house with my partner if my dumb ass had not have listened."[25]

BJ, playing the loyal soldier, did as he was told and walked back across the street to where the firemen stood. He had also been told not to leave "until you see the body of the brother." He made a mental note that this was the wrong thing to do. As he remembered it, BJ informed the firemen that there might be a body in the basement. They checked and sure enough, Sam Napier's tortured and bullet-riddled body lay smoldering in smoke and flames that fought to stay alive under the pressure of the water. BJ saw a woman he knew from the neighborhood and attempted to leave the scene with her when he saw a fireman whispering to a detective and pointing at him. This detective asked a plainclothes policeman to "watch this man," BJ said. When it all ended, BJ went to jail as a material witness. Some ten days later, after Napier's body had been flown back to California and buried, neighborhood kids identified BJ in a police lineup, saying "that's BJ, that's Sam's friend. Back then, I guess it's not as sophisticated as it is now, but I heard them say that on the other side of the glass." BJ had been stonewalling the police until he mistakenly told them that Napier was from San Francisco and they began playing the good-cop-bad-cop game with him. FBI agents, Chief of Detectives Albert Seedman, famous throughout New York, and several others interviewed him until he finally told them the story of the rift in the party.[26]

By this time, Napier had been dead for over a week. First, his tormentors had beaten and scalded him. They then shot him in the head and set him on fire. One former Panther noted that his body "was found charred beyond recognition." According to one newspaper, Joseph Kelley, a supervisory fire marshal in charge of conducting the investigation into the blaze, said "Mr. Napier's eyes had been bound shut with tape and his body appeared to have been set afire with flammable liquid." He said the dead Panther showed no signs of having been mutilated and that he discovered "four bullet wounds, not six" as other reports had claimed. Former party members and others close to people in the organization somberly concluded that Cleaver ordered Napier's death to warn Newton's supporters that he had raised an opposition army. This murder signaled another turning point in the party since Napier, according to Emory Douglas, "was not just a newspaper salesman, he was like the spirit of the party," and had been "a vital element in the functioning of the paper." Elaine Brown extolled the virtues of Napier's resourcefulness despite concentrated efforts to sabotage the publication. In fact, he had relocated the distribution operation to New York after printers refused to print the paper and after someone bombed the only printing facility they had in San Francisco. Brown credited Napier with being largely responsible for "miraculously" distributing the party's newspaper "throughout the entire United States and beyond, on time, every week."[27]

After the smoke cleared, amazingly, Panthers began selling papers again throughout New York City. East Coast distribution became the New York state chapter headquarters. The Panthers relocated to Brooklyn and began anew. They even started a book store, called Seize the Time Books, where they sold books, records, posters, buttons, clothes, and anything else that advertised the party. When Panthers had a problem with the mafia trying to get kickbacks, BJ's brother, who ran the store, let them know that "this is a Black Panther Party store and I don't think you'll be getting any kickbacks." After that, there were no problems and the record dealers "began giving them records after a while." BJ remembered that "it was the kind of thing where they left us alone and we left them alone. Besides, we were already getting the paper printed at Baland Printing, a mafia joint." By this time, however, BJ had had enough and he left the party to tour with James Brown as a road manager for the Godfather of Soul's opening act, the Oakland-based Variations.[28]

———————

In April 1971, Huey Newton commented that "Eldridge joined the party . . . after the police confrontation, which left him fixated with the 'either-or' attitude. This was that either the community picked up the gun with the party or else they were cowards and there was no place for them." If what he says of Cleaver is true, one can readily see how little sense this position made. Former communist Dorothy Healy remarked that not only did this all-or-nothing stance alienate black workers, but "people who had any degree of roots in their community were not about to simply pick up a gun and start shooting." She added that clearly "what was influencing Huey to a large extent was the fact that if the Cleaver line continued to dominate, the Panthers would be out of existence," since Newton's group was no match for the better trained and better equipped police.[29]

In many ways, Newton had started to moderate some of his earlier, more violent views. He certainly noted that many of the individuals who sided with Cleaver simply wanted to shoot police and not engage in the Panthers' community organizing efforts. In January 1972, the Panther leader explained that in the party's Ten Point Program, "it was not until Point 7 that we mentioned the gun, and this was intentional." He noted that the party sought to build a political machine "through which the people could express their revolutionary desires." Because Cleaver joined the party after a highly publicized San Francisco confrontation in which the Panthers dared the police to go for their guns (and got away with it), he wrongly assumed this was "the Revolution and the Party." In a *Black Panther* editorial, Newton expounded on Cleaver's choice of immediate armed revolution:

> Under the influence of Eldridge Cleaver, the Party gave the community no alternative for dealing with us. Cleaver influenced us to isolate ourselves from the black community, so that it was war between the oppressor and the Black Panther Party, not war between the oppressor and the oppressed community.[30]

Although all the blame for political miscalculations cannot be placed on Cleaver, his influence and popularity certainly must have impressed upon some members the accuracy of his views. Nevertheless, with the Panthers constantly on the defensive due to police shootouts, the avenues by which politics could have been more openly discussed remained closed.

Bobby Seale told an Oakland journalist that the party had the idea of community organizing and running for office long before 1970. But, he added, "we had a lot of people who didn't exactly relate to breakfast programs, such as Eldridge Cleaver. He wanted to call the children's programs sissy stuff." Seale echoed Newton's claim that while they were imprisoned the party lost ground. He claimed Cleaver wrongly influenced the party, "cussing out preachers and not wanting to work in the church." He posited that this move turned out to be a major tactical error because every Sunday morning, "40 percent of the black nation is sitting in church."[31] Perhaps Cleaver agreed with other Marxists who believed that religion is the opium of the masses, and that it had kept blacks from using strategies that might secure their freedom. That Christianity had protected and sustained blacks in their most difficult periods apparently went unnoticed by both Cleaver and Marx. Whatever his position, Cleaver thought the BPP would achieve success only when it had adequately challenged the oppressor, particularly on the military front. Despite the unlikelihood of success in this area of struggle, the leader of the group's international operations refused to allow room for the possibility of nonviolent change in blacks' quest for respect, recognition, justice, and freedom.

The truth of Elaine Brown's account of Cleaver's reactions to the party's changing tactics, if true, is likely in light of Cleaver's sometimes irrational demeanor. After an intense argument in Algiers, Brown claims that Cleaver said: "I don't give a fuck about some serve the people programs. Anybody who doesn't want to deal with the struggle is going to have his ass dragged down the revolutionary road kicking and screaming if necessary. I'm talking about the same thing I've always talked about, revolution in our lifetime and I mean it."[32] Eldridge Cleaver was not alone in his disappointment with the change in Panther tactics. According to author Ross Baker, Cleaver's supporters in Algiers, New York, and Kansas City maintained that Newton had forced the party "to back down from its position as the revolutionary vanguard. They argued that, rather than betray those principles of armed revolution that Cleaver saw as the basis of the party, it was preferable to take the Panthers underground." Until his shooting death in 1989, Newton insisted that such a move served only to alienate the party from those in the community who might otherwise be willing to support it in its organizing efforts.[33]

There is some evidence that the FBI inspired the dissension between Newton and Cleaver and then exacerbated these problems to the point where the factional differences became irreconcilable. As early as October 1968, J. Edgar Hoover directed his field offices to "take action against the BPP on a national level" and to "consider how factionalism can be created between local leaders as well as national leaders and how BPP organizational efforts can be neutralized." The director also admonished field offices to consider "actions which will create suspicion among the leaders."[34] In a teletype to the FBI's Albany, New York, field office, Hoover instructed field agents to employ the services of cooperative media contacts or "sources available to the Seat of Government" to disrupt and discredit the party. He emphasized that the Panthers were to be publicly ridiculed and "not merely publicized."[35] The bureau's early efforts apparently yielded little success since the organization continued to gain support and notoriety among blacks and whites and across social classes.

In the winter of 1970, Hoover sent out a memo describing Newton's paranoid and "hysterical" reactions to the bureau's counterintelligence activities. He explained that since Newton appeared to be "on the brink of mental collapse," the bureau "must intensify [its] counterintelligence." From this memo, one may conclude that part of the FBI's philosophy in fighting the Panther menace was to push the group's leaders to the brink of insanity and then keep pushing.[36]

Elated about this development, the bureau instructed its field offices to "write numerous letters to Cleaver criticizing Newton for his lack of leadership." The bureau believed that if Cleaver received enough complaints about Newton, he might order his execution. The FBI then fabricated and authorized the transmission of a letter from Connie Matthews, Newton's personal secretary, to the exiled Cleaver. It noted that BPP headquarters was disorganized and described the newspaper as being "in shambles." Taking a shot at Cleaver's easily bruised ego, the letter noted that "the foreign department gets no support." The letter then suggested the elimination of either Newton or "the disloyal members" who contributed to the chaos.[37]

At that point, several bureau offices, including the ones in San Francisco, Atlanta, Boston, and New York City, dramatically increased their pressure on the BPP and its leaders. A barrage of anonymous letters designed to create more chaos flowed from FBI field offices in compliance with instructions from headquarters. In his doctoral dissertation, written at UC Santa Cruz in the late seventies and early eighties and published as *War Against the Panthers,* Huey Newton quotes from several of these memos. The FBI sent one letter from Algonquin J. Fuller, a member of the Youth Against War and Fascism (New York), and a white admirer of Cleaver. It said that "pretty nigger Newton" had failed Cleaver and the party, as he had become "a day time revolutionary, a night time party goer, and [an] African fashion model." The letter told Cleaver the Panthers needed him in the United States to "bring the Party back to the People." Because the letter had come from a so-called white revolutionary, someone not involved in BPP internal politics and an obvious supporter of the revolutionary philosophy that Cleaver espoused, it undoubtedly boosted Cleaver's belief that immediate armed revolution was possible. The bureau sent Cleaver a similar letter signed by the New York Twenty-one. The letter informed Cleaver he was their remaining hope in fighting "oppression within and without the Party."[38] The meddling did not end there.

Attempting to exacerbate the factional violence, the bureau used a fabricated letter to Don Cox, Cleaver's companion in Algiers, to intimate that "the recent disappearance and presumed death of Panther leader Fred Bennet was the result of Party factionalism." Members on both sides quickly assumed the authenticity of these letters and reacted as the FBI hoped they would. Almost immediately they became increasingly distrustful and violent toward each other. Internecine violence then tore away at the fragile foundation of the BPP's political and military infrastructure. Sensing the success of this operation, the FBI director moved to further intensify the group's internal problems.[39]

Newton pointed out that "on February 24, 1971, an urgent teletype from the FBI director authorized the most daring step in the campaign— a falsified message to Cleaver from Elbert Howard, a member of the Party's Central Committee and the editor of The Black Panther." After explaining to Cleaver Newton's ingratiating and extravagant use of party funds, and how many members "were upset about this waste of money," the fabricated letter told Cleaver that he "would be amazed at what is actually happening." The letter's real potential, however, hinged on Cleaver's reaction to the final paragraph, which read:

> I wish there was some way I could get in touch with you but in view of Huey's orders it is not possible. You should really know what's happening and statements made about you. I can't risk a call as it would mean certain expulsion. You should think a great deal before sending Kathleen. If I could talk to you I could tell you why I don't think you should.[40]

By this time, the bureau knew of Cleaver's desire to eliminate Newton. The intra-party murders also heightened the tension between the two factions. The agency hoped that this letter, by alluding to a threat on his wife's life, would be the final straw in provoking Cleaver to murder Newton. Cleaver never questioned the letter's authenticity and even believed, according to the FBI, the correspondence "contain[ed] good information about the party." Having further poisoned Cleaver's mind against Newton, the FBI watched and waited. Only Newton's death would have made Hoover happier.

To ensure the splintering was both domestic and international, the bureau fabricated a letter under a forged David Hilliard signature and sent it to all the Panthers' overseas support groups. The letter read: "You are advised that Eldridge Leroy Cleaver is a murderer and a punk without genitals. D.C. Cox is no better." In reference to Webb's shooting, the FBI wrote: "Leroy's running dogs in New York have been righteously dealt with. Any one giving any aid or comfort to Cleaver and his jackanapes will be similarly dealt with no matter where they may be located." Martin Kenner, a one-time accountant for the party, noted that around this time, "the party began to turn in on itself." Clearly, by the end of 1971, the party's fracturing had become irreversible. The Cleaver faction, primarily composed of BLA members, now robbed banks and killed those policemen they believed had perpetrated crimes against blacks.[41] Proceeds from the robberies went to pay lawyers' fees and bail as well as to Panther programs and those in need. For its part, the Newton faction, in addition to engaging in voter registration drives and getting involved in local politics, became somewhat of a black mafia, extorting funds from legitimate and illegitimate Oakland businesspeople including liquor store owners, clothiers, pimps, and drug dealers.[42]

Elated with the success of this COINTELPRO operation, J. Edgar Hoover issued the following instructions:

> Since the differences between Newton and Cleaver now appear irreconcilable, no further counter-intelligence activity in this regard will be undertaken at this time and now new targets must be established. David Hilliard's key position at National Headquarters makes him an outstanding target. Elbert Howard and Bobby Rush [of the Chicago chapter] are also key Panther functionaries . . . making them prime targets.[43]

On the heels of this bogus mail operation, the BPP became an organization dedicated to working within the system via community action programs and voter registration drives. During his campaign for mayor of Oakland in 1972, Bobby Seale's campaign team had installed about two hundred members as county voter registrars. Seale explained that the "Black Panther Party is more of a threat to the established order with ballots in their hands than with guns." In the end, the Newton faction retained most Panther chapters. The group almost completely deemphasized the use of the gun as an avenue for change and thereafter participated in various community building programs in an effort to enhance the BPP's badly tarnished media image. Seale claimed that the party had returned "to its original vision" after the leadership and rank-and-file had looked "at the party in the past and realize[d] our mistakes."[44]

In the end, neither side scored a victory and the biggest loser turned out to be the party itself. The open warfare compelled members to leave the organization in droves. Seale called valuable leadership to Oakland for his unsuccessful mayoral bid and kept them away from their home chapters long after the election, which left some chapters to languish and disintegrate. Other members were expelled or suspended by one leader or the other. In some instances, whole chapters resigned, resulting in the almost complete deterioration of the party's national base of support. The BPP's international section fared no better. In late 1971, Cleaver, tired of the war and "nervous over Algerian efforts to curtail his movements," left the party and moved to France. His successors in Algiers saw few improvements, and within a year they deserted the international headquarters. For all intents and purposes, the party was over.[45]

At last the phase where violent rhetoric and picking up the gun served as the centerpiece ended. The new phase ushered in an era where the party emphasized community programs pending revolution. During this phase, it channeled its energies and focus into serving the people. In effect, the party modified its rhetoric and its program and in the process became more reformist and pragmatic. Adequate food, clothing, and housing for the people it hoped to someday liberate dominated the party's interests. The party now substituted self-help, economic development, and voter education for an emphasis on guns and violence.

After nearly six years of calling for the government's violent overthrow, Panther leaders, by 1972, had retooled and brought the BPP back to Oakland. A smattering of chapters continued to operate and other locales saw Panther chapters emerge where previously there were none. For the most part, however, the work was concentrated in and around Oakland, where Newton attended his many trials and Elaine Brown and Bobby Seale made their runs for the City Council and city hall, respectively. Once this failed bid for public office petered out, (with Seale taking an amazing 43 percent of the vote) the Panthers took the political capitol they earned while registering voters to build a political movement of their own. By 1977, Elaine Brown could honestly tell a reporter that "there is not a black who can get elected to office in Oakland without us." She was right. The movers and shakers in this port city often consulted the Panthers when making minority political appointments and making minority hires in places like the police and fire departments. Indeed, they succeeded in making this 50 percent black city responsive to the needs of half its residents. How were they able to accomplish such a daunting task? They worked with and for the people and at the same time changed the culture of the party.[46]

Grassroots in nature, the Panther's new political orientation was rooted in serving the people, an area where they already had plenty of practice. In addition to their Free Breakfast for Children Program and Free Health Clinics, the Panthers began providing free transportation to the elderly, paramedic and ambulance services, and dental clinics. They opened an Inter-communal Youth Institute that provided high-quality education to Bay Area children. The group also implemented free pest control programs and continued operating their free busing to prisons programs. Undoubtedly endearing themselves to the various black communities in the East Bay, this new-fangled Black Panther Party made its previous incarnation seem way over the top with its demand for vengeance and blood to the horse's brow. Their weapons now included the boycott, voting, and support for other groups trying to get problems solved in the areas of housing, education, and employment. Though the group had wanted these things all along, Panther rhetoric and poor leadership made it difficult for outsiders to comprehend as much. Doing away with the cursing and cleaning up for its new image, the party, after 1972, with only few exceptions, maintained a public persona that made its one-time enemies proud of it.

As a part of its new look, BPP leadership revamped its members' physical appearances and made them appear more like businesspeople than revolutionaries. For example, females were required to have five "dressy type suits, six dresses, two dressy skirts and six blouses or tops. The brothers needed a tie rack, cuff links, lint brush, a jacket of some kind," and a dozen or so other items to keep them looking dapper. The rules required all Panthers to keep their clothes neat "and repaired at all times" and to keep their shoes polished and "clean of all mud, crud, dirt, etc." Their fingernails had to be filed and kept cleaned at all times, along with their nostrils and toenails. If they had beards, they had to be trimmed and neatly groomed at all times and if they did not, their faces had to be "clean-shaven at all times." Leadership also did not tolerate "offensive smelling body odors." Infractions were handled immediately and usually through a verbal reprimand, whereas before, rule-breaking could possibly get members physical punishment.[47]

The new Panthers were also required to carry pens and pencils, a bound notebook, a date book or address book, a watch, an alarm clock, and a "brief case of some kind on a daily basis." This briefcase had to hold at least one of the following: a booklet on the well-baby clinic, a S.A.F.E. program brochure, a busing program brochure, a twelve-inch ruler, and a pack of five cent tissues, along with a pack of tissues they were "required to have on or about [them] at all times." BPP leaders even required Panther cars to have a whistle broom, chrome polisher, and two boxes of S.O.S pads. All of these things had to be in the required wash bucket along with the rags and sponges. A list of required books, articles, toiletries, Son of Man Temple guest cards and two dozen other must-haves rounded out the requirements. Carefully screened local leaders and members had to discipline themselves to meet the high standards of this new and improved Black Panther Party.[48] Party Chairwoman Elaine Brown, who took over in 1974 once Newton fled to Cuba after authorities charged him in the killing of a prostitute, said that the party raised the standards because "it was too easy for reactionary elements and police and FBI infiltrators to enter the party" before. But what kind of results did these new changes bring?

In February 1972, a Mr. Johnson called Central Headquarters and offered the party a building he owned. John George, a black attorney and one-time member of the Alameda County Board of Supervisors, put it best when he said "the leadership of the Panthers from Newton to Elaine Brown recognized that to survive they had to keep in touch with the people's needs." They survived, he noted, because, even though they had a new face, they continued to "express the needs of the most exploited sections of the population. The conditions they were speaking for in the beginning," he added, "remain the same; in fact [conditions were] worse, including unemployment, inflation, and housing."[49] Soon after the Los Angeles chapter reopened on January 17, 1977, they had "hundreds of curious young people" pass "through the office seeking information." Obviously taking care of the needs of the community, the party received "letters of support from numerous community groups, including a food cooperative, the Watts Summer Festival and even a credit union," according to one reporter. Working to alleviate some of these concerns, the Panthers showed the world that they were back to fight another day and they represented "a 'concrete alternative' to the crime-and-poverty-infested ghettos." Looking at the situation from a holistic point of view, party members also worked on themselves internally.[50]

People in leadership were required to periodically evaluate the work and attitudes of those who worked under and alongside them. A typical report, labeled "Individual Evaluations," might read: Joan—"Gets involved in too many of the minute details of an operation or area of work. . . . and expects a lot from people and gets disappointed when they don't produce the quantity or quality of work she had expected"; Omar—"just arrived, no concrete basis for evaluation"; Herman—"a very good worker and organizer, although he tends to overload himself at times. . . . sometimes does not listen when others are talking . . . has difficulty accepting criticism"; Audrea—"a very good worker and organizer . . . sometimes acts a trouble shooter" and sometimes "become too involved in the details and miss the overall point"; Big Man—"very good organizer . . . [but] has so many responsibilities in other areas that he often is isolated from daily campaign activities"; Phyllis—"has a lot of personal problems which make it difficult for her to communicate with other Comrades." This criticism and self-criticism served to keep members sharp and learning from their experiences. It also helped the leadership keep tabs on everything and everybody.[51]

During this period, communal living arrangements remained the method by which the rank-and-file were housed. If a person held a part-time job or somehow received outside money, he or she had to report it to the Central Committee. Even if one had college work study money, it had to be reported. For example, Elbert Howard turned in a "Section Financial Report" in December 1972 that indicated that his $240 work study check went toward paying the $210 office lease, copying fees, and cleaning supplies. He had nothing left from this check when all the bills were paid. These conditions might not have endeared some members to the leadership.[52]

Eventually some of the members began to complain of the communal living spaces. They complained about not being able to take jobs of their choosing or of not being allowed to go to college when and where they chose. When they made suggestions they were often rebuffed by the higher-ups. So even though the party started receiving foundation money and donations from reputable businesses and the state of California, the leadership remained out of touch with those who did the actual work. In this atmosphere, one might easily be expelled for complaining too loudly. For example, in July 1973, the Central Committee expelled longtime member Michael Rhymes "for undermining the party's leadership and inner-Party structure." He was also branded with "openly displaying a gross disrespect for and lack of faith in [the Party's] policies and [the] Central Body's ability to formulate those policies." Because Rhymes disagreed with members of the party's upper echelon, the leadership banned him from all party facilities and forbid his communication "in any way with Party members." As time progressed, these expulsions became more and more frequent until eventually they, along with people leaving for all manner of reasons, sealed the party's doom.[53]

There were certainly efforts to salvage what was good in the party as the seventies turned into the eighties. By this time, however, too much ground had already been lost. Cleaver and Hilliard had been expelled; Seale left the party in 1974 under strange circumstances. Newton jumped bail that same year and went to Cuba, where he stayed for three years before returning to face charges of killing Kathleen Smith. A jury later acquitted him, but he was never more than titular head of the party after that. Brown had assumed power and under her, the survival programs were strengthened but internal chaos reigned. Some complained that she ran all the good people away from the party with her strong-arm tactics and her either/or personality.[54] The FBI continued to harass party members, though their murderous escapades ended when the Panthers stopped espousing violence as a tactic. To say the least, it had become nearly impossible to hold things together.

In an attempt to do just that, Jo Nina Abron, on October 1, 1980, drafted a three-page memo to Huey Newton. Noting that the party was turning fourteen years old on the fifteenth of the month, Abron questioned Newton on "the direction the Party is moving." Her memo reminded Newton that "most Party members are between 30 to 40 years old, with one-third of us being over 35." This fact meant that they were concerned about their futures and being overworked because at that point, the party only had twenty-seven members. She went on to say that party morale was low and that something had to be done about it.

Abron made specific suggestions to solve some of the party's problems. Since "very few political groups maintain office hours of 40 hours a week as we do," she suggested that Central Headquarters be closed to save the two thousand dollars it cost to keep it open every month. She recommended getting a post office box instead. That way, party members "could continue to do our political work but not have the tremendous overhead of operating Central." Getting to the real point of her memo, Abron talked about comrades reaching the point where "physically and mentally, they cannot work full-time for the Party and part-time elsewhere." She insinuated that if there came a choice between sustaining themselves and sustaining the party through their own labor, many would choose themselves, since fifteen of the twenty-seven remaining party members already worked at the school, the organization's only viable program at that juncture. So as not to appear overbearing, Abron ended the letter by informing Newton that the party needed "to make a public statement about its direction in the 1980's." They needed to take this step for history's sake since "there has never been an organization like us in the history of this country." More importantly, she concluded, leadership needed to provide "Party members with a sense of where we are headed and a feeling of purpose."[55]

Newton obviously did not live up to this request since the party, by 1980, provided its members with little direction and even less of "a feeling of purpose." This notion can best be represented by Panther Tommye Williams, who had joined the party "nine and a half years" earlier. Williams told Newton in a stinging but heartfelt letter that she was growing tired of the internal inequality and squabbling. Indeed, Williams felt compelled to write Newton because it had become impossible to "remain and silently watch the Party wither away." Nor could the loyal Panther leave "without voicing issues which are taking its toll" on the party. "Inequalities such as the haves and the have nots," tore the party apart, she wrote. "Some comrades have to struggle each month to pay rent, bills, food, and buy necessities for their children and some comrades don't have a source of income at all. Other comrades do not have to worry about their financial necessities. So-called comrades were merely tolerating each other" while bad attitudes abounded. "How can we be loving towards the people and unloving towards each other?" In a foreboding tone, Williams pointed out that the party needed a better system of discipline and that the group's leaders needed to cease playing favorites. The letter made it clear that most of the rank-and-file felt that a solution needed to be imminent. Williams explained that she was at a crossroads and needed some reassurance that the party was still viable. Apparently, Newton could not offer satisfactory answers and Williams left the party.[56]

The file from which this letter came contained nearly one hundred others with similar grievances. While a few hard-core party members continued to have faith and worked hard to achieve party goals, many, especially the older veterans, began to leave California and to return to their former homes. Heavy-handed leaders and goon squads lashed out at those who questioned authority such that some even found themselves having to escape the party literally. Others made a life in the picturesque Bear Flag Republic without the organization. Some gravitated to the Nation of Islam and orthodox Islam in an effort to salvage their broken spirits and dashed hopes. In the end, the party evolved into a community service organization that dwindled in its membership and influence until the last person left. It later crumbled, devastated by Newton's drug use, his mishandling of funds, and the external pressure that had always been there.[57]

This experiment in revolutionary ideology and practice foundered when ill-prepared leaders wielded power in an organization that invited both the ire and the bullets of the establishment. Like many other promising organizations of the time, the party died before it could grow to maturity. In the process, it helped to soothe the souls of black folks who yearned to be free in a land where most white citizens took liberty for granted.

In the final analysis, one can see that the party found not purpose, but dissolution. Since 1966, it had come full circle and wound up in much the same place it started: as a local self-help organization dedicated to gaining political and economic power for blacks. It failed to achieve its goal in either incarnation. It did, however, have something to show for all its troubles. Ending on a high note of grassroots community organizing and serving the people, the party found solace in keeping its eyes on the prize of freedom and justice for all. Moving from its violence-laden revolutionary phase, the Black Panther Party evolved to a point where survival pending revolution was the call of the day. The second, more active phase saw the Panthers gain and wield community electoral power in the fashion that Newton called for in one of the first community patrols witnessed by an audience. Historians would do well to dissect the various elements that made up this chameleon-like organization. In the process, they might find that ordinary people discovered a way out of no way to do some truly extraordinary things. This group's work and legacy should be honored. Its mistakes and other foibles must likewise be understood and remembered so that the next generation of activists will know that power grows not from the barrels of guns, but from service to humanity and a willingness to provide that service despite difficulty and life-threatening obstacles.

CONCLUSION

The role violence played in the making and unmaking of the BPP is significant. The violence of dilapidated housing, long-term unemployment, and inadequate education helped lay the groundwork for the Black Panther Party. Once the extreme violence of police brutality entered into this mix, the stage was set for the BPP's commencement. Panther leaders capitalized on the rampant police brutality of their day to get the attention of millions of youth looking for a way to understand the growing tensions and contradictions in the splintering civil rights movement. This external violence, once it prompted the group's beginning, was then used as a sounding board to draw attention to the party.

Hard to contain, the slippery eel of violence then eased its way into the party's command structure. Harsh discipline in some chapters kept group members aware of their revolutionary development and helped them to see the seriousness of their undertaking. Though unpopular or nonexistent in some chapters, this violence was seen as a kind of glue that held things intact. Having been born in the fires of the mid-sixties' radicalism, the BPP took the great leap forward and for the first time presented the American government with the long-feared threat of a minority uprising. Posing this threat cost it its life.

The violence visited upon the BPP by policemen, federal agents, and *provocateurs* guaranteed its demise. Even though it withstood violent challenges for five years, the BPP was unable to replenish its ranks in time enough for the next onslaught. Bringing to bear the might of the powerful central government, authorities made the Panthers pay for venturing into the killing fields where all's fair. It was this violence that unhinged the party and separated it from its base of support. Once the killing and imprisonment of party members became a nationwide pattern, those who might have joined declined and many already in the group headed for the nearest exit. In essence, the BPP's sixteen-year-run took on a cyclic trajectory where, once violence spawned it, it had to use that violence, physically or rhetorically, to stay alive. This move made it a target and the federal government declared open season on the Panthers. When the season closed and the smoking guns were put away, the violence of the federal government stood supreme and seemed to call for all takers in this war of nerves and steel. Having forced the BPP to retreat to its communities, state-sanctioned violence became the benchmark for how to influence people's decisions with the power that grows from the barrels of guns.

Like most radical groups of the era, the Black Panther Party emerged as a result of heightened expectations created by the mainstream civil rights groups of the late 1950s and early 1960s. Because many black and poor Americans, whether they lived in rural or urban areas, had experienced some form of police brutality, the Panthers rallied around the concept of self-defense. Eventually, however, self-defense included armed attacks and ambushes of policemen known to have harmed or killed blacks or other community members. For some, a defensive posture only achieved so much. Some Panthers therefore came to believe that it was useful to go on the offensive. Despite this risky move, and in some cases because of it, thousands of young blacks rushed to join the group.

The group's early success secured for it an ethnically diverse base of support. For example, groups including the Students for a Democratic Society, the Weathermen, the American Indian Movement, the Puerto Rican Young Lords, the North Vietnamese government, the Chinese government, the Palestinian Authority, and the Algerian government offered the BPP real and symbolic support. It stood alone among Black Power organizations in its willingness to ally with progressive whites on certain issues. Its willingness to join with and fight for a rainbow coalition of other organizations also made it popular with students and different nationalities throughout the Third World.

The BPP's popularity, its rhetoric, and its method of getting things done were widely dispersed by television and other media coverage, making it a prime target for government infiltration and police attack. Almost always portraying the Panthers as mad killers, the media refused to analyze the Panthers' genuine contribution to the African American community. Nor did journalists try to understand the group within the context of American history and its symbiotic relationship to the then-flourishing New Left. As a result, BPP members began to spend a lot of their time deflecting police attacks, avoiding arrest by going "underground," and fighting in the courts.

The numerous Panther trials of the late 1960s and early 1970s exhausted the party's coffers and forced its leaders to take a less violent revolutionary road to freedom. Some thirty years after the party started, former chief of staff David Hilliard noted that "the concept of the Party as a liberation army overthrowing the American government [was] unrealistic." He added that the police were always there to kill them. In somewhat of an overstatement, he wrote that when police attacked them, no one would come to their aid. "Party comrades would jump off the moon," he said, "if Huey tells them to. Our allies won't." Hilliard recognized the apparent futility of the Panther revolutionary mission. The Panthers "waged as stiff a resistance to the police as any American revolutionary group," but, he concluded, they "were hardly very effective as fighters."[1] In most cases, police agencies around the country, with an infusion of millions of federal dollars for SWAT teams and tactical squads, found it easy to outgun the Panthers.

As part of their war against this group, the authorities also sought to destroy the party's programs, while at the same time co-opting and implementing those same programs in communities and schools throughout the country. Panther leaders claimed these community-based programs were the means to an end, a way to prepare and to sensitize ghetto residents to the party's ultimate goal of bringing about revolutionary change. Explaining that the programs were part of the group's original purpose, Hilliard noted that "no one got this point." Many people misunderstood the party's purpose because the local police and federal authorities not only dominated what the Panthers did, they also dictated how the public viewed the group. In other words, the state—FBI, CIA, police—decided the party's fate. The government won the war with the Panthers quite handily. Their victory meant that most of the group's leaders and several of its rank-and-file ended up dead, in jail, in exile, or psychologically damaged.[2]

Perhaps the most successful counterintelligence venture aimed at the Panthers was the one that exacerbated the growing factionalism between the party's national leaders. From the beginning, there had been differences within the leadership over exactly how to bring about revolutionary change. For some time before the FBI stepped in, however, this tension simmered below the surface and many party members knew little or nothing about it. When the FBI sent fabricated letters and prompted its agents inside the organization to sow even more dissension, the party's internal dynamics spiraled out of control. This intra-party strife ended in the deaths of several Panthers. When all the smoke cleared, Newton and Cleaver were not speaking to each other and the BPP's public stance on various political issues affecting the black community differed little from the mainstream civil rights organizations that preceded it in the 1950s and early 1960s. In the process, the *Black Panther* newspaper, the one thing that kept the Panthers in the eyes and minds of people in and outside the United States, suffered a tremendous blow from which it never recovered.

It is, however, erroneous to conclude that the BPP was the FBI's only target during this period. COINTELPRO activities were directed at a number of other groups, including the Revolutionary Action Movement, the Black Liberation Army, the Republic of New Africa, the Black Liberation Front, the Congress of Racial Equality, the Council of Federated Organizations, the American Indian Movement, the National Association for the Advancement of Colored People, the Student Nonviolent Coordinating Committee, the Southern Christian Leadership Conference, Students for a Democratic Society, and the Mississippi Freedom Democratic Party. Aside from the watered down versions of the NAACP and SCLC, none of these organizations survived intact. Thus, this program, coinciding with the wedge politics of Nixon and the domestic political shift to the right, was a resounding success.

In retrospect, federal government agencies largely ignored the demands of Black Power advocates. Unlike the entreaties of earlier nonviolent civil rights groups (such as the NAACP, SCLC, the Student Nonviolent Coordinating Committee, and the Mississippi Freedom Democratic Party), "which were directed at reforming basic institutions," black militants' demands "tended to go beyond social reform." These leaders insisted on black control over the political, social, and economic institutions in their communities, which prompted different responses from business leaders and political officials fearful about the danger these demands posed to national security and the existing economic, political, and social arrangement. Any attempt to accede to Black Power advocates' demands, according to sociologist William J. Wilson, "would have generated severe resistance and hostility from the large white majority." For these reasons, government officials felt compelled to deal with the Panthers and their supporters by using "alternative means" of social control, namely, COINTELPRO. These means were themselves frequently more violent and certainly more effective than what the BPP employed to realize its own ambitions.[3] Nevertheless, the sentiments and actions of federal government agencies showed that official response to the Panthers had to include violence.

While such a response seems to be easily understandable, some whites failed to comprehend why blacks responded violently to begin with. Some continued to be persuaded by prejudiced media representations that characterized blacks as violent criminals waiting for their chance to kill whitey. There was no official national discussion of the obvious problems whites had created for ghetto blacks. Consequently, the nation's leaders made the quest for "law and order" fashionable while the methods of maintaining it became increasingly violent and deadly.

Part of the Panthers' demise, however, must be attributed to the members of the group itself. There is no doubt that Huey Newton abused drugs after his release from prison and this fact cannot be justified. There is no doubt that the Panther leader and his henchmen used violence to extort money from people involved in vice in Oakland. Nor is there is any doubt that Newton mistreated and abused fellow party members after the party decided to concentrate its efforts solely in northern California.

In addition, Newton should have responded positively to the requests from other party members that the Central Committee, its governing body, include members from all regions of the country rather than just a few locales. Its undemocratic structure, in open contradiction to its guiding philosophy of democratic centralism, encouraged fear and intimidation rather than an open exchange of ideas, debate, and discussion. It should have gone back to work in the community years before it did. These flaws arrested the party's development by not allowing its best thinkers to exercise their freedom of expression. In effect, as an organization, the party literally could not think as it was at the mercy of individuals whose leadership skills were overshadowed by their egos.

Eldridge Cleaver might have done better to advocate grassroots organizing rather than immediate revolution. His insistence on aggression put the BPP in a position it could hardly come out of unscathed. The preoccupation with guns and strong-arm tactics left little room for those genuinely interested in fighting for black freedom. Had he used his international contacts to put pressure on the U.S. government rather than to thumb his nose at it, blacks might have been more likely to join or support the party. Cleaver's unwillingness to make amends with Newton at a critical point in party history guaranteed that the organization foundered prematurely.

Panther and former BLA member Sheba Haven remembered "the lack of communication within the party and an unwillingness to share power between the East Coast and the West Coast" as a major problem. She explained that there was "amongst different people, an unwillingness to listen to the concerns [of others] in terms of emphasis on what we taught many people in different parts of the country. That goes back to the cult of the personality" that Newton and Cleaver got lost in "instead of the analysis and following the principles of democratic centralism which was what made people say, 'go ahead, I can be committed to this because I will have a voice.' And then when that voice was taken away, it was a similar thing as with this blind patriotism that we have now." There came a time when Newton and a few others became "the final authority" and they were "not making decisions collectively." Noting that such a setup appealed to some people not operating out of Oakland, she added that "some of us who were local saw it, and saw how it was harming the nucleus; that it was not going forward towards revolution, but that it was becoming a way to generate money for the upper echelon. And even when I left, that's what I was arguing over, donations that I was told that were not there, but people had on all new clothes, you know."[4] Surely the leadership could have stood to be more honest and open with the people responsible for doing the actual work.

Another problem was a lack of media savvy. Though the Panthers sometimes took advantage of their access to the media, this particular shortcoming caused the group always to be on the defensive about its position on violence and how its members felt toward whites. The mainstream media capitalized on the BPP's sometimes varying definitions of itself and successfully painted the group as rabid racists. That the overwhelming majority of its members were nothing of the sort was beside the point since news coverage said otherwise. Again, toning down the violent rhetoric earlier than it did might have forestalled some of the skewed government propaganda. That its members were young and unversed in the art of revolution might have been the cause of some of this, but after the blacker-than-thou attitude became prominent in the party's later years, there were few chances to discuss openly ways in which the rank-and-file could go about addressing this issue.

The group's inability to detect FBI complicity in exacerbating internal and external problems also contributed to its demise. Today, many Panthers lament the fact that the party's counterintelligence capabilities left a lot be desired. Since Panther leaders knew little to nothing of what authorities were doing to it and could do even less to affect the outcome of police actions, the party suffered in myriad ways.

To be sure, the media, FBI, and police were not entirely at fault. The manner in which the group operated virtually guaranteed its violent repression. Talking up the gun and sometimes backing up violent talk did not endear them to police departments and government agencies. While nearly all of the killing of police officers was carried out by members of the BLA, the close ties between the two groups compelled authorities to treat the party in similar ways.

On many occasions, Panther rhetoric forced the media to look to the police and local politicians for its information about the group. Haven noted that the Panthers' inflammatory speeches were great propaganda but they had their downside as well:

> I think the rhetoric was a good thing because it attracted people's attention, it kept them focused, and it made them think a new thought. Do you see anybody walking around with their head down, not making eye contact [with white people]? Black people, and actually all people of color and women as well, have more confidence in themselves now. I mean that's the two-edge sword. You know the old African proverb, if you speak with a sword in your mouth you cut your own mouth.[5]

Though they helped inspire a generation, the Panthers lacerated themselves on numerous occasions.

The party lost community support when opposing factions murdered key members of the group. As a result, the organization's infrastructure crumbled. This turn of events forced many members "underground" while others tried unsuccessfully to bring about a peaceful and "bloodless" revolution. In the end, the group reverted to a local phenomenon in Oakland where, over a decade beginning in 1972, it slowly faded from public view. By 1980, few people knew of the group's attempts to reform American politics and values. Even fewer were cognizant of the many sacrifices party members made to ensure that blacks had a decent future.

Upon reflection, Haven remembered that "we didn't have any distinction between the political and the military. That was our problem. One of the things that we criticized ourselves for, is having the political and the military wings identify together. The same people that were serving breakfast were saying 'off the pig.' The same sister that was giving your child a measles vaccine had a shotgun and a .357 Magnum" beside her.[6]

One of the more serious mistakes the party made was its reliance on a justifiably disgruntled but grossly unprepared segment of the black community to bring about significant social change. The "lumpen proletariat," the underclass, made up a significant part of the group's rank-and-file. Though there were students, laborers, and even some middle-class people in the party, it primarily drew members from the very bottom of society—those they insisted had nothing to lose but their chains. BPP leadership believed this group served as the vanguard of a world revolution. The problem with their assumption lay in the fact that this class has rarely played a primary role in any revolution. BPP leadership demonstrated its naiveté concerning the revolutionary process by expecting this group of men and women to understand the complexities and influence of the capitalist system well enough to organize and execute a successful revolution.

Of course, discipline was also a major problem, as party rules were flaunted whenever it was convenient. Bitter Dog, the drink consisting of port wine and lemon juice made famous by the Panthers, was utilized liberally, whether an individual was off-duty or on. In some cases, "Brother Roogie," a euphemism some Panthers used for marijuana because they knew their phones and offices were bugged, often showed up before the work day ended. This is not to say that the "lumpen proletariat" is the only class of people who use these things. Drugs and alcohol would not be multibillion dollar businesses if that were so. It does, however, make it difficult for a leader to prevent such violations if that leader is clearly guilty of the same. In any case, a cursory glance at world history reveals that even the most brilliant Marxists and Communists have failed to dismantle capitalism, so the grand task should not have been left to this group alone.

This is especially true because a minority within this group had a propensity for violence and hot-headedness. Allowing those members easy access to the organization meant the BPP essentially condemned itself to failure. Logic tells us that the easiest people to turn into infiltrators are the poor and those already inclined to criminal activities. Living on the edge and by their wits, as many in this stratum do, makes it a lot easier to become a self-centered opportunist. Author Henry Winston noted that "it is their declassed parasitical status and outlook that sharply distinguish them from the great mass of the unemployed, who are searching for and demanding jobs" while for the lumpen, "a job is unthinkable."[7] The "lumpen," therefore, need strict discipline and education to stay on task. Many of them simply could not keep up with the demands of revolution. Indeed, some of them even tossed their Red Books to the side for lack of understanding.

This does not mean that hundreds of party members from this group were not transformed by their experiences. Indeed, they reaped and continue to reap the benefits as lawyers, counselors, social workers, writers, teachers, mechanics, artists, labor organizers, doctors, business owners, and the like. The party gave them something for which to live and in the process changed their lives. A significant number succeeded in becoming the new men and the new women that sixties activists so often spoke about. Still, the majority failed to make the great ideological and philosophical leaps required for growth and success. It was these, along with the leaders, who ensured the party's demise.

The Panthers' chauvinism and sexism deprived the party of much-needed energy, personnel, and resources. Women came to play crucial roles in sustaining the party—presenting its goals and political perspectives to the public, acting as "front-line soldiers," formulating and implementing party policy, and administering the group's myriad community service programs. Their contribution was clearly equal to or greater than that of the men. Poor treatment diminished this base of support and opened avenues for outsiders to exploit this weakness. When women, who were often the most capable party members, left the organization, a critical link was broken and the group could no longer hold itself together.

Despite the many mistakes the Panthers made, it is inaccurate to dismiss them as a group of violent racists simply out to "off the pig." The

BPP's contributions to African Americans and other poor Americans are numerous. Many of their programs, such as free breakfasts and lunches, free medical clinics, and legal services have become staples in American social and welfare policy. Although it did not originate these concepts, the BPP played a significant role in calling attention to the paucity of these services in poor communities. Today, for example, it is difficult for most people to imagine a poor child going to school and not having free meals or being assured free medical attention if the need arose. The organization's contribution to sickle-cell anemia testing in the United States is immeasurable, since so many lives have been saved because of research and improved treatments. The fact that this disease is not ravaging the black community today can be attributed to the research and screening that the BPP made possible at a time when few in the medical profession and political arena even acknowledged that the disease existed.

Black students and aspiring activists across the country use the BPP as an example of how to struggle by building coalitions. They see the Panther insistence on self-defense as the only sensible way to go about making change. The emphasis the party placed on the learning of black history has inspired uncounted numbers of youth to try to learn from their past. The thousands of black organizations across the country that celebrate African and African American history even when it is not February are testament to the fact that the Panthers' legacy continues to influence today's youth. In places like San Francisco and Oakland, New York City and Washington, D.C., youthful black activists look to surviving Panthers not only for guidance and advice, but for friendship as well. This linkage of young and old can only serve as a catalyst for future sustained action without the many mistakes mentioned above. Not only do some Panthers continue to organize and serve their communities in the guise of social workers, counselors, and mentors, but other black groups and individuals work alongside them to lay a solid foundation for what they hope is the coming revolution. Because the number of people involved is much lower than in the sixties and seventies and even small victories are rare, networking and recruiting have become even more important to these twenty-first-century visionaries.[8]

Few Americans are aware of the political influence the Panthers wielded during most of their existence as a national organization. According to Emory Douglas, the Panthers were partially responsible for the increased hiring and appointment of black and other minority judges and police officers in the Oakland/San Francisco Bay Area. Douglas claimed that during the 1970s, Bay Area politicians and police chiefs often sought the Panthers' approval of certain individuals before they became judges or policemen. Even after the party's demise as a strident voice in the Black Power movement, the group continued to influence local politics in those communities where it still functioned.

For example, the San Francisco *Examiner* credited the Panthers with facilitating the 1977 victories of Lionel Wilson, Oakland's first black mayor, and John George, the first black Alameda County supervisor. Elaine Brown worked on Wilson's transition team and on George's executive committee as head of the Oakland Council for Economic Development. The Panthers' push for restructured "inclusive" high school and college curricula also fit perfectly into the larger development of Black Studies and Ethnic Studies programs throughout the United States. BPP forays into the fields of health and medicine brought party members love and protection in some black communities.[9] As in all attempted revolutions involving guerrilla tactics, this relationship proved necessary.

Another BPP contribution is the legacy of struggle it left behind. In terms of its place among young, black urban dwellers, the BPP easily ranks as one of the most popular organizations in the twentieth century. Its displays of bravado and boldness in confronting established authority in unconventional ways are not only sources of pride, but they continue to reflect an attitude and behavior that many blacks find difficult, if not dangerous, to display openly themselves. In a world where blackness continues to be looked down upon, the Panther legacy continues to provide a confidence and a sense of purpose for those lucky enough to have learned about the group.

Nowhere is the spirit of the BPP more loved and revered than in today's young black activist community. Black Panther politics, symbols, language, and songs have somehow survived and remain part of contemporary urban culture. This phenomenon can be clearly seen in the multibillion dollar black urban music industry, popularly called rap or hip-hop.

Included among these artists are California rappers O'Shea Jackson (Ice Cube), Paris, the "Black Panther of Rap," whose logo is a black panther, and Tupac Shakur, whose mother, Afeni Shakur, was an outspoken member of the BPP chapter in New York City and one of the New York Twenty-one defendants. Tupac's songs often quoted verbatim from the BPP's Ten Point Program. Though he was murdered in a senseless shooting in Las Vegas in 1998, Shakur's music continues to influence younger artists with its politically laced lyrics that demand that blacks become self-sufficient in all areas of public life. While space prohibits a thorough exposition of Shakur's music and that of the other musicians who write and sing about the legacy of the Panthers, it is accurate to say that many ghetto youths are thoroughly cognizant of Panther history and the legacy of struggle from which it sprang. They advocate a similar struggle that seeks to empower blacks to take control of their own destinies. The Fugitives, a group of rap artists who have taken California, especially the Bay Area, by storm, is made up of children of former party members. Their lyrics too are laced with the party's history and accomplishments, furthering the attempt to disseminate knowledge about the group by any means necessary.

Like the Panthers, these young adults also advocate the building and strengthening of black institutions like schools, hospitals, and the like. All these individuals, who grew up in areas of Panther strongholds, are selling millions of records to ghetto youth who strongly identify with the philosophy of self-defense. They have also begun to articulate and understand the internal-colony discourse espoused by the Panthers and other nationalists of the period. This characterization of the black experience served to link African Americans to their Third World counterparts, also struggling against colonial domination and oppression. In *Racial Oppression in America,* Robert Blauner argued that "the experience of people of color in this country does include a number of circumstances that are universal to the colonial situation." He wrote that blacks had been subjugated to the point where their labor did not bring them social and political advancement. Cultural policies inside the U.S. destroyed blacks' original value system and ensured that their way of life followed that of their oppressors.[10] This colonial situation in black America informed Newton's and Seale's analysis of the black dilemma and served as a springboard from which the group launched its philosophy of the usefulness of armed self-defense. Like Malcolm X before them, the Panthers sincerely believed that they lived in an era of revolution and that their fight against oppression represented a significant part of the global resistance against white domination and colonization.

That they lost this fight is not proof that their efforts were in vain. That they displayed the courage and audacity to fight and teach themselves the rudiments of self-reliance inside a nation they knew could brutally crush their movement at the first sign of success is a testament not just to the Panthers, but to the seminal idea of freedom by any means necessary. In reality, their goal was not to overthrow the government, but to infect the masses with the revolutionary zeal to do it themselves, since it was this group that suffered the most from racism, the most damaging by-product of capitalism. Many of the Panthers were bright, articulate young people with unlimited potential. Instead of concentrating on school or their jobs, they gave their time, indeed their lives, to their people.

It is clear that the Panthers took on the mantle of the martyred Malcolm X. The group co-opted his philosophy of freedom "by any means necessary" and used it to justify black self-defense and violent confrontation with the police, who could often be found oppressing black people. Moreover, their use of Malcolm's words served as an emotional rallying point to recruit frustrated and angry ghetto residents disillusioned by the inability of the civil rights movement to address their economic needs and to empower their communities. Providing fresh thought, as well as new recruits, this emphasis on the memory of Malcolm X created a space for thousands of blacks nationwide to participate in a movement that they once considered "below" them and too passive. Once a critical mass, or something akin to it, had been achieved, these Black Power advocates, according to Timothy Tyson, succeeded in making "a lasting and significant cultural and psychological impact in the lives of African Americans."[11]

Certainly members of the Black Panther Party sought positive social change. They were not the angels their ardent supporters, in an attempt to rewrite history and to excise the seamy side of things, insist they were. Neither were they the demons their detractors portrayed them as, or the gun-toting thugs they are popularly shown as in mainstream history texts, when they show up at all. We must find the middle ground and look to all the available sources to reconstruct this most popular of all Black Power organizations. This study is written in the spirit of assisting in that goal, not as a definitive conclusion to it. As with all histories, we must seek to discover how the participants saw themselves. Sheba Haven, speaking for many of her most dedicated comrades, explained that contrary to popular lore, the "community [police] patrols and the breakfast programs came out of a motivation" to help people, not to hurt others. She concluded that "if this would have been a fair and just country. . . . and if the country had been what it said it was, most Panthers would have been in the military or the police [department]" because serving the people "was [their] motivation."[12]

ACKNOWLEDGEMENTS

Thanks to the Creator for giving us all a place in which to live, work, play, read, and write. I am grateful to a number of wonderful people who in no small way helped bring this project to fruition. Dr. Robert L. Jenkins, my dissertation advisor turned good friend has nurtured and guided me through the brier patch of writing a history of the living. His patience and realistic worldview have helped me to see the light of day on many a dark night. I will always be grateful for his having shown me around Los Angeles and for introducing me to Uncle Leo, Aunt Thel, Flo, and Dimitrea. Drs. Charles Lowery, John Marszalek, and Lorenzo Crowell are also owed a debt of gratitude, not only for their incisive questions about the work, but for the financial, moral, and academic support that was more than enough during my stay at Mississippi State University. Thanks to Dr. Neil R. McMillen, now a retired professor from the History Department at the University of Southern Mississippi, and his wife Beverly, for believing in me and steering me in the right direction. I never understood the real usefulness of history until I met these two.

Thanks to the myriad archivists, librarians, and research assistants across the country who helped make this work a reality. These include the Columbia University Archives and Department of Oral History, New York University Library, University of California at Berkeley Bancroft Library and Special Collections, the Department of Special Collections at UCLA, the Schomburg Center for Research in Black Culture, the Southern California Research Center in Los Angeles, the Department of Special Collections at Stanford University, the Alden Kimbrough Collection, the Roz Payne Archives, and the Cook Memorial Library at the University of Southern Mississippi. Many others, who are not and cannot be traditionally viewed as archives or libraries, but who nevertheless have amassed and provided a mountain of materials and advice include Yasmeen Sutton, John Bowman, Harold Taylor, Frankie Adams, Hank Jones, David Johnson, Shujaah Graham, Billy "X" Jennings, Gail Shaw, Sheba Haven, Yuri Kochiyama, Thomas McCreary, Margaret Block, Hollis Watkins, Bob Moses, Monzel Stowers, Harriet Tanzman, Jan Hillegas,

Owen Brooks, Malik Rahim, Althea Francois, Robert "King" Wilkerson, Marion Brown, Bullwhip, Emory Douglas, Elbert "Big Man" Howard, Cleo Silvers, and a host of other movement activists who not only shared their stories, but who taught me what it really means to be committed to justice and liberation. Charles Jones offered invaluable advice on how to write about and research the BPP.

Department chairs have come and gone, but the three that stand out are Dr. Charles Bolton, currently chair of history at UNC Greensboro. Dr. Richard Crepeau, former chair of history at the University of Central Florida, and Dr. Phyllis Jestice, current chair of history at the University of Southern Mississippi. Thanks, Chuck, for being a good friend, a great listener, and an even better basketball player; your encouragement and work ethic have taught me the value of staying the course and enjoying the ride. Thanks, Dick, for plugging your ears whenever I made excuses for not being finished and showing me the lighter, more human side of practically everything, and for introducing me to your wonderful wife Pat, who can only be described as a breath of fresh air. Thanks, Phyllis, for the confidence you instilled in me to finish and for making it easy for me to get around the country without breaking the bank. Your editorial skills are also very much appreciated and have made this work something that people can read and actually understand. Other colleagues also provided valuable insight in the guise of editing suggestions and nice long conversations. Bradley Bond, Brian O'Neil, Greg O'Brien, Andy Wiest, Tom Ward, Amy Young, Amy Miller, and Shana Walton all helped me learn how to look at an issue from more than one vantage point. Kari Frederickson offered a litany of editorial suggestions that have made the book less confusing and more cohesive than it otherwise might have been. Donna Murch, Kevin Meehan, Lynn and Tino Paz, Ed Kallina, and Adenike Davidson are some of the best teachers living today; they all made valuable suggestions at the times when they were needed most.

Karolyn Thompson, director of Inter-Library Loan at the University of Southern Mississippi, is by far the best and most capable finder of books, newspapers, and other published materials the world will ever know. Her assistance and advice have helped to sustain and keep me sane over the years. Shelia Smith, the department of history's consummate office manager, did so many favors and solved so many problems that I can hardly name them all. Suffice it say that her knack for problem-solving and getting things done quickly and accurately allowed me to pursue the work at hand and kept my mind centered on the truly important aspect of writing. Carol Gonzalez at the University of Central Florida was no less helpful in her position as history department office manager.

A bevy of friends and former students helped to edit, organize files, and verify information during the writing of the book. Huge thanks go to Jacqueline Olive, Rachel Clay, Anna Warren, Marie O'Connell, and Natalie McClellan for all the late nights spent doing this type of mundane, but extremely important, work. Nisha Richmond's critical eye and organizing skills helped keep thousands of disparate sheets of paper together, but more importantly, she kept the fires of perseverance alive as I dealt with so many other pressing issues. Without her invaluable service, this book could not have been written.

Friends and colleagues in the USM Center for Oral History and Cultural Heritage provided me with strong encouragement at every turn. My co-director, Dr. Stephen Sloan, allowed me to miss work without a single complaint. Jeremy Carroll, Stephanie Millet, Linda Van Zandt, Marie O'Connell, and Carol Short stayed in my corner and provided me with the much-needed assurance that this project was worth the time spent and the days laboring outside of the office.

My main man and roadie Xavier Thornton read and reread the manuscript and offered analyses and comments, which all made their way into the final product. His wife Lawanda and their children (and my Godchildren) Joy and John Xavier provided a welcome respite to the long nights spent putting the project together. Khalid and April Shabazz opened their East Bay California home, provided transportation, meals, and a place to sleep, shared their newborns, and, through countless conversations, helped to make sense of the mass of material I collected on my many trips out west. Their love and hospitality made the rough places smooth during this journey and effectively ensured that the project saw the light of day. No truer friends could a person ever want or need. Other California friends that gave of their time, affection, patience, and love include Earl, BIG Game James, Milwaukee Mike, Aaron and Daren, Jeff, Justice, and Pete. Indeed, the "bruhs" in general have supported me over the years and throughout countless cities. Reginald Harris, Robert "Doc" Taylor, Trent Walker, Zenith Dukes, Daryl "Black" Coffee, Hornbuckle,

Alex Raimey, Big Kenny, R. E., C.R., Bennie Foster, Andrew Collins, Andre Burns, Thomas Figures, Sterling Steward Jr., Jason, Jerry, Horry, Dr. Thunder, Buddy Cook, Jeryl Shaw, Ray Buckner, and literally hundreds of others offered up advice, rides, beds, beer, chicken, and camaraderie to make sure that I saw the project through.

My humble thanks and apologies go out to those whose names I have failed to mention but who helped me in ways large and small. You know who you are and the contribution you made; please charge the forgetfulness to my head and not to my heart.

My immediate family, in addition to providing the prayers and confidence-building conversations that have kept me grounded over the years, also watched patiently and approvingly as I disappeared for months at a time to go on yet another research trip. My mother Alice Austin, my aunt Dorothy Rush, my sister Shirley, my cousin Sonja Mallery, her twin sister Tonja Williams, their brother Johnny, and my brothers Tyrone, Charles, Michael, and Patrick all believed in me when I found it difficult to do so. I will always be grateful for their trust and boldness of spirit that buoyed me through graduate school, the research, and the writing phases of this project. I owe a special debt to my daughter Averi, who sat patiently as her daddy went gallivanting around the country in search of yet another interview, document, or archive. Her love and selflessness has been my sustenance through the years. While nothing can replace the time we lost, my love and respect for her has only strengthened during my absence and I have learned that regardless of what is going on, I must always be by her side. It is a valuable lesson and for this reason, this book and anything positive that comes of it is for her. Of course, any mistakes or shortcomings must all be attributed to me and I accept full responsibility for whatever those may be.

Curtis J. Austin
Hattiesburg, MS
June 2006

APPENDIX A

Ten Point Program: What We Want, What We Believe*

1. We want freedom. We want the power to determine the destiny of our black community. We believe that black people will not be free until we are able to determine our own destiny.

2. We want full employment for our people. We believe that the federal government is responsible and obligated to give every man employment or a guaranteed income. We believe that if the white American businessman will not give full employment, then the means of production should be taken from the businessmen and placed in the community so that the people of the community can organize and employ all of its people and give a high standard of living.

3. We want an end to the robbery by the capitalists of our black community. We believe that this racist government has robbed us and now we are demanding the overdue debt of forty acres and two mules. Forty acres and two mules were promised 100 years ago as restitution for slave labor and mass murder of black people. We will accept the payment in currency which will be distributed to our many communities. The Germans are now aiding the Jews in Israel for the genocide of the Jewish people. The Germans murdered six million Jews. The American racist has taken part in the slaughter of over 50 million black people; therefore, we feel that this is a modest demand that we make.

4. We want decent housing, fit for shelter for human beings. We believe that if the white landlords will not give decent housing to our black community, then the housing and the land should be made into cooperatives so that our community, with government aid, can build and make decent housing for its people.

---

*"The Black Panther Party Ten Point Platform and Program, October, 1966, What We Want, What We Believe," http://www.itsabouttimebpp.com/home/bpp_program_platform.html (accessed May 20, 2006).

---

5. We want education for our people that exposes the true nature of this decadent American society. We want education that teaches us our true history and our role in the present-day society. We believe in an educational system that will give to our people knowledge of self. If a man does not have knowledge of himself and his position in society and in the world, then he has little chance to relate to anything else.

6. We want all black men to be exempt from military service. We believe that black people should not be forced to fight in the military service to defend a racist government that does not protect us. We will not fight and kill other people of color in the world who, like black people, are being victimized by the white racist government of America. We will protect ourselves from the force and violence of the racist police and the racist military, by whatever means necessary.

7. We want an immediate end to POLICE BRUTALITY and MURDER of black people. We believe we can end police brutality in our black community by organizing black self-defense groups that are dedicated to defending our black community from racist police oppression and brutality. The Second Amendment to the Constitution of the United States gives a right to bear arms. We therefore believe that all black people should arm themselves for self-defense.

8. We want freedom for all black men held in federal, state, county and city prisons and jails. We believe that all black people should be released from the many jails and prisons because they have not received a fair and impartial trial.

9. We want all black people when brought to trial to be tried in a court by a jury of their peer group or people from their black communities, as defined by the Constitution of the United States. We believe that the courts should follow the United States Constitution so that black people will receive fair trials. The Fourteenth Amendment of the U.S. Constitution gives a man the right to be tried by his peer group. A peer is a person from a similar economic, social, religious, geographical, environmental, historical and racial background. To do this the court will be forced to select a jury from the black community from which the black defendant came. We have been, and are being, tried by all-white juries that have no understanding of the "average reasoning man" of the black community.

10. We want land, bread, housing, education, clothing, justice, and peace. And as our major political objective, a United Nations-supervised plebiscite to be held throughout the black colony in which only black colonial subjects will be allowed to participate, for the purpose of determining the will of black people as to their national destiny.

When, in the course of human events, it becomes necessary for one people to dissolve the political bands which have connected them with another, and to assume, among the powers of the earth, the separate and equal station to which the laws of nature and nature's God entitle them, a decent respect of the opinions of mankind requires that they should declare the causes which impel them to the separation.

We hold these truths to be self-evident, that all men are created equal; that they are endowed by their Creator with certain unalienable rights; that among these are life, liberty, and the pursuit of happiness. That to secure these rights, governments are instituted among men, deriving their just powers from the consent of the governed; that, whenever any form of government becomes destructive of these ends, it is the right of the people to alter or to abolish it, and to institute a new government, laying its foundation on such principles, and organizing its powers in such form, as to them shall seem most likely to effect their safety and happiness. Prudence, indeed, will dictate that governments long established shall not be changed for light and transient causes; and accordingly, all experience hath shown that mankind are more disposed to suffer, while evils are sufferable, than to right themselves by abolishing the forms to which they are accustomed. But, when a long train of abuses and usurpations, pursuing invariably the same object, evinces a design to reduce them under absolute despotism, it is their right, it is their duty, to throw off such a government, and to provide new guards for their future security.

APPENDIX B

Rules Of The Black Panther Party

Central Headquarters
Oakland, California
Originally printed in the *Black Panther*, January 4, 1969

Every member of the **BLACK PANTHER PARTY** throughout this country of racist America must abide by these rules as functional members of this party. **CENTRAL COMMITTEE** members, **CENTRAL STAFFS**, and **LOCAL STAFFS**, including all captains subordinated to either national, state, and local leadership of the **BLACK PANTHER PARTY** will enforce these rules. Length of suspension or other disciplinary action necessary for violation of these rules will depend on national decisions by national, state, or state area, and local committees and staffs where said rule or rules of the **BLACK PANTHER PARTY WERE VIOLATED.**

Every member of the party must know these verbatim and by heart. And apply them daily. Each member must report any violation of these rules to their leadership or they are counter-revolutionary and are also subjected to suspension by the **BLACK PANTHER PARTY.**

THE RULES ARE:

1. No party member can have narcotics or weed in his possession while doing party work.
2. Any party member found shooting narcotics will be expelled from this party.
3. No party member can be **drunk** while doing daily party work.
4. No party member will violate rules relating to office work, general meetings of the **BLACK PANTHER PARTY**, and meetings of the **BLACK PANTHER PARTY ANYWHERE.**
5. No party member will **USE, POINT, OR FIRE** a weapon of any kind unnecessarily or accidentally at anyone.

6. No party member can join any other army force other than the **BLACK LIBERATION ARMY**.

7. No party member can have a weapon in his possession while **DRUNK** or loaded off narcotics or weed.

8. No party member will commit any crimes against other party members or **BLACK** people at all, and cannot steal or take from the people, not even a needle or a piece of thread.

9. When arrested, **BLACK PANTHER MEMBERS** will give only name, address, and will sign nothing. Legal first aid must be understood by all Party members.

10. The Ten Point Program and platform of the **BLACK PANTHER PARTY** must be known and understood by each Party member.

11. Party Communications must be National and Local.

12. The 10–10–10 program should be known by all members and also understood by all members.

13. All Finance officers will operate under the jurisdiction of the Ministry of Finance.

14. Each person will submit a report of daily work.

15. Each Sub-Section Leaders, Section Leaders, and Lieutenants, Captains, must submit Daily reports of work.

16. All Panthers must learn to operate and service weapons correctly.

17. All Leadership personnel who expel a member must submit this information to the Editor of the Newspaper, so that it will be published in the paper and will be known by all chapters and branches.

18. Political Education Classes are mandatory for general membership.

19. Only office personnel assigned to respective offices each day should be there. All others are to sell papers and do Political work out in the community, including Captains, Section Leaders, etc.

20. **COMMUNICATIONS**—all chapters must submit weekly reports in writing to the National Headquarters.

21. All Branches must implement First Aid and/or Medical Cadres.

22. All Chapters, Branches, and components of the **BLACK PANTHER PARTY** must submit a monthly Financial Report to the Ministry of Finance, and also to the Central Committee.

23. Everyone in a leadership position must read no less than two hours per day to keep abreast of the changing political situation.

24. No chapter or branch shall accept grants, poverty funds, money or

any other aid from any government agency without contacting the National Headquarters.

25. All chapters must adhere to the policy and the ideology laid down by the **CENTRAL COMMITTEE of the BLACK PANTHER PARTY**.

26. All Branches must submit weekly reports in writing to their respective chapters.

APPENDIX C

Partial Listing of BPP Chapters and Affiliates*

CALIFORNIA
Bakersfield
Berkeley
Compton
Fresno
Los Angeles
    Watts
Oakland
Richmond
Riverside
Sacramento
San Diego
San Francisco
San Quentin
Santa Ana
Vallejo

COLORADO
Denver

CONNECTICUT
Bridgeport
Hartford
New Haven

DELAWARE
Dover

DISTRICT OF
COLUMBIA

ILLINOIS
Chicago
Peoria
Rockford

INDIANA
Indianapolis

IOWA
Des Moines

LOUISIANA
New Orleans

MARYLAND
Baltimore

MASSACHUSETTS
Boston
Cambridge
New Bedford

MICHIGAN
Detroit
Flint

MINNESOTA
Minneapolis

MISSISSIPPI
Cleveland

MISSOURI
Kansas City

NEBRASKA
Omaha

NEW JERSEY
Atlantic City
Jersey City
New Brunswick
Newark

NEW YORK
Albany
Buffalo
Mount Vernon

*List derived from United States Congress, House Committee on Internal Security, Hearings on the Black Panther Party, *Gun-Barrel Politics: The Black Panther Party, 1966-1971*, 92nd Cong., 1st sess. (Washington, D.C.: United States Government Printing Office, 1971).

New York City
  Bronx
  Brooklyn
  Corona
  Harlem
  Jamaica
  Washington
    Heights
  Peekskill

NORTH
CAROLINA
Winston-Salem

OHIO
Cincinnati
Cleveland

Columbus
Dayton
Toledo

OKLAHOMA
Tulsa

OREGON
Portland

PENNSYLVANIA
Harrisburg
Philadelphia
Pittsburgh

TENNESSEE
Memphis

TEXAS
Dallas
Houston

WASHINGTON
Seattle

WISCONSIN
Milwaukee

NOTES

Introduction

1. Bobby Seale, *Seize the Time: The Story of the Black Panther Party and Huey P. Newton* (Baltimore: Black Classic Press, 1991), 157. This book was first published by Random House in 1970.

2. Philip Foner, ed., *The Black Panthers Speak* (Cambridge: Da Capo Press, 2002), xxxi.

3. Foner, *Panthers Speak*, xxi.

4. David Hilliard and Donald Wiese, eds., *The Huey P. Newton Reader* (New York: Seven Stories Press, 2002), 68–69.

5. Hilliard and Wiese, *Newton Reader*, 70–71.

6. Hilliard and Wiese, *Newton Reader*, 69; Seale, *Seize the Time*, 153. Four years earlier Newton had tried to avoid a fight, but Lee charged him with a steak knife at a party. Newton insisted that he took the knife and stabbed Lee in self-defense. His story convinced the jury, because they let him off with probation only.

7. Seale, *Seize the Time*, 153.

8. Seale, *Seize the Time*, 154; Bill "Billy X" Jennings, interview with the author, cassette recording, January 1, 2002, Sacramento, California. Tape in possession of author; Bobby Seale, interview in Lee Lew Lee *All Power to the People: The Black Panther Party and Beyond*, VHS. Produced and directed by Lee Lew Lee (New York: Electronic News Group, 1996).

9. Seale, *Seize the Time*, 156.

10. Seale, *Seize the Time*, 156.

11. Seale, *Seize the Time*, 157.

12. Seale, *Seize the Time*, 158. Thirty years later when Mario Van Peebles made the movie *Panther*, the doorkeeper's son played this gentleman's role and did things exactly as his father had when the real Panthers arrived.

13. Seale, *Seize the Time*, 159–60.

14. Seale, *Seize the Time*, 161–62.

15. Seale, *Seize the Time*, 161–62.

16. See Appendix A for Ten Point Platform and Program.

Chapter One: Civil Wrongs and the Rise of Black Power

1. Richard Dalfiume, "The 'Forgotten Years' of the Negro Revolution" *Journal of American History* 55 (June 1968): 90–106; Neil R. McMillen, *Remaking Dixie: The Impact of World War II on the American South* (Jackson: University Press of Mississippi, 1997); Herbert Hill and James Jones, Jr., eds., *Race in America: The Struggle For Equality* (Madison: University of Wisconsin Press, 1993); John Hope Franklin and Alfred A. Moss, Jr., *From Slavery to Freedom: A History of Negro Americans, 6th ed.* (New York: Alfred A. Knopf, 1988); Steven F. Lawson, *Running for Freedom: Civil Rights and Black Politics in America since 1941, 2nd ed.* (New York: McGraw-Hill, 1991).

2. Timothy B. Tyson, *Radio Free Dixie: Robert F. Williams and the Roots of Black Power* (Chapel Hill: University of North Carolina Press, 1999), 3.

3. Tyson, *Radio Free Dixie*, 2.

4. *The Untold Story of the Murder of Emmett Till,* DVD. Directed by Keith Beauchamp (New York: Till Freedom Come Productions, 2004); Curtis Austin, *Ordinary People Living Extraordinary Lives: The Civil Rights Movement in Mississippi,* CD-ROM. (Hattiesburg: University of Southern Mississippi, 2001).

5. See Robin Kelley, "'Roaring from the East': Third World Dreaming" in *Freedom Dreams: The Black Radical Imagination* (Boston: Beacon Press, 2002), 60-109.

6. Jacob Drachler, ed., *Black Homeland Black Diaspora* (Port Washington, New York: Kennikat Press, 1975), 134–42.

7. Harold Cruse quoted in Kelley, *Freedom Dreams*, 64.

8. David Farber, *The Age of Great Dreams: America in the 1960s* (New York: Hill and Wang, 1994), 202; Henry Winston, *Strategy for a Black Agenda* (New York: International Publishers, 1973), 214–15.

9. Thomas McCreary, interview with the author, cassette recording, January 2, 2003, Atlanta, Georgia. Tape in possession of author.

10. Griffin McLaurin quoted in Austin, *Ordinary People.*

11. William Van DeBurg, *New Day in Babylon: The Black Power Movement and American Culture, 1965–1975* (Chicago: University of Chicago Press, 1992), 37. For a comprehensive portrayal of the Deacons for Defense, see Lance Hill, *The Deacons for Defense: Armed Resistance and the Civil Rights Movement* (Chapel Hill: University of North Carolina Press, 2004).

12. See John Dittmer, *Local People: The Struggle for Civil Rights in Mississippi* (Urbana: University of Illinois Press, 1994) and Seth Cagin and Philip Dray, *We Are Not Afraid: The Story of Goodman, Schwerner, Cheney and the Civil Rights Campaign for Mississippi* (New York: MacMillan, 1988). At least eight other bodies were found during the search for the three civil rights workers.

13. Tyson, *Radio Free Dixie*, 297; Dittmer, *Local People,* 180–90.

14. Stokely Carmichael with Ekwueme Michael Thelwell, *Ready for Revolution: The Life and Struggles of Stokely Carmichael [Kwame Ture]* (New York: Scribner, 2003), 460–63. The name Carmichael is used throughout the book to refer to Kwame Ture, who changed his name after these events took place.

15. Clayborne Carson, *In Struggle: SNCC and the Black Awakening of the 1960s* (Cambridge: Harvard University Press, 1981), 278; John Hulette in pamphlet titled *Lowndes County Freedom Organization,* 25.

16. Carmichael and Thelwell, *Ready for Revolution,* 464.

17 Hulette, *Lowndes County Freedom Organization* pamphlet, 27.

18. Clayborne Carson et. al., *Eyes on the Prize Civil Rights Reader: Documents, Speeches, and Firsthand Accounts from the Black Freedom Struggle* (New York: Penguin Books, 1991), 275–76.

19. Carson et al., *Eyes on the Prize,* 275.

20. Carmichael and Thelwell, *Ready for Revolution,* 475.

21. Open letter from George Miller to Harlem Community, August 20, 1966, in Huey P. Newton Foundation Records, Special Collections, Green Library, Stanford University, Palo Alto, California (hereafter cited as HPN Foundation Records).

22. Miller, open letter.

23. Tyson, *Radio Free Dixie,* 215.

24. Tyson, *Radio Free Dixie,* 308.

25. Carmichael and Thelwell, *Ready for Revolution,* 488. The gunman used buckshot, so he likely intended to scare Meredith and not to kill him.

26. Terry Anderson, *The Sixties* (New York: Pearson Longman, 2004), 83; Carmichael, *Ready,* 492–500.

27. Carmichael and Thelwell, *Ready for Revolution,* 502–6, 513.

28. Carmichael and Thelwell, *Ready for Revolution,* 506–7.

29. Carmichael and Thelwell, *Ready for Revolution,* 507; Carson, *Eyes on the Prize,* 208–9.

30. Carmichael and Thelwell, *Ready for Revolution,* 507.

31. Matthew 19:26, Philippians 4:13 *The King James Study Bible* (Nashville: Thomas Nelson Publishers, 1975).

32. Carmichael and Thelwell, *Ready for Revolution,* 506–7; Carson, *Eyes on the Prizw,* 208–10.

33. William Chafe, *Civilities and Civil Rights: Greensboro, North Carolina and the Black Struggle for Freedom* (New York: Oxford University Press, 1980), 197.

34. Carmichael and Thelwell, *Ready for Revolution,* 527.

35. Carmichael and Thelwell, *Ready for Revolution,* 523–4.

36. Carmichael and Thelwell, *Ready for Revolution,* 527.

37. Huey Newton, *Revolutionary Suicide* (New York: Harcourt, Brace, Jovanovich, 1973), 13. For one of the best studies of Huey Long, see T. Harry Williams, *Huey Long* (New York: Knopf, 1969). Newton's father had also run into trouble with racist whites in Louisiana. His wife subsequently convinced him a move would be good for the family. See Digby Diehl, "Q & A: Huey Newton," *Los Angeles Times,* August 6, 1972.

38. Huey Newton, *Revolutionary Suicide,* 36–42.

39. Huey Newton, *Revolutionary Suicide,* 22.

40. Excellent studies covering social conditions and the state of black education in American public schools during the 1950s and 1960s include Reginald Clark, *Family Life and School Achievement* (Chicago: University of Chicago Press, 1983), *Challenging the Myths: The Schools, the Blacks, and the Poor,* (Cambridge: Harvard Educational Review, 1975), and Raymond Wolters, *The Burden of Brown: Thirty Years of School Desegregation* (Knoxville: University of Tennessee Press, 1984).

41. Henry William Brown, *Class Aspects of Residential Development in the Oakland Black Community* (Ann Arbor, Michigan: University Microfilms International, 1980), 169.

42. Huey Newton, *Revolutionary Suicide,* 37–40; see also Howard Zinn, *People's History of the United States* (New York: Harper and Row, 1980).

43. Bobby G. Seale, *Seize the Time: The Story of the Black Panther Party and Huey P. Newton* (Baltimore: Black Classic Press, 1991), 6.

44. Seale, *Seize the Time,* 6–8.

45. Seale, *Seize the Time,* 8–10.

46. Seale, *Seize the Time,* 8–11.

47. Seale, *Seize the Time,* 12.

48. Newton, *Revolutionary Suicide,* 61–63, 70–71.

49. Van DeBurg, *New Day in Babylon,* 73–74; Scholars and students subsequently designed Black Studies departments and Black Student Unions to give blacks a larger voice on campus and to eradicate the intellectual and cultural underpinnings of

American racism. See Mike Thelwell, "Black Studies: A Political Perspective," *Massachusetts Review* 10 (Autumn 1969): 707–708; John Blassingame, "Black Studies: An Intellectual Crisis," *American Scholar* 38 (Autumn 1969): 553; "Black Studies Studied: American Council on Education Report," *America* 21 (June 1969): 698; and Harold Horton, "A Study of the Status of Black Studies in Universities and Colleges in the United States" (Ph.D. diss., Ohio State University, 1974).

50. Seale, *Seize the Time*, 14, 20; Newton, *Revolutionary Suicide*, 71–72; Kelley, *Freedom Dreams*, 73–83; "Mass Poison Plot Laid to Negroes; Extremists in Philadelphia Also Face Riot Charge," *New York Times*, September 28, 1967; Emanuel Perlmutter, "16 Negroes Seized; Plot to Kill Wilkins and Young Charged," *New York Times*, June 22, 1967.

51. Huey Newton, *Revolutionary Suicide*, 76, 86–89, 99.

52. Thomas West and James Mooney, eds., "Malcolm X: A Nationalist Alternative to Elijah Muhammad," in *To Redeem a Nation: A History and Anthology of the Civil Rights Movement* (St. James, New York: Brandywine Press, 1993), 194–95.

53. Huey Newton, *Revolutionary Suicide*, 110; Seale, *Seize the Time*, 20–22; Lee Lockwood, *Conversations With Eldridge Cleaver: Algiers* (New York: McGraw-Hill, 1970), 86; Herbert Haines, *Black Radicals and the Civil Rights Mainstream, 1954–1970* (Knoxville: University of Tennessee Press, 1988), 59. Eldridge Cleaver later explained that he wanted to honor Malcolm X by making the Organization of Afro-American Unity a viable political force. See also Yusuf Naim Kly, ed., *The Black Book: The True Political Philosophy of Malcolm X* (Atlanta: Clarity Press, 1986) and Essien U. Essien-Udom, *Black Nationalism: A Search for an Identity in America* (Chicago: University of Chicago Press, 1966).

54. Huey Newton, *Revolutionary Suicide*, 113.

55. Huey Newton, *Revolutionary Suicide*, 110. Excellent studies on the rise of Black Power and student activism are found in Stokely Carmichael and Charles V. Hamilton, *Black Power: The Politics of Liberation in America* (New York: Random House, 1967); Carson, *Eyes on the Prize;* August Meier, *CORE: A Study in the Civil Rights Movement, 1942–1968* (New York: Oxford University Press, 1973); "As Guns are Added to Campus Revolts: Cornell University Surrenders to Negroes' Demands," *U.S. News and World Report*, May 5, 1969, 30–31; and "Behind Revolt of Black Students," *U.S. News and World Report*, September 12, 1969, 16. See also Peniel Joseph, *Waiting 'Til the Midnight Hour: A Narrative History of Black Power in America* (New York: Henry Holt and Co., 2006).

56. Huey Newton, *Revolutionary Suicide*, 109.

57. Huey Newton, *Revolutionary Suicide*, 109–10; "The Watts 'Manifesto' and the McCone Report," *Commentary*, March 1966, 29–35.

58. Huey Newton, *Revolutionary Suicide*, 106–12; "The Deacons and Their Impact," *National Guardian*, September 4, 1965, 4–5; Roy Reed, "The Deacons, Too, Ride By Night," *New York Times Magazine*, August 15, 1965, 20. The Deacons for Defense and Justice was a militant group founded to prevent police brutality. An excellent biography of Robert Williams is Robert Carl Cohen, *Black Crusader: A Biography of Robert F. Williams* (Seacaucus, NJ: Lyle Stuart, 1972). Robert Williams had been active in Monroe, North Carolina, with a program of armed self-defense.

59. Huey Newton, *Revolutionary Suicide*, 112–13. Curtis Muhammad, formerly Curtis Hayes, of the Student Nonviolent Coordinating Committee, remembered that the Panther logo was drawn by "Betty" in Atlanta. She got the idea from one of the black colleges in the area whose mascot was a panther.

60. Huey P. Newton, *War Against the Panthers: A Study of Repression in America* (New York: Harlem River Press, 1996), 119–22. See Appendix A for a complete listing of the Ten Point Program.

61. Lawrence Lader, *Power on the Left: American Radical Movements Since 1946* (New York: Norton, 1979), 218.

62. Eddie Thibideaux, interview with the author, cassette recording, January 10, 1996, Oakland, California. Tape in possession of author.

63. Newton *Revolutionary Suicide*, 119; Elbert Howard, interview with the author, cassette recording, July 19, 2003, Memphis, Tennessee. Tape in possession of author.

64. Emory Douglas, interview with the author, cassette recording, April 21, 1998, San Francisco, California. Tape in possession of author; Elaine Brown, *A Taste of Power: A Black Woman's Story* (New York: Pantheon Books, 1992), 135, 320.

65. Malik Rahim, interview with the author, cassette recording, August 8, 2002, New Orleans, Louisiana. Tape in possession of the author.

66. Brown, *A Taste of Power,* 135. The Panthers also had to abide by a long list of rules devised by the Central Committee. See Appendix B for rules of the Black Panther Party.

67. Brown, *Taste of Power,* 135; Douglas, April 21, 1998, interview.

68. In 1970, according to a United States Senate committee investigating the group, this newspaper had a circulation of approximately 140,000 copies per week. See United States Congress, House Committee on Internal Security, Hearings on the Black Panther Party, *Gun-Barrel Politics: The Black Panther Party, 1966–1971,* 92nd Cong., 1st sess. (Washington, D.C.: United States Government Printing Office, 1971), 86 (hereafter cited as *Gun-Barrel Politics*). The Panthers claim a circulation of a little over 200,000 a week at this time.

69. Douglas, April 21, 1998, interview; Martin Kenner, interview with the author, cassette recording, March 20, 1996, New York, New York. Tape in possession of the author.

70. In 1966, Attorney Beverly Axelrod aided Cleaver in getting paroled from a California prison. Upon his release, she helped him secure a job with *Ramparts* magazine, where he wrote prolifically about political issues of the period. Cleaver's prison letters eventually became the renowned *Soul On Ice* (Dell: New York, 1968).

71. Akua Njeri, *My Life With the Black Panther Party* (Oakland: Burning Spear Publications, 1991), 13.

72. Elbert Howard, interview with the author, cassette recording, July 19, 2003, Memphis, Tennessee. Tape in possession of author; Elbert Howard, *Panther on the Prowl* (Memphis: Elbert Howard, 2004). This self-published autobiography contains no page numbers.

73. Howard, July 19, 2003, interview.

74. Howard, July 19, 2003, interview.

75. Howard, July 19, 2003, interview.

76. Howard, July 19, 2003, interview.

77. Howard, July 19, 2003, interview.

78. Emory Douglas, interview with the author, digital audio recording, January 1, 2001, San Francisco, California. Recording in possession of author.

79. Douglas, January 1, 2001, interview.

80. Douglas, January 1, 2001, interview.

Chapter Two: The Black Panther Party for Self-Defense

1. Huey Newton, interview, in Henry Hampton et al., *Voices of Freedom: An Oral History of the Civil Rights Movement from the 1950s Through the 1980s* (New York: Bantam Books, 1990), 361; Bobby Seale, *Seize the Time: The Story of the Black Panther Party and Huey P. Newton* (Black Classic Press: Baltimore, 1991), 85, 78.

2. Newton interview; Seale, *Seize the Time*, 86–87.

3. Seale, *Seize the Time*, 87.

4. Seale, *Seize the Time*, 89–91.

5. Seale, *Seize the Time*, 92–93.

6. Sol Stern, "'The Call of the Black Panthers," *New York Times Magazine*, August 6, 1967, 10.

7. See Ten Point Platform and Program in every issue of *The Black Panther* from 1968 to 1971 and in Appendix A.

8. Huey Newton, *Revolutionary Suicide* (New York: Harcourt Brace Jovanovich, Inc., 1973), 120.

9. Huey Newton, *Revolutionary Suicide*, 120.

10. Emory Douglas, interview with the author, cassette recording, August 26, 2003, San Francisco, California. Tape in possession of author; Huey Newton, *Revolutionary Suicide*, 121.

11. Douglas, August 26, 2003, interview; Huey Newton, *Revolutionary Suicide*, 121.

12. Seale description of police stop in Lee Lew Lee, *All Power to the People: The Black Panther Party and Beyond*, VHS. Produced and directed by Lee Lew Lee (New York: Electronic News Group, 1996).

13. Huey Newton, *Revolutionary Suicide*, 123.

14. Seale, *Seize the Time*, 72–73. King quote in speech shown in Lee Lew Lee, *All Power to the People*.

15. Elbert Howard, interview with the author, cassette recording, July 19, 2003, Memphis, Tennessee; Tarika Lewis, interview with the author, cassette recording, September 3, 2003, Oakland, California. Tape in possession of author; Eldridge Cleaver quote on opening fly sheet of William Van Deburg, *New Day in Babylon: The Black Power Movement and American Culture, 1965–1975* (Chicago: University of Chicago Press, 1992).

16. Van Deburg, *New Day in Babylon;* Robert Allen, *Dialectics of Black Power,* a *Guardian* pamphlet, Harlem Papers, Box 238, folder 16, Schomburg Center for Research in Black Culture, New York City, New York.

17. Seale, *Seize the Time*, 91.

18. Thomas Rose, ed., *Violence in America: A Historical and Contemporary Reader* (New York: Vintage Books, 1969), 12–13; King quote in Lee Lew Lee, *All Power to the People*.

19. Huey Newton, *A Consistent Ideology*, December 28, 1970, copy located in Huey P. Newton Foundation Records, Green Library, Special Collections, Stanford University Archives, Palo Alto, California (hereafter cited as HPN Foundation Records).

20. Lewis Baldwin, et al., *The Legacy of Martin Luther King, Jr.: The Boundaries of Law, Politics, and Religion* (Notre Dame: University of Notre Dame Press, 2002), 157.

21. Mario Van Peebles, Ula Taylor, and Tarika Lewis, *Panther: A Pictorial History of the Black Panthers and the Story Behind the Film* (New York: New Market Press, 1995), 177.

22. Safiya Bhukari comment in Lee Lew Lee, *All Power to the People;* Thomas McCreary, interview with the author, cassette recording, January 22, 2003, Atlanta, Georgia. Tape in possession of author.

23. Elbert Howard, Black History Month speech, University of Southern Mississippi, February 10, 2004. Digital video cassette in possession of author.

24. William Brent, *Long Time Gone: A Black Panther's True Life Story of His Hijacking and Twenty-five Years in Cuba* (New York: Crown, 1996), 102.

25. James Forman, *The Making of Black Revolutionaries: A Personal Account* (New York: The MacMillan Company, 1972), 542–3.

26. Robin Kelley, *Freedom Dreams: The Black Radical Imagination* (Boston: Beacon Press, 2002), 80.

27. Seale, *Seize the Time,* 99–102; Lewis, September 3, 2003, interview.

28. Eldridge Cleaver, *On the Ideology of the Black Panther Party,* 1, copy in the Alden Kimbrough Collection, Los Angeles, California.

29. Kelley, *Freedom Dreams,* 72–90.

30. Eldridge Cleaver interview in Hampton et al., *Voices of Freedom,* 364.

31. Seale, *Seize the Time,* 123.

32. Seale, *Seize the Time,* 124; Betty Shabazz interview in Hampton, *Voices of Freedom,* 365–66.

33. Seale, *Seize the Time,* 125–8; Erika Doss, "Revolutionary Art is a Tool for Liberation": Emory Douglas and Protest Aesthetics at the *Black Panther,*" in Kathleen Cleaver and George Katsiaficas, eds., *Liberation, Imagination, and the Black Panther Party: A New Look at the Panthers and Their Legacy* (New York: Routledge, 2001), 180.

34. Van Deburg, *New Day in Babylon,* 156.

35. *"Cause of Riots* Watts Study: 'A Hungry Man Is a Dangerous Man,'" *Sacramento Union* July 31, 1967, clipping in Ronald Reagan Library, Simi Valley, California, (hereafter cited as RRL).

36. "Eldridge Cleaver's Story," undated clipping from magazine, found in Black Panther Party file at Southern California Research Center, Los Angeles, California (hereafter cited as SCRC).

37. "Eldridge Cleaver's Story"; "Eldridge Cleaver," http://www.ghsonline.net/projects/Students/essays/cleaver.htm (accessed January 15, 2004); William J. Drummond, "Eldridge Cleaver: A Black Militant Forged By Life," *Los Angeles Times,* November 29, 1968.

38. Cecil Brown, "The Minister of Information Raps: An Interview with Eldridge Cleaver," *Evergreen,* October 1968, 45; Drummond, "Eldridge Cleaver."

39. Eldridge Cleaver, *Soul on Ice* (New York: Ramparts, 1968), 14–15.

40. Cleaver, *Soul on Ice,* 20–21; Eldridge Cleaver, telephone conversation with the author, February 17, 1997.

41. "Eldridge Cleaver," http://www.ghsonline.net/ (accessed January 4, 2004); "Eldridge Cleaver's Story"; Brown, "The Minister of Information Raps," 82.

42. Hampton, et al., *Voices of Freedom,* 362–64.

43. Hampton, et al., *Voices of Freedom,* 362–64; Emory Douglas, interview with the author, digital audio tape recording, San Francisco, California, January 1, 2001. Recording in possession of author; "Eldridge Cleaver's Story."

44. Hampton, et. al., *Voices of Freedom,* 363–64, 366–67; Seale, *Seize the Time,* 132–33.

45. Seale, *Seize the Time,* 132; David Hilliard and Donald Wise, eds., *The Huey P. Newton Reader* (New York: Seven Stories Press, 2002), 204.

46. Hilliard and Wiese, *Newton Reader,* 204; Hampton, *Voices of Freedom,* 367.

47. Hilliard and Wiese, *Newton Reader,* 85–86.

48. Kelley, *Freedom Dreams,* 95; Van Deburg, *New Day in Babylon,* 156.

49. "Why Was Denzil Dowell Killed?," *Black Panther,* April 25, 1967. This, the paper's first issue, also noted that a black woman had recently been brutally beaten by police in Richmond. In Oakland, the same thing had happened to a fourteen-year-old girl. The paper also reported that police, in September 1966, killed George Thompson in San Francisco.

50. "Why Was Denzil Dowell Killed?"; Huey Newton, *Revolutionary Suicide,* 146.

51. Huey Newton, *Revolutionary Suicide,* 150–51.

52. "George Dowell Interview," *Black Panther* May 15, 1967. For an excellent discussion of manhood and the freedom struggle, see Steve Estes, *I AM A MAN: Race, Manhood, and the Civil Rights Movement* (Chapel Hill, University of North Carolina Press, 2006).

53. Stern, "Call of the Black Panthers," 62.

54. Stern, "Call of the Black Panthers," 62.

55. Hampton, et al., *Voices of Freedom,* 375. Polls in 1957 and 1967 showed that two-thirds of blacks in Detroit "complained of discrimination and mistreatment at the hands of police officers." A 1967 Louis Harris Poll revealed that "blacks felt two to one that police brutality is the major cause" of the riots. The same poll showed that less than one in five whites "believe[d] that there [was] any police brutality to Negroes." Between 1957 and 1960, the NAACP filed 172 complaints with Detroit's Police Commissioner. Only once "was an officer found at fault." See James W. Clarke, *The Lineaments of Wrath: Race, Violent Crime, and American Culture* (New Brunswick, New Jersey: Transaction Publishers, 1988), 241.

56. Hampton, et al., *Voices of Freedom,* 382–83, 397, 387–88.

57. Dwight Eisenhower quotes found in "Rioting Must Be Dealt With Sternly, Ike Says," *San Jose Mercury News* July 26, 1967, clipping in RRL.

58. John Conyers quote in Hampton et al., *Voices of Freedom,* 391.

59. Hampton et al., *Voices of Freedom,* 397–98.

60. "Violence Jars 12 Cities In Nation's Worst Night of Racial Strife in History," *Sacramento Bee,* July 25, 1967. Clipping in RRL.

61. *Gun-Barrel Politics,* 9–10; U.S. Riot Commission, *The Report of the National Advisory Commission on Civil Disorders* (New York: New York Times Co., 1968), 111. This document stated that 164 civil disorders were reported in the first nine months of 1967. The commission noted that the riots involved blacks "acting against local symbols of white American society, authority, and property" in black communities, "rather than against white persons per se." The report also noted that "the typical rioter was not a hoodlum or habitual criminal but a teenager or young adult, a high school dropout, underemployed or menially employed, race proud, extremely hostile to both whites and middle-class Negroes, and distrustful of the political system and political leaders."

62. Lawrence Lader, *Power on the Left: American Radical Movements Since 1946* (New York: Norton, 1979), 227.

63. Huey Newton quote in "Huey P. Newton: Philosophy and Electoral Politics," http://socialjustice.ccnmtl.columbia.edu/index.php/Huey_P._Newton_::_Philosophy_::_Electoral_Politics (accessed June 20, 2006).

64. Huey Newton, interview in Hampton, et al., *Voices of Freedom,* 353, 355;

Kimberle Crenshaw quoted in Richard Delgado, ed., *Critical Race Theory: The Cutting Edge* (Philadelphia: Temple University Press, 1995), 117.

65. Stern, "Call of the Black Panthers," 52.

66. Newton, *Revolutionary Suicide*, 171–73.

67. Lewis, September 3, 2003, interview; See also, Van Peebles, et. al., *Panther,* 55–57.

68. Huey Newton, *Revolutionary Suicide*, 174.

69. Stern, "The Call of the Black Panthers," 64.

70. Kathy Mulhern, "Stalking the Panthers," *Commonweal* (11 October 1968): 58–62; Huey Newton, *Revolutionary Suicide*, 175–76.

71. Huey Newton, *Revolutionary Suicide*, 175–76

72. Huey Newton, *Revolutionary Suicide*, 178.

Chapter Three: Speaking of Violence

1. Kathleen Cleaver, "Race, Civil Rights, and Feminism," in Richard Delgado, ed., *Critical Race Theory: The Cutting Edge* (Philadelphia: Temple University Press, 1995), 38. Cleaver, now employed as a law professor, wrote that "under international human rights law, we saw blacks as colonial subjects just as entitled to fight for human rights and self-determination as Africans, Asians, and Latin Americans who were waging revolutionary wars against imperial domination."

2. Eldridge Cleaver told reporters and a television audience that the Panthers hated police brutality so much that they planned "to pick up guns and drive them out" of the black community. See Cleaver in film footage in Lee Lew Lee, *All Power to the People: The Black Panther Party and Beyond,* VHS. Produced and directed by Lee Lew Lee (New York: Electronic News Group, 1996).

3. Frantz Fanon, *The Wretched of the Earth* (New York: Grove Press, 1963), 45–47; Huey P. Newton, *Revolutionary Suicide* (New York: Harcourt, Brace, Jovanovich, Inc., 1973), 106–11.

4. United States Senate, Hearings Before the Subcommittee to Investigate the Administration of the Internal Security Act and other Internal Security Laws of the Committee on the Judiciary, *Assaults on Law Enforcement Officers,* 91st Cong., 2nd sess. (Washington, D.C.: United States Government Printing Office, 1970), 268, 411, 254 (hereafter cited as *Assaults*).

5. *Assaults,* 252–53, 315. Eddie Thibideaux, interview with the author, cassette recording, January 10, 1996, Oakland, California. Tape in possession of the author; Masai Hewitt and Robert Bowen, interview by Robert Grehle and Brett Eynon, tape recording, Los Angeles, California, April 6, 1984, transcripts in Department of Oral History, Butler Library, Columbia University, New York City, New York. Some police officers believe that the Panther newspaper, with headlines that sometimes read "Fight or Die, Nigger" or "Death to the Pigs," was the cause of the slaying of law enforcement officials. For example, in Baltimore, the police ordered Panthers to cease selling the paper and handing out other flyers that graphically depicted how to assassinate police officers. They were particularly concerned because one of their own, Patrolman Stanley Sager, had been killed after a flier describing how to ambush and assassinate police officers had been widely disseminated in Baltimore. See Gerald A. Fitzgerald, "Panthers Barred From Spreading Anti-Police Flyers," *Baltimore Sun,* May 1, 1970.

6. Claudia Dahlerus and Christian Davenport, "Tracking Down the Empirical

Legacy of the BPP; or Notes on the Perils of Pursuing the Panthers," in Kathleen Cleaver and George Katsificas, eds., *Liberation, Imagination, and the Black Panther Party: A New Look at the Panther Legacy* (New York: Routledge, 2001), 212–228.

7. Information on police killings in *Assaults*, 252–53, 315.

8. *Assaults*, 328.

9. Elaine Brown, *A Taste of Power: A Black Woman's Story* (New York: Pantheon Books), 1992. 13.

10. Hewitt and Bowen, interview; Thibideaux, January 10, 1996, interview.

11. Henry Hampton, et al., *Voices of Freedom: An Oral History of the Civil Rights Movement from the 1950s Through the 1980s* (New York: Bantam Books, 1990), 513.

12. Hewitt and Bowen interview.

13. Robert Moss, *The Urban Guerrilla* (London: International Institute For Strategic Studies, n.d.), 1–2.

14. Lawrence Lader, *Power on the Left: American Radical Movements Since 1946* (New York: Norton, 1979), 268–9.

15. Hollis Watkins, conversation with the author, Jackson, Mississippi, June 19, 2005.

16. Bernard D. Nossiter, "Panther Parley Cheers Call to Kill Authorities: Kill Authorities, Panthers Are Urged," *Washington Post*, September 6, 1970; Belinda (no last name given), "Open Letter to the People," *Black Panther*, March 15, 1970. Long-time activist Roy Wilkins believed that the police made the Panthers by stopping cars at random and "shooting at fleeing men whom they called Panthers." He claimed that in the end their "rhetoric was more lurid than their actions." See Roy Wilkins, "Wilkins Speaks: Panthers Seek Mainstream," *Baltimore Afro-American*, October 3, 1972.

17. Michael Newton, *Bitter Grain: Huey Newton and the Black Panther Party*, (Los Angeles: Holloway House, 1980), 144.

18. Bobby Seale, *A Lonely Rage: The Autobiography of Bobby Seale* (New York: Times Books, 1978), 130–42. Panther rhetoric is evident throughout the *Black Panther*.

19. Gene Marine, "The Persecution and Assassination of the Black Panther Party As Directed By Guess Who," *National Review*, December 30, 1969, 1306–67.

20. Fred Hampton, "You Can Murder a Liberator, but You Can't Murder Liberation," reprinted in the *Movement* magazine, January 1970.

21. Akua Njeri, *My Life With the Party* (Oakland: Burning Spear Productions, 1991), 25.

22. "Jury Begins Panther Deliberation," *Nashville Banner*, May 14, 1969. As a result of Panther rhetoric and violent activities, law enforcement sometimes arrested and charged the Panthers with violation of the Smith Act, "a law mostly used to prosecute Communists advocating violent overthrow of the government. The law, named for Representative Howard Smith of Virginia, made it a crime to 'advocate, abet, advise, or teach the duty, necessity, desirability or propriety of overthrowing or destroying any government in the United States by force . . . to print, publish, edit, issue, circulate, sell distribute or publicly display such ideas; or to organize, belong to, or affiliate with any organizations espousing such doctrines.'" See Timothy Messer-Kruse, "Smith Act," in Paul S. Boyer, ed., *The Oxford Companion to United States History* (Oxford: Oxford University Press, 2001).

23. Sonyika Shakur and anonymous Panther, interview by Lee Lew Lee in *All Power to the People*.

24. Ali Bey Hassan, interview by Lee Lew Lee in *All Power to the People*.

25. Speech by Attorney William Kunstler delivered to The Conference For a United Front Against Fascism, Oakland, California, July 19, 1969. Copy found in Huey P. Newton Foundation Records, Department of Special Collections, Green Library, Stanford University, Palo Alto, California (hereafter cited as HPN Foundation Records).

26. Kunstler speech.

27. Polynesian Panther Party letter found in HPN Foundation Records.

28. Black Liberation Army, "Last Warning," communiqué found in HPN Foundation Records.

29. "Last Warning."

30. Eldridge Cleaver, "To My Black Brothers in Viet Nam," open letter, January 4, 1970, in Black Panther Party file, State Historical Society of Wisconsin, Madison, Wisconsin.

31. Cleaver, "To My Black Brothers."

32. Cleaver, "To My Black Brothers."

33. Thomas A. Johnson, "Negro Expatriates, Military and Civilian, Find Wide Range of Opportunities in Asia," *New York Times,* January 21, 1971; Thibideaux, January 10, 1996, interview; Emory Douglas, interview with the author, cassette recording, August 10, 1997, Oakland, California. Tape in possession of author; Liberation News Service, "The Whole World Revolution Will be Kicked Off . . . An Interview with Huey P. Newton," *Black Panther,* September 20, 1969.

34. Malik Rahim, interview with the author, cassette recording, August 8, 2002, New Orleans, Louisiana; Thomas McCreary, interview with the author, cassette recording, January 22, 2003, Atlanta, Georgia; Douglas, August 10, 1997, interview; Elbert Howard, interview with the author, cassette recording, July 19, 2003, Memphis, Tennessee. Tape in possession of author; Ronald Freeman, interview with the author, cassette recording, February 24, 2003, Hattiesburg, Mississippi. Tape in possession of author.

35. United States House of Representatives, Committee on Internal Security, *Investigation of Attempts to Subvert The United States Armed Services,* part 2 (Washington, D.C.: United States Government Printing Office, 1972), 6977–78. See also Eugene Linden, "The Demoralization of an Army: Fragging and Other-Withdrawal Attempts," *Saturday Review,* January 8, 1972, 12–17, 55.

36. Linden, "Demoralization of an Army," 13–17.

37. Washington Post, *Army in Anguish,* (Washington, D.C.: Pocket Books, 1972), 38.

38. United States Congress, House Committee on Internal Security, Hearings on the Black Panther Party, *Gun-Barrel Politics: The Black Panther Party, 1966–1971,* 92nd Cong., 1st sess. (Washington, D.C.: United States Government Printing Office, 1971), 107 (hereafter cited as *Gun-Barrel Politics*).

39. Eldridge Cleave, "The Black Man's Stake in Vietnam," *Black Panther,* March 23, 1969.

40. Undated letter from Karen Wald to Huey Newton, HPN Foundation Records, series 1, box 2, folder 7. The Panthers also carried on friendly relations with Al Fatah and the Palestine Liberation Organization, which offered military training to some Panthers. See letter from Jewish Defense League to Huey Newton, HPN Foundation Records, series 1, box 6, folder 6, October 1973.

41. *Gun-Barrel Politics*, 103, 106.

42. *Gun-Barrel Politics*, 104–6.

43. Letter from the Central Committee of the Partido Revolucionario Dominicano to Black Panther Party Headquarters, HPN Foundation Records, series 1, box 3, folder 14, September 1971.

44. Letter from Matsuko Ishida to BPP headquarters, May 8, 1973, HPN Foundation Records, series 1, box 3, folder 8. Information on International Committee to Release Eldridge Cleaver in series 4, box 14, folder 1.

45. Cleaver and Katsiaficas, *Liberation, Imagination and the Black Panther Party*, 23, 25.

46. Douglas, August 10, 1997, interview.

47. Martin Kenner, interview with the author, cassette recording, March 20, 1996, New York City, New York. Tape in possession of author.

48. Undated letter from George Jackson to Huey Newton, HPN Foundation Records, series 1, box 3, folder 9.

49. See also George Jackson, *Soledad Brother: The Prison Letters of George Jackson* (Chicago: Lawrence Hill Books, 1994), originally published in 1970 by Coward–McCann; Angela Davis, *If They Come in the Morning: Voices of Resistance* (New York: Third World Press, 1971); and Attica Revisited Website, http://www.talkinghistory.org/attica/, (accessed July 20, 2005).

50. George Jackson and General Staff, People's Liberation Army, A 7th, "Orders," copy in HPN Foundation Records.

51. Jackson, "Orders."

52. American Revolutionary Media, *Media Repression* (Detroit: Revolutionary Printing Co-op, n.d.).

Chapter Four: Publicizing the Party

1. Sara Blackburn, *White Justice: Black Experience Today in America's Courtrooms* (New York: Harper and Row, 1971), 85; Huey Newton, *Revolutionary Suicide* (New York: Harcourt, Brace, Jovanovich, Inc. , 1973), 202–3; Kathy Mulhern, "Stalking the Panthers," *Commonweal* (11 October 1968): 59–62.

2. Blackburn, *White Justice,* 12–14.

3. Blackburn, *White Justice*, 14, 37–44, 85; During Newton's three years in jail, the party grew phenomenally and took on increasingly violent characteristics. For a complete story of the trial see Blackburn, *White Justice*. For an excellent study on black retaliatory violence, see Herbert Shapiro, *White Violence and Black Response: From Reconstruction to Montgomery* (Amherst: University of Massachusetts Press, 1988).

4. Blackburn, *White Justice*, 14, 37–44, 85.

5. "Court Reverses Panther's Term," *Baltimore Sun,* May 30, 1970. "Reversal on Newton," *New York Times,* May 31, 1970. While imprisoned, Newton maintained that he was a political prisoner and as a result "refused to perform any routine assignments."

6. Thomas McCreary, interview with the author, cassette recording, January 22, 2003, Atlanta, Georgia. Tape in possession of author.

7. Mario Van Peebles, et al., *Panther: A Pictorial History of the Black Panthers and the Story Behind the Film* (New York: New Market Press, 1995), 86–7; Mulhern, "Stalking the Panthers," 61.

8. Don Cox, *Just Another Nigger*, 1981, unpublished manuscript, n.p.

9. Michael Newton, *Bitter Grain: Huey Newton and the Black Panther Party* (Los Angeles: Holloway House, 1980), 67–68.

10. Emory Douglas, interview with author, cassette recording, August 30, 2003, San Francisco, California. Tape in possession of author; Bobby Seale, *Seize the Time: The Story of the Black Panther Party and Huey P. Newton* (Baltimore: Black Classic Press, 1991), 225. According to Stokely Carmichael, in 1966 Eldridge Cleaver met SNCC member Kathleen Neale in Nashville when he had gone to do a story on Black Power for *Ramparts* magazine. Neale had been one of the organizers of a SNCC conference in Nashville. Cleaver had been traveling with Carmichael for a week when they got to the SNCC office in the Music City. Once they arrived, "the brother takes one look at our sister Kathleen (and she at him) and boom, pow, that's all she wrote Jack. Revolutionary love strikes again." The two married the following year. See Stokely Carmichael with Ekwueme Michael Thelwell, *Ready for Revolution: The Life and Struggles of Stokely Carmichael [Kwame Ture]* (New York: Scribner, 2003), 551–52.

11. Seale, *Seize the Time*, 222, 204–5. The picture with Newton in the wicker chair, according to Emory Douglas, was Eldridge Cleaver's idea. Cleaver had invited Newton to Beverly Axelrod's house in San Francisco, where the photo shoot took place. According to Douglas, Newton "never really liked that picture" and often commented that he wished he had never agreed to pose for it.

12. Michael Newton, *Bitter Grain*, 69.

13. Michael Newton, *Bitter Grain*, 70. Newton noted "the victory came too late for Coltrale and Carter as both were dead: early victims of the Los Angeles Panther wars." Seale, *Seize the Time*, 223–25.

14. Seale, *Seize the Time*, 224–25.

15. Huey P. Newton, *To Die for the People: The Writings of Huey P. Newton* (New York: Vintage Books, 1972), 11–13.

16. Douglas, August 30, 2003, interview; Seale, *Seize the Time*, 225.

17. Ronald Freeman, interview with the author, February 24, 2003, Hattiesburg, Mississippi. Tape in possession of author; McCone Report located in "Black Panther Party" file in Southern California Research Center, Los Angeles, California (hereafter cited as SCRC).

18. Martin J. Schiesl, "Behind the Badge: The Police and Social Discontent in Los Angeles Since 1950," in Norman Klein and Martin J. Schiesl, eds., *20th Century Los Angeles: Power, Promotion, and Social Conflict* (Claremont, California: Regina Books, 1990), 154–55, 166, 168–69.

19. Schiesl, "Behind the Badge," 168.

20. Akinyele Umoja, "Repression Breeds Resistance: The Black Liberation Army and the Radical Legacy of the Black Panther Party," in Kathleen Cleaver and George Katsificas, eds., *Liberation, Imagination, and the Black Panther Party: A New Look at the Panthers and Their Legacy* (New York: Routledge, 2001), 6–7.

21. Van Peebles, et al., *Panther*, 178.

22. "The 'People's Park': A Report on a Confrontation at Berkeley, California," submitted to Governor Ronald Reagan, July 1, 1969. Report found in clipping file in Ronald Reagan papers, Ronald Reagan Library, Simi Valley, California.

23. "Statewide Peace and Freedom Party Organizing Committee Policy Guidelines," Adopted at Berkeley Planning Convention June 28, 1968, pamphlet found in Alden Kimbrough Collection, Los Angeles, California (hereafter cited as AKC).

24. "Statewide Peace and Freedom Party"; "Racism and colonialism" quote in "Peace and Freedom Party Registration Drive," 2, photocopy in "Black Panther Party" file in State Historical Society of Wisconsin, Madison, Wisconsin.

25. Don Newton, "Black-White Coalition in California," *Guardian*, n.d. Copy found in AKC.

26. Don Newton, "Black-White Coalition".

27. James Forman, *The Making of Black Revolutionaries: A Personal Account* (New York: The Macmillan Company, 1972), 523, 527.

28. Huey Newton, *Revolutionary Suicide*, 155.

29. Huey Newton, *Revolutionary Suicide*, 156; Forman, *The Making of Black Revolutionaries*, 522–42.

30. Forman, *The Making of Black Revolutionaries*, 522–23. Forman wrote that he set up the meeting and that it had been the Panthers who did not show, compelling him to quit the organization because of the way the BPP handled things.

31. Thomas McCreary, interview with the author, cassette recording, January 22, 2003, Atlanta, Georgia; Forman, *The Making of Black Revolutionaries*, 534, 539; Douglas, August 30, 2003, interview.

32. Carmichael and Thelwell, *Ready for Revolution*, 659–72.

33. Cleaver quote in "Open Letter to Stokely Carmichael," *Ramparts*, August 1969; FBI memo, G. C. Moore to W. C. Sullivan, February 29, 1968 found at http://www.icdc.com/~paulwolf/cointelpro/blacknationalist.htm#carmichael (accessed July 10, 2005).

34. Seale, *Seize the Time*, 131; Margaret Block, conversation with the author, July 28, 2001, Cleveland, Mississippi. Margaret Block is a civil rights activist, who, along with her brother Sam Block, worked tirelessly for black rights in the Mississippi Delta before his death. She later moved to San Francisco, although she has since moved back to Mississippi.

35. Block, July 28, 2001, conversation.

36. Carmichael had expressed his desire to go to the mother country to many people. The incident with the Panthers convinced him the time had come to make that move. See Carmichael and Thelwell, *Ready for Revolution*, 586–618.

37. Eldridge Cleaver, "Stokely's Jive." Undated speech in private collection of William Johnson, Bronx, New York.

38. Eldridge Cleaver, "Community Imperialism," speech. Copy in State Historical Society of Wisconsin, "Black Panther" file.

39. Cleaver, "Community Imperialism."

40. See "A Woman's Party" in Mumia Abu-Jamal, *We Want Freedom: A Life in the Black Panther Party* (Cambridge, MA: South End Press, 2004).

41. Gun barrels quote in Eddie Thibideaux, interview with the author, cassette recording, January 10, 1996, Oakland, California, but can be found in virtually every issue of *The Black Panther;* Sonyika Shakur, interview with Lee Lew Lee in *All Power to the People;* Randy Williams, "'Tis the Season," *Black Panther*, October 26, 1968.

42. Foster, *Unrelated Kin*, 139, 161.

43. Gloria Abernethy and Elaine Brown interviews in Etter-Lewis Foster, ed., *Unrelated Kin: Race and Gender in Women's Personal Narratives* (New York: Routledge, 1996), 139, 161.

44. Sheba Haven, interview with the author, cassette recording, September 3,

2003, Sacramento, California. Tape in possession of author. Akua Njeri, *My Life with the Black Panther Party* (St. Petersburg, FL: Burning Spear Publications, 1991), 25.

45. Robert E. Sweet, "Girl Talks, Panthers Set to Fight," *Chicago Tribune,* January 31, 1971.

46. Kathleen Cleaver, "Racism, Fascism, and Political Assassination," *Black Panther,* September 14, 1968; Kathleen Cleaver, interview in Julia Herve, "Black Scholar Interviews: Kathleen Cleaver," *Black Scholar,* 56–57. See also Kathleen Cleaver, "Women, Power, and Revolution," in Cleaver and Katsiaficas, *Liberation, Imagination, and the Black Panther Party,* 123–27.

47. Mary Ellen Leary, "The Uproar Over Cleaver," *The New Republic* (1969): 23

48. Frantz Fanon, *The Wretched of the Earth* (Grove Press: New York, 1963), 94.

49. Yasmeen Sutton and Bullwhip, interview with the author, digital video recording, January 21, 2002, Corona (Queens), New York. Digital video cassette in possession of author. The BPP formed coalitions and alliances with black and white student groups, Hispanics, Asians, Native Americans, as well as poor and well-to-do whites like those in the California-based Peace and Freedom Party.

50. These programs will be discussed in a later chapter.

51. See U.S. Bureau of the Census, "Historical Income Tables—Households" http://www.census.gov/hhes/income/histinc/inchhdet.html accessed June 25, 2006; *United Steelworkers of America v. Weber,* 443 U.S. 193 (1979), http://www.debatingracialpreference.org/WEBER-Brennan.htm (accessed June 25, 2006).

52. Philip S. Foner, *The Black Panthers Speak* (Cambridge: Da Capo Press, 1995), 55. This book was first published in 1970.

53. Sol Stern, "The Call of the Black Panthers," *New York Times Magazine,* August 6, 1967, 10.

54. Minister of Information, "On Violence," *Black Panther,* March 28, 1968.

55. Huey Newton, "The Correct Handling of A Revolution" in Foner, *The Black Panthers Speak,* 41, 43.

56. Seale, *Seize the Time,* 14.

57. This quote is taken from the text of a famous poster of Malcolm X. It is probably the most famous poster of the Muslim leader. It depicts him with a menacing sneer and pointing an unusually long index finger during a speech. The speech was given first to the United Nations and later to the British Parliament in late 1964.

58. BJ, interview with author, January 17, 2004, Bronx, New York. Tape in possession of author.

59. Emory Douglas, interview with author, cassette recording, June 28, 2001, San Francisco, California. Tape in possession of author.

60. Huey Newton, *Revolutionary Suicide,* (Harcourt Brace Jovanovich: New York, 1973), 127; Douglas, June 28, 2001, interview.

61. *Black Panther Party Platform and Program,* March 29, 1972. HPN Foundation Records.

62. Malcolm X quoted in reprint of "Speech" in *Black Panther* May 19, 1969, 4.

63. Newton, "The Correct Handling of a Revolution," 41–42.

64. "Rise and Fall of the Panthers: End of the Black Power Era," in *What Strategy For Black Liberation?: Trotskyism vs. Black Nationalism, Key Documents and Articles, 1955–1978* in *Marxist Bulletin 5* (New York: Spartacist Publishing Company, 1994, fourth printing of revised edition), 34.

65. Thomas McCreary, interview with the author, cassette recording, January 22, 2003, Atlanta, Georgia. Tape in possession of author.

66. Newton, *Revolutionary Suicide*, 89.

67. Bill Jennings, interview with the author, cassette recording, January 1, 2002, Sacramento, California. Tape in possession of author.

68. "Rise and Fall of the Panthers"; McCreary, January 22, 2003, interview.

69. "Castro Hails Negro Rioting Around U.S.," *Washington Post* July 27, 1967.

70. Nicholass von Hoffman, *Left at the Post*, (Chicago: Quadrangle Books, 1970), 84.

71. "Rise and Fall of the Panthers," 35.

72. "Rise and Fall of the Panthers," 35.

73. McCreary, January 22, 2003, interview.

74. Sundiata Acoli, "A Brief History of the Black Panther Party and its Place in the Black Liberation Movement," http://www.thetalkingdrum.com/bla2.html, (accessed December 17, 2003); BJ, interview with author, digital video recording, January 21, 2002, Corona (Queens), New York. Digital Video Cassette in possession of author; Malik Rahim, interview with author, tape recording, New Orleans, Louisiana, August 8, 2002.

75. McCreary, January 22, 2003, interview.

76. Joseph R. Brandt, *Why Black Power* (New York: Friendship Pres, 1968), 65.

77. Acoli, "A Brief History."

78. Jennings, January 1, 2002, interview.

79. Acoli, "A Brief History."

80. Jennings, January 1, 2002, interview.

Chapter Five: Growth and Transformation

1. Martin Luther King Jr., *Where Do We Go From Here?: Chaos or Community* (New York: Bantam Books, 1967), 30; Bayard Rustin and Glenn Smiley quotes in Jenny Walker, "Black Violence and Nonviolence in the Civil Rights and Black power Eras," (Ph.D. diss. University of New Castle Upon Tyne, 2000), 26 and 27, respectively. King quote on white men losing blood in Walker, 127 and on falsifying issue of "self defense" in Walker, 172. Walker notes that King told people at one Montgomery Improvement Association meeting that "what needs to be done is for a couple of those white men to lose some blood; then the Federal Government will step in."

2. Mark Bauerlein, et al., *Civil Rights Chronicle: The African American Struggle for Freedom* (Lincolnwood, IL: Legacy, 2003), 340–41.

3. Bauerlein, et al., *Civil Rights Chronicle*, 342.

4. Bauerlein, et al., *Civil Rights Chronicle*, 342. King's murder came in the wake of Malcolm X's, the Congo's Patrice Lumumba's, and dozens of other well-known and not-so-well-known freedom fighters. It preceded John F. Kennedy's, Bobby Hutton's, and dozens of others who died at the hands of those who opposed black equality, justice, and liberation.

5. BJ, interview with author, cassette recording, January 18, 2003, Bronx, New York. Tape in possession author.

6. BJ, January 18, 2003, interview.

7. BJ, January 18, 2003, interview.

8. Bobby Seale, interview in Lee Lew Lee, *All Power to the People*, VHS. Produced and directed by Lee Lew Lee (New York: Electronic News Group, 1996). Seale added

that racist whites, most of whom were from the South like the black newcomers to the West Coast, had infested the police department and made it impossible for blacks to live in peace; "How the Black Panthers Lost the FBI's War of Dirty Tricks," 2–6, a pamphlet published by The Friends of Eldridge Cleaver, a loosely knit group of residents (most of whom were rich and white) in the San Francisco Bay Area.

9. Kathleen Cleaver, interview in Henry Hampton, et al., *Voices of Freedom: An Oral History of the Civil Rights Movement from the 1950s Through the 1980s* (New York: Bantam Books, 1990), 514.

10. Huey Newton and Eldridge Cleaver, interviews in Hampton, et al., *Voices of Freedom*, 514–15.

11. Cecil Brown, "The Minister of Information Raps: An Interview with Eldridge Cleaver," *Evergreen* (October 1968), 77–78.

12. Cleaver interview in Hampton et al., *Voices of Freedom;* Emory Douglas, conversation with author, August 30, 2003; Elbert Howard, speech at University of Southern Mississippi, February 10, 2004, Hattiesburg, Mississippi.

13. Richard Jensen, interview in Hampton et al., *Voices of Freedom.*

14. "8 Held in Wake of Panther Shootout," *Oakland Tribune,* April 8, 1968; *San Francisco Chronicle,* May 21, 1968; "Ex-Officer Disputes Police Account of Panther's Slaying," *Los Angeles Times,* April 18, 1971. Pearson claimed that during the shootout the police "were all worked up for various reasons. They were getting ready to do almost anything."; "How the Black Panthers Lost," 5. See also "The Death of Bobby Hutton: different stories," http://sunsite.berkeley.edu/calheritage/panthers/hutton.htm (accessed June 11, 2006).

15. James W. Clarke, *The Lineaments of Wrath: Race, Violent Crime, and American Culture* (New Brunswick, New Jersey: Transaction Publishers, 1988), 243.

16. "How the Black Panthers Lost," 7.

17. "How the Black Panthers Lost," 7; David Wise, *The American Police State: The Government Against the People* (New York: Random House, 1976), 195.

18. Excerpt from Kerner Commission quoted in Jill Nelson, *Police Brutality: An Anthology* (New York: W. W. Norton and Company, 2000), 11.

19. "Let Us Organize to Defend Ourselves," *Black Panther,* April 25, 1967; Hampton, et al., *Voices of Freedom,* 349; Bobby Seale, *Seize the Time: The Story of the Black Panther Party and Huey P. Newton* (Baltimore: Black Classics Press, 1991), 37, 38; Robert Fogelson quote in Walker, "Black Violence and Nonviolence," 227–8; Information on robbing or burning black establishments by accident from Watts riot participant and Los Angeles resident Ronald Freeman. Freeman also noted that most of the deaths in the Watts rebellions can be attributed to stragglers waiting too long to vacate the area or to those who came on the scene too late. He noted that, on several occasions, "we told them to come on let's get out of here, the police are coming. Our snipers had held them off as long as they could in that particular area and were moving on to take up new positions in a different part of the city." Freeman also remembered "an army, not a National Guard, tank," firing on a carload of people who refused to halt when ordered. "They just blew those people up for no reason, their brakes jerked a little and that was all," he remembered. Ronald Freeman, interview with author, Washington, D.C., April 19 and 20, 2002. For a detailed explanation of the political implications of the rebellions, see Joe R. Fagin, *Ghetto Revolts: The Politics of Violence in American Cities* (New York: Macmillan, 1973), Lewis Killian, *The Impossible Revolution: Black Power and the American Dream* (New York: Random House,

Notes to Pages 164–72 377

1968), and Francis Fox-Piven and Richard Cloward, *Poor People's Movements: Why They Succeed, How They Fail* (New York: Vintage Books, 1979).

20. Aaron Dixon, interview with the author, cassette recording, April 20, 2001, Washington, D.C. Tape in possession of author.

21. Dixon, April 20, 2001, interview.

22. Dixon, April 20, 2001, interview.

23. "Hands Off Aaron Dixon, Captain Seattle black Panther Party," pamphlet in SCRL.

24. Dixon, April 20, 2001, interview; "Hands Off Aaron Dixon."

25. Dixon, April 20, 2001, interview.

26. "Hands Off Aaron Dixon," 5–6.

27. "Hands Off Aaron Dixon," 5–6.

28. "Hands Off Aaron Dixon," 5–6.

29. Dixon, April 20, 2001, interview.

30. Dixon, April 20, 2001, interview.; E. Patrick McGuire, *Target for Terrorists—an assortment of bombers zero in on business,* report issued by Conference Board Management Research found in "Black Panther File" in Ronald Reagan Library, Simi Valley, California, (hereafter cited as RRL).

31. Terry Anderson, *The Sixties* (New York: Pearson, 2004), 120.

32. Anderson, *The Sixties,* 121–23.

33. Michael Newton, *Bitter Grain: Huey Newton and the Black Panther Party,* (Los Angeles: Holloway House, 1980), 144.

34. Kathy Mulhern, "Stalking the Panthers," *Commonweal* (October 11, 1968): 61.

35. Henry Weinstein, "Conversation With Eldridge Cleaver," *The Nation,* January 20, 1969, 75.

36. "How the Black Panthers Lost," 7.

37. Mary Ellen Leary, "The Uproar Over Cleaver," *The New Republic;* "Cleaver," report to governor, August 22, 1969, in RRL; Douglas, June 28, 2001, interview.

38. Leary, "The Uproar Over Cleaver"; "Cleaver," report to governor, August 22, 1969.

39. "Cleaver," report to governor, August 9, 1968, in RRL. The following year, in January 1969, San Francisco State University students, who had started the first Black Studies Program in the country, shut the university down with protests. They had been incensed at the firing of George Murray, at the time a graduate student who taught English and served as Panther minister of education. The students, under the leadership of the BSU, which had Danny Glover (later to be a famous actor of *Roots* and *Lethal Weapon* fame) as its rally committee chairman, also demanded more black student enrollment; a School of Ethnic Studies; that Dr. Nathan Hare, chair of the Black Studies Department, receive a full professorship; an independent Black Studies Department controlled by black students and professors; and a half dozen other things. The student strike, with thousands on and off campus participating, succeeded. See "San Francisco State BSU Demands," *Black Panther,* January 25, 1969, 10.

40. Eldridge Cleaver, "Education and Revolution," undated speech found in Alden Kimbrough Collection.

41. Michael Fallon, "Risk U.S. Anarchy, Cleaver Shouts," *Sacramento Union,* October 3, 1968.

42. "How the Black Panthers Lost," 7.

43. United States Congress, House Committee on Internal Security, Hearings on the Black Panther Party, *Gun-Barrel Politics: The Black Panther Party, 1966-1971,* 92nd Cong., 1st sess. (Washington, D.C.: United States Government Printing Office, 1971), 52.

44. "How the Black Panthers Lost," 1–2.

45. "How the Black Panthers Lost," 2.

46. "How the Black Panthers Lost," 3.

Chapter Six: Unjustifiable Homicides

1. United States Senate, *Final Report of the Select Committee to Study Governmental Operations With Respect to Intelligence Activities,* Books I–III, (Washington, D.C.: United States Government Printing Office, 1976), 197, (hereafter cited as *Final Report*); Frank Donner, *The Age of Surveillance: The Aims and Methods of America's Political Intelligence System* (New York: Vintage Books, 1981), 224; Fred Hampton and Ramsey Clark quoted in Lee Lew Lee, *All Power to the People: The Black Panther Party and Beyond,* VHS. Produced and directed by Lee Lew Lee (New York: Electronic News Group, 1996).

2. *Final Report,* 197; Donner, *The Age of Surveillance,* 224; Ramsey Clark quoted in Lee Lew Lee, *All Power to the People;* The June 25, 1969, issue of the *Washington Post* reported that raids on Panther offices under false pretenses, where Panthers were arrested then released for lack of evidence, "[had] become almost routine in the past few months." It further noted that this "police activity. . . has also nearly stripped several of the organization's chapters of their leadership." See also Ronald Koziol, "Bobby Rush Acting Chief of Panthers: Succeeds Slain Hampton," *Chicago Tribune,* December 11, 1969.

3. Huey P. Newton, *War Against the Panthers: A Study of Repression in America* (New York: Harlem River Press, 1996), 75–76.

4. Roy Wilkins and Ramsey Clark, *Search and Destroy: A Report by the Commission of Inquiry into the Black Panthers and the Police* (New York: Metropolitan Applied Research Center, 1973), 3–4; Trial transcripts quoted in Ward Churchill and Jim Vander Wall, *Agents of Repression: The FBI's Secret Wars Against the Black Panther Party and the American Indian Movement* (Boston: South End Press,1990), 72–73, 398; Dennis D. Fisher, "'Panther Raid Success' — Agent," *Chicago Sun Times,* April 30, 1976. See also Thomas J. Dolan, "Charge FBI 'Plot' to Risk Police Lives," *Chicago Sun Times,* January 17, 1967, and Dennis D. Fisher, "FBI Memo on Panthers Bared," *Chicago Sun Times,* February 28, 1976. Churchill and Vander Wall also noted the following concerning "Gloves" Davis: he "was notorious in Chicago for his wanton brutality, mostly directed against blacks. . . . His personal record . . . contained upwards of 60 disciplinary actions," most of which "involved similar sorts of physical assault." To be fair, the "more arrests, tickets, and general abuse" black officers directed toward other blacks, the more they were "rewarded with promotions, more money, and a reputation for being bad," noted one Chicago policemen in an interview with a reporter for the *Chicago Defender.* There were, however, eight hundred black Chicago policemen who joined the Afro-American Patrolmen's League, an organization set up to fight against police abuse and murder of blacks in the Windy City. Description of the raid was also taken from Leo Harris and Jerry Wade (former Chicago Panthers), interview with the author, Chicago, Illinois, May 25, 1995; and Kenneth O'Reilly, *"Racial Matters": The FBI's Secret File on Black America, 1960–1972* (New York: The Free Press, 1989), 312. After the murders, defense

minister Bobby Rush, now Democratic state representative for Illinois, took the reins of leadership. See Ronald Koziol, "Bobby Rush Acting Chief of Panthers: Succeeds Slain Hampton," *Chicago Tribune*, December 11, 1969.

5. Seth S. King, "Police in Chicago Demote Three Involved in Panther Raid Inquiry," *New York Times*, May 16, 1970.

6. FBI memo from Director to SAC Albany, New York, in series 1, box 3, folder 7 in Huey P. Newton Foundation Records Special Collections, Green Library, Stanford University, Palo Alto, California (hereafter referred to as HPN Foundation Records).

7. Mumia Abu-Jamal, interview with Lee Lew Lee in *All Power to the People*.

8. Lee Lew Lee, *All Power to the People*. See also Brian Glick, *War at Home: Covert Action Against U.S. Activists and What We Can Do About It* (Cambridge, MA: South End Press, 1989) and Huey P. Newton, *The War Against the Panthers: A Study of Repression in America* (Baltimore: Black Classic Press, 1995).

9. Don Terry, "Los Angeles Confronts a Bitter Racial Legacy in a Black Panther Case," *New York Times*, July 20, 1997.

10. Memorandum from G. C. Moore to W. C. Sullivan quoted in *Final Report*, 187.

11. Ridgely Hunt, "The People vs. The Police," *Chicago Tribune*, September 7, 1969.

12. Hunt, "The People vs. The Police."

13. Hunt, "The People vs. The Police."

14. Hunt, "The People vs. The Police."

15. Renault Robinson, "Racist Power Is Black's Downfall," Facts on Film clipping file of *Chicago Defender*, n.d. Located in Cook Memorial Library, University of Southern Mississippi, Hattiesburg, Mississippi.

16. Bobby Rush, interview in Henry Hampton et al., *Voices of Freedom: An Oral History of the Civil Rights Movement from the 1950s Through the 1980s* (New York: Bantam Books, 1990), 520; Jon Rice, "The World of the Illinois Panthers," in Jeanne Theoharris and Komozi Woodard, eds., *Freedom North: Black Freedom Struggles Outside the South, 1940–1980* (New York: Palgrave Macmillan, 2003), 50.

17. Hampton et. al., *Voices of Freedom*, 521.

18. Rice, "The World of the Illinois Panthers," 50–51.

19. Bud and Ruth Shultz, *Price of Dissent: Testimonies of Political Repression in America* (Berkeley: University of California Press, 2001), 238; O'Reilly, "*Racial Matters*," 311.

20. Rice, "The World of the Illinois Panthers," 50.

21. William Braden, "The Illinois Black Panthers: Leader Talks About his Aims," *Chicago Sun Times*, May 25, 1969.

22. Joseph Boyce, "Gang Again Charges Brutality," *Chicago Tribune* August 28, 1969.

23. See Nicholas Lemann, *The Promised Land: The Great Migration and How it Changed America* (New York: Vintage Books, 1992), 246–48.

24. Lemann, *The Promised Land*, 248.

25. *Final Report*, 195–96. The Chicago Gang Intelligence Unit also worked to prevent a merger between the Rangers and the Black Disciples, another Chicago street gang. Michael Shane, a spokesman for the Disciples, during a hearing protesting widespread police brutality and the fact that nothing has been done after years of complaints, noted that Mayor Richard Daley "wanted to keep the two gangs apart so that state's attorney Edward Hanrahan can become mayor."

26. Wilkins and Clark, *Search and Destroy*, 18–19; Rice, "World of the Illinois Panthers," 54–5; Boyce, "Gang Again Charges Brutality."

27. Wilkins and Clark, *Search and Destroy*, 18–19.

28. Wilkins and Clark, *Search and Destroy*, 18–19.

29. Wilkins and Clark, *Search and Destroy*, 19–22; Boyce "Police Brutality."

30. Wilkins and Clark, *Search and Destroy*, 22–26.

31. *Final Report*, 195–96.

32. Churchill and Vander Wall, *Agents*, 66; David Hilliard and Lewis Cole, *This Side of Glory: The Autobiography of David Hilliard and the Story of the Black Panther Party* (Boston: Little, Brown & Co., 1993), 221.

33. *Final Report*, 197. Hampton also formed the now famous Rainbow Coalition in Chicago by making alliances with whites, Asians, and Puerto Ricans. See also "Minority Coalition Linked to Panthers Sought Here," *St. Louis Post-Dispatch*, February 5, 1970.

34. *Final Report*, 197.

35. *Final Report*, 197.

36. Donner, *The Age of Surveillance*, 227.

37. Wilkins and Clark, "Search and Destroy," 26.

38. Donner, *The Age of Surveillance*, 224.

39. Donner, *The Age of Surveillance*, 224.

40. See Earl Caldwell, "Declining Panthers Gather New Support," *New York Times*, December 14, 1969.

41. Churchill and Vander Wall, *Agents*, 65–66.

42. Hampton, et al., *Voices of Freedom*, 522, 524.

43. Hampton, et al., *Voices of Freedom*, 68.

44. Hampton, et al., *Voices of Freedom*, 227.

45. O'Reilly, *"Racial Matters,"* 310; May 1969 memo quoted in Donner, *The Age of Surveillance*, 225; Churchill and Vander Wall, *Agents*, 400. Clearly the federal government did not want blacks controlling their own communities.

46. For popularity of BPP Free Breakfast program, see Leroy Aarons and Robert C. Maynard, "Panther Leadership Hurt By Sweeping FBI Raids," *Washington Post*, June 25, 1969.

47. Churchill and Vander Wall, *Agents*, 68; Shultz, *Price of Dissent*, 240; The free breakfast programs also fed adults in the community, which meant the Panthers were not confined to communicating their ideas solely to children.

48. Rob Warden, "Explosives Offer to Panthers Told," *Chicago Daily News*, July 2, 1976.

49. Schultz, *Price of Dissent*, 218.

50. *Chicago Daily Defender*, July 21, 1976; Churchill and Vander Wall, *Agents*, 67.

51. Wilkins and Clark, *Search and Destroy*, 26–7.

52. Wilkins and Clark, *Search and Destroy*, 27.

53. Wilkins and Clark, *Search and Destroy*, 27.

54. *Gun-Barrel Politics*, 115–16; "Chicago Policeman, Panther Associate Killed in Shootout," *Washington Post*, November 14, 1969.

55. William O'Neal, interview in Hampton et al., *Voices of Freedom*, 532.

56. Churchill and Vander Wall, *Agents*, 70–71; Donner, *Age of Surveillance*, 225; *Chicago Sun Times*, November 15, 1969. Hampton had also gone to jail after having been convicted of robbing an ice cream truck of seventy-one dollars worth of ice cream. He allegedly kept the driver from stopping children who took merchandise

from his truck. See "Long Live Deputy Chairman Fred," *Black Panther,* July 5, 1969. In addition to this police officer refusing to cooperate, the mayor of Seattle, Washington, also spurned FBI overtures to make an illegal raid on the party's headquarters in that city.

57. Churchill and Vander Wall, *Agents,* 70, 401; Chip Berlet, "Panthers Demand Pell Recused in Hampton," *Chicago Lawyer,* November, 1979; Christy Macy and Susan Kaplan, *Documents* (New York: Penguin Group, 1980), 188.

58. Churchill and Vander Wall, *Agents,* 70, 401.

59. Macy and Kaplan, *Documents,* 189.

60. Macy and Kaplan, *Documents,* 189.

61. Wilkins and Clark, *Search and Destroy,* 5.

62. Wilkins and Clark, *Search and Destroy,* 5.

63. Wilkins and Clark, *Search and Destroy,* 5; Deborah Johnson, interview in Hampton et al., *Voices of Freedom,* 533.

64. Churchill and Vander Wall, *Agents,* 70.

65. Nicholas Lemann, *The Promised Land: The Great Black Migration and How it Changed America* (New York: A. A. Knopf, 1991), 271–72.

66. Wilkins and Clark, *Search and Destroy,* 37–8, 159–77.

67. Wilkins and Clark, *Search and Destroy,* 139–40; Johnson interview in Hampton et al., *Voices of Freedom,* 534.

68. *Search and Destroy,* 140–42.

69. Johnson interview in Hampton et al., *Voices of Freedom,* 534.

70. Wilkins and Clark, *Search and Destroy,* 144, 155, 157.

71. Wilkins and Clark, *Search and Destroy,* viii–ix.

72. Wilkins and Clark, *Search and Destroy,* x.

73. *Final Report,* 223.

74. Frank Donner, *Protectors of Privilege: Red Squads and Police Repression in Urban America* (Berkeley: University of California Press, 1992), 229.

75. Churchill and Vander Wall, *Agents,* 73–76.

76. Churchill and Vander Wall, *Agents,* 73–76; "Panther Tried," *New Times,* February 18, 1977, newspaper clipping in SCRC. See Robert McClory, "Black Watergate: Did FBI 'arrange' Panther Murders?," *Pittsburgh Courier,* December 29, 1973.

77. "The Police and the Black Panthers," *Washington Post,* May 25, 1970.

78. Federal Grand Jury report quoted in Churchill and Wall, *Agents,* 75–76, "Excerpts from Grand Jury's Report on Chicago Police Raid on Black Panthers," *New York Times,* May 16, 1970. There were however, "three high ranking Chicago police officers" who were demoted because of their involvement in the raid. See Seth S. King, "Police in Chicago Demote Three Involved in Panther Raid Inquiry," *New York Times,* May 16, 1970.

79. McClory, "Black Watergate."

80. William J. Eaton, "Charge FBI Informer Was 'Hit Man'," *Chicago Daily News,* December 3, 1975; Berlet, "Panthers Demand." See also Churchill and Vander Wall, *Agents,* 75–76.

81. Churchill and Vander Wall, 76–77.

82. Michael Newton, *Bitter Grain: Huey Newton and the Black Panther Party* (Los Angeles: Holloway House, 1991) 151–53; Churchill and Wall, *Agents,* 76–77.

83. "5 Chicagoans Charged in Police Death," *Washington Post* June 20, 1970;

United States Congress, House Committee on Internal Security, Hearings on the Black Panther Party, *Gun-Barrel Politics: The Black Panther Party, 1966–1971*, 92nd Cong., 1st sess. (Washington, D.C.: United States Government Printing Office, 1971), 117 (hereafter cited as *Gun-Barrel Politics*); Wilkins and Clark, *Search and Destroy*, 27.

84. Churchill and Vander Wall, *Agents*, 77. For a complete account of the Chicago raid, see The Citizens Research and Investigation Committee and Louis E. Tackwood, *The Story of an Agent Provocateur and the New Police-Intelligence Complex* (New York: Avon Books, 1977). See also *Final Report*, 968.

85. O'Reilly, *"Racial Matters,"* 324.

86. Church League of America, *SPECIAL REPORT: Discussion and Death—US Style,"* April 6, 1969, 5. Located in "Black Panther" file, Special Collections, University of California Los Angeles, Los Angeles, California.

87. Church League, *SPECIAL REPORT*, 6.

88. Church League, *SPECIAL REPORT*, 1.

89. Elaine Brown, conversation with the author, April 12, 2001, Washington, D.C. Some Panther members, who prefer to remain anonymous, argued that Elaine Brown instigated a dispute with the Simbas to help facilitate this tense situation. This contention has not been substantiated.

90. Brown, April 12, 2001, interview.

91. Clearly, this version of events does not represent the entire story. On at least two occasions prior to the student meeting, Carter and Huggins had met with Ron Karenga and other US leaders in an attempt to reduce tension between the two groups. Carter had informed the Oakland headquarters that the Southern California branch of the Party had no "beef" with US and that the situation that spawned from turf battles and competition for members had been settled amicably. Ron Karenga also insists that the tension between the two organizations had been resolved and that the FBI, which constantly monitored and harassed both groups, had to have masterminded the murders. For a similar version of these events from the US perspective, see Scot Brown, *Fighting for US: Maulana Karenga, the US Organization, and Cultural Nationalism* (New York: New York University Press, 2003).

92. Brown, April 12, 2001, interview; *Final Report*, 190; Anonymous Panther, interview with Lee Lew Lee in *All Power to the People*; Elaine Brown, *A Taste of Power: A Black Woman's Story* (New York: Pantheon Books, 1992), 169–77; Michael Newton, *Bitter Grain*, 95–96.

93. Church League, *SPECIAL REPORT*, 2. In interviews with people who witnessed the shootout and confrontation, in which some insist Bunchy jumped Tawala, the US member who grabbed Brown's coat, the author discovered that every person interviewed believed the Stiners had been used as scapegoats to cover the tracks of an FBI operative who committed the murders. Of course, all these interviewees have refused to name the individuals allegedly involved.

94. *Final Report*, 189.

95. *Final Report*, 193; Churchill and Vander Wall, *Agents*, 43. The cartoons reproduced in this book were obtained from the FBI through Freedom of Information Act requests and are located in the HPN Foundation records.

96. Edward J. Epstein, "The Black Panthers and the Police: A Pattern of Genocide?" *New Yorker*, February 13, 1971, http://www.edwardjayepstein.com/archived/panthers_print.htm (accessed October 20, 2004).

97. Churchill and Vander Wall, *Agents*, 42.

98. *Final Report,* 191; Douglas, June 28, 2001, interview.

99. *Final Report,* 191.

100. *Final Report,* 193–94. Both US and the BPP attracted considerable support in the black communities where they operated. Having worked together on a number of different issues and occasions, the two groups should have analyzed more closely why they experienced so much strife.

101. *Final Report,* 193–94.

102. *Final Report,* 221.

103. *Final Report,* 221.

104. Geronimo Pratt, "Political Prisoners," lecture given at Anderson United Methodist Church, Jackson, Mississippi, February 21, 1998, copy in possession of author.

105. Douglas, June 28, 2001, interview.

106. Douglas, interview.

107. Churchill and Vander Wall, *Agents,* 79.

108. Memo from FBI headquarters to all SAC's, December 23, 1970, *Final Report,* 530–31.

109. Churchill and Vander Wall, *Agents,* 79.

110. Churchill and Vander Wall, *Agents,* 81. The authors noted that Diggs was Butler's immediate superior in the party and might have figured out the agent's true identity "and could have easily suffered his execution style fate as a result." Still, no one has been prosecuted for Diggs's murder.

111. Geronimo Pratt, "L.A. Shootout Before and After," in Revolutionary Peoples Communications Network, *Humanity, Freedom, and Peace* (Los Angeles: Revolutionary Peoples Communication Network, n.d.), 4.

112. Hilliard, *This Side of Glory,* 299–300. Malik Rahim of the New Orleans chapter explained that "Chuckie," the guy from New York who helped set up the Panther chapter in the Crescent City, was one of these fugitives.

113. Geronimo Pratt interview in *Humanity, Freedom, and Peace,* 8; Anonymous Panther, interview with Lee Lew Lee in *All Power to the People.*

114. "Interview with L.A. P.O.W.'s," in *Humanity, Freedom, and Peace,* 8–10. In his autobiography, David Hilliard claims that he and Pratt came up with the idea that "members in trouble with the law" could be "put on ice" down south, since no white person in Rockville or Jackson would ever notice them. He added that in the meantime, the members "could hone their military skills" in relative obscurity. See Hilliard, *This Side of Glory,* 299.

115. "Interview with L.A. P.O.W.'s," 10.

116. Don Terry, "Los Angeles Confronts Bitter Racial Legacy in a Black Panther Case," *New York Times,* July 20, 1997.

117. Douglas, June 28, 2001, interview; Cleaver, interview in *All Power to the People; Los Angeles Times,* July 20, 1997.

118. Terry, "Los Angeles Confronts." Butler was the pastor of the very influential First African Methodist Episcopal Church in Los Angeles.

119. United States Senate, Select Committee to Study Government Operations with Respect to Intelligence Activities, *Huston Plan,* 94th Cong., 1st sess. (Washington, D.C.: United States Government Printing Office, 1976).

120. *Huston Plan.*

121. *Final Report,* 188.

122. *Final Report,* 188; Summary of a report entitled "The FBI's Covert Action Program to Destroy the Black Panther Party," in Southern California Research Center, Los Angeles, California.

123. Letter from J. Edgar Hoover to William Sullivan in *Final Report,* 942.

Chapter Seven: Southern Discomfort

1. Memo from Black Panther Party National Headquarters (ministry of information) to all chapters and branches of the BPP concerning the distinction between Black Panther Party Community Information Centers and NCCF centers of operation, in Federal Bureau of Investigation, *Black Panther Party Activities in North Carolina,* n.d., 142a, microfilm, Department of Special Collections, University of Wisconsin, Madison (hereafter cited as North Carolina microfilm).

2. United States Senate, Final Report of the Select Committee to Study Governmental Operations With Respect to Intelligence Activities, Books I–III, (Washington, D.C.: United States Government Printing Office, 1976), 56, 89, 97, (hereafter cited as *Final Report*); Charles "Cappy" Pinderhughes, interview with the author, November 3, 1996, Baltimore, Maryland. Another reason the group might have used this tactic was because individuals and groups claiming to be Panthers throughout the United States committed a number of senseless crimes (from robbery and extortion to rape and murder) in the name of revolution and the BPP. The party's leadership therefore resorted to a purge. The purge officially began in January 1969 and the party did not take in members for three months. About one thousand members were expelled and many local chapters were disbanded. Senate investigators also claimed that the Panthers used "The People's Community Information Center" and "The Sons of Malcolm" as front names for the party, as Emory Douglas did in an interview with the author. Emory Douglas, interview with the author, cassette recording, May 25, 1995, San Francisco, California. Tape in possession of author.

3. For excellent examples of violence directed against blacks in the South, see Neil R. McMillen, *Dark Journey: Black Mississippians in the Age of Jim Crow* (Urbana and Chicago: University of Illinois Press, 1989); Geroge C. Rable's *But There Was No Peace: The Role of Violence in the Politics of Reconstruction* (Athens: University of Georgia Press, 1984); and Herbert Shapiro's *White Violence, Black Response: From Reconstruction to Montgomery* (Amherst: University of Massachusetts Press, 1988). There were also instances of violence between the two groups in the other southern cities but space does not allow for all those stories. See "Partial List of Local Affiliates of the Black Panther Party, Active and Inactive" in *Final Report,* 88–89. There were BPP chapters and/or affiliates in all the southern states, except South Carolina and Arkansas. See list of BPP chapters and affiliates in Appendix C.

4. United States Senate, Hearings Before the Subcommittee to Investigate the Administration of the Internal Security Act and other Internal Security Laws of the Committee on the Judiciary, *Assaults on Law Enforcement Officers,* 91st Cong., 2nd sess. (Washington, D.C.: United States Government Printing Office, 1970), 96–98 (hereafter cited as *Assaults*); United States, Bureau of the Census, *New Orleans Public Attitudes About Crime* (Washington: Department of Justice, Law Enforcement Assistance Administration, National Criminal Justice Information and Statistics: United States Government Printing Office, 1980).

5. *Assaults,* 100.

6. Geronimo Pratt, "Political Prisoners," lecture given at Anderson United Methodist Church, Jackson, Mississippi, February 21, 1998, copy in possession of author (hereafter cited as lecture); Emory Douglas, interview with the author, cassette recording, August 10, 1997, Oakland, California. Tape in possession of author.

7. *Assaults,* 100–101; Newspaper clipping of a *New York Times* article, no title, no date, found in *Facts on Film* archive at Cook Memorial Library, University of Southern Mississippi.

8. Malik Rahim, interview with author, cassette recording, August 8, 2002, New Orleans, Louisiana. Tape in possession of the author.

9. *Assaults,* 101.

10. *Assaults,* 102, emphasis in original.

11. *Assaults,* 102, Douglas, August 10, 1997, interview.

12. Rahim, August 8, 2002, interview.

13. Don Hughes, "Two Badly Beaten Spies Recall Horrors of Panther Justice," New Orleans *Times-Picayune,* September 19, 1970. At the press conference on which the story was based, Fields's right wrist and both hands were bandaged as a result of chipped bones. His eye appeared red and swollen and his ear had the markings of the nail that had penetrated it and plunged into his neck. Because of his shaven head, reporters could also see more nail holes. Howard's afro concealed signs of his head having been beaten with a .357 magnum.

14. *Assaults,* 108.

15. "11 Are Shot; 16 Arrested: Police, Black Panthers Clash Anew Near Project Tuesday Night," *New Orleans Times Picayune,* September 16, 1970. According to the paper, "many people left the area in an exodus remindful of wartime refugees. Some people carried duffle bags and suitcases packed with belongings. Police, however, limited what they could carry to small items only."

16. "11 Are Shot." See also "Reign of Terror Hits New Orleans," *Jackson Daily News,* September 15, 1970.

17. Rahim, August 8, 2002, interview; "11 Are Shot." On at least two occasions, hundreds, if not thousands of Desire project residents used their bodies as human shields to prevent the authorities from storming the BPP headquarters. Only after police had begun to work with local priests from Tulane University were they able to penetrate Panther defenses. Ingeniously, the police dressed as priests, thereby making it possible for them to walk through the projects unmolested. Upon reaching the door of the Panther office, they were immediately detected by a female Panther who screamed "pigs" when she noticed a shotgun protruding from the one of the officer's coats. This incident brought about the last shootout between these combatants.

18. "11 Are Shot." A similar situation occurred in Detroit when members of the NCCF in that city allegedly shot and killed a policeman from the top floor of its headquarters. Community residents threw rocks and bottles and destroyed four parked police cars with Molotov cocktails. Like in New Orleans, firemen who came to the scene were also "driven away by rocks and other missiles hurled from the crowd," according to one reporter. Only after the police brought in their armored car "and fired teargas projectiles into the house" did the three Panthers inside surrender. See Roy Courtade, "Seeking Killer of Ambushed Comrade: Angry Cops Hold Fire in Black Panther Siege," *National Observer,* November 2, 1970.

19. Paul Delaney, "New Orleans Blacks Say They Shelter a Wounded Panther," *New York Times,* September 20, 1970. Because of the extreme hatred of the police in the Desire Project area, ostensibly created by Panther agitation, this same article noted that "the police stopped nighttime patrols inside the 12-block housing project, patrolling only the periphery."

20. "11 Are Shot." When the Panthers made it to central lockup, or the New Orleans Parish Prison, they continued their organizing even though harassment, mistreatment, and beatings by prison guards were common. They succeeded in attracting dozens of new recruits, one of whom was New Orleans native Robert "King" Wilkerson, the now famous member of the Angola 3, who was released in 2000 after nearly thirty years in Angola, the country's largest and arguably most brutal state penitentiary. Wilkerson and others eventually formed a Panther chapter in Angola. Currently, 85 percent of the people who are sent there die. There they endured harassment, beatings, legal chicanery, and all manner of torture at the hands of guards and their inmate minions. Wilkerson, Albert Woodfox, and Herman Wallace refused to cop pleas or cease demanding their rights, so they have spent nearly three decades in solitary confinement on this 18,000-acre farm named for the Africans who once worked its land as slaves. Woodfox and Wallace remain incarcerated, while an indefatigable Wilkerson crisscrosses the planet giving speeches to raise money for the two he left behind. See "Lockdown at Angola: A History of the Angola 3 Case," http://www.angola3.org/ accessed October 11, 2002.

21. Don Hughes and Danny Thomas, "Truce Ends Tense Day," New Orleans *Times Picayune,* November 20, 1970. See also, "Black militants refuse to give up building they took over," *Birmingham News,* November 19, 1970.

22. *Assaults,* 127, 128.

23. *Assaults,* 128.

24. *Assaults,* 128.

25. *Assaults,* 129; Hughes, "Two Badly Beaten Spies"; Althea Francois, interview with the author, August 10, 2002, New Orleans, Louisiana. The arrests began when officers set up a roadblock at I-10 and Paris Road. They stopped four cars containing nineteen Panthers after they learned the cars "had been rented on Tuesday by actress-turned-activist Jane Fonda who was in the city for a speaking engagement and a show of support for the Black Panthers," said New Orleans Police Superintendent Clarence Giarrusso. The night after the shooting, the police fired on four men they believed were attempting to firebomb the grocery store where one of the spies hid. Three were shot and sent to the hospital while another, twenty-one-year-old Kenneth Borden, lay in the street for more than two hours dying of a gunshot wound to the head. The police claimed not to be able to reach him because of the heavy sniper fire from the militants. According to the September 16, 1970, issue of the *Jackson* [Miss.] *Daily News,* the "police waited for an armored car so he could be moved without officers being exposed to possible sniper fire." See Donald Hughes article in New Orleans *Times-Picayune,* November 27, 1970, and Jack Wardlaw, "Two Die as Police-Panther Wars Erupt Again," *National Observer,* September 21, 1970. The imprisoned Panthers continued to organize in the Orleans Parish Prison, where they were held for a year. They ended the rape of male prisoners by other male prisoners. Inmates sent by the warden to kill Panther leaders were transformed into revolutionaries. As a result of a hunger strike and the Panthers' refusal to go to court because of the terrible prison conditions, the Orleans Parish

Prison was torn down and rebuilt. The jailed Panthers won their case a year later, returned to their offices, and continued organizing the people.

26. "From the Program: Survival Programs of the Black Panther Party," *The Black Panther: Black Community News Service* 1 (Spring 1991): 20–21; Bill Keller, "Breakfast, Clinic Programs Belie Militant Panther Image," *Oakland Tribune*, November 12, 1971; Eldridge Cleaver, "On Meeting the Needs of the People," *Ramparts* September 8, 1969, 34–35.

27. Marsha (no last name given), "Serving the People," *Black Panther*, April 6, 1969.

28. See Paul Wolf et. al., "COINTELPRO: The Untold American Story," http://www.thirdworldtraveler.com/FBI/COINTELPRO_Untold_Story.html (accessed June 13, 2006); Huey Newton quote in HPN Foundation Records, series 1, box 2, folder 16; Douglas, August 10, 1997, interview; David Hilliard, *This Side of Glory* (Boston: Little, Brown, and Company), 258; Edward J. Epstein, "A Reporter at Large: The Panthers and the Police: A Pattern of Genocide?," *New Yorker*, February 13, 1971, 61–62.

29. Frank Donner, *Age of Surveillance: Aims and Methods of America's Political Intelligence System* (New York: Vintage Books, 1981), 225.

30. Elaine Brown, *A Taste of Power: A Black Woman's Story* (New York: Pantheon, 1993), 157; Earl Caldwell, "Black Panthers Serving Youngsters a Diet of Food and Politics," *New York Times*, June 15, 1969. See also Ward Churchill and Jim Vander Wall, *Agents of Repression: The FBI's Secret Wars Against the Black Panther Party and the American Indian Movement* (Boston: South End Press, 1990), 37–99.

31. "Interview with Ericka Huggins, Director: Oakland Community School Offers Quality Model in School Education," *Black Panther*, September 29, 1975.

32. "Interview with Ericka Huggins."

33. Philip S. Foner, ed., *The Black Panthers Speak* (Philadelphia: Lippincott, 1970), 127; G. Louis Heath, ed., *Off the Pigs: The History and Literature of the Black Panther Party* (Metuchen, NJ: Scarecrow Press, 1976), 98–100.

34. Dr. Paul B. Cornely, "Panthers Work for Health Through Free Care Clinics," *Baltimore Afro-American*, May 9, 1970; Hilliard, *This Side of Glory*, 259.

35. Huey P. Newton, "Black Capitalism Re-Analyzed I: June 5, 1971," in David Hilliard and Donald Weise, eds., *The Huey P. Newton Reader* (New York: Seven Stories Press, 2002), 230; "From the Program," 20.

36. Douglas, August 10, 1997, interview; "Free People's Medical Clinic Model in Community Health Care," *Black Panther*, February 7, 1976. For an analysis of how the mainstream media portrayed the BPP, see D. P. Williams, III, "The Contribution of Selectively Focused Print Coverage to the Negative Stereotyping of A Challenging Group" (Ph.D. diss., Arizona State University, 1987). Dr. Mutulu Shakur, interview with Lee Lew Lee in *All Power to the People*, VHS. Produced and directed by Lee Lew Lee (New York: Electronic News Group, 1996).

37. "From the Program," 20; Hilliard, *This Side of Glory*, 339.

38. For an in-depth analysis of ghetto conditions, see William J. Wilson, *The Truly Disadvantaged: The Inner City, the Underclass, and Public Policy* (Chicago: University of Chicago Press, 1987) and Charles Murray, *Losing Ground: American Social Policy, 1950–1980* (New York: Basic Books, 1984).

39. Lincoln Webster Sheffield, "People's Medical Care Center," *Daily World*, May 16, 1970; Information about ambulance services from Douglas, August 10, 1997,

interview; material on success of clinics from Martin Kenner, interview by author, tape recording, March 20, 1996, New York City, New York.

40. FBI memo from Headquarters to Charlotte Division, March 2, 1969, North Carolina microfilm, 60. The Panthers were joined in their radical activities by campus groups like the Weathermen and Students Against Fascism. See Robert A. Jordan, "Panthers, SDS Group Unite," *Boston Globe*, December 7, 1969.

41. FBI memo from Director to SAC, Charlotte, February 17, 1969, North Carolina microfilm, n.p.

42. Pratt, lecture.

43. FBI memo from Headquarters to the Special Agent in Charge (SAC) in Charlotte, March 22, 1969, *North Carolina* microfilm, 60, 61. The memo noted that Deputy Minister of Education Bob Collier sent Avant to North Carolina to organize the A&T campus January 5–15, 1969.

44. FBI teletype from SAC, Charlotte, to the Director of the Domestic Intelligence Division, February 10, 1971, North Carolina microfilm, n.p.

45. Ibid. After learning that the police confiscated a 12-gauge pump shotgun, an M-1 rifle, a 30-30 rifle with a telescopic sight, and a large quantity of ammunition, the court held "the High Point 4" on a fifty thousand dollar bond each. Douglas, August 10, 1997, interview; Pratt, lecture.

46. See John E. Moore, "People of the Community vs. The Slumlords and Fascist Pigs of Winston-Salem," *Black Panther*, March 28, 1970. This issue of the *Black Panther* carries several pages of in-depth articles on the North Carolina branch of the BPP. FBI airtel from Director to SAC, Charlotte, May 13, 1970, North Carolina microfilm, 10, 36, 41.

47. FBI airtel, 41; Charles McEwen, "'This is a White Man's World and I'm Black,'" *Winston-Salem Sentinel*, February 27, 1973.

48. FBI memo from SAC, Charlotte to Mr. W. C. Sullivan, September 29, 1969, in North Carolina microfilm, 3.

49. Information on convention in North Carolina microfilm, 4. The conference convened on November 28, 1970, at the All Saints Unitarian Church, with more than a thousand people (mostly white) attending. New York Panther Michael Tabor did most of the talking. Workshops at the conference ranged from "Means of Production," "Control of the Military," and "Self-Determination for Street People and National Minorities" to "Women's Liberation," "Gay Liberation," "Control of Land," and "Internationalism." The first plenary session of the convention took place at Temple University in Philadelphia on September 5, 1970. The group obviously failed to get its proposed constitution accepted by the majority of American citizens.

50. NCCF press release, November 28, 1970, North Carolina microfilm, n.p.

51. "Panthers Say Police Set Fire," *Winston-Salem Journal*, December 1, 1970.

52. "Panthers Say Police Set Fire."

53. FBI memo from Charlotte to Director captioned "Racial Matters: Smith Act of 1940; Seditious Conspiracy; Rebellion and Insurrection," January 22, 1971, North Carolina microfilm, n.p.

54. North Carolina microfilm "Racial Matters," 66, 67, 114, 115.

55. David DuBuisson, "Police Raid on Panther House Brings Questions," *Winston-Salem Journal*, January 17, 1971, and "Showdown on 23rd Street," January 19, 1971; "Panther Says Police 'Set Up' Theft That Led To Shootout," *Charlotte Observer*,

January 16, 1971, and "Winston Police Fire on Panther Building," *Charlotte Observer*, January 13, 1971. See also Jim Grey, "2 Arrested After Gunfir at House," *Winston-Salem Journal*, January 13, 1971.

Chapter Eight: The the East...and Back

1. Michael Newton, *Bitter Grain: Huey Newton and the Black Panther Party* (Los Angeles: Holloway House, 1991), 173–74; BJ, interview with the author, cassette recording, January 17, 2004, Bronx, New York. This Panther has asked that his given name be withheld and his nickname be used.

2. Cleo Silvers, interview with the author, cassette recording, January 17, 2003, New York City, New York. Tape in possession of author.

3. Silvers, January 17, 2003, interview.

4. Silvers, January 17, 2003, interview.

5. Silvers, January 17, 2003, interview; Bullwhip, interview with author, cassette recording, January 17, 2003, Corona, New York. Tape in possession of author.

6. Cheryl Foster, diary entry "Seize the Time" Schedule. Diary located in "Black Panther Party" folder, Schomburg Center for Research in Black Culture, Harlem, New York. Foster left few dates in her diary, so it is difficult to determine exactly when some of these activities took place.

7. Foster, "Seize the Time" schedule.

8. Michael Newton, *Bitter Grain*, 174–75; Bill Jennings, interview with the author, cassette recording, January 1, 2002, Sacramento, California. Tape in possession of author.

9. Michael Newton, *Bitter Grain*, 176–83.

10. Silvers, January 17, 2003, interview; Thomas McCreary, interview in Lee Lew Lee, *All Power to the People: The Black Panther Party and Beyond*, VHS. Produced and directed by Lee Lew Lee (New York: Electronic News Group, 1996).

11. Thomas McCreary, interview with the author, cassette recording, January 22, 2002, Atlanta, Georgia. Tape in possession of author.

12. McCreary, January 22, 2002, interview; Silvers, January 17, 2003, interview; BJ, January 17, 2004 interview.

13. McCreary, January 22, 2002, interview.

14. "The Black Panther Party and the Case of the New York 21," published by The Committee to Defend the Panther 21, 9–10, n.d. Copy found in Alden Kimbrough Collection, Los Angeles, California.

15. "Case of the New York 21," 9–10.

16. Silvers, January 17, 2003, interview.

17. Bill Jennings, interview with author, cassette recording, January 1, 2002, Sacramento, California. Tape in possession of author.

18. Emory Douglas, interview with the author, cassette recording, June 28, 2001, San Francisco, California. Tape in possession of author; Curt Gentry, *J. Edgar Hoover: The Man and the Secrets* (New York: Penguin Group, 1992), 620; Frank Donner, *The Age of Surveillance: Aims and Methods of America's Political Intelligence System* (New York: Vintage Books, 1981), 226. Taking advantage of this purge, the bureau used membership lists its informants stole "to dispatch letters on forged stationery and over forged signatures to scores of others, telling them they too had been purged."

19. Yohuru Williams, *Black Politics/White Power: Civil Rights, Black Power, and the Black Panthers in New Haven* (St. James, New York: Brandywine Press, 2000), 138.

20. Williams, *Black Politics/White Power*, 140; Elbert Howard, interview with the author, cassette recording, July 19, 2003, Memphis, Tennessee. Tape in possession of author.

21. Williams, *Black Politics/White Power*, 140.

22. Williams, *Black Politics/White Power*, 140.

23. George Edwards, interview with the author, cassette recording, New Haven, Connecticut, August 13, 2003. Tape in possession of author.

24. Edwards, August 13, 2003, interview.

25. Edwards, August 13, 2003, interview.

26. Williams, *Black Politics*, 140–41.

27. Joseph B. Treaster, "Seale in Connecticut for Murder Trial," *New York Times*, March 14, 1970. See also "Black Panther Pleads Guilty in Slaying," *New York Times*, December 2, 1969.

28. Treaster, "Seale in Connecticut"; William Bastone, "The Hillary Clinton Cheat Sheet: A Guide to the Scandals and Issues that Could Stall Her Senate Run," *Village Voice*, June 16, 1999, http://www.villagevoice.com/news/9924,bastone,6495.1.html (accessed May 20, 2006).

29. Brewster quote from an editorial in the *Washington Post*, May 5, 1970, see Suzy Platt, *Respectfully Quoted: A Dictionary of Quotations from the Congressional Research Service* (Washington, D.C.: Library of Congress, 1989) quote 117 (available at http://www.bartebly.com/73/117.html accessed June 25, 2006). Because of the "Ivy League infatuation" surrounding Seale and the Panthers, Yale faculty were "authorized to suspend classes indefinitely" or until the murder trial ended and things cooled down. See also Mark Bailey, "Guide to the Inventory of May Day Records, 1970–1972, 1976, Record Unit 16," http://mssa.library.yale.edu/findaids/stream.php?xmlfile=mssa.ru.0016.xml (accessed June 25, 2006); "Pantheritis," *Chicago Tribune*, May 3, 1970.

30. Treaster, "Seale in Connecticut."

31. "Text of Judge Mulvey's Decision," *New Haven Register* May 26, 1971.

32. McCreary, January 22, 2002, interview.

33. Don Cox, *Just Another Nigger*, (unpublished manuscript, 1981), 76, 139.

34. Cox, *Just Another Nigger*, 141; Bill Jennings, interview with the author, cassette recording, January 1, 2002, Sacramento, California. Tape in possession of author.

Chapter 9: The Rift

1. Emory Douglas, interview with the author, cassette recording, August 30, 2003, San Francisco, California. Tape in possession of author.

2. Mario Van Peebles, et al., *Panther: A Pictorial History of the Black Panthers and the Story Behind the Film* (New York: New Market Press, 1995), 117.

3. Anti-Imperialist Delegation–1970, "Eldridge Cleaver Attempts to Organize a Murder Conspiracy Against David Hilliard, Chief of Staff of the Black Panther Party," n.d., n.p. Copy found in Huey P. Newton Foundation Records, Special Collections, Green Library, Stanford University, Palo Alto, California (hereafter cited as HPN Foundation Records). The author of this report may be Elaine Brown, as it indicates the deputy minister of information as its writer; it also makes mention of songs being sold

for money, something Brown did often to help raise funds for the party. See Elaine Brown, *A Taste of Power: A Black Woman's Story* (New York: Pantheon Books, 1992); and Brian Ward, *Just My Soul Responding: Rhythm and Blues, Black Consciousness, and Race Relations* (Berkeley: University of California Press, 1998), 279, 412–15.

4. Brown, *A Taste of Power,* 322.

5. BJ, interview with the author, cassette recording, January 17, 2004, Bronx, New York. Tape in possession of author; Conversation found in FBI wiretaps of Panther headquarters in HPN Foundation Records.

6. BJ, January 17, 2004, interview; Cleo Silvers, interview with the author, cassette recording, January 17, 2003, New York City, New York. Tape in possession of author.

7. BJ, January 17, 2004, interview.

8. "New York Twenty-one Open Letter to the Weather Underground" found in Alden Kimbrough Collection.

9. Douglas, August 30, 2003, interview; Don Cox, *Just Another Nigger,* (unpublished manuscript, n.p.)

10. Michael Newton, *Bitter Grain: Huey Newton and the Black Panther Party* (Los Angeles: Holloway House, 1980), 206; Huey P. Newton, *War Against the Panthers: A Study of Repression in America* (New York: Writers and Readers Publishing, 1996), 69.

11. Michael Newton, *Bitter Grain,* 206.

12. BJ, January 17, 2004, interview.

13. BJ, January 17, 2004, interview; Thomas McCreary, interview with the author, cassette recording, January 22, 2002, Atlanta, Georgia. Tape in possession of author.

14. BJ, January 17, 2004, interview.

15. BJ, January 17, 2004, interview.

16. Albert A. Seedman and Peter Hellman, *Chief* (New York: Avon Books, 1974), 487. See also Robert K. Tannenbaum and Philip Rosenberg, *Badge of the Assassin* (New York: Pocket Books, 1979).

17. BJ, January 17, 2004, interview.

18. BJ, January 17, 2004, interview.

19. BJ, January 17, 2004, interview; Michael Knight, "Death Here Tied to Panther Feud," *New York Times,* March 10, 1971, 29.

20. BJ, January 17, 2004, interview.

21. BJ, January 17, 2004, interview.

22. BJ, January 17, 2004, interview.

23. BJ, January 17, 2004, interview.

24. BJ, January 17, 2004, interview.

25. BJ, January 17, 2004, interview.

26. BJ, January 17, 2004, interview.

27. "Radicals: Destroying the Panther Myth," *Time* March 22, 1971, 19–20; Martin Kenner, interview with the author, cassette recording, March 20, 1996, New York City, New York. Tape in possession of author. See also John Darnton, "8 Seized on Gun Charges Here After Black Panther is Slain," *New York Times,* April 19, 1971, and Darnton, "7 Panthers Indicted in Slaying of Party Official in Corona," *New York Times,* July 30, 1971; Douglas, June 28, 2001, interview; Brown, *A Taste of Power,* 266. Those arrested on gun charges in a hotel across town after Napier's body was found included Elbert "Big Man" Howard, the group's deputy minister of information and

editor of the *Black Panther,* William Babour, James Young, Allen King, Annette Rogers, Corliss Martin, Lola Wilson, and Betty Schertzer. The police found no evidence that any of the arrested took part in Napier's heinous torture and murder.

28. BJ, January 17, 2004, interview.

29. Huey P. Newton, "On the Defection of Eldridge Cleaver from the Black Panther Party and the Defection of the Black Panther Parth from the Black Community," in David Hilliard and Donald Weise, eds., *The Huey P. Newton Reader* (New York: Seven Stories Press, 2002), 205; Dorothy Healy, interview with Joel Gardner, 1972, 1973, 1974, Los Angeles, California. Tapes in possession of UCLA Special Collections. Copyright 1982 by UCLA Oral History Program, 1054–55.

30. Healy, UCLA interview; Huey Newton, *War Against the Panthers,* 70, 71.

31. Jeannine Yeomans, "Peaceful Panthers Now Vote Threat, Seale Says," *Arkansas Gazette,* September 18, 1972.

32. Brown, *A Taste of Power,* 223.

33. Ross K. Baker, "Panthers Outgrow Their Rhetoric," *The Nation,* July 16, 1973. In 1989, Tyrone Robinson, an Oakland gang member aspiring higher status, shot and killed Newton on an Oakland street. Newton had apparently demanded that Robinson give him free drugs, primarily crack cocaine, on earlier occasions. For a detailed explanation see Hugh Pearson, *Shadow of the Panther: Huey P. Newton and the Price of Black Power in America* (New York: Addison-Wesley Publishing Co., 1994), 311–15.

34. FBI memo from J. Edgar Hoover to the San Francisco field office, September 30, 1968, HPN Foundation Records, series 1 box 3, folder 7.

35. FBI memo, September 30, 1968.

36. Curt Gentry, *J. Edgar Hoover: The Man and the Secrets,* (New York: Penguin Group, 1992), 620.

37. Huey Newton, *War Against the Panthers,* 65–66; Kenneth O'Reilly, *"Racial Matters": The FBI's Secret File on Black America, 1960–1972* (New York: The Free Press, 1989), 319.

38. Huey Newton, *War Against the Panthers,* 66–67.

39. Huey Newton, *War Against the Panthers,* 67–68.

40. Eddie Thibideaux, interview with the author, cassette recording, January 10, 1996, Oakland, California; Hoover also ordered his lieutenants to "be alert to determine evidence of misappropriation of funds on the part of militant nationalist leaders . . . so any practical or warranted counterintelligence may be instituted."

41. Martin Kenner, interview with the author, cassette recording, March 20, 1996, New York City, New York. Tape in possession of author; Douglas, August 30, 2003, interview.

42. Hilliard, *This Side of Glory,* 326.

43. Hilliard, *This Side of Glory,* 70.

44. HPN Foundation Records, series 1, box 2, folder 6; Yeomans, "Peaceful Panthers." In August 1972, Seale's brother John and other Panthers had been elected to "six of 18 seats on a board that helps to allocate $4.9 million a year in anti-poverty funds," according to the *Arkansas Gazette.* Althea Francois, conversation with the author, August 10, 2002, New Orleans, Louisiana; Marion Brown, interview with the author, cassette recording, August 10, 2002, New Orleans, Louisiana. Tape in possession of author.

45. Michael Newton, *Bitter Grain,* 207–8.

46. Jeff Gottlieb and John Stewart, "Black Panthers Launch National Comeback," *Scribe* 5: (5–11) 1977; Emory Douglas, interview with author, cassette recording, San Francisco, California, May 20, 1995. Tape in possession of author.

47. Panther Inspection Checklist found in HPN Foundation Records.

48. Panther Inspection Checklist; Gottlieb and Steward, "National Comeback."

49. Gottlieb and Steward, "National Comeback."

50. Gottlieb and Steward, "National Comeback"; "Communications Central Headquarters, B.P.P.," February, 29, 1972. Report found in HPN Foundation Records.

51. "Individual Evaluations," report found in HPN Foundation Records.

52. Elbert "Big Man" Howard, "Section Financial Report," December 30, 1972. Copy found in HPN Foundation Records.

53. Memo from John de Menil to Grants Committee, Menil Foundation, Inc., November 15, 1972. The John De Menil Foundation gave the party in Houston, Texas, four thousand dollars to operate its breakfast program and the state of California gave the party ninety thousand dollars a year to operate an alternative school for delinquent males under the age of eighteen. Memo from Central Committee, Black Panther Party to Comrade Bob Rush, "RE Expulsion of Michael Rhymes," July 1, 1973. Copy found in HPN Foundation Records

54. George Edwards, interview with the author, cassette recording, August 13, 2003, New Haven, Connecticut. Tape in possession of the author; Elbert Howard, interview with the author, cassette recording, July 19, 2003, Memphis, Tennessee. Tape in possession of author.

55. Jo Nina Abron, "RE: Direction of Party," memo to Huey Newton, October 1, 1980. Copy found in HPN Foundation records.

56. Tommye Williams to Huey Newton, Box 5 folder 1, HPN Foundation Records.

57. Sheba Haven, interview with the author, cassette recording, Sacramento, California, September 3, 2003. Tape in possession of author.

Conclusion

1. David Hilliard and Lewis Cole, *This Side of Glory: The Autobiography of David Hilliard and the Story of the Black Panther Party* (Boston: Little, Brown, & Co., 1993), 284; Herb Boyd, "Power to the People," *Emerge*, 1 February 1993, 40–42.

2. Hilliard and Cole, *This Side of Glory*, 284; Boyd, "Power to the People."

3. William J. Wilson, "Black Demands and American Government Response," *Journal of Black Studies* 3 (September 1972): 24.

4. Sheba Haven, interview with the author, cassette recording, Sacramento, California, September 3, 2003. Tape in possession of author.

5. Haven, September 3, 2003, interview.

6. Haven, September 3, 2003, interview.

7. Henry Winston, *Strategy for a Black Agenda* (New York: International Publishers, 1973), 215.

8. At the BPP thirty-fifth reunion/conference held in Washington, D.C., in 2001, networking and community building strategies were discussed along with the workshops, fellowship, and reunions that go with these events. Some three hundred Panthers, whose attendance attracted the attention of CNN, CSPAN, NBC, CBS, BET, *The Village Voice*, local television stations, and a host of other media outlets,

made the trek from all over the country. As a result of this gathering, in October 2002, the BPP in Oakland, California officially resumed its once-loved community service activities. See http://www.itsabouttimebpp.com/, accessed August 30, 2002.

9. Emory Douglas, interview with the author, cassette recording, August 10, 1997, Oakland, California. Tape in possession of author; Tim Breitman, "Panthers Long Road From Bullets to the Ballot," *San Francisco Examiner,* July 17, 1977; Elaine Brown, *A Taste of Power: A Black Woman's Story* (New York: Pantheon, 1993), 436. See letter from Ezell Ware to Huey Newton, February 1, 1979, and letter from California legislative Black Caucus to Governor Edmund G. Brown, July 26, 1979, Huey P. Newton Foundation Records, series 1, box 2, folder 6, Special Collections, Green Library, Stanford University, Palo Alto, California.

10. Robert Blauner in Stephen Howe, *Afrocentrism: Mythical Pasts and Imagined Homes* (New York: Verso, 1999), 92.

11. See Timothy B. Tyson, "Civil Rights Movement," in William L. Andrews, Frances Smith Foster, and Trudier Harris, eds., *The Oxford Companion to African American Literature* (New York: Oxford University Press, 1997), 147–152.

12. Haven, September 3, 2003, interview.

BIBLIOGRAPHICAL ESSAY

In Panther lore, there are many voices. Among the first of these voices were those who lived in and survived the party and the turbulent times that spawned it. Huey Newton's *Revolutionary Suicide* and *To Die for the People* give readers an up close and personal glimpse into the life and motivations of one of its founders. Cofounder Bobby Seale's *Seize the Time* remains the standard volume on the party's early years and its development into a national phenomenon. Former chairwoman Elaine Brown's controversial *A Taste of Power* uncovers much of the internal violence that permeated the group and also showed how gender dynamics contributed to the party's stifling growth. Eldridge Cleaver's *Post-Prison Writings* give us a glimpse into the mind of this once-respected radical. Chief of staff David Hilliard's *This Side of Glory* is a masterfully written piece of history that pulls the curtain back on the party's radical period and provides a glimpse into the decision-making apparatus that later ensured the party's demise after only sixteen years.

Other rank-and-file members have tried their hand at writing history. Earl Anthony did so as early as 1972, with his *Spitting in the Wind*. Anthony exposed the party's weak underbelly when he wrote about its leaders' shortcomings and criminal proclivities. Bill Brent's *Long Time Gone* and Assata Shakur's *Assata: An Autobiography* provide much-needed insight into the inner workings of the group and individual interpretations of how one grows and evolves in an organization. Both these texts describe how their authors fled to Cuba due to their trouble with the law. Shakur's flight can be viewed as the more noble of the two, as she continues to resist in Cuba today. Fred Hampton's former fiancé Akua Njeri's *My Life With the Black Panther Party* demonstrates that the party swam or sunk based on the rank-and-file's impression of local leaders. All these works provide a view of the party that is otherwise unavailable. Dhoruba Bin Wahad's *Still Black Still Strong* is a piercing view of the movement in the Northeast and its international implications. Most recently, Evans Daryl Hopkins's *Life After Life: A Story of Rage and Redemption*, chronicles the life of a southern black man whose revolutionary dreams often stood at odds with his sobering realities. Hopkins describes his journey from country bumpkin to urban revolutionary to prison inmate to prolific writer. His is a story of trial and triumph, perseverance and faith in one-self and one's dreams. The guideposts these works provide are invalu-able to understanding the party as a whole.

Other Panthers who weighed in on one of the 1960s' most exciting groups include Mumia Abu Jamal, a Philadelphia radio personality and news reporter currently incarcerated for his alleged role in the killing of a Philadelphia police officer. Jamal has recently been the beneficiary of worldwide demonstrations to get him released. He has effectively become the poster child for political prisoners in the United States. His most recent book, *We Want Freedom: My Life in the Party*, offers an eye-opening analy-sis of the principles the Panthers stood for. His chapter on women in the party is arguably the best written to date. Jamal wrote this treatise while awaiting execution on Pennsylvania's death row. Geronimo (Ji Jaga) Pratt wrote of his life growing up in Louisiana, going to Vietnam, then joining the Black Panther Party's Los Angeles chapter, where he became respon-sible for preparing all offices for self-defense. His treatment of the party in *Last Man Standing* focuses on his illegal incarceration for the murder of Caroline Olsen, a Santa Monica school teacher. Pratt provides vivid details about life on death row in California prisons and his legal battles over a twenty-seven-year period. His lawyer, the late Johnnie Cochran, finally convinced a judge of his innocence and he emerged from jail in 1998. George Jackson's *Soledad Brother* and *Blood in My Eye* remain the standard works on revolutionary prison literature. Both these books offer an inci-sive critique of prison life and the revolutionary's role behind bars. They offer the best examination of the history of black political prisoners inside the United States.

In a near-slanderous critique of the party, Hugh Pearson's *Shadow of the Panther* has done more to give the party a black eye than the fed-eral government in the group's years after 1972 ever did. While some of Pearson's conclusions hit the mark, much of what he writes about Newton and the Black Panther Party must be taken with a grain of salt. Pearson's foray into the life of Huey Newton left the party looking like a lawless group of drug dealers and drug addicts who sought only to fool white people out of their money. There are several inaccuracies and, in a few places, outright lies told about the party in what could other-wise have been a much-needed analysis of the organization.

For example, he falsely states that the Louisiana-born Deacons for

Defense were started by Robert Williams in Monroe, North Carolina. His claim that Stokely Carmichael and Willie Ricks initiated the substitution of the term black for Negro can hardly be true since Malcolm X and other black leaders had long insisted on the same. Furthermore, he argues that the FBI-directed COINTELPRO checked itself whenever activist lives were at risk. Pearson clearly did not read the numerous FBI memos that showed how agents took credit for the lawlessness, violence, and chaos in many areas where the Panthers set up chapters. He also could not have read the memos outlining various ways in which COINTELPRO agents had been ordered to destroy the party or that these tactics often included the use of violence, where many Panthers lost their lives and other activists' lives were clearly at risk. The murders of Fred Hampton, Mark Clark, John Huggins, and Alprentice "Bunchy" Carter all contradict this assertion. Pearson's claim that the Panthers cast an image that was "principally . . . of defiant posturing over substance" does not take into account all the Free Breakfast for Children Programs, Free Health Clinics, the thousands of people Panthers registered to vote, the political candidates the party put in office, its liberation schools and Inter-communal Youth Institute, and the deep sense of pride the group instilled in countless blacks. His claim that COINTELPRO only directed a small amount of energy to the party flies in the face of the facts: of the 295 operations directed against protest groups during the movement, 233 were directed at the Panthers.[1]

At one point, Pearson intimated that Newton did not begin "what became known as survival programs" until 1972 because he had "been shaken by the declaration" a year earlier of one woman who "declared that Newton and the Panthers had lost their souls and were going to hell." Even a cursory glance at the party's history, and particularly its newspaper, demonstrates that these programs began nearly four years earlier. He claims that the Black Liberation Army was "begun by one group of Cleaver loyalists." Again, a check of the party's newspaper, especially where it lists "Rules of the Party," might have helped avoid this mistake. Pearson would have immediately discovered the BLA existed long before Cleaver's defection and, according to BLA functionary and former Panther Geronimo (Ji Jaga) Pratt, even before the formation of the BPP.[2] At one point, Pearson describes Panther headquarters as "short staffed" and in the next paragraph asserts the group organized a "permanent national staff" in and out of Oakland because it was "fat in funds."[3]

Inconsistencies like these abound. Pearson's work is an injustice to the sacrifices made by so many during that tumultuous and exciting period. To be sure, Huey Newton abused drugs after his release from prison, and this fact cannot be justified by anyone. However, Pearson's characterization of Newton as solely a murderous rapine psychopath is inaccurate and fails to get at the heart of the BPP phenomenon. As author Errol Henderson points out, "only if we reduce the BPP to Newton then reduce Newton to his criminal behavior while ignoring all else can this claim be substantiated." He adds that these kinds of conclusions "are ahistorical and inaccurate."[4]

Pearson's claim that Newton's "destructive behavior continued killing the party" is no doubt true, however, he does not provide a discussion of the external pressures brought to bear on the organization and the reader is left to conclude that Newton alone is to blame for the party's failure to succeed. Even a brief glance at how the FBI and local police decimated the ranks of the Los Angeles, New York, Denver, Winston-Salem, and New Orleans chapters, to name but a few, illuminates the negligible role Newton played in the murder, imprisonment, and exile of Panther members throughout the country. This failure to explore the main issues affecting the party deprives Pearson's book of substance. For example, he admits that "essentially, for the life inside the party from the point of view of party veterans I was left with those who would never forgive Huey for what he did to the party." As a professional journalist, Pearson should know heavy reliance on such sources is insufficient if one is to get an accurate picture of what transpired. Upon reading this work, however, one notices not only the misstatements of fact, but the very negative manner in which the entire party is portrayed.[5]

Pearson's claim that the Panthers had some serious problems in their structural makeup is accurate, but to place the entire party in this light is not only false, but unfair. Pearson's dismal portrayal of the BPP did have its silver lining, however. His inaccuracies and suspect interpretations galvanized a tired generation of fighters into a flurry of revivals. When party members read Pearson's book, they began to organize forums to fight the harangue and to make plans to write their own histories. Uncounted party members now have their memoirs on the front burner instead of the back because of the negative fashion in which Pearson portrayed the group.

Still other scholars looked at the group while it remained a viable organization. The best contemporary view came from Gene Marine, author of *The Black Panthers*. Marine provided a short history of the party through 1969. His concise narrative of events situated the party in the context of the larger movement and succeeded in offering the reader a fair assessment of the group's successes, failures, trials, and tribulations. Equally valuable in this vein are Reginald Major's *A Panther is a Black Cat* and Gail Sheehy's *Panthermania*. G. Louis Heath brought together major speeches and events in the life of the party in *Off the Pigs: The History and Literature of the Black Panther Party*.

A lull in the writing of Panther history ensued with the onset of the 1980s. Former actor Ronald Reagan's capturing of the presidency ushered in the super-conservative era the George Bush-led Republican party continues to expand today. The irony was not lost on the original Oakland cadre that suffered at the hands of Gov. Ronald Reagan of California. As President Reagan's unprovoked invasion of the Caribbean island of Grenada tried to salve the pain of America's pitiful performance in the Vietnam War, a rollback of the gains sixties' activists made came with this new administration. This reversal coincided with a lack of good scholarship being published on the more radical aspects of the 1960s. Cedric Robinson's *Black Marxism: The Making of the Black Radical Tradition* seemed to have been read primarily in universities. Herbert Shapiro's masterful *White Violence and Black Response* cut off in 1963, leaving the Panther story to be told by someone else. People barely paid attention to Michael Newton's brief but detailed critique of the party in *Bitter Grain*. It is true that more works, including Newton's University of California–Santa Cruz doctoral dissertation "War Against the Panthers" (which later appeared in book form) and Ward Churchill and Jim Vander Wall's *Agents of Repression* made an appearance during this decade, but it was not until the Republicans left town and southern-bred William Jefferson Clinton took control of the Oval Office that a new crop of books on radical sixties' politics began to make their mark on posterity. The Vietnam War–dodging Clinton and his once student-activist wife Hillary apparently made people comfortable enough to talk and write about what "really" happened during that still misunderstood epoch. As Spike Lee and Oprah Winfrey made splashes on movie and television screens, so did good scholarship on the civil rights movement's radical wing.

Bobby Seale's *Seize the Time* was reissued on the heels of nemesis David Horowitz's *Destructive Generation*, which claimed the Panther movement had no merit since its members were thugs and hooligans out to make a buck. Horowitz, a "red diaper baby," one-time heavy in the student left, and former member of Students for a Democratic Society, no doubt had time to fester in his anger toward the party, likely because it was he who introduced Betty Van Patter to the organization. An intelligent woman with the acumen for numbers, Van Patter had become the party's accountant under Huey Newton and Elaine Brown and somehow wound up in Brown's disfavor. One day, after weeks of internal party squabbling over financial improprieties, someone discovered Van Patter's body in San Francisco Bay. The police questioned Brown, but found no cause to indict or take her to trial for the mysteriously killed bookkeeper. Horowitz's book is venomous and leaves the Panther's reputation in tatters. Horowitz, after a whirlwind tour of television studios and packed houses of sympathizers at venues large and small, was left to pout in his corner office in the beautiful Bay Area.

The decade, however, continued to produce good work. Filmmaker Lee Lew Lee made an important contribution with his documentary *All Power to the People*. Using interviews from Panthers and retired CIA and FBI agents, Lee demonstrated that the Panther menace was a mostly manufactured image and the organization sought to right past wrongs. The indelible black-and-white footage forces the viewer's understanding and propels the discussion into other radical groups like the American Indian Movement. Coupled with older films like Newsreel's *Off the Pig* and *Mayday*, this two-hour-plus documentary can be used to help young people see and hear the sounds of the radical sixties. An entire archive of this type of footage can be found in the University of California at Berkeley's Bancroft Library and in Pacifica News's archives, also in California's Bay Area. Charles Jones's *The Black Panther Party Reconsidered* helped close out the decade with a wide-ranging look at the party's history. With articles from scholars and party members, this book set the stage for a comprehensive reevaluation of the party's place in American history.

By the time the twenty-first century dawned on the horizon, writers had picked up the pace on their evaluation of this important organization. Aside from the thousands of articles that had been written in past years (an inordinate amount of which are in German), books on the party began to materialize. Though few historians were in on this sudden turn of events, journalists, political scientists, sociologists, and other non-historians began to focus a critical eye on the group. Kathleen Cleaver's and John Katsiaficas's *Liberation, Imagination, and the Black Panther Party* picks up where Jones's edited volume left off. It too is a well-rounded collection of essays by former party members and scholars and it too provides a detailed analysis of the major events in the life of the party. This thin but information-packed volume takes the reader into a world where few have gone. It shows the day-to-day functioning of the party as well as its oft-neglected international aspects. Providing a rare look into the origins and development of the Black Liberation Army and a candid discussion about Panther shortcomings, this publication will be a reference for years to come. Akinyele Umoja's article on the BLA—the first chapter in this volume—is by far the most comprehensive and balanced piece on this mysterious organization aside from the BLA's own writings. The Black Panther Party's close ties to the BLA are chronicled in Robert K. Tannenbaum's *Badge of the Assassin,* John Castelucci's *The Big Dance,* and Albert Seedman's and Peter Hellman's *Chief.* An up-close-and-personal, inside view of this organization can be found in political prisoner Jalil Muntaqim's *We Are Our Own Liberators.* Muntaqim not only provides a history of the BLA, but he also offers a prescription for future radical formations. Nicholas Henck's *On the Black Liberation Army* raises serious issues concerning armed action inside the United States.

Perhaps the best outside view of the black radical tradition was put forth by Robin Kelley, who, among other things, wrote *Freedom Dreams.* In addition to looking at the Revolutionary Action Movement, the Republic of New Africa, and radical feminism, he turned his attention to the BPP and leaves the reader with a more than adequate understanding of the Panthers' place in the sixties pantheon of organizations seeking change by any means necessary.

Other authors have written histories detailing the spade work of activists who made "black power" possible before it became popular in the sixties lexicon. Foremost among these writers are Timothy B. Tyson and Lance Hill. Tyson's *Radio Free Dixie* has already become a classic. His treatment of North Carolina's Robert Williams and armed self-reliance is thorough and convincing. This work proves beyond a shadow of a doubt that the elements that eventually came to make up the Black Power movement existed in the forties and fifties in Monroe, North Carolina, and other locales. Tyson followed this scholarly work with a popular book on protest and change in the fifties, sixties, and seventies in the state of

North Carolina. *Blood Done Sign My Name* takes the murder of a black man and situates it in the burning caldron of racial violence in the Tarheel state. Hill's *The Deacons for Defense: Armed Resistance and the Civil Rights Movement* provides a birds-eye view of one of the most neglected organizations in civil rights history. Hill shows that when local people became fed up with racial violence and the unwillingness of authorities to protect protesters, church deacons and others joined to form a group that vowed to do the job. Placing the movement in its national and international context, Hill succeeds in demonstrating that armed self-reliance, despite what its detractors said, had merit and value in the sense that uncounted lives were saved.

Michael Thelwell's and Stokely Carmichael's masterful autobiography of the Carmichael is by far the best look into the life of this monumental figure. *Ready for Revolution: The Life and Struggles of Stokely Carmichael [Kwame Toure]* is a collaboration of these two movement veterans. Told in the first person with the exception of editor's notes throughout, this 835 page volume details the life and times of one of the most honored, yet misunderstood, personalities of the movement. Tracing his life from Trinidad to New York, New York to Washington, D.C., Washington, D.C., into the movement, and then on to Africa and back, this volume satisfies the thirst so many have endured for a comprehensive look at the consummate agitator. Its style and flow are so natural that those who have heard him speak might think he is there in person. Carmichael's take on the Black Panther Party of Oakland, though not flattering, is fair and balanced. His extensive knowledge of movement people from one side of America to the other is a testament to this man's involvement in every major action in the 1960s. His life shines as bright as he did that dark night in Greenwood, Mississippi, when he emerged from jail yelling "Black Power, Black Power, Black Power!"

Carmichael's colleague and one-time comrade James Forman wrote his own personal account and titled it *The Making of Black Revolutionaries*. Not quite as massive as Carmichael's work at 553 pages, this volume details the evolution of a University of California at Los Angeles political science major into a movement icon. Working in places like Mississippi and Alabama, New York and Washington, Forman describes how black revolutionaries are made and not necessarily born. He shows how heartache, disappointment and official violence turned otherwise well-meaning youths into radical, militant activists. His work is one of the standards on the Student Nonviolent Coordinating Committee and holds its own with others in the fields of civil rights and Black Power. It also offers a valuable glimpse into the early days of the Black Panther Party and the forces that shaped it. Cleveland Sellers's *River of No Return* traces the life a South Carolina student from near obscurity to the front pages of the *New York Times*. Sellers not only provides an examination of his own experiences in the Student Nonviolent Coordinating Committee, but details of the lives of other, lesser-known SNCC workers who helped pave the way for the Panthers. A riveting autobiography, *River of No Return* helps us to see how behind-the-scenes tactical and ideological discussions helped propel individuals toward a more radical stance.

Yohuru Williams's *Black Politics/White Power* traces black political mobilization in post-war New Haven, Connecticut, one of the country's first meticulously planned cities. His exploration of the roots of the Black Panther Party in this "model city" is by far the best treatment of the group in the Northeast. Williams is able to place the party in its local, national, and international contexts while at the same time paying close attention to the individuals that made the organization so feared by city, state, and federal police agencies. His is a model that should be consulted by all seeking a synthesis of civil rights activities before and after the party.

New Orleans native and freelance writer Orissa Arend recently finished a case study of the Panthers in New Orleans. Her *Piety and Desire: The Story of the Black Panthers in New Orleans,* sponsored by the Louisiana Endowment for the Humanities, is the first full-length study of this oft-forgotten but hard-working chapter in the South. Filled with the recollections of police officers, leading politicians of the time, business owners, and Panthers, Arend's work is invaluable to students and researchers who are looking for a case study on political decision making with militant organizations. Her use of oral histories is a testament to this technique's value to the profession.

There are hundreds of book chapters and articles on the Black Panther Party. They dissect various elements of the group, including the role of women, the newspaper, decision making, police/Panther shoot-outs, federal involvement, and deradicalization. Most of these are worthy contributions in the field of black protest. While space prohibits an exposition on all these various and conflicting works, it is important to note at least a couple. Peniel Joseph's Fall/Winter 2001 *Black Scholar* article, "Black Liberation Without Apology: Reconceptualizing the

Black Power Movement," does a grand job of situating the BPP in its proper historical context and in its relationship with other movements of the period. A great reference work, this article demonstrates that scholarship on the party and other radical movements is growing more sophisticated. Joseph's incisive eye and knack for subtlety make this piece a joy to read and a must for teachers of this period of American history. Charles Jones and Judson Jeffries's "'Don't Believe the Hype': Debunking the Panther Myth," in Jones's *Black Panthers Reconsidered* is a welcome balm to the many slanderous pieces put out about the Panthers. A hard but fair estimation of the BPP's evolution, this article helps to demonstrate how myth can create serious problems for historians who write about the past. Candid and objective, it holds together the other essays in the book. The final chapters in Thomas West's and James Mooney's *To Redeem a Nation* are likewise accessible and easy to understand. Relying primarily on oral histories, this work allows activists to do their own talking and leaves little room for misinterpretation. Alexander Bloom's and Wini Breines's *Taking it to the Streets* encapsulates the entire era and provides a comprehensive overview of the major happenings of the period. The women's movement, the sexual revolution, drugs, and countercultures are blended with the speeches of Malcolm X, Richard Nixon, Ronald Reagan, and the supporters of Black Power. The consummate primary source for studying the late sixties, this volume is a standard for edited works.

The federal government, though not always voluntarily, did a commendable job keeping the American people abreast of some of its dealings with radical groups. National lawmakers held a plethora of hearings on the party between 1968 and 1976. The House of Representatives's Committee on Internal Security published *The Black Panther Party: Its Origin and Development as Reflected in Its Official Weekly Newspaper, the Black Panther Community News Service* in 1971. It primarily analyzed and critiqued various statements made by party leaders and other functionaries who wrote for the paper. Five years later the Senate published *The FBI's Covert Program to Destroy the Black Panther Party.* This government study looked at various COINTELPRO operations directed at the party and, without debate, concluded that the federal government had overstepped its bounds in pursuing the group. While no one was actually held responsible for the deaths and incarcerations, not to mention mangled lives and relationships, the study proved the Panther claim that there was a federal conspiracy to destroy the party. With the Internal Revenue Service and Alcohol Tobacco and Firearms Division being used to persecute the group, the study demonstrated that the Panthers had little chance of doing serious harm to the government.

A half dozen other hearings on the party also took up the time of these national lawmakers. One of these resulted in a massive volume. In 1971, the House of Representatives Committee on Internal Security published *Gun Barrel Politics: THE BLACK PANTHER PARTY, 1966–1971.* This report outlined Panther activities, strategies, and goals. It also provided an analysis of the group's difficulties with law enforcement. Together with its minority views, the report sounded the alarm for the federal government to act before it was too late. The lazy bureaucracy, however, was loathe to do anything that might significantly change the status quo. As a result, the BPP continued to grow.

Three years prior, in 1968, the U.S. Riot Commission published its *Report of the National Advisory Commission on Civil Disorders.* This study detailed the causes of the riots and concluded that white racism had been at their roots. Most police departments and government agencies ignored the report and carried on with business as usual. Activists and other Americans used the many statistics in the report to demonstrate that their complaints had merit. From employment and housing to education and a willingness to engage in violence, the report encapsulated the ills of America's ghettos and recommended sweeping changes if further violence were to be avoided. Again, few people in decision-making positions even read the report and those who did pretended they had not.

In the early seventies when activists broke into FBI headquarters in Media, Pennsylvania, and broadcast their findings in the *New York Times,* the government had to cut back on its domestic spy hunting. It had a lot to cut back on. Kenneth O'Reilly's *Racial Matters* and Ward Churchill's *The Cointelpro Papers* help tell the story of federal spying on local organizations. A lesser known but well done work on this aspect of the movement is David Wise's *The American Police State.* This well-written and meticulously researched volume retraces the efforts of the CIA and FBI to contain and, in most cases, to prevent legitimate protest against systemic American injustices. A sort of exposé that details fabricated letter-writing campaigns, wiretapping, and break-ins, this work succeeds in demonstrating that all branches of the federal government took part in silencing the voices of protest for change inside the United States.

Not long after the break-in in Media, Pennsylvania, Congress passed the Freedom of Information Act, and private citizens began demanding any and all files the government held on them. Some people received twenty pages of garbled messages about their domestic duties while others received two thousand or more pages of heavily redacted surveillance notes. The Black Panther Party alone, by no means the largest organization of the period, took up nearly two million pages of these government documents. Only about eighty thousand of these pages are available for public (or private) viewing, as the rest might violate the sanctity of national security.

These numbers demonstrate the priority national leaders placed on this otherwise small organization. They assumed, correctly, that it was the members who made the organization move, and not anything else. Taking this fact as a given, federal, local, and state authorities put pressure on the group whenever and wherever they could. Their gambit worked and eventually helped to push the party out of existence.

They did not, however, push all its members out. For this reason, the author consulted with many former members of the party at one point or another. Indeed, oral histories comprise a significant amount of the evidence used to tell this story because of the difficulty involved in doing research on the party. That aspect of the research process is a story in itself.

My Journey

I was born September 2, 1969, in Yazoo City, Mississippi, when the Black Panther Party was at its height. A premature child (I was born on the back seat of a Chevrolet on the way to the hospital), I was for all intents and purposes a scrawny runt, the fifth of six children, or as country folks call it, the knee-baby. It did not help that when I was born I was not breathing because of the caul over my face. To this day, my mother refuses to go into detail about it, but at some point after the midwife could not remove this troublesome piece of skin, Gertrude Gainwell, my grandmother, came to the rescue and showed them all how to do it. She has been my hero ever since. My low birth weight stayed with me for years, and I was so skinny my great-grandfather, who stayed with us until he died at age 92, dubbed me Po-boy.[6]

My mother thought I was too little to play with the big boys, so she gave me books. When she went off to clean white folks' houses, I played with the big boys anyway and cleaned myself up before she got home because I still wanted the benefits that came with people thinking I was too small to do for myself. I also read whatever books she had given me so I had the best of both worlds. She did not know I played with the "bigger boys" so often until I came in the house hurt one day—and got a whuppin for it.[7] In any case, her gift of books translated into good marks when I went to the Headstart at St. Francis Catholic School, which had recently come into being because some lunatic activists in the Mississippi Delta had the gall to create the Child Development Group, which led to preschool for the state's poor children. I recently met some of those crazy people and have been in debt to them ever since.

From the time I was a small child, I have been enamored of the sixties and all its implications. Because I was born on the edge of the Mississippi Delta in Yazoo City, however, my thirst for knowledge about this period went unquenched due of the paucity of information and human sources available to me. I did not make a fuss, but as I matriculated into primary and secondary school, it became more and more apparent that at some point I had to drink from that sixties cup. When I still could not find it, I decided in the ninth grade that school was a waste of time and I needed to find something more important to do with my life.

I told my mother, who grew up in a place and time where blacks could *only* go through the eighth grade, that if I ever made out of high school she did not have to worry about me going to any other school after that. I do not recall her response or whether she gave a response at all. She was a single mother with five boys and one girl and often allowed us to make our own decisions since she was busy trying to figure out what we were going to eat the next day. Even though I was a great student (I graduated fifth out of 289) and took all the AP classes my counselor made me take, I still felt a void. Senior year came and went and I prepared to make good on my promise to my mother to stay out of school and to do something better with my life.

At the time, that something consisted of working at McDonald's for $3.50 an hour and driving fast in my 1981 black Grand Prix. Gas was eighty-nine cents a gallon and I was loaded because my mother did not make me pay bills with my check. I guess she thought I was saving it. I was not. It got to the point where my work at McDonald's was so superior that I took on the job of training others and, before long, I was in good with all the managers. This development meant that I could work or take off pretty much whenever I wanted to. I took advantage of the situation and made a lot of road trips. Because most of my friends went to college after high school, it became difficult and then impossible to find a consistent riding partner and the long distance trips had to be cut out.

Occasionally, I bumped into those old high school buddies in the clubs, at the grocery stores, or on the streets, since Yazoo was such a small place—then and now. To the person, my white and black classmates raved about how college was the best time of their lives and how I ought to at least try it. Those offers came in one ear and went out the other, as I had not thought about school since I was threatened with expulsion the week of graduation after the principal, who sneakily pulled up behind me, caught me drinking beer on campus. My aunt knew the mayor and my mother knew how to pray. Principal Charles "Charlie" Brown called me the night of graduation an hour before the ceremony and told me I had better come now because if I were late he would not let me walk. I liked to drive fast so I made it there in no time. I had graduated, and I was trying to explain to my pals the promise I had made about staying out of school. They just laughed and kept telling me how grand college was.

This went on for a year or so and I had modified my road trips to in-state destinations only. When some friends discovered that I was always on the road anyway (and still am), they invited me to visit them at their universities. I thought it was odd since I had seen all their schools at one point or another during the high school trips we took with our classes or on those rare occasions when we skipped school and tried to pretend to be freshmen at a various colleges. It never worked. I took them up on their offers and made a few visits. They had softened me up. One weekend, there was to be this huge party in Hattiesburg so my friends invited me to the University of Southern Mississippi to join them. I obliged and drove the two hours south and had a ball! When I asked them if it were "like this" all the time, they said "yeah man, we've been trying to tell ya." Boy, what a sucker I am, I believed them; now I know that no one can party that hard all the time! At any rate, Sunday came and we were still partying, or drinking, to be more exact. They managed to get me in the school cafeteria and inside other buildings on campus and I must admit I was a tad impressed—I think it was the liquor though. By Sunday night we were back in their dorm room across Hardy Street in Elam Arms. I did not have to work the next day so everything was cool. The drinking continued so much that we had to get more beer. This is where I get to the point of the story.

We went across the street to the Jr. Food Mart to buy beer and returned to the dorm. I remember vividly that it was a case of tall cans of Budweiser. One of our number, I don't remember who, suggested we have a contest to see who could drink the most. We all took up the challenge and started chugging; never mind the fact that we had been drinking heavily since Friday morning. To make this long story a little less long, I won. I drank eleven cans and the nearest person only made it to nine and he did not finish that one. To make him happy—actually I was being snide—I drank it for him, so that made twelve. All this drinking took a few hours and at some point during the evening someone, I do not remember who, bet me twenty dollars that I would not go over to Student Services (now the [Clyde] Kennard/Washington Building) and take the ACT. I had never taken it in high school because I knew I was not going to college. For the same reason I dropped typing four years in a row because I thought it was for sissies and that only people who were going to college needed to know how to type. I was drunk so I took my friend up on his bet and someone else held our money.

We shut down about two o'clock that morning and from about three to about seven thirty I intermittently puked my guts out, literally, I believe, because there was blood and a lot of pain to go with it. To this day I cannot stand the smell or the sight of a tall can of Budweiser. Undaunted by this unfortunate turn for the worse, I dragged myself away from the toilet as my friends slept and stumbled across Hardy Street onto campus so I could win my twenty bucks. I must have looked disheveled because I received a number of strange looks. I imagine that the people who worked in Student Services were used to seeing strange people. I informed them that I wanted to take the ACT and they sent me upstairs to a set of offices. I asked again if I could take the ACT and an older black woman replied, "sure baby, we'll even grade it for free for you." She gave me the test, which reminded me of the California Achievement Tests we took in first, second, and third grades. She said "I won't time you so take your time." I thought to myself, thanks but no thanks I won't need much time.

I quickly went through the test and to try to make it look like I actually cared, I stayed another ten minutes so my total time there was twenty minutes—one dollar per minute that is.

Upon leaving, the nice older black woman gave me something that looked like a receipt and wished me well, after she asked if I was OK. I stumbled back across the street and into the dorm and produced the proof that I had just taken the ACT. My friends were still all asleep so my friend did not want to pay up. I was still sick so I went back to sleep. Several hours later, and after several more trips to the bathroom, we woke up and found food. I threw that up, too. At this point, everybody was around so I demanded my twenty bucks, which my friend, after checking the slip, promptly paid. Happy, I put gas in my car and slowly made my way back to Yazoo City. I went back to my job at McDonald's and to doing whatever I chose after that. Ahhh, sweet freedom.

Something like six or eight weeks went by and one night, after a particularly busy day at work, I came home to a beaming but stern mother. It was a strange scene to say the least because she was usually in her room reading the Bible—or so we always thought, anyway. She greeted me with that big, bright smile of hers and informed me that I was going to school. Mustering up all the respect I could, I gently reminded her that I had already told her that I was not going to school and that I planned to do something with my life. Not one of those mothers that likes to be told anything by her children, she replied, "I think you're going to school." I said, "No momma, I'll do whatever you want me to do but I am not going to school." My respect at the end of its line, I began, in a perturbed voice, to explain to her that I was nineteen and grown and had the right to make my own choices. She simply looked at me with the customary blank look that people give you when they are trying their hardest not to let you in on the fact that they are ignoring you.

She then explained to me why she had brought this issue up a year after my high school graduation. She pointed out that a letter had come in the mail saying I had been accepted into the University of Southern Mississippi. Accepted! What? "What do you mean?" I asked. She said this letter here says you can come to school whenever you register. I did not care what the letter said, I just knew that I was not going to school. Who'd have thunk that if you take the ACT at a university that they would just assume that you wanted to go to that university? I certainly would not have and I certainly would not have given them my mother's address if I had known. Why was she reading my mail anyway, isn't that a federal offense, I thought, as I tried to come up with something that would make her change her mind. At her wits end and not wanting to slap me or do something else drastic like that, her final words were, "well you gettin' the hell out of here!" I knew I was getting the hell out of there then because my mother never cusses, or at least she had not since we were little and she had to. That was a Tuesday and by that Thursday I was at USM filling out paperwork for the dorm and for Pell Grants. I started classes the following Monday and have been in school ever since.

After I discovered that one did not necessarily have to get up at eight every morning for class and that one could literally take any class one wanted, I began to enjoy school. The learning was fun but I also discovered New Orleans, where I really learned how to have fun. Since I was the first one in my family to go to school, I knew nothing about college. I learned, though, and before I knew it, I was a history major. My mother, above all else, knew of my thirst for knowledge about the sixties and simply wanted to help me quench it. I found that knowledge in many places, but in one place, I was able to drink my fill: that place was any class being taught by Dr. Neil R. McMillen. Though not all his classes were sixties related—in fact most of them were not—he had a way with words and knowledge that made me want more. So even though I missed a bunch of my classes, I never missed any of his and there started an academic and personal friendship that has stood the test of time—I hope.

As a senior at the University of Southern Mississippi in Hattiesburg, I decided after taking Dr. Neil McMillen's "U.S. History Since 1945," to write my term paper on the Black Panther Party. I had already done a paper for another professor based on oral histories that covered school desegregation in Yazoo City. I thought I could use that model to do a project on the Panthers. That paper for Dr. McMillen eventually led to a master's thesis called "Menace to Society: The Black Panther Party in Oakland, California, 1966–1972" and I was then encouraged to go on for the Ph.D. I reluctantly did so, as I was eager to return to my job at McDonald's and to my then three-year-old daughter Averi. Nevertheless, I ventured the three hours to the middle northeastern part of the state to Starkville, Mississippi. There, I enrolled at Mississippi State University (MSU) in the Ph.D. program in American History, with a concentration in black protest. Because I did not want to go, I applied for places I was sure not be accepted. I had applied to the University of Michigan, UC

Berkeley, and Howard University. After three weeks at MSU, I received acceptance letters (as I had applied late for all of them) from two of the above schools. My dissertation director talked me out of going so far away from home and MSU became my place of residence for the next four years. There I learned the art of combining research with teaching. I also received a boatload of money to travel and to find out what I could about the Black Panther Party.

An adventurous young man, I hopped a flight to Oakland and called one of my Omega Psi Phi fraternity brothers to pick me up from the airport. A law student at Berkeley at the time, this young man directed me first to the Bancroft Library and then to the Oakland Public Library and its Oakland History room. In both places I discovered a smorgasbord of information and spent the next five days sifting through it. Not knowing anybody in California, I began asking around to see if anyone knew "where the Black Panthers were." They did not and the jig was up until one night at a fraternity party I met a brother who had once been a community worker for the BPP. He introduced me to Emory Douglas, a longtime graphic artist for the party and one of the first people to join. Douglas refused to do an interview on such short notice and I headed back to Mississippi. Several months later, I went back to California to do my first interview with Douglas. It was uneventful, but he promised to introduce me to some other "comrades," a strange term if I ever heard one (coming from Mississippi, that is). In the meantime, I began scanning the Internet for sources on the BPP and, unlike today, there were precious few. Undaunted, I continued to push, to teach my two classes, and to take my three classes, until I found another opportunity to go to California.

This time, it was 1995 and I was a participant in that year's National Black Graduate Student Association meeting in Claremont, outside Pomona, California, and just a little south of the City of Angels. The conference was a blast, and on the last day I convinced East St. Louis native and University of Wisconsin–Whitewater graduate student Montez Coleman to ride to San Francisco with me so that I could try yet another unscheduled interview. Five hours after he accepted, we arrived in Oakland and had a little fun before we headed over the bridge to San Francisco to the *San Francisco Sun Reporter*'s office, where Emory Douglas continues to work after more than thirty years. Amid the noise of the printing press, telephones, and customers, I conducted my first significant interview with Douglas. He was great and made good on his promise to introduce me to the "comrades." The only problem was that the comrades were in New York City, all the way across the country.

When I arrived in New York three months later, I discovered another problem. The "comrade" I was sent to meet was white. His name was Martin "Marty" Kenner and he did not look like a Panther to me. Well, not being a racist, I went ahead and agreed to do the interview. Of all places, he chose to talk to me on the roof of Butler Library, outside of Ronald Grehle's Oral History Office at Columbia University. Through wind and laughs, we finished the interview three hours later. Kenner, who had once been a member of Students for a Democratic Society, an organizer of the famous 1968 Columbia student strike, and had served as the party's accountant after Newton was released, had to rush off for class. Not having anything to do and not knowing anybody, I made my way to the Schermerhorn Extension and found Manning Marable's office. That building is a maze. Marable was great. Not knowing me from a can of paint, he invited me in and listened to my story about my project. Not one to be upstaged, Marable laughed and produced a student of his own, also working on party history. That student was Robyn Spencer and we have been friends since then. I also had the pleasure of meeting Robin D. G. Kelley on that visit. He had just finished a book on Thelonious Monk and came by Columbia for a presentation. At the time, he was not chair of New York University's history department and all I knew of him was *Hammer and Hoe*. He, too, was great. My trip to New York nearly finished, I went back to the upper west side apartment where I was staying and waited for my host.

This fellow, Jean Marc Ran Oppenheim, now a history professor at Fordham, had no television, but he did have books, something I was used to. I learned a lot reading while I waited for him and discovered Robertson Davies, author of *The Fifth Business*. I have been high on Canadian authors ever since. My stomach also got a treat as every day I had a different cuisine, from Korean and Vietnamese to Japanese, Indian, and Ethiopian food. I enjoyed it all. I also managed to get an invite back.

By this point, the time had come for me to make a decision about which direction my dissertation would go. Suffice it to say that having a crew of southern gentleman and one black man on my committee, that these days were not my best. I was told it would be better to write on the

NAACP or the Masons or some other group, but definitely not on the Black Panther Party. I persevered and the two people on my committee who did not give a hoot what I wrote about gave me the green light, so I worried not over the situation. I finally finished my classes and the time came for me to research. Somehow, Dr. Charles Lowery, chair of the History Department at the time, found the money and I became the recipient of yet another lucrative research fellowship and spent the next year traveling the country and combing the archives.

At this point, the Huey P. Newton Foundation Records, run by Newton's widow and David Hilliard (who subsequently married Newton's widow) had not yet been indexed but the papers were in the Green Library at Stanford. Hilliard, who came upon the papers in Newton's basement after his death, shopped the collection around to several black colleges (which agreed to store them for free) and finally sold the collection to Stanford for a pretty penny. After hearing this news, I went to Beverly, Hills that is, and hung out with a filmmaker friend of mine until it was time to take the 101 north to San Francisco. Once I arrived in Palo Alto, the first thing I noticed was East Palo Alto, one of the poorest municipalities in the country at the time. I wondered how it could be that such a depressed area could sit next to such a rich enclave of big houses, foreign cars, and manicured lawns. I stopped wondering that after I realized that Mississippi was certainly no different. In any case, I proceeded through the beautiful campus until I found the Green Library—back in the days when ticket-writing had not become a habit for campus security. After finding Special Collections and telling the attendant why I had come all the way from Mississippi, I was told that the papers had not been indexed or organized yet and that she had no idea how long it would take since there was so much material. I first tried rationalizing the situation by telling her that Stanford had already advertised the collection on the web and it had to be open. When that did not work, I gave my sob story and before you know it, the woman, who shall remain nameless, brought out a box and made me promise not to lose anything. Well, I did promise, but how was I to know that thirty minutes into my crime all the lights on campus were going to go out? Boy am I in trouble, I thought. I tried to locate the woman who had brought me the papers, but by the time I found my way back to the counter in the dark, she had been evacuated—as had all the other customers and students in the library.[8]

Somehow I found my way to a set of stairs and, in total darkness, bumped into the famous historian Carl Degler. He remembered me from a class visit where he spoke for Dr. John Marszalek a year before. He calmed my fears about the out-of-place-box and showed me where I could get coffee. Not that much of a coffee drinker at the time, I decided to go into this beautiful building next to the library that did not look like it had been affected by the blackout. Its name was the Hoover Institution, and I told myself that Hoover was going to have to deal with me now and not later. I was summarily accosted by an no-nonsense woman after browsing around about ten minutes. The lights then went out in that building and I was stuck in this huge rotunda with nowhere to go. The woman who accosted me earlier escorted me out of the door. I was miffed until I discovered that the building was named after a different Hoover.

Chalking this trip up as a loss, I headed back to Mississippi, where I packed for New York again. This time I went to use the libraries at Columbia and New York University. Columbia's Oral History Program is top-notch, and I found some of the most exciting stuff I had ever seen there. Hilliard's and Cole's book had just come out, and Columbia had all of the interviews. I could take notes, I was told, but copies had not yet been authorized. I do not think taking notes had been, either, but once again, the angels watched over me. Later, after making use of our underused interlibrary loan program, I got a chance to copy much of the authorized material.

NYU's library is massive and impressive, but since purple is my favorite color, I didn't let it bother me. Meeting the right people almost by chance, I happened upon an expert in black protest. I kept interlibrary loan busy with these folks as well.

Back in Mississippi, I began to write. It immediately dawned upon me that I could not finish with what little I had. Because the money was there, I headed back to California. This time my law school friend had graduated into real life and another group of my fraternity brothers picked me up from the Oakland airport. There is nothing like northern California in the spring. One of my fraternity brothers who picked me up was a divinity student at Berkeley (his name is Justice) and he had developed an interest in the movement. He introduced me to several professors and other students and I was on my way once again. I hooked up with Emory Douglas for another interview and this time he gave me the actual name of another Panther. This was also the first interview where Douglas told me something that I could not find in print, either in published sources, the Panther paper, or government documents. After six years of work, I was finally in. He sent me to one of Newton's former body guards and personal aides.

I called William "Billy X" Jennings and told him what my cause was and who sent me. He simply replied, "well come on up." Billy X lives in Sacramento with his wife Dr. Gail Shaw, who happened to be a member of the International Committee to Combat Fascism. Their house is a veritable archive and I hope it is fireproof because he has original everything, from videotapes and photographs to posters, buttons, and at least one gun. This patient man and his wife hosted me like I had not been hosted before. BJ, as many of his comrades call him, is from Alabama and Gail is from Miami, so that might have had something to do with what I took as southern hospitality—though we were only south of Oregon, Washington, and Alaska. Our interview lasted nearly eight hours and I hated to leave. BJ actually gave me the names of other people to interview in New Orleans—ahh, home. So I planned to go there when I returned.

Before that, however, I had to make a stop in Los Angeles, where Alden Kimbrough lives. Kimbrough has roots in Mississippi, so that might be why he accepted Emory Douglas's word about me being OK. I met him at his book store/collectibles shop in LA's Degnan Square. I almost died when I saw all the original Panther materials and other sixties memorabilia. I bought a couple original Panther papers for twenty-five dollars and a few *Liberators* for five dollars, grabbed dinner at El Pollo Loco, and we headed to his place off La Cienaga. When we arrived, I was floored again. This man has wall-to-wall classics on everything from Cabral and Nkrumah to Du Bois and Ida B. Wells. What a collection, in every room. I could have stayed there for days. Had I been raised in this house, my mother definitely would not have had to worry about me playing with the big boys. I would have been too busy reading. The trip was a grand success and I went back twice for more; once having to buy an extra bag to carry all the copies on the plane. Before I knew it, it was time to go to New Orleans.

The first person I interviewed, however, did not live in New Orleans, but literally "across the river," in Algiers. I made the short drive down and we hit it off immediately. When I arrived, Malik Rahim, one of the original members of the New Orleans chapter, was in the backyard of his mother's house washing the longest dreads I had ever seen outside of Jamaica. He immediately started telling me these never-before-heard of (by me) exciting, keep-you-on-the-edge-of-your-seat stories. When I asked him if I could record him, he asked why I had not already been recording since he granted me permission to interview him over the phone. These Panthers are really no-nonsense types (in a good way) and he refused to repeat anything he'd said earlier. I turned on the recorder and followed him while he did his rounds in the city for the rest of day. Rahim had recently run and lost a campaign for alderman-at-large as a member of the Green Party and everywhere we went, people seemed to know him. He introduced me to people who had served as community workers for the party and to others who the party had to run off for one reason or another. Rahim, after thirty years, was still working on programs that the party supported. This day, he was working to bring quality housing and job development to his community in Algiers. It was a sight to see. I also met other New Orleans Panthers and had the honor of being introduced to Robert King Wilkerson, one of the Angola Three, who had been in prison since 1970 on trumped up charges. He had just been released two weeks before. After thirty years? Wow!

He was a strong, upright man who did not seem to have vengeance in his eyes. He treated guests in his home as if it were theirs. He also provided me with some Freelines, pralines he had learned to make while serving time in Angola State Penitentiary in Louisiana. He tried to refuse my donation but by this time I had learned how to spend like the best of them so I insisted that he take the twenty dollar spot for the five dollar candy. His companion, Marion Brown, was equally generous and took the time to tell me her story about joining the party as a Tulane student. The following semester, King, as he is called, came up to the University of Southern Mississippi and gave a talk on his experiences as a Panther in prison. The audience was riveted and my students took a test on it the next class period.

By the time my contacts grew in New Orleans, the dissertation had been finished and I was in the second year of an advance book contract —sorry Larry. I needed to get what I thought of as the whole story. Little did I know that the whole story could hardly be told in one book. At any rate, I kept pressing for more interviews, and more interviews I received.

I went back to California for a week and ended up talking on the phone with Phyllis Jackson, who had once been in the party. I also spoke with a number of US members on this trip but I was not allowed to record them. Most of what I did not write down on the plane I have since forgotten.

While there, one of my dissertation director's sisters informed me that she knew someone who had gone to Newton's funeral in 1989. This turned out to be a great lead as this person, who wants to remain anonymous, had been in the party in Oakland and in Los Angeles. The information just kept rolling in. I found solace in yet another of his sisters and enjoyed a great dinner out with "Flo," short for Florence, her children and nephews. I still, however, do not quite know why In-N-Out Burger joints are so popular. I made my way to Westwood and found the right bus to UCLA, where I discovered its oral history program. After touring the campus and finding and photographing Campbell Hall, the building where Bunchy Carter and John Huggins were murdered, I made my way past all the campus art and immersed myself in the interviews. Communist Dorothy Healy's was by far the best of the bunch.

Three days before returning to Mississippi, I ate a bad piece of fish from the fish joint across from the archives and contracted the worst food poisoning I could ever imagine. I happened to be staying in this gigantic but beautiful house with the niece of my dissertation director, who, by the way, is a California native, and had hoped that this stunningly beautiful woman would take care of me in my time of need. It was not to be. She had recently divorced and could not stand men at the time. When I tried to make even a little conversation after we had lunch one day, she informed me that she was just being nice and told me of her feelings on "niggas, flies, and rats." When I asked her what she meant, she responded that the more she sees "niggas, the more she likes flies and rats." I couldn't make it work, so I left it alone. I hope she is happy somewhere now.

In any case, the best part of that particular trip was the Southern California Research Center. This small library-looking building held a treasure trove of California history. Situated on Vernon Street, which was smack dab in the middle of the Rodney King riot, this place had all you ever wanted to know about the Panthers but were afraid to ask. The curator at this library/museum simply pointed me in the direction I needed to go and eight hours later she was trying to explain that they opened really early the next day. Of course I had to leave the next day, so she agreed to give me two more hours. And they say city folk are rude—not this one. My leads in New Orleans and California led me back to New York but I struck out because my subject failed to remember who I was or what I was coming for. Or so he said. That's how I got to know Manhattan and the other five boroughs of New York City.

Luckily, a few months later, people in the party had scheduled the thirty-fifth reunion in Washington, D.C. Since I was already in D.C. for the Organization of American Historians (OAH) annual meeting, I decided to stay another week. My decision was fortuitous.

Panthers from east and west of the Mississippi had not seen each other—or talked for the most part—in thirty years. This reunion meant that all that would change. People from all over the country, from Seattle and Portland to Cleveland and New Orleans, showed up. I finally got the chance to interview Bobby Seale, even though thirty minutes into the interview he stormed off telling me I sounded "like the fucking FBI or something with all my questions." I had gotten that before, so I handled it wisely—I said nothing—since my recorder still worked and there were many more people to interview. The actual program went off without a hitch except for one tense moment when members of the New Black Panther Party made a grand entrance in their all-black uniforms. Older Panthers immediately pulled the group to the side and left for about an hour—I don't know what was said but Malik Shabazz and his New Black Panther Party came back into the auditorium, sat there, and paid attention. No one caused any problems. This is a big thing because some Panthers had become upset that this new group had taken the Panther name without consulting anybody. Apparently, no one bothered to tell these Panthers that Newton had done exactly the same thing thirty-five years earlier. All the sessions ended and nighttime arrived.

My hotel room was next door to a group of New York Panthers and I had bumped into Omar Babour in the hall that morning before breakfast. He and BJ gave me the green light to go to their hotel room after everything ended that day. I did just that.

About ten o'clock that night, I knocked on the door of the room the New York Panthers had given me and heard a loud voice from inside inquiring about who it was—I stated my name and heard a lot of unmentionables, then said it again. This time I was let in—or really pulled in and had the door slammed behind me. Everyone just looked at me because I was obviously the only person in the room who had not been a member of the party—that is except Michael Garvey, the grandson of Marcus Garvey. Ali Bey Hasssan of New York fame came in shortly afterward with his wife and a few more people who were not Panthers, so I was safe for the moment.

There was talking, laughing, reminiscing, and fun for everybody—except me. I was there because I had a book to write and because I wanted to learn from the people who actually participated in the party's programs. They were there because they had not seen their comrades in thirty years, so our motives conflicted. Some time shortly before midnight, the conversation became hushed and serious. Almost at the same time, all twenty or so people in the room, including members of the BLA, looked at me as if I were supposed to know something. When it was clear that I did not, BJ grabbed me by the arm and said that I did not need to hear the rest of the conversation. I futilely tried to explain to them that I was cool and could be trusted. Before I could finish the sentence, I was on the other side of the door, pouting, headed back to my lonely hotel room.

The next day at the conference was a blast. Bobby Seale spoke. Kathleen Cleaver and her beautiful mother made an appearance at the dinner banquet, and I made a number of contacts with former BLA members. I also met a bevy of New York and other East Coast Panthers like Paul Coates, Yasmeen Sutton, Cleo Silvers, Bullwhip, and a group of Panther sisters from the Baltimore chapter, including Sala. It was a great day, but fortunately, night came again.

I went right back to the room I had been kicked out of so nicely the night before. Again, there were twenty or so people there, still reminiscing, but this time discussing serious issues about the party. When it became clear that "the author" was still in the room, some enterprising brother offered to make democracy work. He asked if the group wanted to take a vote on whether I stayed. I had worked the crowd well earlier in the day and an overwhelming majority voted that I could stay. Only the person who asked for the vote and one other Panther from New Jersey voted against me. I was in!

This session reminded me of a down-home family reunion. With twenty people in the room, no one had to yell or to raise their voices. It was amazing. The men treated the women with the utmost respect and the women seemed like few others I had met, as they were confident in themselves and their ability to analyze a situation and come up with a solution for any problem. I was floored, until finally someone asked me what I had been working on and if they could see it. Well I had just presented at the OAH and had the paper that I read there with me. A few people looked at it, thought it was OK, but they all agreed that it needed some work if it were to appear in print. I thought that was funny because my publisher kept telling me the same thing.

This might be a good time to flash back to the OAH a week before. I presented my paper on a panel with two other scholars, both from the east coast. This was the first time anyone had ever organized an all-Panther panel at any predominantly white conference. We were all ready—or so we thought. With John Dittmer as the commentator and Tim Tyson as the discussant, how could we possibly go wrong? It turned out not to be too difficult.

Once we all finished giving our presentations and getting our hand claps, the commentator took questions from the audience, which at this point was sitting on the floor, lining the walls, and filling up all but one or two chairs. The questions were timely, well thought-out ones that I wish I could have asked—until the bomb was dropped.

One brown-skinned, beautiful woman stood up to ask her question. Rather than standing in front of her chair, she moved slowly out into the aisle, where everyone could see her finely tailored brown pantsuit that matched her skin tone almost exactly. She began by saying that one of our papers was fine and that she had no problem with it but that the other two had absolutely no academic or scholarly merit whatsoever—or something like that. She complained that we were all wrong (the two of us that is, one of them being me) and that we needed to go back to the drawing board. Not content with that, she began to complain about not being quoted in the papers. Then of course, she announced that she was Elaine Brown, former leader of the Black Panther Party, and that no one even bothered to quote her or any other women in the party. That accusation was not true, but that did not matter.

Dittmer asked for rebuttals and the first two presenters did the smart thing and declined to answer. I took the whole situation as an affront to my dignity because I had in fact quoted several women, including the woman making the comment. My response to Dittmer was, "hell yes, I'd like to rebut," and applause came from the audience. I explained that I had quoted her, but reading footnotes was not customary in professional conferences. That did not satisfy her and she fired into me demanding that we tell her why we had not interviewed her.

There is a little history that needs explaining here. I had been in contact with Elaine Brown for about two months prior to this conference. I wanted to conduct an interview with her. A mutual friend of ours hooked us up on e-mail and we wrote back and forth a couple of times. The gist of the e-mails was that I wanted an interview for my book. She agreed but with one condition: that I invite her to my university to give a speech/presentation to the students and then we could do the interview. Well I promised to check on that situation and when I did, the students responded that it was too late in the year but that they could accommodate the request the next academic year.

Back to the OAH in D.C. I tried all I could to ignore the words coming from this person that I had grown to respect because of her work in the party and her fabulous writing. She kept hammering on this same topic, so, finally, after Tim Tyson tried to calm her down, I felt like I had no choice but to speak. The next time she asked why I had not interviewed her, she did so in a threatening manner, waving her finger and coming closer to the table where we all sat. I honestly felt fear racing through my veins, as I had never had a leader of the BPP come so close and be so belligerent toward me. My defense was this: I told her that the only reason that I had not interviewed her was because every time I asked her for an interview she asked for money in return. All the air left the room at that moment, along with a few people who had apparently had enough.

When she shot back that she had not done any such thing, I changed the wording to honorarium to "quote" her more accurately, and this ticked her off even more. She yelled at me, called me a damned liar and a few other names, and stormed out of the room. Another question or two was asked and the session let out—all the while I was thanking goodness. People started coming up to me saying I had done the right thing, including scholars for whom I have great respect, and other people just kind of stared as if they had seen the devil. I shrugged it off as happenstance and before I could gather my things and rise from the table, Brown stormed back in the room with a copy of the e-mail that she had sent. She tried to make me admit that she had not demanded money from me but I would not because the e-mail she waved in my face was a truncated version of our earlier conversations. I knew Brown would be at the conference so I brought her e-mail address along with me to see if I could coax her into giving me at least thirty minutes of her time at the conference. I just happened to bring the e-mails, too.

When I pulled out my copy of the e-mail and showed her where she had demanded money, she denied it again and stormed out of the room. All I could think of was that she was going to get me. I had read her book three times at this point and knew people had suffered punishment for less. I was still afraid.

But I had my admirers. People continued to come up to congratulate me and ask more specific questions about my work. When Dittmer told me he thought I had no choice and that I had done the right thing, I felt comfortable about leaving the room. I had not walked ten yards when I saw Brown in a hushed conversation with the other two panelists.

As I approached, I saw a very good friend I had not seen in years and we just so happened to meet in the hall next to where Brown's conversation was taking place. Barely three feet away, all I could hear was "that guy" this and "that guy" that and every time I looked over, I could see the uneasiness on everyone's face. I hugged my friend and asked to excuse myself because this situation was way too close for comfort to ignore.

As soon as I approached the three, one of them left. I merely stood there listening. Anyone would have been able to tell that they had just changed the conversation for my benefit. After I boldly asked a few innocuous questions, the other person left and I was standing there in the middle of this large foyer with someone I was sure five minutes prior was going to off me. As it turns out, I was totally wrong and simply insane to be thinking such silly thoughts.

As soon as it was clear that there was no one else around—it was break time at the conference and most people left for lunch—we started talking. After I apologized for my behavior, Brown perked up. I said while I have you here, I would like to ask you a few questions. I had been working on my study of the party at that point for ten years and still had several unanswered questions. She replied that I could ask her anything I wanted and she would answer. I asked her about the Bunchy Carter and John Huggins killings at UCLA. She explained everything as it is written in this book (with a few exceptions) and when she finished she burst out in a flood of tears. We were standing so close to each other that all we had to do was lean forward just a little bit and we would be hugging, and I'll be damned if that's not what happened. Sobbing uncontrollably about having to carry that burden around for thirty-two years, she just stood there, hands around my neck, my arms around her torso, and me thinking this is the wildest s——t I have ever been involved in. I spied one of the people who had been in the session as they walked by, and they looked as if they had seen a ghost. I felt the same way.

When we were done with our moment, our mutual friend miraculously showed up and suggested we all go to the wine-and-cheese reception the conference was sponsoring for a small fee. I found myself bringing Brown wine and grapes an hour later and still have not figured out how we got to that point from the session earlier. I ended up in her room, along with her roommate, and we had more conversation to clear the air. By the end of this session, I had been drafted into service to carry Brown's new book, *The Condemnation of Little B,* downstairs, where she had a book signing. I did my duty and that followed with even more small talk. Brown and I promised to squash the whole thing and she promised to speak at my school one day. Unfortunately, Brown has since left Atlanta, where she was staying at the time and moved to Brunswick, Georgia, to run for political office. We have since lost touch.

That brings us back to the hotel at the Panther reunion/conference. Once they finished looking at and critiquing my paper, more discussion ensued. I told them about the Brown episode and pointed out to them that even though they may not have liked Brown's book, they and Brown did agree on one thing: that my paper needed work. We had a good laugh and continued the conversation. Again, even though there were twenty people in the room and all of them were talking at the same time, the room was eerily calm. Though many of us were drinking, no one said a curse word and no one displayed any anger, despite the fact that some of the issues under discussion required that emotion.

By the end of the night, I had passed whatever test I had been given and everyone in the room gave me their contact information. I had already asked BJ for an interview because I knew he had worked with Sam Napier and I knew he knew some of the underground members. I did not find out until later that Hoover's tactics had left Napier a little less than friends with the radical wing. That reunion went a long way in mending those friendships, however. BJ's challenge to me was to interview the other people in the room, then he would consider giving me an interview. We have been friends ever since.

I made contact with all the people in the room and ended up in places like Atlanta on Super Bowl weekend, Sacramento, San Diego, New Jersey, Connecticut, and a half dozen other cities and states. After a year passed and I had done all the interviews, I showed up in New York, ready to interview BJ. He kept his promise and I had to make three trips to the Big Apple to finish the interview. This seeming inconvenience was no inconvenience at all.

In the process, I discovered the Harlem Black Panther collection at the Schomberg Center for Black Culture. I met with people who walked and talked with Malcolm X. I got to know Queens, Harlem, Brooklyn, the Bronx, and Manhattan. I was even in New York City, in Bryant Park, when the lights went out that fateful day a few years back. And yes, I too, along with a sea of other New Yorkers (and visitors, too, I imagine) walked for miles from Manhattan to the South Bronx (and other places) and not a single person bothered BJ and me as we made our way—crazy New Yorkers my foot, those are nice people when they are not mad at you.

I also got to interview a group of Panthers at the home of Yasmeen Sutton in the Dorie Miller Homes. If you ever want to have some fun, try interviewing a group of Panthers at once and see if you can figure out who's right about what "really" happened forty years ago. You will have a good story at the end of the night. And I say night because they all work in the day time, but they still have the habit of staying up really late like good revolutionaries. Speaking of which, I also traveled to Sullivan County Correctional Facility north of New York City to visit former BLA member Bashir Hamid. He is a knight in shining armor and was the inspiration for one my next projects: a video documentary on the history of political prisoners in the United States.

In the process of completing this journey, I was fortunate to make the acquaintance of librarians at the Library of Congress in Washington, D.C., the National Archives and Records Administration in Baltimore, the Amistad Center at Tulane University in New Orleans, the archives of UC San Diego, San Diego State University, the University of Southern

California, and the magnificent library at Yale University. The State Historical Society of Wisconsin in Madison also provided me with a cornucopia of information on the Panthers and other movement activists. James P. Danky is one of the best finders of anything in print that I ever met. All these places provided respite and information for a weary but still hungry soul.

Roz Payne, a resident of Burlington, Vermont, who once worked for both California and New York Newsreel, also allowed me to use her extensive archive. She has trial transcripts, thousands of government documents, hundreds of hours of videotape, books, cassette tapes, and personal papers of any number of activists, including Panthers. Her work to collate and disseminate this material is arduous and expensive, and interested parties should help her with this enormous task. She has just finished a DVD with never-before-circulated moving and still pictures, audio, text, and other scanned files. A $50 donation makes the DVD yours. Visit www.newsreel.us for more information.

Other important collections reside in the closets, garages, and storage facilities of former Panther members and their loved ones. These individuals have looked up and come to grips with the fact that they did not die for the revolution, yet. They have invaluable materials that need to be centrally located so all can access them. These personal collections represent by far the most important reservoirs of information on the Panthers. An enterprising oral historian could easily spend the rest of his life collecting this one-of-a-kind material. Former Panthers are willing to talk if you are willing to listen. They still have intelligence networks that let them know if someone is an officer of the law or not so it might take a little time, but patience and perseverance will land you an interview—that is, if you are not the police. These individuals, in places as varied as New York, Texas, Nevada, and Oklahoma, in addition to having a story to tell, possess artifacts. They might be willing to part with them if a space is made available to keep them forever. Now is the time to make this project a reality. Like their World War II forbears, they are passing on at an alarming rate, and once they are gone, their stories will be gone with them. We must serve them as they once served the people, and show them the way to the nearest archive—or aid them in building and maintaining one of their own. If this were to happen, one day, we might have the true story of the rise and decline of the Black Panther Party.

Some people are already working toward that goal. Research on the Black Panther Party, while not voluminous, is rapidly growing. Graduate students in universities across the country have made this topic one of the hottest since historians started looking at the movement from a bottom-up perspective. In addition, scholars in every field of the humanities have done their part in resurrecting this oft-forgotten and almost always misunderstood organization.

From Stanford's Clayborne Carson and the Black Panther Party Research Project to Berkeley's Waldo Martin, currently working on a history of the party and a larger Panther research institute of his own, many historians have found value in exploring the contours of this radical organization. Dr. Charles Jones of Georgia State University in Atlanta is finishing up research on a comprehensive history of the group with particular emphasis on southern chapters, while his colleague, Dr. Akinyele Umoja, has delved into a history of the underground wing. He is fast becoming an expert on armed resistance in the civil rights movement, and his work on the history of the Black Liberation Army is refreshing and timely.[9]

Other scholars, including Yohuru Williams at Delaware State and Jama Lazarow at Wheelock College in Boston, are unraveling the not-so-mysterious grassroots organizing efforts that produced the party, years before it knew it was going to become a force in local politics. Penn State's Robyn Spencer will soon complete her opus on the group during the ten years after its heyday when it sought to off the pigs. Looking at the years from 1972–1982, Spencer will show that rather than dying on the vine, the party went through a resurgence and flowering and became intimately involved in local politics wherever it went. She will also demonstrate that this was a period when women held many of the decision-making positions in the party. Kathleen Cleaver's memoirs are also due out soon, and they promise to give the reading public a behind-the-scenes look at the party both inside and outside the United States. Seattle's Aaron Dixon and California-based Elbert "Big Man" Howard are working on their memoirs, too. Bobby Seale continues to keep his dream of a Panther movie alive.

Other ongoing projects on the party's relationship with various and sundry white and ethnic organizations are sure to prove what the party said all along—that people possess the power to effect change as long as they are willing to use that power. Groups like the Third World Liberation Front and the Chinese Red Guards will figure heavily into these comparative histories. All the new scholarship will help shed light on an organization and a movement that served as the focal point for a new generation of activists.

On another front, many Panthers are trying to publicize the fact that America has political prisoners now. Mumia Abu Jamal, they say, is not the only one. Ruchell Magee, Russel "Maroon" Shoats, Herman Bell, Sundiata Acoli, Bashir Hamid, Jamil Al Amin, Kamau Sadiki, Mutulu Shakur, David Gilbert, and a long list of others wait as their comrades drum up publicity for their causes. They, along with Bob Moses and his Algebra Project, are also interested in making education a civil right and in fashioning a movement around this demand. They may one day link up with the group of Mississippi civil rights veterans that just organized in Jackson, Mississippi, to revive the movement, this time based on access to good education and better paying jobs. We do well to assist in this effort, because those who do not know their history have to be taught it. Otherwise, bad things happen.

Notes

1. Hugh Pearson, *Shadow of the Panther: Huey P. Newton and the Price of Black Power in America,* (New York: Addison-Wesley Publishing Co., 1994), 261
2. Pearson, *Shadow,* 233–5; Geronimo Pratt, speech, Anderson United Methodist Church, Jackson, Mississippi, 1998. Tape in possession of author.
3. Pearson, *Shadow,* 184–5.
4. Errol Henderson, "The Lumpenproletariat as Vanguard," *Journal of Black Studies,* Vol. 28 No. 2, November 1997, 171–99.
5. Pearson, *Shadow,* 261, 345.
6. The word "po" is pronounced poe. It is a corruption of poor, in this case, poor meaning skinny.
7. Whuppin is the country word for whipping.
8. This mishap helps explains why some of the documents from the Stanford Archives are labeled with series, file, and folder names. Even when the collection first opened for public use, the materials had not been fully indexed. It was another two years after this incident before all the files had been put in order and by then, some had been moved and others removed. Some were removed because word got out that personal and or medical files were in the collection and Stanford had to remedy that problem.
9. See Akinyele Umoja, "Repression Breeds Resistance : The Black Liberation Army and the Radical Legacy of the Black Panther Party," *New Political Science,* 21, June 2, 1999, 131–55.

BIBLIOGRAPHY

Government Documents

United States Bureau of Labor Statistics. *Income, Education, and Unemployment in Neighborhoods, Oakland, California.* Washington, D.C.: United States Government Printing Office, 1963.

United States Congress. House Committee on Internal Security Hearings on the Black Panther Party. *Gun-Barrel Politics: The Black Panther Party,1966–1971.* 92nd Cong., 1st sess. Washington, D.C.: United States Government Printing Office, 1971.

United States Department of Labor, Bureau of Labor Statistics. *The Negroes in the United States—Their Economic and Social Situation.* Bulletin no. 1511. Washington, D.C.: United States Government Printing Office, 1966.

United States House of Representatives. Committee on Internal Security. *Investigation of Attempts to Subvert the Armed Forces.* Part 2. Washington, D.C.: United States Government Printing Office, 1972.

United States President's Commission on Law Enforcement and Administration of Justice. Task Force Report. *Crime and Its Impact—An Assessment.* Washington, D.C.: United States Government Printing Office, 1968.

United States Senate. Select Committee to Study Government Operations. *The FBI's Covert Program to Destroy the Black Panther Party.* 94th Cong., 1st sess. Washington, D.C.: United States Government Printing Office, 1976.

United States Senate. Final Report of the Select Committee to Study Governmental Operations With Respect to Intelligence Activities. *Books I, II & III.* 94th Cong., 2nd sess. Washington, D.C.: United States Government Printing Office, 1972.

United States Senate. Hearings Before the Subcommittee to Investigate the Administration of the Internal Security Act and other Internal Security Laws of the Committee on the Judiciary. *Assaults on Law Enforcement Officers.* 91st Cong., 2nd sess. Washington, D.C.: United States Government Printing Office, 1970.

United States Senate. Hearings Before the Select Committee to Study Government Operations With Respect to Intelligence Activities. *Huston Plan.* Volume 2. 94th Cong., 1st sess. Washington, D.C.: United States Government Printing Office, 1976.

Collections

Alden Kimbrough Collection. Los Angeles, California.

Black Panther Party Collection. Southern California Research Center. Los Angeles, California.

Department of Special Collections. University Research Library. University of California, Los Angeles. Los Angeles, California.

Huey P. Newton Foundation Records. Department of Special Collections. Green Library, Stanford University. Stanford, California.

Oakland History Collection. Oakland History Room. Oakland Public Library, Oakland, California.

Oral History Collection. Butler Library. Columbia University. New York City, New York.

Unpublished Documents

Cleaver, Eldridge. "On the Ideology of the Black Panther Party." Undated pamphlet. Alden Kimbrough Collection. Los Angeles, California.

Committee of Returned Volunteers. "Repression, Rebellion, Revolution," no.4. May, 1970. Southern California Research Center. Los Angeles, California. Alden Kimbrough Collection.

The Black Panther Party. "Free Bobby Seale, Free the NY 21, Understand the Black Panther Party." Undated pamphlet. Alden Kimbrough Collection. Los Angeles, California.

Heinze, Laura J., Edward Kirshner, and Linda Ludlow. "An Income and Capitol Flow Study of East Oakland." 1979. Oakland History Room, Oakland Public Library. Oakland, California.

Newton, Huey. "The Black Vanguard: Rules and Laws." Undated pamphlet. Southern California Research Center. Los Angeles, California.

People's News Service, Black Panther Party Southern California. "Legalized Genocide," July 14, 1970. Alden Kimbrough Collection. Los Angeles, California.

The Friends of Eldridge Cleaver. "How the Black Panther Party Lost the FBI's War of Dirty Tricks." Undated pamphlet. Southern California Research Library. Los Angeles, California.

Video Recordings

Lew Lee, Lee. *All Power to the People: The Black Panther Party and Beyond.* Produced and directed by Lee Lew Lee. 126 min. Electronic News Group, 1996. videocassette.

Newsreel. *Black Panther: Off the Pig.* 15 min. Newsreel Productions, 1968.

_____. *May Day.* 15 min. Newsreel Productions, 1969.

Books

PRIMARY BOOKS

Blackburn, Sara. *White Justice.* New York: Harper and Row, 1971.

Blackstock, Nelson. *COINTELPRO: The FBI's Secret War on Political Freedom.* New York: Random House, 1975.

Breitman, George, ed. *Malcolm X Speaks: Selected Speeches and Statements.* New York: Grove Press, 1966.

Brown, Elaine. *A Taste of Power: A Black Woman's Story.* New York: Pantheon Books, 1992.

Carmichael, Stokely and Charles V. Hamilton. *Black Power: The Politics of Liberation in America*. New York: Random House, 1967.

Carson, Clayborn, et al., eds. *The Eyes on the Prize Civil Rights Reader: Documents, Speeches, and Firsthand Accounts From the Black Freedom Struggle*. New York: Penguin Books, 1991.

———. *In Struggle: SNCC and the Black Awakening of the 1960s*. Cambridge, MA: Harvard University Press, 1981.

Citizens Research and Investigation Committee and Louise E. Tackwood. *The Glass House Tapes: The Story of an Agent Provocateur and the New Police-Intelligence Complex*. New York: Avon Books, 1973.

Citizens in Defense of Civil Liberties in Cooperation with the National Lawyers Guild Civil Liberties Committee. *Counter Intelligence: A Documentary Look at America's Secret Police: The FBI's Counterintelligence Operations Against Black, Puerto Rican, Native American, and Chicano/Mexicano movements*. Chicago: Citizens in Defense of Civil Liberties, n.d.

Cleaver, Eldridge. *Soul on Ice*. New York: McGraw-Hill, 1968.

Commission of Inquiry into the Black Panthers and the Police. Roy Wilkins and Ramsey Clark, Chairmen. *Search and Destroy*. New York: Metropolitan Applied Research Center, Inc., 1973.

Erickson, Erik H. *In Search of Common Ground: Conversations With Huey P. Newton*. New York: Norton, 1973.

Fanon, Frantz. *The Wretched of the Earth*. New York: Grove Press, 1963.

Foner, Philip S., ed. *The Black Panthers Speak*. Philadelphia: Lippincott, 1970.

Foster, Michelle, and G. Etter-Lewis, eds. *Unrelated Kin: Race and Gender in Women's Personal Narratives*. New York: Routledge, 1996.

Genet, Jean. *Prisoner of Love*. Hanover, NH: Wesleyan University Press, 1992.

Hampton, Henry, et al. *Voices of Freedom: An Oral History of the Civil Rights Movement From the 1950s Through the 1980s*. New York: Bantam Books, 1990.

Heath, G. Louis., ed. *Off the Pigs: The History and Literature of the Black Panther Party*. Metuchen, NJ: Scarecrow Press, Inc., 1976.

Hilliard, David. *This Side of Glory: The Autobiography of David Hilliard and the Story of the Black Panther Party*. Boston: Little, Brown, and Company, 1993.

King, Martin Luther, Jr. *Where Do We Go From Here?: Chaos or Community*. New York: Bantam Books, 1967.

Lockwood, Lee. *Conversation With Eldridge Cleaver, Algiers*. New York: Dell Publishing, Co., 1968.

Mao, Tse-Tung. *Quotations From Chairman Mao Tse-Tung*. Peking: Foreign Languages Press, 1968.

Newton, Huey P., ed. *Black Panther Leaders Speak*. Metuchen, NJ: Scarecrow Press, 1976.

———. *Revolutionary Suicide*. New York: Harcourt, Brace, Jovanovich, 1973.

———. *To Die For the People*. New York: Harcourt, Brace, Jovanovich, 1972.

———. *War Against the Panthers: A Study of Repression in America*. New York: Harlem River Press, 1996.

Njeri, Akua. *My Life With the Black Panther Party*. Oakland: Burning Spear Publications, 1991.

Macy, Christy and Susan Kaplan. *Documents: A shocking collection of memoranda, letters, and telexes from the secret files of the American intelligence community*. New York: Penguin Books, 1980.

Moss, Robert. *The Urban Guerrilla*. London: International Institute For Strategic Studies, n.d.

Pratt, Geronimo. *The New Urban Guerrilla*. Los Angeles: Revolutionary Peoples Communications Network, n.d.

Seale, Bobby. *A Lonely Rage: The Autobiography of Bobby Seale*. New York: Times Book, 1978.

_____. *Seize the Time: The Story of the Black Panther Party and Huey P. Newton*. New York: Random House, 1970.

Sheer, Robert., ed. *Eldridge Cleaver*. New York: Random House, 1972.

Skolnick, Jerome. *Justice Without Trial*. New York: John Wiley & Sons, 1966.

United States Riot Commission. *Report of the National Advisory Commission on Civil Disorders*. New York: Bantam Books, 1968.

Williams, Evelyn. *Inadmissible Evidence: The Story of the African-American Trial Lawyer Who Defended the Black Liberation Army*. Brooklyn: Lawrence Hill Books, 1993.

Williams, Julian. *The Black Panthers Are Not Black . . . They Are Red*. Tulsa, Oklahoma: Christian Crusade Publications, 1970.

X, Malcolm. *The Autobiography of Malcolm X as told to Alex Haley*. New York : Grove Press, 1966.

SECONDARY BOOKS

Alphonso, Pinckney. *Red, Black, and Green: Black Nationalism in the U.S.* New York: Cambridge University Press, 1976.

Andrews, Tony. *Black Liberation and Socialism*. New York: Harcourt and Brace, 1972.

Altshler, Alan A. *Community Control: The Black Demand for Participation in Large American Cities*. New York: Western Publishing Co., 1970.

Avakian, Bob. *Summing Up the Black Panther Party*. Chicago: RCP Publications, 1979.

Bennet, Lerone. *Before the Mayflower: A History of the Negro in America*. New York: Penguin Books, 1962.

Bloom, Alexander, editor. *Long Time Gone: Sixties America Then and Now*. Oxford: Oxford University Press, 2001.

Blumenthal, Sid and Harvey Yazijian. *Goverment by Gunplay: Assassination Conspiracy Theories From Dallas to Today*. New York: Penguin Books, 1962.

Bracey, John, et al., eds. *Black Nationalism*. New York: Bobbs-Merrill, 1970.

Brandt, Joseph R. *Why Black Power?* New York: Friendship Press, 1968.

Brietman, George. *The Last Year of Malcolm X*. New York: Pathfinder Press, 1970.

Brown, William Henry. *Class Aspects of Residential Development and Choice in the Oakland Black Community*. Ann Arbor, MI: University Microfilms, 1970.

Bunch, Lonnie G., et al. *Visions Beyond Tomorrow: The History of the Eastbay Afro-American Community, 1852–1977*. Oakland: Northern California Center for Afro-American History and Life, 1989.

Chafe, William H. and Harvard Sitkoff. *A History of Our Times: Readings on Postwar America*. New York: Oxford University Press, 1987.

Churchill, Ward and Jim Vander Wall. *Agents of Repression: The FBI's Secret Wars Against the Black Panther Party and the American Indian Movement*. Boston: South End Press, 1990.

Cleaver, Kathleen and George Katsiaficas, eds. *Liberation, Imagination, and the Black Panther Party: A New Look at the Panthers and Their Legacy*. New York: Routledge, 2001.

Crawford, Vicki, et al. *Women in the Civil Rights Movement: Trail Blazers and Torch Bearers, 1941–1965*. Brooklyn: Carlson Publishing, 1990.

Donner, Frank J. *The Age of Surveillance: The Aims and Methods of America's Political Intelligence System*. New York: Alfred A. Knopf, 1980.

_____. *Protectors of Privilege: Red Squads and Police Repression in Urban America*. Los Angeles: University of California Press, 1990.

Feagin, Joe R. and Harlan Hahn. *Ghetto Revolts: The Politics of Violence in American Cities*. New York: Macmillan Publishing Co., 1973.

Fredrickson, George M. *Black Liberation: A Comparative History of Black Ideologies in the United States and South Africa*. New York: Oxford University Press, 1995.

Gentry, Curt. *J. Edgar Hoover: The Man and the Secrets*. New York: Penguin Group, 1992.

Haines, Herbert. *Black Radicals and the Civil Rights Mainstream, 1954–1970*. Knoxville: University of Tennessee Press, 1988.

Haskins, James. *Power to the People: The Rise and Fall of the Black Panther Party*. New York: Simon & Schuster, 1997.

Institute for the Study of Labor and Economics. *The Iron Fist and the Velvet Glove: An Analysis of the U.S. Police*. Berkeley: Center for Research on Criminal Justice, 1977.

Johnson, Loch K. *A Season of Inquiry: The Senate Intelligence Investigation*. Lexington: University Press of Kentucky, 1985.

Johnson, Marilyn S. *The Second Gold Rush: Oakland and the East Bay in World War II*. Berkeley: University of California Press, 1993.

Jones, Charles, editor. *The Black Panther Party Reconsidered*. Baltimore: Black Classic Press, 1998.

Jones, Jacqueline. *Labor of Love, Labor of Sorrow: Black Women, Work, and the Family From Slavery to the Present*. New York: Vintage Books, 1986.

Keating, Edward. *Free Huey!* Berkeley, CA: Ramparts Press, 1971.

Killian, Lewis and Charles Grigg. *Racial Crisis in America: Leadership in Conflict*. Englewood Cliffs, NJ: Prentiss-Hall, Inc., 1964.

Knowles, Lewis and Kenneth Prewitt., eds. *Institutional Racism in America*. Englewood Cliffs, NJ: Prentiss-Hall, 1969.

Lader, Lawrence. *Power on the Left: American Radical Movements Since 1946*. New York: W. W. Norton and Company, 1979.

LaFeber, Walter. *America, Russia, and the Cold War, 1945–1996*. 8th edition. New York: McGraw-Hill, 1997.

Lemann, Nicholas. *The Promised Land: The Great Black Migration and How It Changed America*. New York: Vintage Books, 1992.

Logan, Rayford., ed. *What the Negro Wants*. New York: Van Press, 1944.

Lokos, Lionel. *The New Racism: Reverse Discrimination in America*. New Rochelle, NY: Arlington House, 1971.

Lucien, Thomas and Vincent Blair. *Retreat to the Ghetto: The End of a Dream*. New York: Hilliard Wang, 1977.

Major, Reginald. *A Panther is a Black Cat*. New York: W. Morrow, 1971.

Marable, Manning. *Race, Reform, and Rebellion: The Second Reconstruction in Black America, 1945–1982*. 2nd ed. Jackson: University Press of Mississippi, 1984.

Marine, Gene. *The Black Panthers*. New York: New American Library, 1969.

Matusow, Allen J. *The Unraveling of America: The History of Liberalism in the 1960s*. New York: Harper and Row, 1984.

McAdam, Doug. *Political Processes and the Development of Black Insurgency, 1930–1970*. Chicago: University of Chicago Press, 1982.

Meier, August and Elliot Rudwick. *The Emergence of Negro Nationalism: A Study in Ideologies*. Urbana: University of Illinois Press, 1977.

_____. *CORE: A Study in the Civil Rights Movement, 1942–1968*. New York: Oxford University Press, 1973.

Muse, Benjamin. *The American Negro Revolution: From Nonviolence to Black Power, 1963–1967*. Bloomington: Indiana University Press, 1968.

Newman, Edna S. *We Also Serve*. Berkeley: Tilghman Press, 1945.

Newton, Michael. *Bitter Grain: Huey Newton and the Black Panther Party*. Los Angeles: Holloway House, 1980.

Moore, Gilbert S. *A Special Rage*. New York: Harper and Row, 1971.

Olsen, Jack. *Last Man Standing : The Tragedy and Triumph of Geronimo Pratt*. New York: Doubleday, 2000.

O'Reilly, Kenneth. *Racial Matters: The FBI's Secret File on Black America, 1960–1972*. New York: The Free Press, 1989.

O'Shinsky, David. *A Conspiracy So Immense: The World of Joe McCarthy*. New York: The Free Press, 1983.

Pearson, Hugh. *The Shadow of the Panther: Huey Newton and the Price of Black Power in America*. New York: Addison-Wesley, 1994.

Rose, Thomas, ed. *Violence in America: A Historical and Contemporary Reader*. New York: Vintage Books, 1969.

Scott, Robert L. and Wayne Brockriede. *The Panther Paradox*. Garden City, NY: Doubleday, 1971.

Shapiro, Herbert. *White Violence and Black Response: From Reconstruction to Montgomery*. Amherst: University of Massachusetts Press, 1988.

Smith, Jennifer B. *An International History of the Black Panther Party*. New York: Garland, 1999.

Tyson, Timothy B. *Radio Free Dixie: Robert F. Williams and the Roots of Black Power*. Chapel Hill: University of North Carolina Press, 1999.

Van DeBurg, William L. *New Day in Babylon: The Black Power Movement in American Culture, 1965–1975*. Chicago: University of Chicago Press, 1992.

Wheeler, B. Gordon. *Black California: The History of African Americans in the Golden State*. New York: Hippocratus Books, 1992.

Woodson, Carter G. *The Miseducation of the Negro*. Washington, D.C.: Associated Publishers, 1933.

Wolfe, Thomas. *Radical Chic & Mau-Mauing the Flak Catchers*. New York: Farrar, Strauss, and Giroux, 1970.

Wright, Nathan. *Black Power and Urban Unrest: Creative Possibilities*. New York: Hawthorn, 1967.

Articles

"A Close Look at Black Panther Shootouts." *U.S. News and World Report* 22 (December 1969): 25–26.

"Black Scholar Interview: Kathleen Cleaver." *Black Scholar* 3 (December 1971): 55–65.

Boyd, Herb. "Power to the People." *Emerge* 4 (February 1993):36–41.

Carmichael, Stokely. "Power and Racism: What We Want." *New York Review of Books* 7 (September 1966): 5–8.

Carmichael, Stokely and Charles V. Hamilton. "America's Racial Crisis: White Power and Institutional Racism." *Current* 93 (March 1968): 38–45.

Cleaver, Eldridge. "On Meeting the Needs of the People." *Ramparts* 8 (September 1969): 34–35.

_____. "Tears for the Pigs." *Humanist* 29 (March 1969): 29–37.

Cobb, Charlie. "Ready for the Revolution: From Stokely Carmichael to Kwame Ture." *Emerge* (June 1997): 38–43, 46.

Cover, Robert. "A Year of Harassment." *Nation* 21 (February 1970): 210–18.

Crenshaw, Kimberle. "Race, Reform, and Retrenchment: Transformation and Legitimation in Antidiscrimination Law," in Kimberle Crenshaw et al., eds. *Critical Race Theory: The Key Writings That Formed the Movement.* New York: The New Press, 1995.

"Crisis That Won't Go Away." *Newsweek* 70 (August 1967):17–19.

Dalfiume, Richard M. "The Forgotten Years of the Negro Revolution." *Journal of American History* 55 (June 1960): 90–106.

Ferry, William H. "Blacktown and Whitetown: The Case for a New Federalism." *Saturday Review* 15 (June 1968): 14–17.

"Gatherings of the Clan: Three Day Conference in Oakland." *Newsweek* 41 (August 1969): 32–34.

"Guns and Butter." *Newsweek* 53 (May 1969): 40–41.

Hahn, Harlan. "Black Separatists: Attitudes and Objectives in a Riot-torn Ghetto." *Journal of Black Studies* 52 (September 1970): 35–53.

Hamilton, Charles V. "An Advocate of Black Power Defines It." *New York Times Magazine* 27 (April 1968): 79–83.

_____. "Blacks and the Crisis of Political Participation." *Journal of Black Studies* 54 (October 1972): 56–59.

Harding, Vincent. "Black Power and the American Christ." *Christian Century* 28 (January 1967): 10–13.

Hare, Nathan and Julia. "Black Women 1970." *Trans Action* 8 (November-December 1970): 65.

Harris, Michael. "Black Panthers: The Cornered Cats." *Nation* 8 (July 1968): 122.

Haughley, John C. "Those Black Panthers." *America* 17 (January 1970): 212–16.

Marine, Gene. "The Persecution and Assassination of the Black Panthers as Performed by the Oakland Police Under the Direction of Charles R. Gain, Mayor John Redding, et al." *Ramparts* 29 (June 1978): 18–28.

"More on the Panthers." *Nation* 209 (December 1969): 717.

McSwain, Donald. "A New Breed of Blacks." *Economist* 31 (August 1968): 228–32.

"Negro Problem Keeps Growing: The Reason." *U.S. News and World Report* 62 (March 1967): 58–62.

Newton, Huey P. "The Black Panthers." *Ebony* 11 (August 1969): 32–37.

"Police and Panthers at War." *Time* 94 (December 1969): 20–21.

"Radicals: Destroying the Panther Myth." *Time* 97 (March 1971): 14–16.

Scanche, Ron A. "The Black Panthers Are Coming: America on the Eve of Race Revolution." *New Statesman* 20 (May 1969): 176–83.

Seale, Bobby. "A Rap From Bobby Seale." *University Review* 18 (February 1970): 98–104.

Shakur, Assata. "Women in Prison: How We Are." *Black Scholar* (November-December 1981): 50–57.

Smith, Paul M. "Black Activists Want Liberation, Not Guidance." *New Republic* 25 (May 1971): 15–19.

Steale, Ronald. "Letter From Oakland: The Panthers." *New York Review of Books* 11 (September 1969): 216–21.

Swain, Lawrence. "Eldridge Cleaver." *North American Review* 36 (July 1968): 33–39.

"Three Revolutions." *Nation* 205 (August 1967): 98–99.

"The Persecution and Assassination of the Black Panther Party as Directed by Guess Who." *National Review* 21 (December 1969): 102–104.

Wilson, William J. "Black Demands and American Government Response." *Journal of Black Studies* 1 (September 1972): 24–36.

"Too Late For the Panthers? Chicago and Los Angeles Confrontations With the Police." *Newsweek* 22 (December 1969): 18–28.

Dissertations

Brown, Hubert Owen. "The Impact of Worker Migration on the Public School System of Richmond, California from 1940–1945." Ph.D diss., Stanford University, 1973.

Crowe, Daniel. "The Origins of the Black Revolution: The Transformations of San Francisco Bay Area Black Communties, 1945–1969." Ph.D. diss., University of Kentucky, 1998.

Drabble, John. "COINTELPRO-White Hate, the FBI, and the Cold War Political Consensus." Ph.D. diss., University of California, Berkeley, 1997.

Hopkins, Charles W. "The Deradicalization of the Black Panther Party, 1967–1973." Ph.D. diss., University of North Carolina at Chapel Hill, 1978.

Johnson, Bruce Carl. "Discretionary Justice and Racial Domination: A Study of Arrest without Prosecution in Urban America." Ph.D. diss., University of California, Berkeley, 1973.

Karlsson, Ann-Marie. "Signs in Blood: Racial Violence and Antebellum Narratives of Resistance." University of California, Berkeley, 1995.

Matthews, Tracye. "No one Ever Asks What a Man's Place in the Revolution is: Gender and Sexual Politics in the Black Panther Party." Ph.D. diss., University of Michigan, 1998.

Ogbar, Jeffrey. "From the Bottom Up: Popular Black Reactions to the Nation of Islam and the Black Panther Party." Ph.D. diss., Indiana University, 1997.

Rice, Jon. "Black Radicalism on Chicago's West Side: A History of the Illinois Black Panther Party." Northern Illinois University, 1998.

Strain, Christopher. "Civil Rights and Self-Defense: The Fiction of Nonviolence, 1955–1968." Ph.D. diss., University of California, Berkeley, 2000.

Waggener, Tamara. "Gender, Race, and Political Violence in U.S. Social Movements, 1965–1975." Ph.D. diss., University of Texas, Austin, 1999.

Williams, D. P., III. "The Contribution of Selectively Focused Print Coverage to the Negative Stereotyping of a Challenging Group." Ph.D. diss., Arizona State University, 1987.

INDEX